D1602120

The Lied

The Lied

Mirror of Late Romanticism

Edward F. Kravitt

Yale University Press   New Haven and London

For Lenore

Designed by Sonia L. Scanlon.
Set in Caslon type by The Composing Room of Michigan,
Inc., Grand Rapids, Michigan.
Printed in the United States of America by BookCrafters,
Inc., Chelsea, Michigan.

Library of Congress Cataloging-in-Publication Data

Kravitt, Edward F.
    The lied : mirror of late romanticism / Edward F.
Kravitt.
        p.   cm.
    Includes bibliographical references and index.
    ISBN 0-300-06365-2 (c : alk. paper)
    1. Songs, German—19th century—History and
criticism.   2. Songs, German—20th century—
History and criticism.   I. Title.
ML2829.K7   1996
782.42168'0943—dc20   95-42761
                        CIP
                        MN

A catalogue record for this book is available from the
British Library.

The paper in this book meets the guidelines for perma-
nence and durability of the Committee on Production
Guidelines for Book Longevity of the Council on Library
Resources.

10 9 8 7 6 5 4 3 2 1

Contents

Prologue vii

Acknowledgments xi

Part I Introduction

The Fin de Siècle—Modernism versus Tradition

1 Innovation 3

2 Preservation of Tradition 17

3 End of the Romantic Era 35

Part II The Disparate Aesthetic

Naturalism, Nationalism, Symbolism, and Other Trends

4 Declamation 51

5 Naturalistic Description and the Reaction It Provoked 75

6 The Height of Naturalism in Music: The Actor
and Musician in Collaboration 87

7 Pan-German Nationalism 106

8 The Ballad and the Kinderlied 124

9 The Twilight of Late Romanticism 142

Part III The Unifying Aesthetic

10 Expressive Aesthetics in Performance 177

11 Structural Principles and the Common Aesthetic 199

12 Late-Romantic Expansiveness 229

Notes 247

Glossary 297

Select Bibliography 305

Index 315

Prologue

In the debate over the clashes between innovators and traditionalists in the fin de siècle, two opposing arguments emerge. The one generally accepted today identifies the fin de siècle with the rise of modernity and the decline of the anciens régimes. Advances in science, technology, industrial capitalism, and political democracy—such as the rise of the social democrats in Germany—signaled the destruction of Europe's seignorial establishment. According to this argument, Europe moved into the modern age before World War I. Studies, especially of the past twenty years, provide a contrary argument: that the crossover took place *after* World War I.

The German lied is an ideal medium for studies of these arguments as they affect Germany and Austria. Further, the lied clearly mirrors the influence of dominant trends of the fin de siècle through its music and texts. Owing to its brevity, the lied reflects a particular trend more easily than do lengthier genres. Then, too, the diversity of styles stimulated by such trends was increased by each composer's approach. Through the lied, for example, we can see Hugo Wolf responding strongly to naturalism in "Prometheus," less so in "Und willst du deinen Liebsten sterben sehen," and rejecting its influence in "In der Frühe." The lied also reflects the social aspirations that unified fin-de-siècle Germans. To say that the lied played a significant role under the influence of nationalism understates the issue. More accurately, the lied became a principal vein to the hearts of a German people shaken in the late nineteenth century by social and economic upheaval. How better to discover a nation's roots than through the folkish songs of its people?

In music, adherents of the thesis that the fin de siècle marks the rise of modernism are more preoccupied with the spirit of innovation and "experiment" than with the influence of tradition. They concentrate on the remarkable advances of Gustav Mahler and Richard Strauss, who brought music to the outer fringes of the old tradition, and by Arnold Schoenberg, who went beyond those fringes. These scholars conclude that the crossover of music into modernity in Germany and Austria occurred before World War I.

But this thesis ignores the fact that the fin de siècle was a time of conservatism, certainly in central Europe. Austria and Germany swung to the right in reaction to the failed liberalism of the 1860s. This reaction permeated the tissue of their society. Even their youth was driven by "anti-modernist *völkisch* (populist)" sentiment. And a majority of their composers sought to preserve inherited tradition. Innovations in technology, political democracy, and industrial capitalism met with powerful resistance. "Forces of inertia . . . curbed this dynamic . . . new society . . . within the *anciens régimes* that dominated the historical landscape," Arno Mayer argues: "The Great War was an expression of the decline and fall of the old order fighting to prolong its life rather than of the explosive rise of industrial capitalism bent on imposing its primacy."[1]

This thesis slights another fact. Before the war, the musical world regarded Wolf and Strauss as moderns. Schoenberg and his followers—a tiny handful of composers—broke new ground in isolation from that world.[2] Their modernist rebellion, reviled by contemporaries, rumbled under the surface. (The famous Viennese "Skandalkonzert" of March 31, 1913, indicates with accuracy the hostility of prewar audiences to the avant-garde. The tumult that interrupted the concert has no parallel in twentieth-century music other than the first performance in Paris, two months later, of Stravinsky's *Rite of Spring*.)[3]

World War I shattered the dominance of the old tradition. The new era saw the acceptance in Germany and Austria of egalitarianism: democracy and popular elections instead of monarchy. Avant-garde artists felt freer to experiment in the twenties and thirties: they were ignored rather than attacked—except of course in communist and fascist countries. Conservatives simply disregarded the avant-garde, a reaction that today is international.

In music, traditionalists fell on the defensive. Hans Pfitzner raged against the avant-garde in 1920, but to little avail. By 1924 even Strauss, as Norman Del Mar observes, "was no longer in the foreground . . . but wholly out of step . . . with Hindemith, Stravinsky, Les Six, and most of all with the mature Schoenberg. . . . The world to which he really belonged had passed with the war." Although Del Mar's verdict may seem a bit harsh—it ignores Strauss's Weimar innovations, some critics argue—nevertheless, it confirms Strauss's stylistic estrangement from these avant-garde composers. So, too, does Strauss's final, distinguished contribution to the lied, *Vier letzte Lieder*, a remarkable reaffirmation of the old tradition.[4]

The lied mirrors the shattering of the old tradition. Because the nineteenth-century lied embodies romanticism—the old tradition in music—enthusiasm for the genre declined in postwar years. After producing many lieder Strauss, Pfitzner, Joseph Haas, Schoenberg, and Alban Berg virtually abandoned the genre. By 1930 the practice of offering twenty *Liederabende* (song recitals) in a week, once common in Berlin, had ceased. It would be naive to conclude from the enthusiastic response to an occasional performance by outstanding recitalists—like Christa Ludwig (with Leonard Bernstein, in Vienna, 1972)—that contemporary audiences still hunger for lieder. On the contrary, in the past decades we have read more often about "The Vanishing Lieder Ritual."[5] The lied has taken its place at concerts as simply another genre from our past.

Today, with the lied of minor importance in modern concert life, one tends to overlook its earlier great significance. Fin-de-siècle composers turned to the lied for many reasons, even for radical experiment. The lied also reflects changes of nineteenth-century aesthetics. This one small genre supplies an abundant yield, especially with regard to the fin de siècle, when enthusiasm for the lied climaxed. Nearly all of the more than fifty active composers discussed here wrote lieder. Many composed hundreds. Small wonder that in so many subjects, styles, and moods—in fact, in our whole concept of the period—we find the lied an ideal mirror of the fin de siècle.

Acknowledgments

I chose my parents well for my ultimate specialization in lied. My father, who sang internationally—in Bayreuth (Fafner, Hagen, Titurel) and in Berlin's three opera houses—was my primary source for questions on vocal techniques. Earliest memories are of him and my mother, a concert pianist, rehearsing lieder and opera. Latest are of the triumvirate of dear friends without whom this book would not have been possible: my wife, Lenore, for penetrating queries on style, suggestions, and, whenever necessary, consolation; Burnett Cross, who brought his remarkable linguistic skill to bear in reading the manuscript; and Harold Diamond, for obstinate insistence on clarity of many a fuzzy thought.

This book has a long history, and it has put me under obligation to many. When I began my research in Germany under a Fulbright grant, GEMA *(Gesellschaft für Musikalische Aufführungs- und Mechanische Vervielfältigungsrechte)* provided an impressive list of addresses of composers and their descendants, which was increased by publishers Bote und Bock, Universal Edition, and F. E. C. Leuckart. I am grateful for detailed responses to my inquiries from Wolfram Humperdinck, Heinz Reinhart Zilcher, and especially Dorothea Ansorge-Lippisch. My letters led also to interviews: I was a guest in the homes of Franz and Alice Strauss, Joseph Haas, Richard Trunk, Carl August Weismann, and Emilie Bittner. My worldwide correspondents included composers Leo Blech, Karl Bleyle, Justus Hermann, Hermann Stephani, Justus Hermann Wetzel and relatives of Waldemar von Bausznern, Wilhelm Berger, Walter Braunfels, Eugen d'Albert, Georg Göhler, Paul Graener, Hugo Kaun, Wilhelm Kienzl, Friedrich Klose, Armin Knab, Paul Scheinpflug, Franz Schreker, Bernhard Sekles, Rudi Stephan, and Felix Woyrisch.

To the generous Carmen Weingartner-Studer, conductor, author, and widow of Felix Weingartner, I remain ever thankful. She introduced me to many luminaries, including the Schubert scholar Otto Erich Deutsch and Robert Heger, conductor of the Bavarian State Opera, and provided essential information about Weingartner, as both conductor and lied composer. I am equally grateful to Hedwig Courvoisier-Thuille, daughter of Ludwig Thuille and wife of Walter Courvoisier, and to Ludwig Voss, grandson of Ernst von Possart.

Special thanks must go to Mali Pfitzner, the composer's widow, and Willi Kössel, whose kindness knew no bounds in helping me when I was a young scholar.

Performers who offered invaluable information regarding changing styles of lied performance include the eminent accompanist Michael Raucheisen, on lied performance throughout western Europe and New York in the early years of our century; Elena Gerhardt; Julia Culp; Frau Bender, widow of the celebrated bass;

August Schmid-Lindner; Karl Hallwachs; and the conductor Bernhard Paum-gartner, whose father was a close friend of Hugo Wolf's and whose mother, the contralto Rosa Papier, was among the earliest performers of Wolf lieder. I wish in particular to thank Gerhard Huesch, who responded to my persistent inquiries—he lived a short distance from my home in Munich—and also arranged for me to be a guest in the home of his teacher Hans Emge to discuss vocal techniques.

I am happy finally to record my debt to Frank Walker, outstanding Wolf and Verdi scholar, friend and mentor, who until his tragic death was a fundamental source on Wolf, putting me in touch with his associates, the Schubert scholar Maurice J. E. Brown, and Wolf's family and friends, Cornelia Strasser and Ilse Kautsky. I am also indebted to the ever-helpful Edward R. Reilly of Vassar College, who read earlier chapters of my manuscript and responded immediately to many questions.

Libraries were rich sources. I wish to thank the following: in Munich, the staffs of the Städische Musikbibliothek, the Theater-Museum, and the magnificent Musiksammlung of the Bayerische Staatsbibliothek—particularly its curators, Hans Halm and his assistant, Joseph Klingenbeck—Gertrud Strobel of Bayreuther Festspiele, and Ottmar Güntzel of the Max Reger-Archiv, Meiningen; in Vienna, Hedwig Krauss of the Gesellschaft der Musikfreunde, Leopold Nowak of the National-Bibliothek, Ernst Hilmar of the Wiener Stadbibliothek, and several members of the Internationale Gustav Mahler Gesellschaft; in New York, J. Rigbie Turner of the Pierpont Morgan Library, Jean Bowen and members of the Music Division of the New York Public Library, and Daniel R. Rubey (chief librarian), Harold Diamond (fine arts librarian), Edward Wallace (cataloguer), and Gene Laper (interlibrary loan) of the Lehman College library of the City University of New York.

I am also indebted to Walter Abendroth, Bernyce Berman, C. Russell Crosby, Ursula Hoffmann, Hans Jancik, Henry-Louis de la Grange, Philip Lieson Miller, Donald Mitchell, Robert Münster, Carl Orff, Morse Peckham, Barbara Petersen, Susanne Popp, Hans Rectanus, Zoltan Roman, Franz Trenner, and James L. Zychowicz.

Grateful thanks are due to two members of Yale University Press: Harry Haskell, music editor, for offering imaginative suggestions, overcoming obstacles, and replying informatively to all my concerns, and Susan Laity, for her editorial work, which she accomplished with an eagle's eye for detail.

Portions of this book appeared in earlier form in the following journals: *Acta Musicologica, Journal of the American Musicological Society, Musical Quarterly, Music Review, Seminar,* and *Studies in Romanticism.*

part one

Introduction: The Fin de Siècle—
Modernism versus Tradition

chapter one

Innovation

The great transformation of Germany from an agrarian society of separate states into an industrialized empire, which began in 1871, signaled extraordinary advances in science, technology, and political democracy. When Wilhelm II was crowned emperor in 1888, he became sovereign of a nation that had become dominant on the Continent. Frenetic activity gripped the new empire as it entered a period of industrial growth. The magnitude of the change staggers belief: in three years Germany produced as many new factories, iron works, and blast furnaces as it had in the seventy previous years. In raw iron production, for instance, Germany had been fourth on the Continent in 1870, but by 1914 it had nearly outstripped the combined productions of England, France, Italy, Holland, and Belgium. This was the *Gründerzeit*, the period of great destiny, of economic boom but also of dizzy speculation.[1] Politically, the social democrats also recorded a spectacular increase. They polled 1,750,000 votes in elections in 1893 and more than four million in 1912. The bourgeoisie and the professional middle class, meanwhile, were making demands for political democracy and civil liberty.[2] And music reflected these changes.

In music, the phrase *New German*—the party cry of the avant-garde in Austria and Germany—signified modernism, the expression of innovation. The New German label was coined in the mid-nineteenth century to indicate the radical reforms of Liszt and Wagner. By the fin de siècle it connoted a general easing of classical formal restriction. Composers were encouraged to breathe intensity of feeling into their music, such as was found in the works of Liszt and Wagner. Innovators in vocal music now concentrated on declamation, vivid characterization, and the use of leitmotives. Modern composers wrote music drama rather than opera; symphonic poems rather than symphonies.

New German music provoked severe censure from conservatives, as is evident in the verdict Wolf received from the publishers Breitkopf and Härtel, to whom he submitted masterpieces of lied. "The songs are among the most absurd that the extreme left wing of the New German school has as yet brought forth," stated the firm's reader. "They have nothing more in common with my conception of the musical art than the bare elements of sound and rhythm."[3]

The press responded similarly. "The Modern Lied," identified as the creation of Wolf, is *"poetry* in the eminent sense of the word," Rudolf Louis objected. "This is the first time in the history of the lied that the musician has merged [himself] completely with the poet." Wolf's objective, Louis continued, is to make "evident with music that which the poet could only suggest with words," with the result that the poetry receives greater attention than the music. The danger of this "new practice" is that declamation becomes ubiquitous: it destroys melody and "dissolves poetry into prose."[4]

Disputes on musical prosody were intense. The endless debate—should music or poetry receive priority in vocal music?—was referred to as the *Wort-Ton Problem* (the problem of unifying words and music). Conservatives argued that concentration on prosody brought the lied into decline. They criticized even Wolf's sensitivity to prosody. The critic of *Der Kunstwart* pointed out just how badly Wolf, "the highly praised master of declamation[,] . . . can upon occasion declaim." And in a long article the scholar Edmund von Freyhold cited the composer's errors and made suggestions for "improvement." Even Wolf's biographer Ernst Decsey noted what he thought were subtle errors in Wolf's declamation. Other radicals, too, were criticized: the critic Max Steinitzer, for instance, lists "errors" Strauss made in setting "Ständchen," Op. 17, no. 2.[5]

His critics condemned Wolf as "the gifted but unfortunate creator of the Modern Lied." Walter Niemann contended that Wolf and other New Germans "destroyed the traditional lied," the purely "lyrical genre" conceived for "performance in the home," and created an "unsingable pianoforte song meant for the concert hall." Niemann specified: "The main interest [in the Modern Lied] is no longer [in lyrical vocal melody] but in a rich, radiantly colored, and symphonically conceived instrumental part." He concluded that "the rich development of instrumental program music" had stimulated radicals "to flood the piano part with color, tone painting, characterization, realism and naturalism," with the result that "the natural balance between voice and piano suffered dire consequences."[6]

Critics used the term *modern* pejoratively, to mean drastic change, the repudiation of tradition. Niemann described the Modern Lied as "false pathos, exaggerated emotional and dramatic perception." For Louis, "the preferred form of the Modern Lied is *intensification [Steigerung]*—according to the Wagner prototype—a [continual] swelling and ebbing of intensity."[7]

The terminology applied to the lied reflects the clashes of the innovators with the resisters of innovation. The wish to distinguish the out-of-date from the up-to-date led to the formulation of several opposing lied categories. One of these juxtaposes simplicity and brevity with sophistication and expansiveness. In this antithesis, the traditional lied—"a modest little violet that blossomed hidden from the world"[8]—was contrasted with its modern representative, the enormous *symphonic lied† (for voice and piano), so called because its sonority suggests the multicolors of the late nineteenth-century orchestra. The terminol-

---

† Words marked with an asterisk (*) are discussed in the glossary.

ogy also showed what we may call generic antitheses, juxtaposing the traditional, "old-fashioned" group—the *Melodielied* (lyrical song), the *volkstümlich* (folkish) song, and the *Stimmungslied* (songs with gentle evocative mood)—with the modern group of *declamatory song, *symphonic lied, and orchestral song.

A third and more fundamental antithesis, a musico-literary polarity, arose from the *Wort-Ton Problem. Many terms were devised for speechlike settings of texts: *Deklamationslied* (declamatory song), *gesteigerte Sprache* (elevated speech), *lyrische Rezitativ* (lyric recitative), *parlando ballad style, *prose lyrique* (lyrical prose), *Sprechgesang, and *Sprechlied. These antitheses—the musico-literary in particular, with its stress on declamation—were sharpened in heated argument.

Critics of Wolf's declamation failed to recognize the many other kinds of expression inherent in the Wolf lied. None of his songbooks is primarily declamatory—only individual songs or passages in some lieder are speechlike. When Wolf sought to mirror a poem's inner meaning in music, he might ignore speechlike declamation entirely (see ex. 48d). Indeed, his *Moerike-Lieder* is profusely lyrical. It comprises a variety of lied genres, ranging from the "modern" symphonic lied to the conservative volkstümlich song. On the other hand, in *Goethe-Lieder* Wolf often assigned the melody to the piano, subduing the lyrical flow in the voice part. These songs are settings of complex philosophic verse (such as the *West-östlicher Divan* group) that are interpreted in Wolf's vocal line through protean melodic or rhythmic motives or, as in "Prometheus," through theatrical declamation. In some songs, which might be called pathological studies, characterization involves pathological subjects, such as the embittered, half-crazed harper and the mysterious Mignon of "Wilhelm Meister." The *Spanisches Liederbuch* (Spanish songbook) touches new nerves. Here a small group of sacred songs, some on religious themes, is followed by a larger group of secular songs with Spanish features, dance rhythms, and guitar and tambourine effects. No national features exist in the *Italienisches Liederbuch* (Italian songbook), which Wolf called "children of German origin." These songs are delicate, limpid, exquisite miniatures, some only a page long, in which Wolf raised nuance to supreme heights. Small changes of harmony or melodic contour alter mood and declamation subtly but unmistakably. Also this is the only songbook for which Wolf provided metronome markings.

In spite of the broadside fire of his critics, Wolf's innovations never provoked "scandals" like those Schoenberg and his followers experienced at concerts. On the contrary, within a few years Wolf rose in Vienna from a local eccentric to a local celebrity. Autumn 1888, just after he had completed his *Moerike-Lieder,* marked the beginning of Wolf's rise to fame. In that year came the first performance in the Vienna Wagner Verein (society) of some of these songs. "The name of Hugo Wolf, which was almost completely unknown," Theodor Helm noted, "was suddenly on everyone's lips." The press in Vienna sought to temper the audiences' immediate enthusiasm for Wolf, for when he had been music critic on the *Salonblatt* (1884–87), his reviews had systematically antagonized them. When a well-known singer, Marianne Brandt, planned to include three of Wolf's songs in her concert of January 4, 1890, she was surprised by a visit from a leading Viennese critic. "Unless the three songs of this socially undesirable person were removed from her program," he warned, "not one of the Viennese music critics would attend." The intimidated singer substituted three songs by Edvard Grieg.[9] In later years, Brandt regretted her decision, when in the 1890s favorable articles about Wolf appeared in Vienna, Berlin, Cologne, and Munich.

The press's negative influence was brief. Audiences outside Vienna were enthusiastic. "'Der Feuerreiter' struck home like a bomb," Wolf wrote in 1894 from Berlin: "Endless applause, calls, and clamor, 'da capo!'" Soon even Wolf's old adversary in Vienna, Eduard Hanslick, wrote favorably. Helm quipped: "Singers who had been afraid to perform even one Wolf song publicly in Vienna now vied with each other to be the first to introduce groups of new lieder."[10]

Further, Wolf was widely discussed before World War I in Germany and Austria—even in England, where he received a substantial entry in the second edition of *Grove's Dictionary of Music and Musicians* (1904–10). Wolf's influence extended to literary taste and to a composer's selection of poetry. His influence upon Max Reger, Engelbert Humperdinck, Schoenberg, Joseph Marx, Alban Berg, Othmar Schoeck, Yroe Kilpinen, and a long list of lesser masters, had become "overwhelming."[11]

For composers at the turn of the century, to create a Modern Lied meant to follow Wolf. Reger's development of the lied illustrates the point. The young Reger was out of touch with contemporary musical thought—that of the New Germans—partly because he had spent his early years in small Bavarian towns. Brahms was his principal model for Opp. 4–23, especially for the piano parts of Op. 12. "My piano parts are exactly like those of Brahms," Reger prided himself. "It is his figuration that I love so much." Many of these songs are Melodielieder, on texts by early nineteenth-century poets. Reger's change of residence to Munich in 1901, where he made contact with contemporary musical thinkers, accelerated his change of style to a more declamatory one. Yet Reger had attempted this innovation earlier. Hoping to impress his publisher, he wrote in 1899: "I have, of course, striven everywhere (in Op. 23), to write music that has the closest possible relationship to the text."[12] After 1901 he strove to master techniques of adapting the musical to the literary style of the lied. To master the art of declamation, Reger studied the Wolf lied carefully. He became a missionary for Wolf, writing articles and arranging, editing, and performing Wolf's music. Perhaps his greatest homage was his emulation of the Wolf style in lied cycles such as his Op. 51, *An Hugo Wolf*.[13]

After Wolf's death, Richard Strauss became "without question the most important representative of the Modern Lied."[14] Mahler, Reger, and Schoenberg never came under consideration. Mahler's contemporaries, save a small cadre of admirers, never understood his individuality. The fact that Mahler was Jewish greatly hindered his struggle for recognition during the fin-de-siècle rise of aggressive nationalism. Even friendly critics censured elements in Mahler's unfamiliar style as products of his Jewishness. Niemann proclaimed that Mahler's music sometimes expressed "the scandalous Semitic race, too strongly. . . . Jewish blood flows through Mahler's creativity." In those days such criticism was not necessarily a mark of anti-Semitism, as I shall show in Chapter 7. For Niemann warned readers not to follow "blindly the folly of [Mahler's] anti-Semitic adversaries," and not to overlook the "numerous brilliant" aspects of his creativity.[15]

When Strauss was proclaimed "leader of the moderns" and "head of the avant-garde," he inherited some familiar invective, such as this, from Louis: "wild, radical, fanatical progressive." The Strauss lied received special scorn: "When Strauss emancipated himself from the influence of Liszt," Henry Finck charged, "he followed Wolf [to create songs that] are appallingly arid and uninteresting." Even Ernest Newman, an early admirer, denounced this modernist of the lied: Strauss "often experiments in his songs in audacities from which even he would shrink in his orchestral works." Fritz Gysi censured Strauss for the "melodic decomposition of the lied." Others charged that Strauss, like Wolf, had destroyed the traditional lied, a lyrical genre, and created a new type of song. Steinitzer inauspiciously dubbed the contributions of Strauss *Sprechlied*.[16]

His adherents, however, spoke of Strauss as a brilliant innovator. In early maturity he mastered the union of words and music in both opera and lieder (see Opp. 26–56, 1891–1905). In "Ruhe, meine Seele!" (Op. 27, no. 1), Strauss called for as many as six different musical analogues for the trochaic meter in one line of verse (mm. 17–25). And he sought unconventional ways to emphasize words. One is through long "florid" melismas of descriptive intent, which I shall discuss in Chapter 5. Another is by setting emotive words to extremely long time values, as if to extract musically the utmost feeling the words can convey. See, for example, his setting of the word *Liebe* (love) in "Pilgers Morgenlied" (Op. 33, no. 4, mm. 88–91). The third, most forceful, means is through the use of wide leaps, which is evident in opera and lieder alike. Wide leaps, incidentally, became an important part of Strauss's expressionistic style, which he started to develop during these years. They serve to galvanize melody (exx. 1a and 1b), to give an image to words of direction (ex. 1c), and even to create humor, as in "Für funfzehn Pfennige" (ex. 1d). Here a leap on the *funfzehn* (fifteen; dialect spelling) from the top to the bottom of the singer's vocal range helps to suggest the ludicrous situation of a clerk offering his beloved his entire fortune—fifteen pennies—if she will marry him.

Example 1. Strauss: (a) "Lied an meinen Sohn" (Dehmel), Op. 39, no. 5, mm. 34–36; (b) "Ich sehe wie in einem Spiegel" (Rückert), Op. 46, no. 5, mm. 58–59; (c) "Am Ufer" (Dehmel), Op. 41a, no. 3, mm. 49–52; (d) "Für funfzehn Pfennige" (*Des Knaben Wunderhorn*), Op. 36, no. 2, mm. 84–85.

Such early critics as Newman were quick to criticize the "formlessness" of the Strauss lied.[17] They failed to recognize that Strauss had developed not one but three basic vocal styles—lyrical, dramatic, and speechlike—and that his "lyrical arioso" shades into each of the three. Although he preferred the lyrical style for the lied, he wrote fewer purely lyrical songs than usually assumed. His dramatic style ranges widely, from lyrical arioso to intense, wide-arched, and jagged vocal lines. The speechlike song shades from the straightforwardly declamatory through a kind of *recitativo secco* to the lyrical arioso. Strauss experimented with these three styles even within a single song, seeking always to fuse text and music intimately.

Early critics saw weakness in precisely the kind of vocal writing that Strauss, the innovator, had tried so long to develop: vocal music engendered by the text. They failed also to understand that melody in Strauss is of a special kind—a long undulating lyrical line expanded from melodic fragments. Some songs have no rests in the vocal lines for from sixteen to twenty bars. "[Only] two measures of a melody come to me spontaneously," Strauss explained. "I then begin to spin these out by adding . . . stone upon stone until I have succeeded in bringing the melody into its final shape . . . which is a long path, indeed." No composer of the nineteenth century, Strauss insisted, created melody in this way.[18] In successful songs, this melodic style is a thing of ingratiating beauty.

In spite of the scathing attacks of critics, or perhaps partly because of them, Strauss achieved great stature before World War I. His art of the lied, however, continues to provoke criticism. Even books on the romantic lied written as recently as the 1970s neglect the Strauss lied entirely.[19] Their authors charge that Strauss's inspiration was not consistently high throughout his lieder. But this complaint could be leveled as well against extended passages of his operas and symphonic poems. Critics also claim that he gave the lied only secondary consideration. Actually, he lavished attention on it. As Willi Schuh keenly observed, Strauss "experimented first in the lied with daring harmony"—"audacities" to Newman—developed in his symphonic poems and operas.[20] It is possible that he performed at concerts of his own lied more than any other contemporary composer. He orchestrated neglected pianoforte songs specifically to attract attention to them. Of Strauss's eighty-six opus numbers, thirty are devoted entirely to the lied. Included are his first and last compositions and some of his finest music.

New German aesthetics influenced even the conservative Hans Pfitzner during the years 1894 to 1916, when he wrote some of his finest songs (Opp. 9–26). In these works, intense dissonance touching on expressionism occurs along with a symphonic development—motivic manipulation—both of which are demonstrated by the impressive "In Danzig" (Op. 22, no. 1). Accordingly, their form is freer and their harmony richer than those of earlier lieder. Further, Pfitzner began to cultivate the orchestral song, writing several that contain sharp musical imagery (see Chapter 12, below). Yet in other orchestral songs, like "An den Mond" (Op. 18), musical imagery serves to mirror the poem's symbolism. Pfitzner's triumphs in Strasbourg, Berlin, and Munich during these years brought him in close contact with contemporary music.

In spite of their heated clashes, innovators and conservatives agreed on at least one aspect of lied composition—the obligation of composers to select poetry of outstanding quality. Composers were expected to be far more sophisticated in their selection and treatment of poetry than their predecessors had been, Schubert included. "It is no longer possible today to compose music for a poor text the way Schubert did" without receiving censure, Wolf stated. "Schubert could compose something beautiful even on a 'cheese label' and still be admired." Composers who set verse that might be dismissed as kitsch, Reger complained, received sharp critical stings. "I am often rebuked because of my choice of texts." But of the older masterpieces, "Goethe is completely set to music. And in all of Hebbel, I found only two suitable poems." Unlike his predecessors, who altered poetry they set, Pfitzner apologized for occasionally quoting a poem incorrectly in his lieder. These mistakes resulted from "slips of memory."[21]

Like missionaries, lied composers drew their public's attention to neglected poetic masterpieces. In 1888, when Wolf set fifty-three of Eduard Moerike's poems, the poet was appreciated mainly by German literary specialists. Today, through Wolf's efforts, Moerike is internationally regarded as one of Germany's greatest poets.[22] I shall discuss Mahler's similar efforts on behalf of *Des Knaben Wunderhorn*, a large collection of folk poetry, equally noteworthy, below. Composers also discovered young giants like Stefan George, Rainer Maria Rilke, and Hugo von Hofmannsthal. Although they were also attracted by poets whose verse quickly faded, these composers drew attention to a seemingly endless list of contemporary poets.[23]

But conflicts arose when innovators set the poetry of dangerous radicals: for instance, the verse of Richard Dehmel (1863–1920), whose challenges to the puritanical brought him into a police court on charges of obscenity. "The young generation of today cannot imagine the enthusiasm with which the youth at the turn of the century exalted the poetry and personality of Dehmel."[24] Progressives were attracted not only to Dehmel's verse on sexual liberation, but also to his socialistic poems—verse influenced by Friedrich Nietzsche—and poems for children written with his first wife, Paula. Conrad Ansorge (1862–1930) was one of the first to set Dehmel's texts, in 1895. Strauss's early protest lieder "Arbeitsmann," "Befreit," and "Lied an meinen Sohn" (all 1898) are among his ten famous Dehmel songs. And Dehmel's poetry gave direction to Schoenberg's early works. "Your poems have had a decisive influence on my development as a composer," Schoenberg wrote to the poet.[25]

The contempt of many intellectuals for modern materialism was clearly mirrored in the late nineteenth-century lied. The flight into nature of the Wandervogel movement and the poetry of Hermann Löns (1866–1914) afforded one escape.[26] Detlev von Liliencron (1844–1909) provided another. His vivid and sensuous nature poetry, as well as his erotic, Rabelaisian verse, had a strong appeal for lied composers. For his part, Liliencron was particularly receptive to the new lied: he was one of the first to champion Hugo Wolf, for whom he wrote a poetic panegyric. The biting satire of Christian Morgenstern (1871–1914) offered still another stimulus for composers. Morgenstern's satirical verse caught the eye of Paul Graener, who made particularly good use of it in his "Palmström singt" of the *Galgenlieder* (Gallows songs).[27]

The search for a beauty beyond the modern industrial world led some composers into the mystic realm of Stefan George (1866–1933), which he expressed in an unconventional and severe style that had been influenced by the French symbolists. Yet he and the little-known Alfred Mombert (1872–1942), who offered dark visions of a world beyond reality, were quickly discovered by lied composers. George's influence on Schoenberg's modernist breakthrough was fundamental. But Schoenberg was not the first composer to enter George's hidden realm. Ansorge, in his fine *Waller im Schnee* (1899), is one of several lesser lights who set George's verse before Schoenberg.[28]

Finally, innovative composers extended the horizons of the lied beyond the poetry of German-speaking Europe. Many followed Wolf's example and set the verse of Michelangelo and other Italian poets, in addition to Spanish poets, in German translation. Others found inspiration among the radicals of French and American literature.[29] Exotic poetry (in German translation) once more became a passion, as it had been earlier in the nineteenth century. Settings of Persian, Turkish, Kurdish, and Indian verse, as well as of Chinese and Japanese poetry (the new rage, stimulated in part by Mahler, as I shall detail in Chapter 9), produced songs of musical luminescence. Composers of the Modern Lied, traditionalists now alleged, were denying their roots even in their selection of poetry.

The censure of the modernists by their critics is ironic, for Wolf, Mahler,

Strauss, and Reger—like most of their critics—were fierce Wagnerites. When those critics attacked the New German Modernists, they were actually censuring Liszt and Wagner, whose innovations had served as the foundation of New German aesthetics.

The conversion of Strauss and Reger to modernism makes this irony particularly clear. Young Strauss had been confined to the study of classical masters by his father, who condemned the "moderns, particularly Wagner." Indeed, the fifteen-year-old Richard was instructed to recompose three of his lieder with simpler modulations "to please papa." Strauss's earliest songs keep to the old traditions. All but two in his first published song cycle, Op. 10, are in conventional strophic form.[30] They reflect little more than the mood of the poetry; few have passages of descriptive music. There is none of the soaring dramatic writing that characterized the later Strauss. Turgid vocal rhythms (see "Die Zeitlose," mm. 9–15) and careless yet conventional accentuation of words occur in all the early songs (1885–91). Yet traces of the later style are already evident. The vocal line in some songs often ranges from the captivatingly lyrical to a speechlike arioso, suggesting Strauss's later fabulous melodic gift. Further, his mature skill in opera and lieder, his mastery in developing instrumental motives drawn from the rhythm of words, is foreshadowed in such songs as "Die Georgine" (Op. 10, no. 4).

The expressive style developed by Strauss in his early maturity, which became the model of the Modern Lied, arose from his conversion to New German aesthetics. Alexander Ritter (1833–96) "urged me . . . like a windstorm," Strauss confessed, to "develop the poetic, the expressive in music as exemplified in the works of Liszt, Wagner, and Berlioz." Powerfully dramatic lieder, dense in texture, now make their appearance. Voice parts are chromatic, florid, and, especially in dramatic songs, of extensive range. In some songs, no rests appear in the voice parts for from sixteen to twenty-three measures. Piano parts are also of extensive range; they are rhythmically enriched and harmonically opaque. Descriptive music abounds. Relatively simple accompaniments can still be found, however, but only in the lieder that critics called "late-romantic salon music." Like his opera libretti, Strauss's lied texts are deeply expressive. Many are erotic. Verse of social protest by Richard Dehmel and Karl Henckell, poetry that "seethes with the confused and unsettled ethical ideas of its time," also gives these songs that New German stamp.[31]

As we have seen, Wagnerian principles of composition also stimulated Reger to develop the New German aesthetic. Under the influence of Wolf, Reger had already introduced into early songs some of these principles: dramatic vocal lines, involved piano parts, and complex harmony. Reger completed his conversion to New German aesthetics when he moved to Munich and fell under the influence of Wagner, particularly that of *Tristan*.[32] He now sought to surpass Wolf, especially in highly dramatic lieder that are similar to Wolf's "Prometheus." Reger refined and enriched his harmonic language, while developing a passion for orchestral music. The piano parts of Opp. 51–75 (1900–1903), Op. 51 in particular, attained such magnitude that they have been identified as symphonic lieder. Reger gave detailed performance directions for these songs, emphasizing soft and delicate shading even within single measures (see exx. 49a, 56, and 62). When Reger accompanied his lieder, using his celebrated light touch, with the piano lid closed, the sonority of the piano enveloped the voice in multicolors. In these lieder he selected deeply expressive, even erotic, verse and evocative symbolist poetry. Vocal lines became jagged, especially in dramatic songs (in "Hymnus des Hasses," Op. 55, no. 1, for instance), which won Schoenberg's praise. Rhythmically, some voice parts are so fluid that they seem to obscure the meter of their poetry. In such songs, which Grete Wehmeyer and other Reger specialists identify as being in his "prose style," the composer elevated the literary lied to supreme heights.

Compositions such as these invited controversy even from Wagnerians, who, during the fin de siècle, had split into opposing groups. Wolf had felt the wrath of the old guard during early performances of his music in the Vienna Wagner Verein. The breach widened. Strauss polemically characterized the two well-established factions as innovative Wagnerians who sought "progress in art . . . futurist music" and the conservative "narrow Wagnerians," who "sinn[ed] against the spirit of their master" by "making things difficult for those who wish[ed] to go forward."[33]

Although fin-de-siècle masters of the lied considered their harmonic and tonal innovations advances on tradition, their critics deemed them breaches. These critics had no mercy. "Vienna publishers who used to object to Schubert's piano parts," Finck proclaimed, "would stand aghast at Strauss, whose pages sometimes look like a wilderness of flats and sharps, with the head of a note timidly peeping out here and there." The Strauss lied was "sheer harmonic nonsense" for Newman. "One finds sins not only against beauty but against sanity."[34]

Reger's former teacher, the distinguished Hugo Riemann, was equally critical of Reger: "Even a dilettante who has learned nothing would shrink from heaping up so many incorrectly written notes. . . . But when a Reger does this one may ask: is the composer permitting himself an ugly joke? Does he wish to mystify us, pose as a dilettante, or simply renounce our art of writing music as it is conceived?"[35] Riemann dubbed Reger's "needless" harmonic experiments "Konfusion in der Musik" and advanced the astonishing thesis that much of the harmonic complexity of the period was the result simply of incorrect notation. Riemann insisted that the entire "Ein Drängen" (ex. 2a) is in the key of E and that its harmonic language is really simpler than appears from Reger's notation (ex. 2b).

But Riemann's notation does not resolve the music's intricacies. The first bar passes through A-sharp major! Riemann's third bar (he did not print it) would have included a B-sharp major chord. The harmonic complexity in "Ein Drän-

Example 2. (a) Reger: "Ein Drängen" (Zweig), Op. 97, no. 3, mm. 1–3; (b) Riemann: *Grosse Kompositionslehre*, 3:235 ("Ein Drängen" in Riemann's notation).

gen" is not just orthographic but an intrinsic feature of the music. Chords that seem unrelated follow each other in profusion. According to Reger's principle of harmony: "Any chord may be followed by any other, even immediately." Reger often modulates with lightning speed to unexpected keys. Yet he believed firmly that all his progressions, even his radical ones, were derived from classical tradition.[36] He often concluded radical progressions with clear-cut cadences. Although of unquestionable individuality, Reger's harmonic language is characteristic of its day.

Fin-de-siècle composers were expanding tonal concepts by ending works in different keys from which they began. Critics did not always praise this innovation. Louis Elson wrote sarcastically in the Boston *Daily Advertiser* (November 26, 1899) that a musical dictionary of the day would have defined a key as "any succession of tones; but the succession which is indicated by the signature must be avoided, especially at the close." In a calculated attempt to startle, Strauss concluded "Wenn" (1896) in D major, although it began in D flat, adding as a footnote at the point where the modulation began: "The composer advises any singer who wishes to perform this song, while the nineteenth century is still in existence, to transpose it, from this point, a half-step down (i.e., into D flat) so that the piece may end in the key in which it began." He published "Wenn" in the avant-garde magazine *Die Jugend* as an example of the music of the future. "Progressive tonality" fascinated Mahler in his youth. "Erinnerung" (1880–83) presents an impressive early example—one of many—gliding from G minor to A minor.

But fin-de-siècle composers were by no means the first to treat tonality in this manner.[37] An early example, though not a lied, comes immediately to mind: Osmin's first aria from Mozart's *Entführung aus dem Serail,* which opens in F major and closes in A minor. But Mozart applied limits to progressive tonality. "Since passions, whether violent or not, must never be expressed to the point of exciting disgust, and as music, even in the most terrible situations, must never offend the ear . . . , I have not chosen a key as remote from F (in which the aria is written) . . . , but one related to it."[38]

The five masters of the lied—Wolf, Mahler, Strauss, Pfitzner, and Reger— recognized no such restrictions. They modulated to remote keys, reaching them through side roads, as Wolf did in Mignon II: "Nur wer die Sehnsucht kennt." One may question the song's underlying tonality. Although two flats appear in the key signature, the song seems to begin in A-flat major and end in D. But Wolf's puzzle is easily solved. The central key is, of course, G minor. The opening A-flat chord is a Neapolitan harmony and the closing, the dominant of G. The fascinating point is that the actual tonic (G minor) sounds only once (in m. 52) in the entire song—and on a weak beat.[39]

Fin-de-siècle composers dissolved tonality, that rocklike foundation of music, only temporarily in their lieder. Though the swift and frequent harmonic changes in "Ein Drängen" disorient the listener's feeling for tonality, Reger establishes the key firmly in the song's final bars. Despite vehement criticism that they had destroyed tonality, these composers carefully avoided a final break with tradition. Schoenberg, of course, did not.

Like Strauss, the young Schoenberg lavished attention upon the lied but with fundamentally different consequences. He followed inherited tradition in his earliest published lieder (Opp. 1–3, 1898–1903). Like Reger, he modeled the piano parts of his early songs, particularly those of Op. 1, after Brahms. Also like Reger he ventured to surpass his model with force and mass. He released great torrents of sound in songs in the symphonic-lied style and even intensified these fortissimos to achieve utmost impact (for example, *ffff* in "Dank," m. 76). Another important Schoenberg mentor—not sufficiently acknowledged—was Wolf. Admiration for Wolf was then at its height in Vienna, especially among progressive musicians like Schoenberg's teacher, Alexander von Zemlinsky. Schoenberg's "Erwartung," "Jesus Bettelt," and "Waldsonne" mirror the finely wrought declamation of Wolf's Italian and Spanish songs, with their tight motivic structure and their characteristic chromatic color.[40] Like Wolf, Schoenberg also contoured the piano part more strictly than the voice part, as is evident in the folkish "Hochzeitslied" and "Freihold," Schoenberg's strictest strophic songs. In Chapter 11, I discuss form in Schoenberg's lieder.

Characteristics of Schoenberg's better-known style begin to appear in the second phase of his early development of the lied (Opp. 6–12, 1903-07). Tonality is prominently stretched in "Die Aufgeregten" (November 1903) and particularly in "Lockung," in which the composer went beyond Wolf's "Nur wer die Sehnsucht kennt," sidestepping tonal points of rest almost entirely. Yet these lieder are still tonal. All are provided with firm cadences. The extended tonality in "Der Wanderer" (1905) and the quartal harmony at the close of "Jane Grey" (1907), however, brought Schoenberg to his famous crises with tonality.

His voice parts also underwent change after 1903. The vocal line of earlier lieder (see Op. 1) is lyrical and broadly phrased. Finely wrought speechlike contours appear in Op. 2, where Schoenberg made ample use of syncopation in the Wolfian manner, to reflect nuances of speech. Although he had carefully followed the rhythm of speech in his voice parts, he began after 1903 to neglect its inflections and to twist his vocal line expressionistically. Wide melodic leaps, already prominent in "Traumleben" (Op. 6, no. 1), foreshadow his later well-known liking for melodic angularity.

Schoenberg's piano parts also evolved rapidly from opaque polyphonic (Op. 1) to light-colored linear textures (Op. 15). Freeing himself from piano configurations influenced by Brahms, Schoenberg sought greater linearity. The texture of several songs of Op. 6 ("Verlassen," "Alles," and "Ghasel") is already taut linear polyphony. And the piano and voice parts of "Der Wanderer" show rhythmic independence and, at key phrases (such as mm. 71 ff.), daring dissonance. Such writing climaxes in *Das Buch der hängenden Gärten* (The book of hanging gardens, 1908–09). There texture is sparse to the point of austerity. The voice part is often treated as another linear line. Mood is tense even in soft passages.

Schoenberg's transition into maturity involves his famous breach with tradition in *Hanging Gardens*. Even "Jane Grey" differs markedly from this first song cycle in the idiom known since as atonal. Schoenberg had suspended tonality extensively in "Ich darf nicht dankend" (December 1907). But this song—provided with key signature and with touches of tonality—is not the first in the new land. The question of priority, however, is moot.[41] For several lieder of *Hanging Gardens* (see below, Chapter 9, note 32) are also tonally oriented.

Of greater significance is the fact that Schoenberg's modernist break with tradition was no simple step into a new world of sound. The composer had sought new paths for years, first in poetry and painting. "My first attempts to compose settings for your poems," Schoenberg wrote to Richard Dehmel, "contain more of that which had subsequently developed in my work than there is in many a much later composition."[42] Dehmel and, particularly, August Strindberg, whom Schoenberg read with enthusiasm, had entered an inner realm that fascinated Schoenberg. So, too, had the painters Oskar Kokoschka and Richard Gerstl. To convert such artistic expression into music, Schoenberg became a painter (1907–10). The ultimate stimulus for his modernist break-through, however, which I shall detail in Chapter 9, came from a fresh source: the poetry of Stefan George.

Hanging Gardens, the composer conceded, signifies a new aesthetic of the lied, a new way of fusing words and music: "With the George songs I have for the first time succeeded in approaching an ideal of expression and form which has been in my mind for years. Until now, I lacked the strength and confidence to make it a reality. But now I have set along this path once and for all. I am conscious of having broken through every restriction of a bygone aesthetic. . . . I suspect that even those who have so far believed in me will not want to acknowl-edge the necessity of this development."[43]

Schoenberg's new aesthetic signified an end to certain nineteenth-century lied traditions: the paralleling of tension and release in the poetry with tonal dissonance and consonance; the correlation of changes of place and situation in the poem with modulation in the music; the echoing of the movement to climax in poetry with functional harmonic progression to musical climax; and the underscoring of key words with dissonant chords. Traditional lied structures, too, were to be discarded, as I show in Chapter 11. Schoenberg's entrance into the new aesthetic in *Hanging Gardens* represents another basic change: the end of the composer's great love for the pianoforte lied.[44]

Late in life Schoenberg modified his assertion that he had "broken off the bonds of a bygone aesthetic" in *Hanging Gardens:* "This music is distinctly a product of evolution, no more revolutionary than any other development in the history of music."[45] Artistic innovation is more often the consequence of evolu-tion than revolution. Parallels exist even in mechanics: for example, the first automobile was called a "horseless carriage" to affirm its position in the process of evolution. The automobile signified fundamental change, nevertheless. We do Schoenberg an injustice if we fail to recognize the magnitude of his innova-tion.

Before World War I, however, Schoenberg had reason to fear that few would "acknowledge the necessity of this development." Anton Webern was equally apprehensive of the reaction to his own suspension of tonality in Op. 3, *Fünf Lieder* (1908), also on George poetry: "Naturally it was a fierce struggle, there were inhibitions of the most fearful kind to overcome, a panic fear as to whether it was possible." Webern added: "Never in music has such resistance been shown as there was to these things."[46]

chapter two

Preservation of Tradition

The unification of Germany allied old and new forces, as the old, autocratic Junkers and the new German monarchy lent powerful support to German industry. Adherents of the thesis that the fin de siècle marks the rise of modernism hold that the entrepreneurs wished to abolish the old regime in order to allow modern capitalism free development. But other theorists contend that entrepreneurs, bankers, and industrialists alike revered the old aristocracy. They competed for titles, which represented status in the late nineteenth-century feudal hierarchy. The German monarchy, responsive to the change, ennobled more than a thousand men between 1871 and 1918.[1] Even the Social Democrats, despite their spectacular rise to power, never challenged the old autocracy. They remained monarchist, venerating God and kaiser, and even sanctioned Germany's entrance into World War I. We may, indeed, conclude with Tom Kemp: "The rise of German industrial power took place within an archaic framework of autocracy, traditionalism, and militarism."[2]

Conservative sentiment swayed fin-de-siècle musicians as it did the magnates of capital, the professionals, and the bourgeoisie. Far from being bohemian nonconformists, musicians zealously sought the imperial seal. Their wish was not to overturn the "seignorial establishment but to break into it." Titles like Königliche Kammersinger (Royal Chamber Singer) and medals awarded by royalty remained principal objectives of performers and composers as evidence of eminence. Even concert attire indicated adherence to this old tradition. "It was the custom on the continent," according to George Henschel—singer, conductor, and friend of Brahms—"for gentlemen to wear evening dress at any official function, even in the morning" and at concerts for a "singer to appear displaying the gold medals he had been awarded."[3] Although musicians no longer depended on the monarchy for employment—they received most of their support from wealthy patrons—concert life in Germany and Austria showed performers and patrons alike exhibiting fawning loyalty to royalty.

Austrians tended to be particularly conservative. For while Germany was growing both socially and economically, Austria was decaying under a regressive autocracy.[4] Its youth was driven by antimodernist, nationalist thought, even the Pernerstorfer circle, whose leaders were socialists and whose members included Hugo Wolf, Gustav Mahler, the philosopher and poet Siegfried Lipiner, the writer (and patron of Bruckner and Wolf) Friedrich Eckstein, and the physician—and founder of the Austrian Social Democratic Party—Viktor Adler. Most Austrian students were, above all, German nationalists, united in hatred of the Hapsburgs, passionate for the union of Austria with the new Germany. Wagnerism unified many Pernerstorfers, giving them common ground even with the offshoot right-wing group led by Georg Schönerer, who was later one of Hitler's mentors. In lively discussions on the German spirit and its ancient culture, both groups formed a strong Austro-German bond within their multi-ethnic empire. In music, these feelings spawned even this "double dose of nationalism"—the group singing of "Deutschland, Deutschland über Alles!" to the piano accompaniment of "O du Deutschland, ich muss marschieren" played by Gustav Mahler, William McGrath notes. Nationalism became aggressive, anti-Semitic, and disruptive, even at concerts. At a performance in the Vienna Wagner Verein, with the composer at the keyboard, Wolf's "Heimweh" (poet: Eichendorff) "was made the occasion for a pan-Germanic demonstration" at the song's concluding line: "Grüss dich, Deutschland, aus Herzensgrund" (I greet thee Germany, with all my heart). Pandemonium again broke forth at the song's repetition, preventing its completion—to Wolf's fury.[5]

Concert life clung so dearly to antiquated practices—some from the late eighteenth century—that reforms instituted after 1900 actually affirmed earlier nineteenth-century aesthetics. The lied—that most distinctive expression of nineteenth-century romanticism—had been excluded from public concerts in Austria and Germany throughout the first half of the century and later. "Not even the remotest thought was given to the public performance of the lied." Yet it had been a great favorite in concerts given in private homes.[6] After 1850, however, a few enterprising singers dared to offer public concerts that featured lieder. The celebrated baritone Julius Stockhausen was the first to sing as complete cycles the *Müllerlieder* (in 1856), and the *Dichterliebe* (1861). Reaction from resistors of innovation was swift. These concerts—referred to by Eduard Hanslick as "experiments"—were not commended. Clara Schumann, ignoring Stockhausen's innovation, performed her husband's *Frauenliebe und Leben* (Op. 42) in two separate parts (see fig. 1), only four songs at a time.

Conservatives delayed the change until around 1870; but in the fin de siècle the lied became omnipresent in public concert life.[7] The public regarded the lied—especially Schubert's and Schumann's miniature miracles of lyricism—as revered national treasures. Gustav Walter (1834–1910), a singer at the Royal Opera, gave his first Schubert evening in 1876 and met with such success that he offered evenings of Schubert's songs every year thereafter. These concerts became an important feature of Viennese musical life. Theodor Helm commented: "Gustav Walter's remarkable evenings of Schubert, which are unprecedented, have become a stable feature of our Viennese musical life. It has come to pass that these enjoyable concerts of lieder are presented on a . . . fixed date— March 1, in Bösendorf Hall. One might say . . . that it is a mark of good taste to

Zweites
CONCERT
Clara Schumann

(k. k. Kammer-Virtuosin)

Donnerstag den 1. Februar 1866,

Abends halb 8 Uhr,

im Saale der Gesellschaft der Musikfreunde.

PROGRAMM:

1. **Sonate** B-dur . . . . **F. Schubert.**
   - Molto moderato.
   - Andante sostenuto.
   - Scherzo.
   - Allegro ma non troppo.
2. **Nr. 1, 2, 3, 4 aus Frauenliebe und Leben** . . . . **R. Schumann,**
   vorgetragen von Frln. **Bettelheim,**
   k. k. Hofopernsängerin.
3. **Variationen** C-moll op. 36 . . . **Beethoven,**
4. **Duo** für 2 Klaviere . . . . . . **Ernst Rudorff,**
   vorgetragen von Fräulein **Julie v.
   Asten** und der **Concertgeberin.**
5. **Nr. 5, 6, 7, 8 aus Frauenliebe und Leben** . . . . **R. Schumann,**
   vorgetragen von Frln. **Bettelheim.**
6. a) **In der Nacht** op. 12.
   b) **Schlummer-Lied** op. 124. } **R. Schumann.**
   c) **Novelette** D-dur Nr. 2 op. 21.

Cercle à 3 fl., Parterresitze à 2 fl., Galleriesitze à 1 fl. 50 kr.,
Entrée à 1 fl. sind in der k. k. Hof-Kunst- und Musikalien-
handlung des Herrn C. A. SPINA am Graben und am
Abende des Concertes an der Kassa zu haben.

Figure 1. Concert Program: Clara Schumann, *Frauenliebe und Lieben*, February 1, 1866
(Archive of the Gesellschaft der Musikfreunde, Vienna)

meet each year on March 1 . . . to hear Walter sing Schubert. Of course, this custom still has not been imitated by other singers. . . . Where can one find a more wonderful singer?"[8]

Walter's daring grew with his success, but he was still the only singer in Vienna to attract any attention to the lied before 1880. Albert Gutmann, his concert manager, understood the reason for Walter's "monopoly on the lied" to be the apparent demand by the public for lieder and the reluctance of other singers to satisfy it. Gutmann explains that he urged Walter "to extend his monopoly on the lied by giving a series of three or four evenings of songs. . . . Next, I decided to arrange a series of Liederabende by [other singers]. . . . I engaged in addition to Viennese singers, Hermine Spiess, Amalie Joachim, Eugen Gura, Johannes Messchaert, Raimund von zur Muehlen, Ludwig Wuellner, Lilli Lehmann, Lula Gmeiner, Julia Culp et al."[9]

By the late 1880s, "Liederabende have grown into an epidemic," Wolf, then critic on the *Salonblatt*, wrote in 1887: "Walter's lucrative idea of offering Liederabende has in recent years found many imitators. Our native singers were suddenly seized with a deep need of also 'making' Liederabende, and even singers in other cities are captured by the spell of his lieder humbug."[10]

The height of public enthusiasm for the lied occurred between 1900 and 1914. The number of *Liederabende* (song recitals) offered between 1900 and 1914 was staggering. In Berlin alone the outstanding accompanist Michael Raucheisen reckons that an average of twenty were offered weekly, and these were generally sold out. Raucheisen estimates that he accompanied at eight Liederabende each week.[11] The lied became one of the principal musical expressions of the period. "Lieder recitals of all types and hues," the composer Karl Bleyle (1880–1969) informed me, were presented in Munich. Concert programs on file in Munich's city library support Bleyle's claim. Lieder were also performed at musical soirées in Germany and Austria. The organization of these sophisticated gatherings warrants a brief description since the lied played a major role there.

According to Emilie Bittner, a concert singer and the widow of the composer Julius Bittner (1874–1939), performances of Viennese *Hausmusik* ran along these lines: Various musicians—Wilhelm Kienzl, Julius Bittner, Alma Mahler—and wealthy music lovers would make their homes available for regular weekly evenings of music, to which forty to sixty people would be invited.[12] Dinner was generally served first, after which the guests would retire to the music salon for the concert. Often composers associated with the group—Mahler, Kienzl, Bittner, Schoenberg, and Berg—would present evenings of their compositions. Although songs with piano accompaniment were favored, works for voice and concerts by chamber groups were offered occasionally. Schoenberg's *Pierrot Lunaire* had its first Viennese performance at the home of Alma Mahler.[13] "Lieder," Emilie Bittner continued, "fitted particularly well into the atmosphere of these intimate social gatherings. The poem was generally read before each setting was sung. One could easily lose oneself in the mood produced. Vienna had a rich, sophisticated society that sought the best in art and was willing to support it."

Lieder played a major role also at concerts given by the Vereine dedicated to the arts, since they were relatively inexpensive to perform. As with the soirées, the poem was usually read before the lied was sung. The Ansorge Verein, typical of many such societies, was founded in 1903 by Wilhelm von Wymetal and Paul Stefan to promote the works of the pianist and composer Conrad Ansorge. Its formation was announced not only in Vienna but even in distant cities, in the journal *Vossische Zeitung* of Berlin, for instance.

Events planned by the Ansorge Verein during its first year indicate its high cultural objectives and its missionary work for art in general:

- An evening of Ansorge's compositions (including the lied cycles Op. 10, 11, 12, 14, and 17).
- A Liederabend of Ansorge and Pfitzner.
- A Liederabend of Ansorge, Gutheil, Streicher, and Zemlinsky.
- A Schoenberg evening.
- A Goethe Liederabend (*Urworte* and *Orphisch* by Ansorge and *Mignon-Lieder* by Zelter, Beethoven, Schubert, Liszt, Wolf, and Tchaikovsky).
- A Richard Dehmel evening.
- A Friedrich Nietzsche evening.
- A reading of works by Stefan George and his school.
- An evening of pianoforte music by Ansorge, Schubert, Liszt, Chopin, and Beethoven.
- An evening of chamber music (Ansorge's *Vigilien* Quartet, Op. 13).
- A theatrical evening.
- An evening of authors.
- A Liliencron evening.

Attendance at the opening concert was beyond expectation: "People were standing in the artist's room and in the corridors. . . . University professors sat on the steps and, as the concert began at 8:15, a group of aristocratic people, who had come too late, were forced to leave simply because there was not room for them to enter. . . . The evening was a sensation! Almost all of Vienna was there."[14] Though brilliantly successful, the life of this society was short, but new societies sprang up almost as rapidly as old ones dissolved.[15]

Around 1900, lieder were frequently performed in exclusive hotels and even in the *Überbrettl* and *Elf Scharfrichter* (artistic cabaret entertainments). "The lied also played a prominent role at concerts in vocal schools and even of choral societies, which were seemingly innumerable at that time," Bleyle noted. Not only were arias and lieder performed together in concert programs but singers would begin their programs with a lied instead of an aria, as had been traditional. As late as 1866 Clara Schumann wrote to Brahms that the audience at a Stockhausen concert in Berlin "was annoyed because . . . he charged one-and-a-half thalers, sang only little lieder, and gave the *Loewenbraut* as his first number instead of an aria by Handel, which would have been more appropriate."[16]

Concert programs before 1900 still clung to outdated practices. Walter's famous evenings of Schubert, for instance, were not song recitals in the modern sense (concerts at which only lieder were performed) but events at which instrumental solos were interspersed with groups of songs. Such programs persisted in Vienna until at least 1890, and sporadically thereafter. In a Liederabend that Wolf attended in Munich in 1890, "the intervals were passed off, God be thanked, without the piano thumping customary in Vienna." These early practices persisted even longer in Berlin.[17]

In addition, singers performed from printed music instead of singing from memory, a custom that continued throughout the nineteenth century into the early twentieth (see fig. 2). The time of the singer who was trained to concentrate on the lied was yet to come. The recitals that Gutmann arranged before 1900, according to Helm, were "lieder recitals by opera stars."[18] The different types of singers who performed the lied during the nineteenth century reflect its slow change of status. Before 1850, as we have seen, it was sung primarily by amateurs in private homes. When it was later performed in public, the lied became the domain first of opera singers and, after 1900, of trained specialists.

Distribution of lied texts at recitals became customary in the fin de siècle (see fig. 3). "Why haven't you ever supplied your audience with lied texts? Everyone does," Hanslick asked the well-known artist Alice Barbi, in great surprise.[19] This practice was no innovation. Libretti of newly performed operas had been furnished without charge from at least the 1780s. Fin-de-siècle artists adopted this practice to support an old ideal of the lied: the fusion of music and poetry. Pfitzner provided the texts of his songs before a concert (in Essen, 1904) to prepare his audience with an understanding of the poetry before hearing his settings.

The rapid growth of concert life during the last two decades of the nineteenth century led to a reappraisal of concert practices early in our century. Reform was sought for practices that had remained unchanged for well over a hundred years. The mixed program, which combined chamber music, pieces for solo instruments, symphonies, and lieder, was strongly attacked. "It is absolutely necessary," Paul Ehlers wrote, "to ban lyric solo pieces from symphony concerts. The performance of works for solo piano and violin or of songs with piano accompaniment directly after symphonic music hurts one's aesthetic feeling for program unity."[20]

Reformers urged that the number of soloists at recitals be limited to two and that programs have organic unity. A well-organized program should build up to a climax and be unified with respect to the nationality and period of the composers, yet it must contain variety as well, Richard Batka argued in his monograph *Handbuch für Konzertveranstalter*.[21] Chamber music and lieder, reformers

Figure 2. Johannes Messchaert and accompanist Julius Röntgen, after a drawing by Otto Böhler

urged, should be presented in small halls only. "I consider it barbarous to drag into our giant modern concert halls string quartets, sonatas for one or two instruments, and *Gesänge* with piano accompaniment. . . . These genres are, in the noblest sense of the word, Hausmusik and should be heard only at informal gatherings with indirect lighting by musicians and music lovers who take part in their performance."[22] This conservative reform threatened the lied, after its

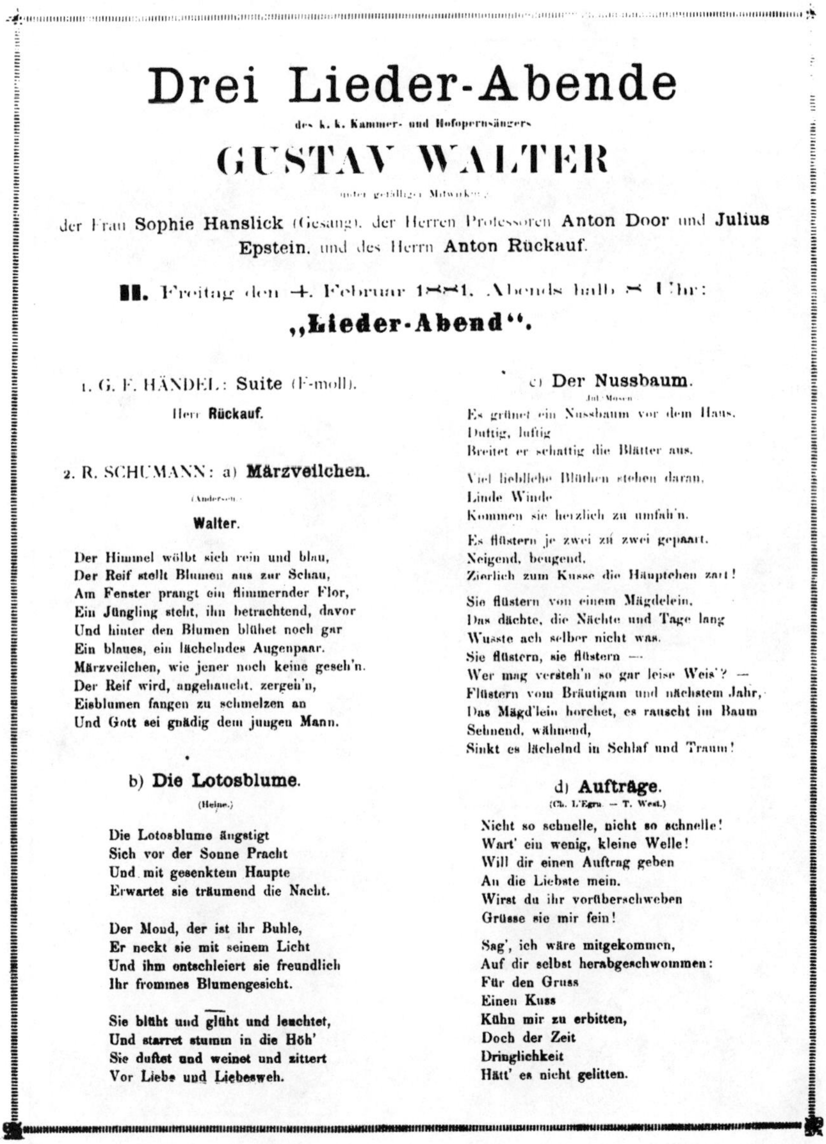

Drei Lieder-Abende

des k. k. Kammer- und Hofopernsängers

GUSTAV WALTER

unter gefälliger Mitwirkung

der Frau Sophie Hanslick (Gesang), der Herren Professoren Anton Door und Julius Epstein, und des Herrn Anton Ruckauf.

II. Freitag den 4. Februar 1881. Abends halb 8 Uhr:

„Lieder-Abend".

1. G. F. HÄNDEL: Suite (F-moll).

Herr **Rückauf.**

2. R. SCHUMANN: a) **Märzveilchen.**

(Andersen.)

Walter.

Der Himmel wölbt sich rein und blau,
Der Reif stellt Blumen aus zur Schau,
Am Fenster prangt ein flimmernder Flor,
Ein Jüngling steht, ihn betrachtend, davor
Und hinter den Blumen blühet noch gar
Ein blaues, ein lächelndes Augenpaar.
Märzveilchen, wie jener noch keine geseh'n.
Der Reif wird, angehaucht, zergeh'n,
Eisblumen fangen zu schmelzen an
Und Gott sei gnädig dem jungen Mann.

b) Die **Lotosblume.**

(Heine.)

Die Lotosblume ängstigt
Sich vor der Sonne Pracht
Und mit gesenktem Haupte
Erwartet sie träumend die Nacht.

Der Mond, der ist ihr Buhle,
Er neckt sie mit seinem Licht
Und ihm entschleiert sie freundlich
Ihr frommes Blumengesicht.

Sie blüht und glüht und leuchtet,
Und starret stumm in die Höh'
Sie duftet und weinet und zittert
Vor Liebe und Liebesweh.

c) **Der Nussbaum.**

(Jul. Mosen.)

Es grünet ein Nussbaum vor dem Haus.
Duftig, luftig
Breitet er schattig die Blätter aus.

Viel liebliche Blüthen stehen daran.
Linde Winde
Kommen sie herzlich zu umfah'n.

Es flüstern je zwei zu zwei gepaart.
Neigend, beugend,
Zierlich zum Kusse die Häuptchen zart!

Sie flüstern von einem Mägdelein.
Das dächte, die Nächte und Tage lang
Wusste ach selber nicht was.
Sie flüstern, sie flüstern —
Wer mag versteh'n so gar leise Weis'? —
Flüstern vom Bräutigam und nächstem Jahr,
Das Mägd'lein horchet, es rauscht im Baum
Sehnend, wähnend,
Sinkt es lächelnd in Schlaf und Traum!

d) **Aufträge.**

(Ch. L'Egru — T. West.)

Nicht so schnelle, nicht so schnelle!
Wart' ein wenig, kleine Welle!
Will dir einen Auftrag geben
An die Liebste mein.
Wirst du ihr vorüberschweben
Grüsse sie mir fein!

Sag', ich wäre mitgekommen,
Auf dir selbst herabgeschwommen:
Für den Gruss
Einen Kuss
Kühn mir zu erbitten,
Doch der Zeit
Dringlichkeit
Hätt' es nicht gelitten.

Figure 3. Gustav Walter, Liederabend, February 4, 1881: Concert Program with lied texts (Archive of the Gesellschaft der Musikfreunde, Vienna)

century-long struggle for acceptance at public concerts, with a return to its former status as Hausmusik.

Reformers also sought ways to make the concert hall more suitable for the reception of the lied. They demanded that applause be curtailed since it destroyed the mood of the music. Lights should be dimmed during performance, for darkness creates atmosphere. "The transformation of a hall into a comfortable, festival, or social room in which lights are dimmed during recitals," Ehlers argued, "creates an atmosphere that is uncommonly charming . . . intimate . . . and particularly suitable for the performance of the lied."[23]

Radical reformers urged the use of different colored lights in the concert halls, the choice of color depending upon the mood of the music. Alexander Dillmann performed against a lighting effect of purple twilight in a recital in the Odeon Hall in Munich.[24] Extremists recommended that halls be scented with various types of perfumes during Liederabende, the fragrance to be chosen according to the mood of the particular song. Critics also suggested that singers be concealed from view, in order to produce effects of mystery and to eliminate the distraction of seeing musicians in performance. "When one listens only to the music and to the clearly enunciated word," Ehlers wrote, "one's imagination is given greater room to operate." Paul Marsop added: "One will readily admit that gesticulation and pantomime have no place in the execution of songs." Concealing performers at Liederabende "covers [their exaggerated] motions" from view. Several methods of concealing performers at concerts were attempted. Flowers, palms, and laurel trees were placed between the audience and performers. At a concert in Nuremberg, "the decoration of plants was illuminated by green light" (see fig. 4).[25]

Today the most extreme reforms seem like a reductio ad absurdum of the reform movement. Nevertheless, those suggested by Wilhelm Mauke deserve attention. They were printed in one of Europe's most prestigious newspapers, the *Frankfurter Zeitung* (August 10, 1899), and actually adopted. Further, they touched off heated debate between their author and the composer and conductor Felix Weingartner. Mauke considered the following conditions ideal for the performance of lieder:

Figure 4. Plants and palms concealing performers (from Marsop, "Von Musiksaal der Zukunft")

25

The auditorium, whose seats are arranged in the shape of an amphitheater, affords only enough light to permit the audience to read the text of the lieder. Neither the piano nor the pianist is visible. The singer is not dressed in tasteless attire, but in the symbolic broad, white robe of an Apollonian priest, or is clad in the attire of a singer of Bacchus—costumes which he changes according to the mood of each song. His voice touches our hearts by being heard through a sea-green web of liana plants. An aroma of Heliotrope passes through the hall when sensuous sultry love songs are sung. Serious lieder are heard with incense that comes from rows of columns that are embraced by holy groves or cypress. The hymns of summer night rock one to sleep in the midst of large umbellated buds, violet-colored clouds, stars that glitter gently—everything is in mystical darkness. Passionate cries of erotic songs speak to the imagination and to intimate emotions of the audience, which is thrilled with perplexity and pain.[26]

The concert reform movement was no bold venture into musical modernism but an eleventh-hour endeavor—it began after 1900—to implant nineteenth-century aesthetics into concert practices that had undergone no real change since the late eighteenth century. As will be shown in Chapter 11, the campaign to unify concert programs was, in a sense, a late expression of the movement toward unity and integration initiated by Beethoven a hundred years earlier. The idea of linking hall size to specific genres, of introducing atmospheric lighting effects, of curtailing applause and concealing performers from view descended from the Wagnerian aesthetics introduced at Bayreuth.[27]

The reform of linking hall size to genre differs markedly from modern practice: Mahler wrote to Strauss, "Despite all commercial considerations, I have given these songs in a *small* hall only. . . . They are appropriate only there. To perform them in a large hall . . . is *without question in poor taste* and really would expose both of us to [commercial] reproaches!"[28] Today the performance of lieder in large concert halls, to sold-out capacity, marks a performer's renown. It evokes praise, not reproach!

Strauss sought to reintroduce this Wagnerian reform after the devastation of World War II. He proposed that three kinds of opera houses be constructed, each with a different repertory. For Paul Henry Lang, Strauss's proposal, was a "manifesto of a bygone age[,] . . . pathetic because . . . it shows that its author has outlived his own times and speaks from a vantage point that is no longer clearly perceptible to us."[29]

Schools of music were strongholds of conservatism during the fin de siècle, unlike those of today, in which modern works are studied and performed. Brahms, Joachim, and the composers and academics Bernhard Scholz (1835–1916) and Julius Otto Grimm (1827–1903) had signed the famous manifesto against radical New German aesthetics in 1860. A generation later, professors of composition throughout Germany, idolizing Brahms, continued to respond negatively to the "new" aesthetics. An unimpeachable witness, the composer Julius Weismann (1879–1950), found his one year (1898) of internship in Berlin to have a heavy *verbrämte* and *verbramste* atmosphere (his humorous quip on the name Brahms). Study in the "masterclass (that dreadful word) of Herrn v. H. was overbearing." The Hoch Conservatory of Frankfurt, which attracted students from all over the world—among them Percy Grainger (Australia), Cyril Scott (England), Hermann Sandby (Denmark)—was another stronghold of Brahms tradition. Iwan Knorr (1853–1916), professor of composition, was, for Pfitzner, a "Brahmin" and the conservatory—"in contrast with the revolutionary, heaven-storming New German" aesthetic—a "temperance league." Instructors regarded compositions by students that betrayed Wagner's influence as "life threatening." Scholz "ruled with the authority of an absolute prince," Peter Cahn writes. "Each new generation of students performed the exact same pieces." Although change began after Scholz's retirement in 1908, it was not until Bernhard Sekles's directorship (1924–33) that the school finally threw off its conservatism. The Königliche Musikschule of Munich had another stern disciplinarian at its helm, Joseph Rheinberger (1839–1901), who ignored the works of Wagner and Liszt, as well as more recent musical currents. Change came to the Munich conservatory in 1902 when Ludwig Thuille (1861–1907) succeeded Rheinberger as director. He helped found the famous Munich School. "In the Thuille circle there was one supreme god, R. Wagner and two living gods, Max Schillings and L. Thuille," Weismann wrote about study there. Evidently, Thuille was only a moderate adherent of New German modernism, even after his conversion by Alexander Ritter. Weismann discloses: "It was, indeed, curious how seldom R. Strauss and his work was mentioned and how hostilely Reger was rejected."[30]

Pfitzner confided: "It was far better to have studied under [Knorr] than with any one of the wild New Germans."[31] The degree to which professors—often regarded by students as supreme authority figures—influenced young fin-de-siècle composers remains an important but elusive topic. Pfitzner's early lieder show the strong influence of his conservative training. Many of his early songs—the *Jugendlieder* (ca. 1883–87) in particular—are conservative Melodielieder, some so attractive that he arranged them for violin and piano (for example, "Ich hört ein Vöglein locken," Op. 2, no. 5). The early lieder of Strauss and Reger, as mentioned, also show the strong influence of conservative training. The subtle influence in their late years of their earlier orientation is not to be ignored.

The resilience of tradition is best illustrated by the response of Strauss, Mahler, and Reger to innovations that challenged the very foundation of inherited tradition: the advances of Schoenberg. Mahler and Strauss did not consider Schoenberg's breach of tradition an inevitable consequence of their innovations, although his advances were stimulated by theirs. Note that Strauss opposed straining music beyond what he considered its limits. As early as 1902 he found Schoenberg's music "a bit over-charged at the moment." Of Schoenberg's later radical advances, Strauss was less indulgent: "It would be better for him to be shoveling snow than scrawling on music paper." Mahler, perplexed by Schoenberg's radical innovations, couched his reactions more kindly: "I don't understand his music, but he's young and perhaps he's right."[32]

Nearly all the lied composers who achieved prominence during the fin de siècle sought new ways to advance tradition. But none, not even Schoenberg's former teacher, brother-in-law, and lifelong friend, Zemlinsky, considered Schoenberg's modernist breakthrough, when it occurred, as having been the inevitable consequence of the innovations of Mahler and Strauss.

The predilection of Wolf, Mahler, and Strauss for ever more intense expression—for bolder ventures in harmony at moments when expression ran high—created crises of tonality. Analysts correctly pointed out that these composers had, in some passages, entered the domain of new music. The crucial point, however, is that the ultimate aim of these composers was to preserve tradition. They delighted in occasional brinkmanship, to be sure, but they always returned to safe traditional harbor. Schoenberg's course was the opposite of theirs. "I believe it is not possible to trifle with freedom while being shackled[,] . . . to loosen the bonds of tonality . . . and, despite this, suddenly to reaffirm them at [a work's] end . . . or somewhere else."[33]

Reger, Strauss, and Mahler endeavored in their later years to dilute or even to discard the very aesthetic on which part of their early reputations as avant-gardists was based. Reger began his retreat from radical New German aesthetics after 1903. Although he had often stretched tonality to the breaking point, Reger abjured a complete break. Singers capable of meeting his fierce demands were becoming increasingly difficult to find, and he felt that his radical experiments hindered the expression of his true individuality. Consequently, he made an about-face after completing Op. 75. "I understand everything that you have written about Op. 75," Reger confessed to Karl Straube about 1903. "I have taken . . . the *Schlichte Weisen* (Op. 76) intentionally as a remedy. . . . These songs will certainly prove to you that I have, in some lieder, found a cure for what in Op. 75 was sick." In a subsequent letter: "My new lieder . . . will be genuine Reger."[34] He now aimed at lucidity and transparency. He simplified the texture in the piano part and eliminated excessive demands on the singer by smoothing out his former New German jagged vocal line. But although the mood in these later lieder is cooler than that of his middle years, the harmonic language of some of them ("Ein Drängen," for instance) still provoked hostile criticism.

Reger persisted. His predilection for absolute music came to dominate his late style. Unlike Wolf and Strauss, Reger arranged twelve of his *Schlichte Weisen* for violin and piano (Op. 103c) and more than fifty songs by Brahms, Wolf, and Strauss for piano solo. Purely musical elements prevail in his late songs, especially in Op. 137 and Op. 142. Reger regarded his new style as a retreat from radical New German aesthetics. Late twentieth-century scholars regard his new style as foreshadowing neoclassicism.

Mahler, too, began a retreat. His early death, however, prevented its fulfillment. "In earlier years, I used to like to do unusual things in my compositions. . . . If a piece began in D major, I would make a point of concluding it in A-flat minor. Now, on the contrary, I often go to a great deal of trouble to end a work in the key in which I began."[35] Mahler's statement rings true with respect to his later songs. Progressive tonality appears only once in *Lieder und Gesänge, Knaben Wunderhorn,* and *Sieben Lieder aus letzte Zeit* and not at all in *Kindertotenlieder.*

Strauss's retreat from New German "excesses" is evident in the songs of his late years (1918–49). Hofmannsthal's catechism of Strauss in 1908 alerts us to Strauss's impending change of style: "If I rightly understood you . . . your intention is to write something quite new in style, yet which—since every new development in art acts like a swing of the pendulum—will resemble the *older* type of opera . . . with set pieces . . . and old-fashioned recitativo secco" (emphasis mine). Strauss's intention—"I give you my word I have definitely cast off the whole armor of Wagner forever more"—was not always realized.[36] With respect to the lied, Strauss's avowed new style also does not represent a complete about-face. Familiar traits of Strauss's musico-literary synthesis persist. But the composer often attenuates literary effects to strengthen purely musical ones. He tends to develop rhythmic motives in *both* the piano and the voice parts, as in his setting of the first line of Heine's "Schlechtes Wetter" (see ex. 87), where he introduces a rhythmic motive into the voice part that he develops in the piano part—at the expense of careful declamation.

Further, powerful dramatic songs and challenges to tonality also are rare in Strauss's late lieder. So, too, is detailed musical imagery, the *Krämerspiegel* excepted. In short, the flame of his earlier lieder appears in the late songs only as a deep glow. Lyrical passages, arabesquelike figures, and finely spun coloraturas, such as are found in Zerbinetta's music from *Ariadne auf Naxos,* predominate. High and light color—songs for soprano—are abundant. The older Strauss seems increasingly to regard the voice as a medium primarily for producing beautiful sound rather than for articulating language to convey thought. This tendency is highly developed in the last four orchestral songs (1948), where the voice part is often enveloped in luxuriant orchestral fabric and treated as another orchestral instrument.

Pfitzner's late lieder do not show extensive change in style. As conservative, Pfitzner never yielded to the excesses of New German aesthetics, even though he was influenced by them. Nearly all his late lieder express his lifelong aim for lyricism, careful musical organization, and, above all, evocative mood—aspects of the traditional lied, which he endeavored his entire life to preserve.

In later life Pfitzner issued a crucial challenge against a group of critics we may identify as New German theorists. He described three methods of lied composition, rejecting entirely the declamatory method of the New Germans: "The more attention . . . a composer pays to the text . . . the more he is bound to neglect . . . the purely musical organization of his songs, which, as a consequence, often becomes musical nonsense—despite declamation." Pfitzner was critical, too, of a second long-established method, which he considered a relic of the past. "The composer shapes his melodies . . . as if they were instrumental . . . later adjusting the text more or less to fit the music." According to his ideal, composers should follow the third method: "There are times . . . when, from two different springs, the same spirit streams in word and tone together . . . into one channel like the tones of a perfect interval." To create such fusion, the music "must come from its own sphere and evoke the same mood as that of the poem; this can occur *wholly* independently, *before* knowledge of the poem."[37]

New German theorists, early in the twentieth century, were attracting much attention in Germany and Austria. Ernest Newman was this rapidly growing group's best-known English spokesman. Wolf was their idol. They revered his declamatory methods, censuring other composers' methods, as did Newman: when Strauss leafs through "a volume of poetry" and discovers a poem that "agrees with the mood he is in . . . the appropriate music is instinctively fitted to it," Newman notes. If not, the results are labored. Newman vigorously censured this method as lied composition begun from the wrong end and demonstrated the correct way, Wolf's way. Wolf started from the poem, "absorbing himself so utterly in it" that "the music . . . was simply the equivalent in tone of the emotion that had penetrated the poet when he wrote the words."[38]

Early adherents of Wolf particularly praised his declamation. They applauded the skillful ways he accented key words according to their importance in the central meaning of a poem, often producing a subtle gradation among the words. For example, the climax of "Was soll der Zorn" (from the *Italian Songbook*), which concerns a girl who would rather be killed by her lover than face his scorn, illustrates the point:

nimm des Dolches Stahl	take a dagger's steel
und wasch' in meinem Blut	and wash in my blood
all meine Qual	all my anguish.

Wolf set these lines with great subtlety, using traditional means of stressing words. He uses as many as five different time values, whose lengths are in proportion to the relative importance of the words within the poem. The five time values are shown by X's in example 3. He rhythmically contrasts the three groups of words—"nimm des Dolches Stahl," "und wasch' in meinem," and "Blut all meine Qual"—by obliging the singer to stress the first moderately, hasten over the second, and place heaviest emphasis on the third, where the thought is centered. (This heightened interest, incidentally, is reinforced with a crescendo in the piano part.)

Example 3. Wolf: "Was soll der Zorn" (Heyse), mm. 14–17.

Wolf's extensive use of less conventional methods of word emphasis (syncopation, chromaticism, and sudden changes of dynamics) distinguishes his "literary" procedures from those of early nineteenth-century composers. He often applies these devices to carefully selected syllables in key words. The second syllable of *uralte* (primeval) in "Grenzen der Menschheit" (m. 8), for instance, is brought into special prominence on a syncopated chromatic note that produces a strong dissonance with the harmony in the piano part. Panegyrics of Wolf's declamation centered on fine points such as these.

The influence of Newman and the New German theorists was enormous. Although it produced positive results, it also incurred negative consequences that linger. It conceals some important facts. For instance, Wolf himself, upon occasion, composed lieder "from the wrong end." Like Strauss, he, too, set poetry that fit the mood he was in. And so, too, did most fin-de-siècle composers—radicals and conservatives alike. When Pfitzner spoke of "two streams" with the same spirit (mood) uniting in a lied and Strauss spoke of "two firestones being struck together," both were stressing the same point: the fundamental importance of mood in lied composition. Pfitzner even praised Brahms's "Minnelied" (Op. 71, no. 5), which was unanimously censured by New German theorists as poorly declaimed, because the mood of the poetry and the music fused perfectly. Some New German theorists, in contrast—centering attention on declamation—censured not only Brahms but even Wolf on occasion, ignoring the fact, as noted above, that Wolf's magnificent contributions to the lied extend beyond the art of declamation. Pfitzner's crucial challenge thus draws attention to a vital old aesthetic of the lied, one that persisted into and beyond the fin de siècle: the importance of *Stimmung* (mood) in lied composition.

This point leads to crucial evidence about the preservation of tradition, evidence that seems incompatible with the objectives of Wolf, Mahler, Strauss, and Reger as radical lied composers: the influence of the gentle lyricism of Schumann's Stimmungslied. This influence perhaps reveals most about the aim of these modern composers to preserve tradition. For while they were creating radical crises of tonality, they endeavored also to preserve a style rooted in the 1840s, when Schumann composed many of his greatest lieder.

It may seem surprising that Schumann's lyricism influenced Strauss nearly eighty years later, in the turbulent year of 1918 no less. Yet Strauss's long Schumannesque introduction to "Von Händlern wird die Kunst bedroht" from the *Krämerspiegel* (Op. 66) is not an isolated instance. Actually the five masters all expressed aesthetic delight in developing Schumann's gentle lyricism in the fin-de-siècle lied. One finds examples in Mahler, whose innovative style is at the same time vastly different from Schumann's. A comparison of the conclusion of Schumann's *Dichterliebe* no. 9, mm. 79–84, with the ending of Mahler's "Des Antonius von Padua Fischpredigt" (1893) shows an almost note-for-note similarity, on which several scholars have commented. Yet the passage from Schumann sounds thoroughly Mahler-like in its "new" context, evidence that fifty-three years later Schumann's style did not seem out-of-place in the Modern Lied. Mahler loved the "restrained feelings, true lyricism, and profound melancholy" of the Schumann lied. Norman Del Mar found another similarity in the same Schumann song within the closing bars of both Mahler's "Wer hat dies Liedlein erdacht" and Strauss's "Muttertändelei" (Op. 43, no. 2).[39]

Schumann's far-reaching influence on the fin-de-siècle lied has gone largely unnoticed, partly because of its subtle expression by the masters. They developed an entire genre of the lied that Schumann created, the Stimmungslied. They shaped it as did Schumann, aiming to create and sustain one central mood, giving the voice part an all-pervading delicate lyricism and the piano part sensitive, florid configurations and ostinato-like figures. Schumann's well-known examples, such as "Im wunderschönen Monat Mai," served as models. Mahler absorbed the style, expressing it with individuality, in "Ich atmet' einen linden Duft." So, too, did Wolf, Strauss, Pfitzner, and Reger.

We can easily document Schumann's influence upon Wolf. We know that the young Wolf regarded Schubert, Carl Loewe (1796–1869), and Schumann as models. But though he admired Schubert, only few of Wolf's early songs show Schubert's mark: "Ein Grab" (1876), "Wohin mit der Freud?" (1882–83), and "Spätherbstnebel" (1878), for instance. The influence of Schumann is most evident in "Der Schwalben Heimkehr" (1877), "Liebesfrühling" (1878), and "Liebesbotschaft" (1883). Wolf scribbled across the manuscript of "Was soll ich sagen" (1878): "Too much like Schumann—on that account not finished." Of some other early songs (from 1877), Wolf stated: "A strong Schumannian trait runs through the songs, especially in *Traurige Wege*." Wolf even tried to pass off some of his early songs (at a concert in the Austrian Alpine Society, 1882) as Schumann compositions.[40] Wolf's concept of the Stimmungslied descended from Schumann. At first he copied Schumann's long evocative piano solos. Later he created his own examples. The early masterpiece "Nachtzauber" (1887) is a Stimmungslied enchanted by Schumann.

Pfitzner's admiration for Schumann ran especially deep. It stimulated a variety of creative efforts: an uncompleted comprehensive biography written with his first wife, Mimi; a sonnet dedicated to Schumann; and the orchestration of a half-dozen of Schumann's pianoforte songs and eight of his choral pieces for female choir, which Pfitzner himself conducted.[41]

As a lied composer, Pfitzner owed a special debt to Schumann. Hans Joachim Moser had considered Pfitzner's songs a mere repetition of the Schumann lied. After careful restudy, however, Moser's opinion changed to one of admiration: although Schumann comes unabashedly through in some of the Stimmungslieder, in most, Pfitzner made the genre his own. The Stimmungslied enabled Pfitzner to explore a favorite subject, nature. His object was to suggest nature's depths through mood rather than imagery, for which he used an exceptionally broad scale of dynamic shadings. He depicted the rumbling reverberation of nature's inner core with undulating, ostinato-like piano figures. To intensify the effect, he instructed the pianist (in the footnote in "Abschied" [Op. 9, no. 5], for instance) to play "the accompaniment *ppp* and somewhat blurred" by extensive use of the pedals. "An den Mond" (Op. 18), however, bursts the confines of the Stimmungslied as conceived by Schumann. Pfitzner's shimmering music suggests colors far beyond those of the pianoforte lied. Pfitzner accordingly orchestrated "An den Mond," "one of the most melodious of Goethe's poems," to capture its lyricism, its rich colors, and its inner world, where humans and nature become one.[42]

The Stimmungslied became so much an inner part of Strauss's oeuvre that Schumann's influence seems all but lost. Schumann, nonetheless, peers out from Strauss's earlier and later efforts (see "Die Nacht," 1885, Op. 10, no. 3, my *Krämerspiegel* example). But his mature songs more frequently bear his own individual stamp. Some became popular favorites: "Freundliche Vision" (Op. 48, no. 1), "Traum durch die Dämmerung" (Op. 29, no. 1), "Nachtgang" (Op. 29, no. 3), and "Waldseligkeit" (Op. 49, no. 1). Strauss also expanded the genre in breadth and concept, as is illustrated by "Im Spätboot" (Op. 56, no. 3), a song worthy of more attention than it generally receives. The poem, by Conrad Ferdinand Meyer, depicts a boat from which shadows disembark at tiny ports (coffins). "At long last my brow is cooling, my heart is sweetly chilling," is one passenger's sinister confession. Strauss scores this morbid subject for deep basso and sets it in the piano's lower register. Yet he touches the poem's gloom lightly. All is calm, even comforting. The piano part, orchestral in dimension, covers the song with glowing warmth. Its short, undulating motive, melodically reminiscent of Brahms's famous "Wiegenlied," gives the song the curiously appropriate aura of a lullaby. Ever the optimist, Strauss—who even in such a frightening subject turned to the Stimmungslied—confronted death without the soulwrenching dread of Mahler.

Reger's Stimmungslieder also descend from Schumann. They comprise a large, radiantly colored, special category of song, beginning with Op. 35 (see no. 2, "Der Himmel hat eine Träne geweint") and continuing sporadically, through intermittent cycles, into the composer's late works (like "Aus dem Himmelsaugen," Op. 98, no. 1). Reger selected poetry with a deeply evocative mood for his Stimmungslieder. Piano and voice contribute equally to the creation of that mood. The piano weaves undulating ostinato figures that, in early examples, often consist of triplets, in order to create and sustain the song's basic feeling. Reger tended in later years to be especially careful in selecting evocative poetry, and to rely more on harmonic color than on undulating triplet figures, to parallel the mood in the poetry. He enriched harmony with chains of chromatic chords (see "Notturno," Op. 88, no. 1) that produce ever-flickering new colors. Such dense texture cushions the voice in a kaleidoscope of sound, an innovation that prompted critical censure. His champions countered that Reger's rich chromaticism led the composer to impressionism.[43]

Schumann reintroduces the term *Gedichte* as a title for sets of songs to draw attention to the importance of poetry in the artistic fusion the lied represents. Although the term never achieved widespread application, later composers became continually more conscious of the artistic fusion inherent in the lied. The fin de siècle saw the height of this fusion.

The influence of Schumann and the Stimmungslied on Wolf, Mahler, Strauss, and Reger makes evident that these fin-de-siècle innovators had a double aesthetic aim. We may call it a "dialectical aesthetic": they wished both to advance music into modernity and to preserve inherited tradition. Schoenberg, the radical, abandoned this dialectic aesthetic. But the great majority of late nineteenth-century composers held it dear.

chapter three

End of the Romantic Era

In perpetuating traditions, some of centuries' duration, did fin-de-siècle composers also prolong the vital shift to romanticism associated with the earlier nineteenth century? Music historians have several answers to this perplexing question. Some interpret the fin de siècle as romanticism's continuation, others as its gradual demise. Still other historians see it as the time of revolt against romanticism or as the period that followed romanticism. To complicate the problem, various historians have amassed a clutch of conflicting names to describe the music of Germany and Austria: *post-Wagnerian, neo-romantic, postromantic, late romantic,* and, of course, *modern.*

The old imbroglio—What is romanticism?—lies at the bottom of this perplexing musical problem. Fortunately, literary critics M. H. Abrams and Morse Peckham provided ways out of the dilemma decades ago. They formulated two separate theories that, applied to music—and to German music in particular—serve our discipline well.

Abrams demonstrated that the romantics introduced a new aesthetic into Western art, centered on the artist as creator, which he called "expressive aesthetics": "A work of [romantic] art is essentially the internal made external, resulting from a creative process operating under the impulse of feeling, and embodying the combined product of the [artist's] perceptions, thoughts, and feelings."[1] This new focus on self is evident in Beethoven's famous remark: "Do you suppose I think of your miserable fiddle when the spirit takes hold of me?"

Before the romantic period aesthetics was founded on a theory formulated by the Greeks, the mimetic: the arts imitate life. A later theory grew out of it: the pragmatic. In pragmatic theory, the creative artist is audience-oriented; the aim is to please patron or public. "The Pragmatic view, broadly conceived, became the principal aesthetic attitude of the Western world," Abrams noted.[2] Examples in music are as extensive as in literature, as this letter of Mozart's about his *Paris Symphony* suggests: "The last Allegro [found favor] because, having observed that all last as well as first Allegros begin here [in Paris] with all the instruments playing together and generally unisono, I began mine with two violins only, *piano* for the first eight bars—followed instantly by a forte; the audience, as I expected said 'hush' at the soft beginning, and when they heard the forte, began at once to clap their hands."[3]

Pragmatic aesthetics restrained the accent on self-expression. "Expressive aesthetics" removed those restraints by shifting the focus from the patron and audience to the artist. This new romantic aesthetic, "centered on the relations between consciousness and consciousness of self[,] . . . [was] already expressed in the expulsion from Eden."[4] In a sense, patronage provided an Edenic protection for composers, which the romantic artist lost.

Instead of creating primarily to please patron or public, the romantic composed mainly for self-expression. Romantic art is introversive, generated by a consciousness of self, stimulated by and embodying the artist's own perceptions, thoughts, and feelings. "The artist himself becomes the major element generating both the artistic product and the criteria by which it is to be judged," as Abrams asserted. Curt Sachs distinguished expressiveness in the nineteenth century from that of previous times, the baroque, for instance. "The expressive of the Baroque was much less introvert in a romantic sense than it was extrovert, indeed, rhetorical. The *Oxford Dictionary* defines rhetoric as 'language designed to persuade or impress'; and this is indeed what all the arts, including architecture, were then meant to do. Whether visual or auditory, they aimed at a public that willingly followed and reacted." Abrams calls such art "patron-orientated" because "the final cause [is] the effect intended upon the audience."[5] Romanticism, for Abrams, involved a new focus, the shift to an *introvert art generated by a consciousness of self,* which, for Abrams, is the core from which the numerous attributes of romanticism radiated.

Abrams's concept of romantic art as introversive meets with no fundamental disagreement from music authorities. They see romantic music as subjective, egocentric, and autobiographical.[6] Fin-de-siècle music is also introversive, as illustrations from three composers with disparate styles—Mahler, Strauss, and Schoenberg—indicate. Mahler's art has been considered compulsively autobiographical. Yet Mahler withheld personal commentary from the public, while Strauss drew attention to it. Schoenberg, in contrast, is hardly associated with autobiographical music by the general public.

Mahler blended life and lied intimately in *Lieder eines fahrenden Gesellen* (Songs of the wayfarer). Letters to a friend and a poem to Johanna Richter—with whom he had an unhappy love affair—indicate that Mahler, himself, is the wayfarer ("ich, fahrender Gesell"). Yet years later Mahler requested of a critic: "Please . . . do not touch on the 'Fahrenden Gesellen' episode of my life." Mahler's letters reveal that each of these four songs arises from involvement with Johanna. The first song, of the Wayfarer's unrequited love, expresses Mahler's torment over Johanna, his *sphinx:* she "never ceases to threaten [me] with riddles. . . . I can only say, God help me!" The Wayfarer seeks release from his grief in nature—in the first song: "How the world is fair," and in the second: "I went this morning into the field." The composer, too, sought liberation in nature: "My window is open, sunny, fragrant spring shines upon me," from a letter. But liberation in life, as in the lied, was brief, as Mahler reveals: "The most painful was yet to come . . . to lose everything in one stroke." A further letter reveals that the "burning knife" of the third song ("never lets you rest . . . even when I sleep") expresses his personal agony: "I had but one somber wish: to sleep but not to dream." Mahler resolved this torment in life, as in the *Wayfarer* songs, in the characteristic fashion of Ahasuerus, the wandering Jew—by departing in silence and pain. "It is highly probable that I will leave without saying a word of farewell."[7]

Strauss's autobiographical works depict the composer as a hero conquering his adversaries, his critics and publishers. *Krämerspiegel,* Op. 66 (1918), on texts by Alfred Kerr (1867–1948), satirizes Strauss's publishers, especially Oscar von Hase of Breitkopf and Härtel. The song, "Es liebte einst ein Hase," concerns a hare (*Hase*) whose diet is composer's blood, which it sucks 'til it bursts. Von Hase is linked not only to a hare but also to the word *Hasse* (hate). Strauss slips musical quotations from his well-known works into the songs to sharpen the autobiography and delight the listener. Years later (1931) he urged the publisher Bote und Bock to publish his harmless joke. "Success of recent performance . . . warrants publication." His entreaties, however, received no response. The burlesque apparently retained its sting.[8]

Young Schoenberg also blended life and lied through song texts—but with great subtlety. Some texts suggest Schoenberg's resolve never to compromise ideals for public acceptance, as, for instance, in "Wie Georg von Frundsberg" (Op. 3, no. 1): "He who sells himself goes far. . . . My services remain unrecognized." "Freihold" (Op. 3, no. 6) discloses the consequence of this resolve: "He who would be free travels alone." So, too, does "Am Wegrand" (Op. 6, no. 6): "Thousands pass me by." "Litanei"—particularly the words "Kill my longing, close my wounds"—reveals another kind of rejection Schoenberg experienced, when his wife, Mathilde, ran off with their mutual friend, the artist Richard Gerstl. *The Book of Hanging Gardens* expresses this rejection indirectly. The songs begin with love's fulfillment in a paradisal garden but conclude with the disappearance of the lover and the disintegration of the garden. Schoenberg set the closing poems in September 1908, after his wife had abandoned him. Most interesting, in "Alles" (Op. 6, no. 2), a song with striking passages of suspended tonality, comes the textual suggestion of positive consequences of Schoenberg's struggles with tonality: "You blessed child of thirty, you will soon discover everything." He set these words when he was thirty years old.[9]

The theory that romantic art is introversive extends beyond the narcissism the quotations above might suggest. It involves a nineteenth-century idea, elevated in the fin de siècle that artists are privileged, endowed with supreme powers of clairvoyance—an extravagant idea, but not necessarily egotistical.[10] Mahler, for one, believed that his creativity sprang from a hidden world. (In Chapter 9, on symbolism, I shall discuss this important aspect of romanticism, which is rarely considered.)

By the late nineteenth century, if not earlier, the public had come to regard music as an introversive art. Masterworks were revered as almost sacred and the process of their composition as mystical. The fin-de-siècle composer, as Frank Walker perceptively observed about Wolf, seemed to his public like "an instrument through which music sounded, to be recorded thankfully as the divine gift of the gods to humanity."[11]

Widespread acceptance of expressive aesthetics in the fin de siècle brought about a relationship between composers and public that is the direct opposite of what it had been under eighteenth-century patronage, when patrons sometimes made imperious demands on artists. Fin-de-siècle composers themselves might make imperious demands. Wolf, for instance, rejected "suggestions" from patrons, publishers, or public regarding his choice of lied texts, their composition as songs, or their publication and performance. "It falls to my judgment and not that of the publishers," Wolf protested, "to choose poems that are suitable or unsuitable for setting to music." In the printing and performance of his lieder, "every detail . . . had to be precisely [according] to [Wolf's] specifications."[12] Mahler served his musical ideals no less uncompromisingly. Befriending such composers implied accepting their musical ideals without question.

Changes in nineteenth-century social life explain why the shift to expressive aesthetics took place. Bereft of patronage, the artist relied on a public that was often hostile. Peckham linked alienation and isolation to expressive aesthetics in a theory that paints another vision of romanticism. He explains that social changes made the artist feel estranged from society's values and vexed by its norms and prohibitions. The artist sought to escape the monotony of daily life, the shackles of decorum. Unable to find happiness in the social world, the romanticist looked for it in dreams. Upon realizing that the search is endless and the goal unattainable, the romanticist's yearning becomes increasingly painful. Johann Gottlieb Fichte describes this torment of unsatisfied longing as the "impulse towards something entirely unknown which reveals itself only in a sense of need, in a feeling of dissatisfaction or emptiness which though craving to be satisfied does not indicate how it possibly might obtain satisfaction."[13] Craving, yearning, longing, the romanticist's ultimate lot, form the undercurrent of his thought and art.

When did this theory of romanticism's cause arise? Peckham dated its origins in a letter to me: "I have never encountered any reference to alienation as a theme of romanticism from early in this century. I believe it was first used in the sense of cultural alienation by Kenneth Burke in the 1930s. Since the 1950s the notions of alienation and isolation have been so widely used in literary studies that they are now pretty much an unquestioned attribute of Romantic culture." The two have been subsumed explanatorily within Abrams's theory. But they have not, as Peckham accurately observes, "had much impact on historians of music." Music historians do agree that social changes from the eighteenth to nineteenth centuries were portentous for composers vis à vis their public. For Peckham, however, this is the central concern: "The problem of understanding romanticism is the problem of locating with accuracy its problem." Romanticists met these crises "through cultural alienation and social isolation." In music, Kurt Stephenson, Hans Tischler, and Wilibald Gurlitt had the same understanding, which Stephenson expressed as a tripartite theme: "It is only in flight from the world of man, in longing, and in fulfillment of dreams—all three interlaced— that the true nature of the romanticist can be recognized."[14]

The self-consciousness that is the core of romanticism, when allied with alienation, results in a pessimistic view of life. Romanticists view society as oppressive because it thwarts them. They can fulfill their hopes only in fantasy.[15] Society's delights cannot gratify, since society's conventions are those the romanticist wishes to escape. But neither does self-imposed isolation bring gratification, since it engenders solitude and sadness. Worse still, when the romanticist perceives his goal as unattainable, endless yearning ultimately dissolves into melancholia. The result is this paradox: the romanticist seeks happiness in a way that leads to despair, even to suicide. German romantics in particular were drawn to this pessimistic creed, to the chagrin of their elder, Goethe: "All these poets write as if they were ill, and as though the whole world were a hospital." Caspar David Friedrich's paintings of lone, isolated figures in desolate environments have, for modern writers, become symbols of German romanticism. The climax of the paradox was, however, expressed in music, in the "obsession" with Wagner, his "enchanted *oeuvre*," which, as Thomas Mann perceives (notes Leon Botstein), will reveal that the past century's "deep pessimism, its musical attachment to night and death . . . will probably come to be seen as the dominant characteristic of the age."[16]

In romantic art, pleasure is indeed often linked to pain, longing to lamentation, and search for fulfillment to frustration. We find an example in Keats's "Ode on Melancholy":

Ay, in the very temple of Delight
Veil'd Melancholy has her sovereign shrine,
   Though seen of none save him whose strenuous tongue
Can burst Joy's grape against his palate fine;
His soul shall taste the sadness of her might,
   And be among her cloudy trophies hung.

Longing is expressed as an end in itself. In romantic love, the object is the pursuit rather than the winning of the fair lady. The romantic Don Juan is one such dreamer. In extreme cases the pursuit becomes frenzied, and the frenzy itself becomes a romantic illness. Insatiable passion for the unattainable permeates the yearning: "The nympholepsy of some fond despair," is Byron's expression.

The shattering of a dream-ideal is often a traumatic experience for the romanticist. The poet Nikolaus Lenau (1820–50), depressed by the political reactionism of Austria under Metternich, cherished a dream of America as a land of primeval forests and freedom. But a winter spent near Pittsburgh shattered his illusion. It aroused "contempt for a country which 'had no wine nor nightingales,' whose national beverage, cider 'rhymes with *leider* [sorrow, regret],' and whose citizenry's main interest is in insurance."[17] Lenau's dream of a serene and free world persisted, but since he could find no realization for it in the actual world, his suffering continued.

The romanticist may, however, relieve a trauma through artistic expression by what is now called "romantic irony," a manifestation perceived by Irving Babbitt: "When [the romanticist] finds that he has taken some cloud bank for terra firma, he continues to cling to his dream, but at the same time wishes to show that he is no longer the dupe of it; so 'hot baths of sentiment,' as Jean Paul (1763–1825) says in his novels, 'are followed by cold douches of irony.'" Romantic irony, the intentional destruction of an illusion, seems to be another of those "romantic contradictions." Why would the romanticist so recklessly destroy the prime objective: the creation of illusion? The answer is "to inflict upon the reader the disillusion from which he [the poet] has himself suffered."[18] The poet—certainly Heinrich Heine—creates a delicate image or mood in the body of a poem only to shatter it with one final line. The destruction of the image is as swift as it is stinging.

The romanticist uses many symbols to express this creed. Among them, the role of night in German romanticism, is crucial. For example, in Wagner's *Tristan und Isolde* the ceaseless yearning, the quintessence of this drama, finds fulfillment only in the fantasy of night. "The longing for holy night" is Tristan's impassioned plea. Day, cruel and detestable, belongs to the world that separates Tristan from Isolde. But night, although it unites and covers them, provides escape only in death. Thus, in *Tristan,* night is closely linked to death, the ultimate evasion of life's torment. Heine, too, opposed night and day similarly in his "Der Tod, das ist die kühle Nacht" (set as a lied by Brahms, Op. 96, no. 1): "Death is the cool night / Life is the sultry day." Romanticists equated day with reason and society's conventions, night with romance and escape from those conventions. In fact, German romanticists were so preoccupied with the mysterious night, moonlight, darkness and the like, that their artists were called, as Babbitt reminds us, "twilight men."

Ruins, of all shapes and sizes, are another of the romanticist's symbols. Masonry ruins surrounded by entangled vines were seen as symbolic bridges linking the past to flights of fantasy. Urns, churchyards, and archaic sculpture are tinged with melancholy, connoting a past happiness never to be recaptured. But all such subjects acquire that singular romantic coloration only when they incorporate the tripartite theme of escape, longing, and fulfillment of dreams. As Stephenson observed, "The spell of elves dancing in a midsummer night is wonderfully enchanting—as long as the romantic spirit does not come into the picture. Genuine romantic ghosts come and haunt their creators, punishing them by scoffing at everything human: created by abnormal imaginations, they are phantoms at large."[19]

Strauss's "Nächtlicher Gang" (Op. 44, no. 2) presents a fine illustration of man as victim of his own sinister fantasy. The text, a ballad by Friedrich Rückert, is set in the hostile world of spirits. It tells of a ghastly night ride, filled with apparitions, the rider at the mercy of loathsome unseen creatures. With a deft hand Rückert allows readers to draw their own imagery and conclusions about the poem's ending. Strauss, however, converts suggestion in poetry into vivid scenes. With a huge orchestra, he paints each image in detail in his lied: the choir of the dead in the house of bones, the cracking of the winter's ice, and the fierce yawning throats of two sinister dogs. More important still, Strauss provides the poem with his own conclusion—a graphic scene of horror, in which the beloved is a victim of some monstrous act conveyed in the song's savage instrumental coda. Through the music, Strauss thus highlights the concept that fantasy in romanticism ultimately ends in tragedy.

Finally, nature served the romanticist as an escape from society. Through nature the romanticist's fantasy is freed, only to become melancholia as the romanticist's unfulfilled yearning is reawakened. As we recall, the Wayfarer, in Mahler's first two *Gesellen* lieder, yearned to mitigate his torture in the sunny canvas of springtime. He eventually asked: "Now won't my happiness begin?" The response is a recollection of his personal woes. Mahler's view of nature here is precisely that of the early German archromanticist Ludwig Tieck, in one of his *Sternbald* poems. In its opening stanzas, happiness attained through love of nature seems complete.

> Hands are beckoning from the clouds,
> Red roses on every finger;
> They beckon with flattering caresses.
> "Whither," you pause and ask, "goes the way?"
>
> Then all the spring zephyrs commence to sing;
> The flowers are fragrant and tinkle;
> Delicate rustling echoes down the valley:
> Be brave and do not fear.

But in that characteristic romantic way, happiness cannot long endure. Tieck's personal sorrows soon find expression in the poem, and it closes with melancholy.

> It seems as though the springs were silent;
> He fancies dark shadows arise
> And quench the queen flames of the forest;
> And flowers withdraw their finery.
>
> Gracious flowers are gone now;
> Fruits stand in the self-same places;
> The nightingale conceals its song in the forest;
> Only echoes reverberate through the solitude.[20]

Only a few German nineteenth-century musical works focus directly on the underlying pessimism characteristic of romanticism. But these works include some of the century's monuments: Schubert's *Winterreise;* Schumann's *Manfred;* Wagner's *Fliegende Holländer, Lohengrin,* and *Tristan;* and many lieder of Brahms, whom his biographer Walter Niemann called "the greatest master of resignation, pessimism, and *Weltschmerz,* even in nineteenth-century song." Each of these works involves negation of the world and a path that ultimately leads out of it. Stephenson's penetrating comment on *Tristan* merits attention: "The evasion of the world, in its ultimate form as evasion into the sanctuary of death's redeeming darkness—which had appeared to Novalis in his 'Hymn of the Night' visions—was given large dramatic proportions in *Tristan.*"[21] Romanticism appears grim in these works.

Artists' feelings of alienation persisted throughout the fin de siècle. For the gulf between creative artists seeking recognition and their public continued to widen. In sculpture and painting, "the artist reached a high point of isolation from the public" according to the art historian Bernard Myers. "Deprived of the traditional patronage that had made him responsible in some measure to a public, he fell back on the approval of the few like-minded individuals he could find." In music, this alienation was critical for Wolf, Mahler, and Pfitzner. "I don't see why I . . . should publish my things [and] . . . sacrifice time and money . . . for judgments from sundry unwashed mouths," Wolf remonstrated. "Is it not . . . finer to be loved and understood by a few men than to be hated and reviled by thousands?"[22] Although admirers provided protection, encouragement, and the means for him to attain considerable success, Wolf remained an "outsider" his entire career. He never held a public position in music save his brief period as a critic on the magazine *Salonblatt.*

If Wolf presents a classic expression of the romantic conflict in his professional life, Mahler, in a sense, wrote its peroration. The underlying reason Mahler was attracted to the conflict seems evident. "I am thrice rejected," he told his wife, "as a native of Bohemia in Austria, as an Austrian among Germans, and as a Jew throughout the world. Everywhere an intruder, never welcome."[23] Mahler regarded himself as Ahasuerus, the tormented and alienated wandering Jew. He often gave his rejection subtle expression, as he did in "Urlicht." A simple folk lyric (from *Des Knaben Wunderhorn*), the poem's symbolism for Mahler was nonetheless profound. Its protagonist resolves to flee man—who "lies in deepest distress"—to God. But his path is barred by an angel, who tries to turn him aside. For Mahler, this rejection mirrors his lifelong feelings of alienation as Jew in a Gentile world. "Oh no! I would not turn aside! I am of God and would return to God," Mahler insisted. He set the first line twice (see *Y* in example 74, unit 4) to an impassioned climax, a yearning for acceptance by the infinite.[24]

The theme of the wanderer in Mahler's art runs deeper than ethnic isolation. A theme that "has haunted literature since the Romantic period," and, according to the critic Geoffrey Hartman, bears the full weight of the romantic conflict, "is that of the solitary, or Wandering Jew. He may appear as Cain, Ahasuerus, Ancient Mariner, and even as Faust." For Hartman, Peckham, and others, this theme encapsulates the romantic conflict. Hartman explains: "These solitaries are separated from life in the midst of life, yet cannot die. They are doomed to live a middle or purgatorial existence which is neither life nor death, and as their knowledge increases so does their solitude. . . . [The] consciousness that alienates them from life imposes the burden. . . . [They] are compelled to repeat their experiences in the purgatorial form of words. Yeats, deeply affected by the theme of the Wandering Jew, records a marvelous comment of Mme. Blavatsky's: 'I write, write, write, as the Wandering Jew walks, walks, walks.'"[25]

As a solitary, Mahler, like Yeats, assumed the mien of Ahasuerus to evade the world of man. Mahler's song "Ich bin der Welt Abhanden gekommen" reveals his pleasure in living apart from that world "on which I wasted much time." Peaceful resignation evoked through effusive lyricism fills the composition. "It is my very self!" Mahler confided, while convalescing "away from the world," following a brush with death.[26] He had survived and experienced a productive summer in Abbazia, but once the summer idyll ended, he had to return to the world of human problems. Mahler's autobiographical vocal works—from the earliest mature examples to *Das Lied von der Erde*—often picture alienated wanderers seeking release. In Mahler art and life are uniquely entwined with the romantic conflict.

Some critics suggest that composers express alienation in music mainly through the texts they choose. But music can play an essential role and, in the lied, even a unique one. Pfitzner's "Hast du von den Fischerkindern" (Op. 7, no. 1) is one of several lieder that shows music rather than poetry conveying the essence of the romantic crisis.[27] The text, by Wolfgang Müller von Königswinter, poses the question: Have you understood the meaning of the tale of the fisherman's children? They sailed out to sea in a rickety skiff, playing in blissful innocence. The second stanza paints this idyllic scene. The third transforms it into catastrophe as we learn the children have vanished at sea. The final stanza discloses the tale's hidden meaning, an ominous romantic twist: the children are really you and I, and our love, like the sea, will be our grave.

Pfitzner captures the folkishness of the poem masterfully in an enchanting lyrical song. He seems to provide fresh music for each of the poem's events. The first vocal melody (ex. 4a), poignantly melancholy, expresses the poem's fantasy and foreshadows its unhappy conclusion. The second (ex. 4b) expresses the joy of the happy voyage, while the final melody (ex. 4d) embodies the poem's ominous ending. Actually this musical idea, the work's main theme, serves also as the song's short instrumental prelude (ex. 4c). Further, the "happy" melody for the idyllic period (ex. 4b) is not new melody but a transformation of the main theme. At the song's conclusion, the transformed theme (ex. 4d) descends grimly to image the word *grave* in the poem's last thought: "the sea is like our love / it will be our grave." Pfitzner wrote just one melody (ex. 4c) for the entire song. He shaded it joyfully for the second stanza and tragically for the end, thereby bringing out the poem's inner message: life's essence is melancholy, for joy is brief and always linked to sorrow. He underscores this message imaginatively, by seeming to conclude the song at the point where the happy scene fades. Attention is then focused on the final section yet to be heard: the fairy tale's dire ending.

Mahler's expression of the romantic crisis in the first of his *Wayfarer* songs is remarkably similar. The Wayfarer's motive of sorrow (voice part, m. 5) is the same music, transformed, as the happy wedding motive (mm. 1–3). By linking both motives in measure 8, Mahler reveals the romantic credo: the inevitability of pain in pleasure. That Mahler and Pfitzner expressed romantic pessimism in much the same way—through thematic transformation—is striking. Their personalities and musical styles could scarcely be more dissimilar. Apparently, expression of the romantic conflict transcends ethnic, stylistic, and national differences.[28] The masterpieces of Schubert, Schumann, Wagner, and Brahms mentioned above show similar transcendence of individual stylistic differences. We might, therefore, conclude that romantic aesthetics—rooted in introversive art—persisted in Germany and Austria throughout the nineteenth century into the fin de siècle.

During the postwar years, a new aesthetic arose, which replaced the introversive aesthetic of the romantic. In literary criticism this aesthetic, which Abrams calls "objective orientation," took decades to develop and involved a shift of focus as fundamental as the one from pragmatic to expressive aesthetics. A literary work was to be regarded "as a self-sufficient entity constituted by its parts in their internal relations," not as the self-expression of the artist. Objective orientation "sets out to judge" a work "solely by criteria intrinsic to its own mode of being"—to sanitize the work, while analyzing it, from factors considered extraneous: to wit, the social and cultural.[29] In modern music, objective criteria evolved into concepts as diverse as neoclassicism and the twelve-tone system. Emphasis on expressive aesthetics was also passé for Paul Hindemith, who stressed that music must be useful and practical. Further, social changes of the postwar years gradually brought composers into a new relationship with their public. We recall how antiquated the concept of commissions had seemed to such fin-de-siècle musicians as Wolf, who responded with humor to a commission: "Can you fancy me as court composer and tone-poet of occasional music?"[30] The modern age, however, signaled the revival of commissions in music, but now they came from radio stations, foundations, and universities.

These fundamental changes, when viewed in their totality, reaffirm a basic premise of this book: that the fin de siècle represents the era's end.[31] Which, then, of the names mentioned on this chapter's first page serves as the best designation for music of the fin de siècle in Germany and Austria: post-Wagnerian, neoromantic, postromantic, or late romantic? Each, in its time, was

Example 4. Pfitzner: "Hast du von den Fischerkindern" (Königswinter), Op. 7, no. 1, (a) mm. 5–8; (b) mm. 13–14; (c) mm. 1–2; (d) mm. 37–38.

carefully chosen. And specialists have added more labels: music in transition, turn-of-the-century music, twilight of the gods, expanded resources.[32]

Post-Wagnerian—the designation of fin-de-siècle critics for the music of Wolf, Mahler, Strauss, Reger, Pfitzner, and a host of lesser figures—arose during the time of Wagner's greatest influence. The contribution of these masters, critics narrowly generalized, was to assimilate and advance the style of Wagner: "It appears to me that the attempt was being made here to transplant Wagner's dramatic principles to the lied," Felix Weingartner wrote after his first study of Wolf lieder.[33] The five masters and their important propagandists were, indeed, fierce Wagnerites, as we have seen.

But although the post-Wagnerian label secured the attention of good-sized audiences at the turn of the century, it had negative consequences even then. It stamped the composers involved with a kind of artistic transparency, that is, they had no definite color of their own. Witness Rudolf Louis's negative assessment of Wolf: "A shining constellation in the heavens of modern music, but a planet, not a fixed star . . . because he shines with no light of his own, but rather with reflected light from the sun of the Bayreuth master." This evaluation overlooks other important influences on the five composers and, of course, their commanding individuality. Though *post-Wagnerian* is being applied with less frequency, especially following the reassessment of Mahler that began in the 1960s, echoes of it, nevertheless, recur.[34] In my discussion of naturalism in Chapters 4 to 6 I shall endeavor to enlarge *post-Wagnerian*'s narrow focus. For naturalism, rooted in the nineteenth century, stimulated not only Wagner but his predecessors and his immediate followers.

Neoromantic was a designation used throughout the nineteenth and early twentieth centuries to "distinguish each successive kind of romanticism from the preceding one," Carl Dahlhaus stresses. *Neoromantic*, however, has its own special problems. Fin-de-siècle specialists like Riemann and Niemann applied the term to post-Wagnerians. More recent scholars, like Alfred Einstein and Dahlhaus, apply it to the previous generation, that of Wagner himself.[35]

The term *postromantic* has more serious problems. To some critics, it implies "revolt against" the romantic age (Machlis), to others it means "the dying nineteenth century without appreciably entering . . . the nascent twentieth century" (Lang).[36] But *post* means "after, subsequent to, following, succeeding, later than" (*OED*). The label thus gives the fin de siècle these different meanings: *continuation* of, *revolt* against, *demise* of, and the period *after* the romantic age. Since nearly all the composers surveyed above aspired to expand or heighten inherited traditions, this book rejects "after" romantic as its designation for German fin de siècle.

Late romantic is the most germane of the terms listed for music of the fin de siècle. *Late* evokes two images, each more appropriate than *post* or *neo* for our historical context: a summit and the season of fall. The first suggests height, while *fall* suggests rich, intense color (fall foliage), followed by decay. Both are fitting images for the avant-garde harmony of Wolf, Mahler, and Strauss, and for the later "decay," the dissolution of tonality. *Late*, of course, also suggests "further on" in the same period. Since fin de siècle composers expanded inherited traditions, this term is most appropriate for the artists of the end of the past century.[37]

Late romanticism, as applied in this book, indicates a specific period—the fin de siècle, final period of romanticism. As continuation, climax, and close of an era, the time when late romanticism began is difficult to pinpoint. No work or year can be given to mark its precise beginning since its rise was gradual. We can at least cite a work within the field of the lied that indicates late romanticism had, in its initial development, become a dominant aesthetic force: Wolf's *Moerike-Lieder* of 1888. I select this work for its influence, achievement, and size. The *Moerike-Lieder*, a huge set of fifty-three masterpieces, achieved success the first year it was performed, an indication that late romanticism was already in vogue. Yet the style of the cycle seemed radically modern to some critics. Recall one critical comment on Wolf's songs: "They have nothing more in common with . . . musical art than the bare elements of sound and rhythm."[38] The year

1888, when Wilhelm II was crowned kaiser, has further significance. It marks the final period of monarchy in Germany.

A terminal date for late romanticism is also difficult to establish, even for the lied. Older composers continued to create in their familiar "late romantic" style long after the avant-garde made its mark. The question is, therefore, when did late romanticism cease to be a major artistic force. Two dates indicate general boundaries. The first, about 1910, is the time when the schism between "old" and "new" became evident in music, painting, and literature. The second, during the 1920s, designates the time neoclassicism began to exercise supreme authority. The 1920s, of course, also mark the dawn of a new social and political era, after the old aristocracies had received crushing defeats. Our concern with late romanticism ends about 1920, therefore, though some more recent works in this style will be considered, such as Strauss's *Vier letzte Lieder* (Four last songs, 1948). I shall center my attention on the period between 1888 and 1910, when significant composers, including Schoenberg, contributed monuments to the late-romantic lied.

We have become increasingly aware in these three introductory chapters that the view of the fin de siècle formulated by our contemporaries is radically different from the view during the period. This realization makes us ever more conscious of "a double awareness: of the actual differentials—political, economic, ideological—which separate the Romantic period from our own as well as of the persistent illusions that these differentials do not exist."[39]

part two

The Disparate Aesthetic: Naturalism, Nationalism, Symbolism, and Other Trends

chapter four

Declamation

Curiously enough, German vocal music was rarely performed in Germany and Austria in the early nineteenth century. Italian vocal music was favored. But when the public finally began to accept native vocal music, German composers were faced with a serious problem: audiences could not understand texts in their own language because singers enunciated deplorably. Composers to whom distinct enunciation of German was vital vigorously sought solutions. Wagner was one of the most forceful, since he considered comprehension of his texts essential to his aesthetics. For him, poor enunciation resulted from German singers "trying to imitate what they call 'the Italian production.'. . . Their native language itself, to say nothing of the cultural heredity underlying what is being sung, is an insuperable obstacle to their transplanting the Italian tone, Italian vowels, Italian accents, inflections and phrasing into music the whole life of which is bound up with the genius of another tongue."[1] For Wagner, what was needed was a German school of singing.

Vocal training in Germany was dominated by Italians until about 1830. This trend continued for well over another generation.[2] When the break between the German and Italian styles finally came, it proved to be radical: German singing masters were satisfied only with a complete renunciation of Italian methods and the formation of a German school. Such extremists proliferated during the fin de siècle. They sought to end a tradition of vocal training that had prevailed in Germany for nearly two hundred years.

One of the first to lay the foundation of a German school of singing was Friedrich Schmitt. His *Grosse Gesangschule für Deutschland* (Comprehensive vocal instruction for Germany, 1854) was its cornerstone. Like Wagner, Schmitt thought that the only way to correct the deplorable enunciation of German singers was to repudiate the Italian vocal method. Schmitt, a true child of his age, considered vocal music to be elevated speech. His vocal exercises began with speech instruction rather than tone production.[3] When the student had begun to master good enunciation, the student would proceed, almost imperceptibly, from speaking syllables to singing them. Vocal training "must begin with singing short tones, not long ones (as in the Italian method) because in language one never finds sustained tones that are so essential to singing."[4] The ballad composer and singer Martin Plüddemann (1854–97) explains how far his teacher

Schmitt actually went in trying to bind singing to the German language. Solfeggio, the backbone of Italian training, was abandoned. Instead, students were instructed to apply German words or sentences like "das Wandern ist des Müllers Lust" (wandering is the miller's joy) to vocal exercises.[5]

Schmitt's contemporaries, committed to Italian tradition, did not accept his revolutionary school of singing. For Schmitt, hope for his new method lay in Wagner, who was seeking the type of singer Schmitt thought his method could produce. Wagner, in turn, needed Schmitt to train singers, since none could be found "with the necessary qualifications for the *Ring*." Although collaboration between the two was short-lived, it sowed the seeds for the German style of singing.[6] These flowered in the succeeding generation under Schmitt's disciple, Julius Hey, who systemized and amplified the national school of singing with typical German thoroughness. Schmitt's book was widely attacked. But Hey's giant, three-volume *Deutscher Gesangs-Unterricht* (German vocal instruction, 1884–86) was a great success. It appeared at a time ripe for its acceptance: the late romantic period, when Wagnerian singing and the German school of singing were considered synonymous.

During this period, major changes had occurred in the attitude toward the German style of singing, owing to the public demand for German vocal music. Many singers had been trained specifically to qualify for the *Ring*—singers who enunciated expertly. Since interest was keen in finely spoken language in theater, actors and singers were brought into an ever-closer relationship.

The maze of dialects and regional inflections found in Germany was mirrored on the stage in the speech of both actors and singers. As late as 1878, a questionnaire was sent to numerous authorities in philology, drama, and music (Wagner, Stockhausen, and Hey, among others) concerning the proper pronunciation of the final *g* in selected words; during this period one heard the final *g* in a word pronounced in four different ways by leading performers: correctly, as *g*, and incorrectly, as *k*, *j*, and *ch*. Thus *Sieg* (victory) was frequently pronounced *siech* (sickly). Rules for standard stage-German (*Bühnen-Deutsch*) were not codified until 1898, when Theodor Siebs organized a commission for the purpose.[7] In their common need, Wagner and his followers had catapulted the movement toward polished stage-German. The speech of the singers they trained was exemplary.

Such widespread interest in Bühnen-Deutsch explains why the late-romantic period was an age ripe for Hey's *Deutscher Gesangs-Unterricht*. Although several German singing methods appeared at that time, only Hey's established the criteria of German singing, a style often heard in opera and in concert. His valuable study resulted from years of experience gained from training singers under Wagner's supervision. Reflecting the contemporary preoccupation with stage-German, the first volume is a manual of speech exercises designed for the actor, public speaker, and singer alike. Exercises provided were to be studied by the singer prior to, and in conjunction with, the vocal training in volume two.

The differences between Italian and German vocal pedagogy involve differences in national orientation toward singing as well as in theoretical principles that concern only voice teachers. Italian and German vocal teachers sharply disagree on how singers ought to link a cantilena to a text. Their dispute centers on two elementary facts of singing.

In the first place, vowels, as everyone knows, are ideally suited for singing. But the great variety of vowel shading, particularly in German, sometimes makes smooth vocal connection difficult, as between, for example, the dark German *a* (ah) and the bright *i* (ee). A common way singers solve this problem is by neutralizing such vowels, that is, shading one off into another. Consonants, on the other hand, create a problem of their own. They tend to interrupt melodic flow because many are produced only when the voice is silent. To produce a liquid cantilena performers often avoid emphasizing consonants: the singer who stresses consonants will destroy the cantilena.

Nearly all teachers, whether of the Italian or the German method, accept these two solutions in theory. The discrepancy between the two methods rests on the differences between the Italian and German languages, in addition to the differences between Italian and German attitudes toward singing. Italian, with an abundance of words with many vowels, is made for singing. German, by contrast, is overburdened with consonants, which in singing, as Hugo Wolf deplored, hiss and sound like swords in battle. And German, as Hey points out (see vol. 3.), has many more mixed vowels (*ü, ö, ä*) and diphthongs, in addition to the pure vowel sounds common to both languages.

Italians, according to Hey, are generally inclined to neutralize all vowels toward an *a,* and to treat consonants as linguistic stepchildren. Unlike their northern neighbors, they regard the voice more as a medium for producing beautiful sound than as a means of articulating language. Germans, in their fear of marring enunciation, applied the two vocal solutions—neutralizing vowels and avoiding emphasis of consonants—moderately. In general, singers resolve the two problems noted above according to their preference for the liquid cantilena or for clear enunciation. Perfect fusion or balance of the two—the aim of Wagner and certain Italian teachers and singers—is, perhaps, only an ideal. In post-Wagnerian Germany, the choice was often made in favor of clear enunciation, owing to the influence of composers, critics, and teachers of the German school.

Hugo Wolf's criticism of a singer in *Tristan und Isolde,* act 1, brings our discussion into focus. "Only the following fragments of the introductory song of the young seaman could be understood: 'We(st)-wär(ts) schwei(ft) der Bli(ck), o(s)twä(rts) st(r)ei(cht) da(s) Schi(ff). The letters in parenthesis were swallowed mercilessly." The singer evidently omitted all the consonants that interfered with his rendition of the cantilena he sought for this passage. Richard Strauss made direct demands on the singer to emphasize consonants. "Correctly pronounced consonants, and only they, can penetrate an orchestra even of the most brutal type, while a singer's most powerful vowels are easily covered by a mezzoforte. . . . There is only one weapon for the singer . . . his consonants."[8]

Some critics were as concerned with clear speech as with vocal delivery. "Karl Mayer . . . is one of the best lieder singers. . . . His vocal technique and pronunciation is masterful" is typical of the reviews printed about 1900. The concentration by some critics on stage-German may appear to border on obsession. Many critics actually listed the words, syllables, or even letters that were poorly pronounced: "Frau Gentz-Malten failed in certain of her songs, because of her cool delivery, insecure attack, and defective pronunciation of the d's, t's, and p's." Some over-eager voice teachers, Plüddemann confides, were accused of ruining students' voices because they laid too much emphasis on crystal-clear speech too early in vocal training.[9] Composer and press were responding to the strong influence of naturalism, which prompts artists to regard the traditional goals of their craft as secondary to achieving verisimilitude. Singers, in varying degrees, were induced to sacrifice one goal of singing, the liquid flow of the cantilena, in favor of speechlike enunciation.

Sprechgesang, sometimes confused with *Sprechstimme*, demands extreme naturalism in singing.[10] The style—which was particularly vigorous between 1890 and 1914—was often heard in Wagner's operas and in ballads and, to a lesser extent, in lieder. Probably few leading performers sang exclusively in Sprechgesang, which adheres more closely to the rules of Bühnen-Deutsch than any other style of singing. Its most striking feature is crisp and chiseled enunciation, as precise in singing as in contemporary recitation. To produce the sharp speech so characteristic of the style, letters such as *k, t, d,* and *g* were enunciated explosively, especially in key words. That fine singer and master of the art of recitation Ludwig Wüllner (1858–1938), it was said, pronounced "the individual consonants, such as 'k' in the word 'gehenkt' ("hanged") [in August Strindberg's *Ein Weib*], so that they formed an image of complete barbarism." Perhaps the fear of not being fully understood prompted singers to enunciate some letters so sharply that *g*'s at the end of words would be pronounced like *k*'s: Wagner's *Ring* would thus be pronounced *Rink*. "Ever since Wagner made his influence felt," Lilli Lehmann complained, "most singers strive to exaggerate the distinctness of the consonants, and . . . expel the entire word in a hard, shrill toneless, ugly fashion; you can actually hear the end-consonants flying about in space."[11]

Elision of words was to be avoided. The highly esteemed reciter and actor Ernst von Possart (1841–1921) instructed actors never to slur words: *nicht treu* (not true) must not be pronounced *nich treu*.[12] The advice is as binding on the singer as on the actor, but when followed by the singer, "hard declamation" often results. The most illuminating example of the effect of naturalism on the singer is that in Sprechgesang the rules of Bühnen-Deutsch are supreme even when they conflict with a composer's intention. Had a composer set the short first syllable in *Gipfel* (summit) to a long note-value, the performer would sing the syllable (*Gip*) only as long as a person would speak it and then actually insert a rest for the remainder of that note value.

Crisp and chiseled enunciation is only one feature of Sprechgesang. Another is the effect known as elevated speech—a hovering somewhere between singing and speaking. This effect is produced when inflections of speech are applied to singing. "Emmy Destinn often lapsed into the mannerism of speaking the text, especially while singing in her middle register," a critic wrote in 1903. "This type of performance does not disturb one because it brings the text most plastically before us." Further: about 1900 "most Wagnerian singers, under sanction of Bayreuth, to a certain extent speak their parts more than they sing them."[13]

Even Sprechgesang does not reveal the complete influence of naturalism on the singer. Sprechgesang is but one vehicle for the singer to produce what we may call naturalistic performance. In such performance, suggestion is replaced by vivid representation. Just as operatic directors of about 1890 (as I shall show in Chapter 5) sought to translate mental images into visual stage action, so even in lied performance and poetry recitals performers aimed at the visual. Drama, that ideal medium for the expression of naturalism, lent itself well to the emotional temper of the period.

Concert singers expressed their enthusiasm for drama by applying theatrical techniques to lied performance. In so doing, they were often drawn into close professional relationships with actors. In a number of German conservatories, singers studied declamation with an actor who was a regular member of the voice faculty. They were instructed in academies as well as in books to approach the performance of a song through its text, to study and recite the poem on which a song is based with the care and consideration of an actor.[14] Numerous joint recitals of actors and singers indicate that close professional relationships existed between them: I think, for example, of the Goethe evenings given by Eugen Gura (1842–1906) and Ernst von Possart, in which Gura sang settings by Schubert, Loewe, and Wolf of poems that von Possart recited.[15] The closest possible relation between the two fields was achieved by such performers as Wüllner, who employed techniques of recitation in his performance of lieder. On the other hand, the American baritone David Bispham (1857–1921) applied vocal techniques in his recitation of melodramas (fig. 5).

To what extent did singers during the fin de siècle apply theatrical techniques to their performances of lieder? The best concert singers did not indulge in exaggerated gesturing. The reinforcement of a word or phrase in a song by hand gestures or body movements had been frowned on, in principle. "Such effects," to quote the outstanding singer Julius Stockhausen (1826–1906), "belong on the stage. You must not exhibit your personality in the concert hall, for there you are nothing but an interpreter of poet and composer." In the period that followed Stockhausen's career, however (the time of late romanticism),

"Suddenly there came a tapping"   "Perched upon a bust of Pallas   "Whose fiery eyes now burned
                                     just above my chamber door"   into my bosom's core"

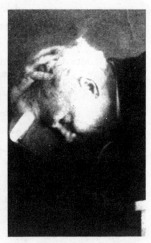

"On this Home by horror haunted"   "Is there—is there balm in   "And my soul from out that
                                     Gilead? Tell me—tell me,   shadow—Shall be lifted—never-
                                     I implore!"   more"

Figure 5. David Bispham in a Dramatic Reading of Poe's "The Raven" (from *Seminar* 14:3 [1978])

minor singers frequently indulged in exaggerated histrionics: "During the course of deeply emotional passages . . . Magda von Dulong . . . exhibited the power of her inner agitation by closing her eyes as if she were dying and convulsively folding her hands." One of the critics who tried to reform concert life suggested that artists perform behind curtains or screens to conceal exaggerated gesturing.[16] Great artists, whether reciters or singers, did gesture, but subtly.

Many parallels existed between contemporary styles of reciting poetry and singing lieder. Like the reciters, singers concentrated on facial pantomime, character delineation, and graphic representation of words. "Facial pantomime," Felix Weingartner (1863–1942) wrote, "is the expression of the emotions that the performing artist experiences during the execution of his art, whether he is a singer or actor." Late romantic performers were expected to mirror vividly in their faces the subtle changes of mood in the works they rendered. "What would one think of a singer," Weingartner continues, "who would use exactly the same facial expression for *Doppelgänger* and *Feldeinsamkeit?*"[17]

Character delineation is obviously important to the singer who wishes to transform lieder or ballads into miniature dramatic scenes. Plüddemann actually instructs the singer on how to delineate the several characters of Loewe's "Erlkönig." "The difficulty of a rendition of *Erlkönig* is the imitation of the four voices, that of the narrator, the father, the child, and the *Erlkönig*. The singer should use a normal high baritone for the narrator, a somewhat deeper bass-like color for the father, and the child should be sung in a falsetto with the minimum of chest tone. The tone of the *Erlkönig* is most difficult to produce. It should also be a type of falsetto but a sort of spiritlike whisper, a murmur that is produced with the mouth nearly closed, a tone that is very soft, almost dull, and sinister." A phonograph recording of von Possart's reading of the Goethe poem indicates that the actor portrayed the four persons in the ballad almost exactly as Plüddemann had instructed singers to do.[18]

Artists were often severely censured if, in performing a ballad, they sang only a beautiful cantilena of homogeneous color, instead of contrasting vocal shades, one for each individual in the ballad.[19] Some singers went to extremes, using exaggerated changes of vocal color on behalf of vivid characterization. Some late-romantic composers delineated character superbly in their songs because they themselves possessed unusual theatrical skills. Wolf could portray characters in reciting poetry and in interpreting his lieder to a point where they were almost visually perceived. Audiences of the time were fascinated by skillful characterization, especially when the artist executed the seemingly impossible. In Plüddemann's "Der Kaiser und der Apt," the singer is expected not only to depict four people but also to portray one of them imitating another. A masterpiece of characterization was said to have been Wüllner's recitation of Mark Antony's famous address to the Roman populace in *Julius Caesar*, a reading that was so vivid that not only Antony but also the various citizens were "as though made visible to the audience."[20]

The graphic representation of words reveals extremes to which actors and singers went on behalf of naturalism. The technique requires the performer to enact such key words of a text as *laugh* and *cry* by actually laughing and crying. This feature of acting in singing, frequently mentioned by critics, was considered an essential ingredient in good interpretation of lieder. Even the conservative Viennese critic Eduard Hanslick urged Stockhausen to apply the technique more extensively. We are fortunate that Plüddemann has illustrated graphic representation in his detailed instructions on the performance of his ballads. "The passage 'Luther lachte' (Luther laughed) is not easy to execute. It must be sung with a real laugh, but without any variation of pitch."[21] But in the music at the word *lachte,* the composer, like so many of his contemporaries, left only a suggestion of what was intended: two staccato signs. Today, the performer would probably sing two staccatos instead of deducing that the staccatos are indications for a laugh.

Singers enacted not only the words that composers had depicted musically but also any others that they themselves thought should be emphasized. They took special pride in skillfully illustrating words that did not lend themselves easily to representation. Some singers took liberties in so doing. Elena Gerhardt (1883–1961) described for me the difference between bad and good taste in depicting words: for bad, "As a result of the excesses of youth I sang the word *Fäden* (threads) in Wolf's 'Und willst du deinen Liebsten sterben sehen' by gliding slowly from the upper to the lower note of the octave to which it is set." But she was very proud of the manner in which she depicted the word *fällt* in "der Schleier fällt" (the veil falls). She thought that her representation enabled the audience "almost to hear the veil touching the ground." Singers today, striving for uniformity of vocal color, generally avoid contrasts as strong as this one used by Wüllner on behalf of graphic representation: "Within a pianissimo (in Grieg's *Lichte Nacht*) he brought out the word *hell* (bright) and contrasted it, by means of a strong and effective vocal coloring, with *erdunkelnd* (to dim) which he allowed to fade away."[22]

The stress on acting in lieder performance induced singers to take liberties with the music to make their renditions more effective dramatically. The press often praised dramatically arresting, emotional performances, even when the artist had distorted the composer's intentions. "The hearer must not be disturbed if Dr. Wüllner takes liberties with rhythms and musical phrases in order to make dramatic effects. Dr. Wüllner is often wholly wrong no doubt, but at the same time he is superbly dramatic."[23] But the performer who took liberties that were deemed inartistic was severely reprimanded.

We have seen that naturalism exercised a strong influence on singing in the nineteenth century. Plüddemann notes that in the early nineteenth century, ballad singers did not portray characters in dialogues but relied instead on the listener to draw mental images. He believes that this "undramatic and impersonal" manner of performance explains why "Loewe sang his powerful *Edward* ballad, while practically smiling." During the latter part of that century, vivid representation replaced suggestion. Singers tended to transform even ballads into miniature dramatic scenes, thereby destroying the form's epic character.[24]

Lieder, especially those of Schubert, were also performed in markedly different manners during the early and late nineteenth century. Here our witness is Schubert's friend Leopold von Sonnleithner (1797–1873), who dates the change in style from shortly before 1860.

> As regards the way in which Schubert's songs should be performed, there are very strange opinions today [1857] amongst the great majority of people. Most of them think they have achieved the summit if they interpret songs in the manner they imagine to be *dramatic*. According to this, there is as much declamation as possible, sometimes whispered, sometimes with passionate outbursts, with retarding of the tempo etc. . . . I heard [Schubert] accompany and rehearse his songs more than a hundred times. . . . He never allowed violent expression in performance. The lieder singer, as a rule, only relates the experiences and feelings of others; he does not himself impersonate the characters whose feelings he describes. Poet, composer, and singer must conceive the song *lyrically,* not dramatically. . . . Schubert demanded above all that his songs should not so much by declaimed as *sung* flowingly . . . to the complete exclusion of the unmusical speaking voice.[25]

The decade 1860 seems to mark the time when the "declamatory-dramatic" style of performance began its ascendancy, which was also the time that Wagner called on Friedrich Schmitt to help him initiate his radical reforms in operatic performance.

The peak of this style of performance occurred about 1890, when composers, critics, and the public alike were all fascinated by it. Dissenting opinions, like those voiced by Sonnleithner in 1857, were nearly forgotten. Witness the esteem in which Wüllner's style of performance was held. Virtually all authorities considered his art the ultimate in lied performance. "After singing to filled halls in four [solo] concerts" in the 1903–04 season in Berlin, Wüllner and Lilli Lehmann (1848–1929) each "announced a fifth popular evening of lieder."[26] Yet curiously enough the critics who praised him, in both the United States and Europe, called Wüllner "the singer without a voice."

The key to the paradox is that, as we have seen, many late romantics considered skill in interpretation a more important feature in lied performance than the cantilena. Wüllner's fame as a singer rests on his interpretations. He was esteemed not only by composers (like Brahms and Weingartner), critics, and the public, but by such fine vocalists as Gerhardt and Julia Culp (1880–1970). Wüllner had temporarily abandoned a successful career as an actor in order to study singing. His Shylock (in *The Merchant of Venice*), Faust (in Goethe's *Faust*), and Nathan (in Gotthold Ephraim Lessing's *Nathan der Weise*) commanded admiration throughout Germany. The lied presented him with another means of expressing his skill as reciter. Consequently, he usually limited his choice of songs to those that lent themselves well to dramatic treatment. He wisely omitted "Mondnacht" when performing Schumann's *Liederkreis* because he realized he could not execute its purely musical requirement, a sustained cantilena in pianissimo.[27] A review of Wüllner's third Liederabend (January 6, 1896) pictures Wüllner, the singer, as characteristically late romantic. As such, it sketches a late-romantic ideal in lied performance.

> His enunciation is of utmost clarity and scrupulousness. . . . There is nothing of consequence to mention about his voice with respect to its quality, but his treatment of text is so full of life, so richly endowed, so saturated with his unique perception that as soon as the singer opens his lips one is at once spiritually gripped by him. Every fiber of his being appears to take part with complete devotion to the subject and content of the poem that he sings. The singer follows the music inwardly even when his voice is silent [during instrumental passages]. His bearing is always composed. But this composure seems to be externally forced because, from his heaving breast, his facial pantomime—his raising and lowering of his brow—the listener can feel the performer's artistic excitement very intensively. The reader should not imagine that his pantomime makes an impression of affectation. It is always genuine and true. His type of interpretation mirrors outwardly the work's inner life, as does a good actor who, never allowing even a momentary gap [in performance], always appears to be the individual he is playing.[28]

Criticism of this kind of performance began even while the style was still in vogue. Some critics charged that German singing had entered a period of decline. "Complaints about the decline of the art of singing in our generation are well known," Rudolf Louis contended. "It would be foolish to claim that they are completely unfounded." German singers, these critics argued, had neglected purely musical aspects of singing and thus harmed their art. "From year to year the art of singing has been going downhill," Arthur Smolian deplored in an extensive article. "On the operatic stage there rages the crassest type of naturalism in singing which offends both the singer's voice and the listener's ear. In the concert hall, the more intelligent performers who propagate this new art of intense expression hide, with all sorts of subtleties, the insufficiency of their voice training under declamatory and mimetic interpretation." The repudiation of the Italian school of singing and the cultivation of Sprechgesang, Smolian believed, were the main reasons for the decline of vocal art in Germany. "Singers who are trained exclusively according to the Italian tradition ruin themselves financially because they have learned only how to sing, not how to enunciate, whereas those who are drilled in Sprechgesang ruin their voices."[29]

When did "naturalism in singing," as Smolian referred to the style, begin to fall into general disfavor? Not in the years between 1897 and 1910. The style was most vigorous then. Rudolf Louis dates the decline after 1910. "Only a few years ago," he writes in 1912, "Wüllner represented the most modern of concert singers. In him the voice, in fact music itself, was of secondary importance to the mimetic-declamatory and literary-poetic [aspects of singing]. His art of inter-pretation exhibits the extremes of the literary spiritualizing of music (in the sense of a conscious permeation of the musical life with extra-musical . . . elements) against which there has set in a reaction in favor of a strong emphasis on the specifically musical."[30]

The decline must have been gradual because J. A. Fuller-Maitland reports in 1911 that "the modern singer, especially in Germany, is so anxious to show off how many different sorts of voice-production he has learnt, that he misses no opportunity of singing songs in which two or more voices can be imitated."[31] Nevertheless, after 1910 composers themselves—Schoenberg, for instance—began to react against the singer who was anxious to show off how many sorts of voice-production he had learned: "The performers are never assigned the task of shaping the character of the individual pieces or of creating an atmosphere from the words but only of rendering the music. All the moods and the examples for tone painting in the text that the composer thought important have been treated musically. The performer should not contribute his own examples where the composer has not required any. This would not be a contribution but rather a distraction."[32]

Naturalism in singing is clearly out of fashion in modern Germany. So, too, is Sprechgesang, even on the operatic stage. The former chief conductor of the Munich opera, Robert Heger, told me that he forbade any singer to over-emphasize consonants in the manner of Sprechgesang. And traditional Italian vocal pedagogy is no longer dismissed in Germany today. The most widely accepted vocal methods combine the best features of both the German and the Italian schools. Further, connoisseurs today regard the dramatic techniques of Wüllner and his contemporaries to lied rendition as belonging more to the operatic stage than the concert hall. Concert singers today use them with extreme care and circumspection.

The reaction against naturalistic singing, broadly viewed, involves an ironic twist: the German school that Wagner and Schmitt fought so vigorously to found in the mid-1860s—and which had become an honored institution in the 1890s—became the center of controversy again after World War I, when the German musical world seriously challenged naturalism and the excesses of the German national school of singing.

Theatrical Declamation and the Composer

The interest in naturalism stimulated late-romantic composers to attempt to transform the lied into a miniature music drama. To create an illusion of reality in the lied, composers vividly characterized the individuals in its poetry. They thus focused attention on the text, feeling that in ideal musico-dramatic representation text should be understood as clearly when sung as when spoken. This objective is illustrated by an incident that occurred after the first performance of *Salome*, in 1905: "A young music student was discussing the Salome tragedy with Mrs. Strauss without even mentioning the musical part of it. Mrs. Strauss, somewhat annoyed, finally asked the young man: 'But what do you think of the music?' The music student replied, 'I didn't even notice it.' Strauss adds to that: 'It was the finest compliment ever paid to me,—there is nothing of which I am more proud.' "[33]

Late-romantic composers with naturalistic inclinations contoured their voice parts after the inflections and accents of speech. "Believe me," Henri Duparc advised Ernest Chausson, "do not write the music of one line [of poetry] without declaiming it yourself aloud, with *accents* and *gestures*" (emphasis mine). Vocal writing of this type was often identified as "intensified speech." Indeed, Friedrich Klose (1862–1942) generalized that music itself "is actually nothing other than emotionally intensified speech."[34]

Some late-romantic composers contoured their vocal line directly after the speech inflections and intonations used by renowned actors and orators of their day.[35] The effect of recitation is so successfully achieved in their lieder that the term *theatrical declamation*, denoting expressive use of language by actors, may justifiably be applied to their treatments of text. We may call such songs "frozen recitation." They document what a composer considered to be his most effective oral reading of a poem. Theatrical declamation in Wolf and Strauss, as well as in lesser masters like Plüddemann and Theodor Streicher, indicates that these composers skillfully translated considerable histrionic ability into musical terms.

Wolf himself possessed all the requirements of a good actor, which he demonstrated in the recitations of his lieder texts, as the drama critic and playwright Hermann Bahr (1863–1934) indicates: "Never in my life have I heard such reading. It is impossible to describe it. I can only say this: when he spoke the words, they assumed a prodigious truth, they became corporeal things: we had the feeling as if his own body had suddenly become an incarnation of the words, as if these hands, that we saw glimmering in the dim light, no longer belonged to a man, but to the words that we heard. He had, as it were, transubstantiated himself with all his body into the words of the poet."[36]

Wolf's reputation as an accomplished reciter was legendary. In his presentation, from memory, of the "Wolfsschlucht" (Wolf's Glen) scene from Weber's opera *Der Freischütz:* "The characters were so vividly portrayed that the frightened beholders expected to see Samiel suddenly appear. . . . When Wolf sang his songs for us, one believed the singer to be an actor. Many passages would actually be spoken: 'da fällt's in Asche ab' [it falls into ashes; "Der Feuerreiter"]. Though he had no singing voice to speak of, one felt transported into the poetic situation through his histrionic skill."[37]

Before writing a song, Wolf would often carefully study the text, weighing the relative importance of each word, seeking out correct inflections and intonations, searching for high points of declamation, and considering all the factors necessary for effective recitation.

Late romantics inserted many equivalents of stage directions into their songs to achieve dramatic presentation. Strauss wrote *mit grösster Verachtung* (with great disdain) over a passage in "Für funfzehn Pfennige." Pfitzner instructed the singer of "Herr Oluf" to perform *die Reden Olufs langsamer als die der Mutter* (the discourse of Oluf slower than that of his mother). Wolf wrote *mit hohler, heisere Stimme* (with a hollow, hoarse voice) in "Zur Warnung." Early romantics inserted fewer directions for dramatic presentation, according to Plüddemann, because they thought such theatrics belonged in opera. In contrast, late romantics searched for means to portray character vividly. "The wish to characterize people in the sharpest manner," Strauss wrote, "brought me to bitonality, since rhythmic devices did not appear to me to be strong enough." Verisimilitude for Wolf was as important in a song as in a stage work. His supreme principle of art was "rigorous, bitter, inexorable truth—truth to the point of cruelty."[38]

Some composers attempted to narrow or even bridge the gap between the spoken and sung word. If we abstract performance directions from vocal scores and arrange them in a series, we can see the subtlety of these gradations: *flüsternd* (whispering), Plüddemann's "Don Massias"; *fast gesprochen* (almost spoken), Liszt's "Kling leise, mein Lied," the 1860 version; *halb gesprochen* (half spoken), Joseph Marx's "Sankta Maria"; *gesprochen* (spoken), Paul Graener's Op. 43, no. 6; *mehr gesprochen als gesungen* (more spoken than sung), Joseph Schmid's Op. 41; *fast gesungen* (almost sung), Schoenberg's *Pierrot Lunaire*; and *ins Singen hineinkommen* (gradually beginning to sing), Alban Berg's *Wozzeck*. It is difficult to determine on the basis of this series exactly where singing ends and speaking begins. These directions all but eliminate the boundaries that separate melodrama, lied, and opera. Strauss observed astutely: "It is astonishing that none of our classical [masters] has made use of the subtle nuances that may result in the transition from spoken prose via the melodrama, the *secco recitative*, and the *recitativo accompagnato* to the lyrical sweep of a broadly flowing vocal melody."[39]

A comparison of the contours of selected vocal passages from some lieder with the speech inflections of skilled actors illustrates an important influence of naturalism on the late-romantic lied. The similarity proves remarkably close when the comparison is made with late-romantic recitation, a style that is markedly different from modern recitation.

Late-romantic actors made constant use of subtle transitions between speaking and singing, thereby giving a musical character to their recitation. The vocal training of actors contributed considerably to the musical character of their delivery. The objectives of most leading actors—von Possart, Josef Kainz (1858–1910), Wüllner, and Alexander Moissi (1880–1935)—with respect to voice placement were the same as those of most good singers: to develop the type of resonance produced by the interaction of the soft palate with the intercostal muscles and flexible diaphragm or chest breathing. Some actors (Moissi, for instance) studied voice placement (tone production) with singing teachers. (Conversely, Lilli Lehmann suggested that voice students observe Josef Kainz in order to learn such vocal techniques as proper breathing.)[40] With voice production of this type, some of the strongly emphasized words these actors recited sounded almost as if they were being sung. Further, actors continually attempted to increase their speaking range. Von Possart prided himself on his nearly three-octave speaking range, which he acquired by diligent exercise with the piano. With a wide speaking range, actors were able to emphasize key words by giving them relatively higher pitches, that is, by *pitch inflection*. They could contrast phrases by reciting each in a different voice register, by *pitch phrasing*, and intensify a climax in poetry by speaking it with a gradually rising pitch. Actors also emphasized words by applying portamenti to them, or by stretching their vowels (*quantitative accentuation*). These techniques produced a speech that hovered somewhere between speaking and singing. Today's actors tend to avoid this kind of stylized recitation. They rely more on changes of dynamics than changes of pitch to stress words and phrases and to build climaxes. Finally, late-romantic reciters were more inclined than are today's actors to enact words and to use an emotional style. Recitation, especially as it developed in Germany, was an emotional and, at times, grandiloquent performance, far removed from everyday speech.

A comparison of Wolf's setting of Goethe's "Prometheus" with readings of the poem recorded by Kainz and Moissi, two fin-de-siècle actors whose styles are remarkably different from each other, affords a rare opportunity to observe how closely the contours of Wolf's voice part resemble the speech inflections of actors of the period.[41] One may assert that Wolf's vocal style is closely interlinked with the late-romantic style of recitation. (That the two readings are dissimilar may allow them to serve as controls.) In addition, a comparison of both Wolf's and Schubert's settings of the poem will allow us to observe general differences between early and late nineteenth-century treatments of a dramatic text.

"Prometheus," one of Goethe's most famous and powerful poems, was written in 1774, during the period of Sturm und Drang. The monologue seethes with protest against tradition. Goethe's dynamic Titan, Prometheus, is fearless. He challenges the all-powerful Zeus by creating human beings in his own image and instructing his creatures to defy the god. This dramatic poem is an excellent vehicle for the display of the dramatic abilities of Schubert and Wolf, as well as those of Kainz and Moissi.

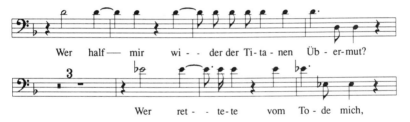

Example 5. Wolf: "Prometheus" (Goethe), mm. 102–111.

Wer half mir   wi- der der Ti - ta- nen Übermut?   Wer ret- te- te vom To- de mich

Example 6. Schubert: "Prometheus," D. 674, mm. 54–57.

Both Schubert and Wolf capture the intense drama of the poem. Schubert creates some of his best dramatic effects by purely musical means: through contrasts of recitative and arioso and changes of mode from minor to major. His lied is shaped into well-constructed sections with formal clarity. Wolf, however, gives clarity of form and contrast between sections a secondary role. Both composers tended to break the frame of the typical lied. With his alternations of ariosos and recitatives, Schubert created a miniature oratorio. Wolf composed a miniature music drama, replete with leitmotives. He pictures Zeus so vividly in a motive in the piano part—which alternates with the speech of the Titan—that he tended to transform Goethe's monologue into an implied dialogue. The dramatic implications of the song prompted Wolf later to orchestrate "Prometheus." His biographer Ernst Decsey felt in 1908 that a preference for Schubert's or Wolf's song "depends on whether one wishes to be modern or not."[42]

The contours of Wolf's voice part are strikingly similar to the vocal inflections of Kainz and Moissi. Both actors recite Prometheus's intrepid challenges in a high vocal register filled with emotion: "Wer half mir . . . " (Who helped me / against the arrogance of the Titans? Who delivered me from death?). In Wolf's composition these lines are similarly emphasized; he even intensifies the second line by setting it higher in pitch (ex. 5). Unlike Schubert, Wolf observed both caesuras in line one. He also carefully differentiated the long and short syllables with long and short time values. But Schubert chose to contrast the passage "Wer half mir . . . " with the one immediately preceding it, "da ich ein Kind war . . . ," by setting the first as a recitative and the second as an arioso. Schubert's setting is more lyrical and less rhetorical than Wolf's (ex. 6).

Kainz and Moissi, in particular, differentiate the emphatic phrase "Hier sitz' ich . . . " from the frustrated challenges quoted in examples 5 and 6 by using a middle-voice register for the emphatic phrase and a high one for the frustrated challenges (ex. 7).

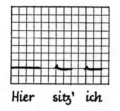

Hier sitz' ich   Wer half mir

Example 7. Moissi: "Prometheus," l. 51; l. 28.[43]

Again Wolf composed these passages as both actors recited them. He requires a high register for the frustrated challenge (see ex. 5) and a middle register for the emphatic phrase (ex. 8).

(Here I sit, / making men in my own image.)

Example 8. Wolf: "Prometheus," mm. 162–164.

Schubert produces his dramatic effects through purely musical means. He emphasizes "Hier sitz' ich . . ." (Here I sit, / making men in my own image) by introducing a sudden and effective change of mode from minor to major directly before the passage (ex. 9).

Example 9. Schubert: "Prometheus," mm. 91–94.

Moissi and Wolf both create a climax in the third stanza by becoming steadily more intense. Wolf's climax, however, is more impressive. He reinforces the rising line of the voice part with a series of harmonic sequences in the piano. His insertion of the equivalent of a stage direction above this passage—"with expression that grows continually more intense"—is further evidence of his dramatic intent (ex. 10).

(I turned my wandering eyes to the sun, as if above there were an ear to hear my lament, / a heart like mine, / to take pity on the distressed.)

Example 10. Wolf: "Prometheus," mm. 80–93.

kehrt' ich mein ver- irr- tes Au- ge zur Son- ne, als wenn drüber wär ein Ohr, zu hö ren meine

Kla- ge, ein Herz, wie mein's, sich des Be- dräng-ten zu er - bar- men

Example 11.   Schubert: "Prometheus," mm. 44–53.

Schubert's interpretation of these lines differs extremely from Wolf's and Moissi's. He envisions Prometheus in deep contemplation rather than frustration and growing anger at Zeus's lack of sympathy. Accordingly, Schubert creates a beautiful arioso (ex. 11).

Schubert's vocal style in "Prometheus" is lyrical. It rarely becomes declamatory, even in powerful dramatic passages. Wolf, on the contrary, shows his willingness to sacrifice lyricism for declamation. In example 13, as in example 5, we can see how Wolf interrupts the flow of melody in the voice part with pauses similar to those a good actor might make when reading the text. The pauses Kainz makes between the word groups quoted in example 12 are about equal in length to those indicated by the rests in Wolf's voice part (see ex. 13).

Kainz and Moissi apply three techniques that fin-de-siècle actors commonly used to stress key words: pitch inflection, quantitative accentuation, and emphasis through portamenti. Moissi makes *Hier* (see ex. 7) not only stand out but sound as if it were being sung. He enunciates the word with an effective pitch inflection and with considerable resonance. Kainz incorporates a series of carefully calculated pitch inflections in reading the last stanza of the monologue. The highest of these, which seems to touch the upper extremity of his voice range, brings *dein* into special prominence (ex. 12):

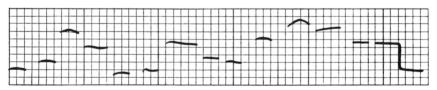

zu   ge-nie-ßen und zu freu- en sich und dein nicht zu ach-ten.

(To enjoy and to rejoice, and to ignore you, even as I!)
Example 12.   Kainz: "Prometheus," l. 55.

Wolf's setting of "und dein nicht zu achten" closely resembles the pitch inflections used by Kainz (ex. 13):

zu leiden, zu wei - nen, zu ge-nie- ßen und zu freu-en sich und dein nicht zu ach - ten,
Example 13.   Wolf: "Prometheus," mm. 167–171.

Kainz, like Wolf, stresses the assonance (quantitative accentuation) of *glüh-test, jung,* and *gut* by stretching the vowels *ü* and *u* (ex. 14a).

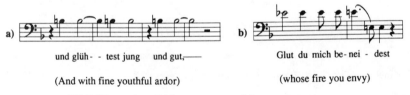

a) und glüh- - test jung   und gut,——

(And with fine youthful ardor)

b) Glut du mich be- nei - dest

(whose fire you envy)

Example 14.   Wolf: "Prometheus," (a) mm. 120–123; (b) mm. 49–50.

Moissi uses not only a portamento but also a slightly tremulous voice to stress the second syllable of *beneidest* (envy), a word that in his reading appears at the peak of a climactic passage (ex. 15).

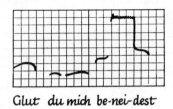

Glut du mich be-nei-dest

Example 15.   Moissi: "Prometheus," l. 10.

The slurred notes to which Wolf set *nei* in *be-nei-dest* (ex. 14b) function as the musical equivalent of the histrionic effect. Fin-de-siècle composers frequently used portamenti to stress words.

Both actors, but especially Moissi, provide excellent examples of the manner in which reciters enacted words. Both read "zu leiden, zu weinen" (to suffer, to weep) with quavering descending intonations and "zu geniessen" (to enjoy) and "zu freuen sich" (to rejoice) with rising vocal inflections. They enact these words in the manner that Wolf paints them (ex. 16).

From the numerous similarities between the voice inflections of Kainz and Moissi and the contours of Wolf's vocal line, we can hypothesize that Wolf was influenced in "Prometheus" by the late-romantic style of recitation. This raises the question, How typical of Wolf's vocal writing is the vocal style of "Prome-

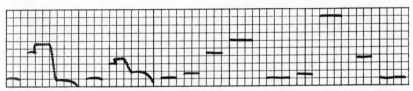

zu lei - den, zu wei-nen, zu ge-nie-ßen und zu freu- en sich

Example 16.   Moissi: "Prometheus," l. 54.

theus"? Its speechlike writing is but one of several kinds developed by Wolf. Here, I would identify this style—apparent in dramatic scenes in Wolf's *Goethe* cycle—as theatrical declamation, since it resembles the grandiloquent recitation of contemporary actors like Kainz and Moissi. Such declamation contrasts sharply with the everyday speechlike idiom of the *Italian Songbook*. Both kinds of vocal writing serve an entirely different purpose from that of composers of the traditional lyrical lied. Unlike these composers, who aim at captivating melody, Wolf's object here is to suggest speech, to reflect its intonation, rhythm, and pacing. Wolf's unique ability to create an extraordinarily wide range of lyrico-dramatic shadings in "naturalistic" lieder and to light the spark of life within them is his great achievement.

Wolf's speechlike styles are as protean as they are polymorphic. His vocal writing is marked by shifts in a continuum that proceeds from actual speech to lyrical melody. Some passages approximate speech closely while others, more lyrical in flow, convey only its impression. Or he might impart to only one phrase, in an otherwise lyrical song, the suggestion of speech in order to draw special attention to that phrase. Subtle variety of speechlike writing is apparent even in a single song, as comparison of the four phrases in example 17 reveals. Although both 1a and 1b are speechlike, 1a is more speechlike than 1b. The first is simply a triumphant statement of the fact "I *am* in love," while the second is a coquettish avowal that "I am *in love*." Appropriately, Wolf gives 1b a warm musical gesture: a lyrical upward portamento sweep. The previous phrase (2a) provides a dramatic break: "but haply not with you." Its consonants sizzle percussively. Both 2a and 2b are more speechlike than 1a and 1b, but 2b, which presents the peak of the poem's humor, is the most speechlike of all. It is often virtually spoken. We might also note that Wolf often sets a repeated word differently each time, to bring out new subtleties of meaning.

Wolf's declamatory writing is not necessarily speechlike. Declamatory writing—whether in Wolf's songs or in late-romantic lieder in general—can be of many kinds, not all speechlike. A song could be lyrical yet declamatory if the composer was seeking to reflect the *prosody of the poetry in the rhythm of his

Example 17. Wolf: "Du denkst mit einem Fädchen" (Heyse), mm. 13–17.

vocal line. Wolf's "In der Frühe" provides a fine example (see ex. 48d): though painstakingly declaimed, its twisted vocal line, as I shall show in Chapter 9, is not at all speechlike.

None of Wolf's cycles is exclusively declamatory. As I noted in Chapter 1, Wolf's declamatory style is confined to individual songs within songbooks, not to entire volumes. For Wolf cultivated a wide variety of vocal styles. His lyrical, volkstümlich songs provide fine examples. Our aesthetic pleasure in them lies in their purely musical features—rhythmic patterns and cantabile vocal melody. Fin-de-siècle critics, captivated by musical prosody, did not appreciate this distinction. The delightful prancing rhythm in the piano part of "Der Gärt-ner"—meant to suggest the canter of horses—permeates the lyrical vocal line, causing Wolf to accent *Leibrösslein* (literally, favorite little steed) incorrectly. Critics quickly censured this as an error in prosody.[44] On the other hand, Wolf might declaim an individual measure or passage of a nondeclamatory lied, as in "Fussreise." There he momentarily interrupts the song's robust tramping rhythm with engaging declamation on *Dann* (m. 16): "Dann wie's Vöglein in Laube" (Then as birds in the branches). The consequence, of course, is a mixture of styles.

The degree to which passages in Wolf may be said to approximate speech depends, in the final analysis, on their performance. The singer who concentrates on the purely vocal (cantabile) aspect of singing is likely to create a different impression of Wolf's intentions from the one who highlights the words. Wolf disliked singers who sugarcoated his vocal lines with "sweet tones." He admired Eugen Gura, whose "fiery" interpretation and immaculate speech were widely applauded. He harshly criticized Theodor Reichmann (1849–1903) and Gustav Walter in particular.[45] And he soon became disillusioned with Friederike Mayer, a young mezzo he wished to train, because she paid too much attention to purely vocal matters and too little to interpretation.[46] Resounding in Wolf's ears from his earliest days were the dramatic and stentorian tones of the Wagnerian singer. The era of the singer trained primarily to specialize in the lied was still some years off. Wolf's letters are filled with ecstatic praise for outstanding Wagnerians. He enthusiastically sought Wagnerians like Lilli Lehmann to interpret his songs. His foremost interpreter was Friedrich Jäger (1832–1902), the Heldentenor who had retired from Bayreuth and opera to devote himself to Wolf. That the tone and temperament of these Wagnerians influenced Wolf's taste in lied singers is more than conjecture.

As I have discussed, many late-romantic composers, both minor and major, sought to suggest the erratic course of speech. Meanwhile, critics debated whether such writing had any place in the lied. Progressives, like Max Steinitzer and Richard Specht, thought it did and identified Strauss's work as *Sprechlied, the most modern kind of song. Conservatives, responding with stern words for such composition, argued that Wolf and Strauss had misapplied Wagner's declamatory operatic style to the lied.

Late romantics had applied aspects of theatrical declamation to the lied even before Wolf made his influence felt. Plüddemann exhorted singers not to captivate their audiences with beautiful singing but to "narrate with utmost clarity of speech" when performing his "Der Kaiser und der Apt." His general performance direction, "to be sung almost entirely in Parlando style," and his occasional directions—"harsh," "shouting," "crying," and "with a disguised voice"—make his naturalistic intentions explicit. After Wolf's ascendancy, Strauss turned, in his middle years, to theatrical declamation. So did Reger, in his early maturity. But good declamation was never easy for Reger. Mahler, by contrast, commented angrily on his dislike for declamation in Wolf in general and particularly in "Gesang Weylas": "How is this a song with such a threadbare melody?"[47] Yet Mahler could on occasion shape a declamatory phrase as well as any master. Pfitzner, too, created some of the finest declamatory songs of the fin de siècle.

Theodor Streicher (1874–1940) was one of many composers who accepted Wolf's authority. He was esteemed by a select group of admirers as a master of musical rhetoric. Streicher's vocal line in example 18 suggests the contour of a good oral reading of a poem, with carefully considered voice inflections. He obliges the singer, as a result of his time values, to linger on the key words "saurer Gang" and to accelerate the pace over the less important "ob es auch ein" with the result that the passage suggests speech.

Strauss's setting in example 19 is even more speechlike. His phrasing is erratic, restricted in range, and composed of more discrete units. The pauses Strauss introduced might be called "contemplative pauses"—the kind a good actor makes to ignite the spark of life in his reading.

Late romantics suggested speech by other means, for example, by inserting many notes of small time value within measures of compound time. So doing, they sought to render indefinite recurring structural beats of the measure and thereby create a free musical rhythm similar to the free rhythm of speech. French composers like Fauré and Debussy—more often than the Germans—suggested speech by this means. Another means was by frequent changes of time signatures. Early in the twentieth century many composers, like Pfitzner, Reger, Mahler, and Strauss, changed time signatures frequently in the lied, although

Example 18.   Streicher: "Was du fordest, es gescheh'!" (Hafis), mm. 1–3.

Example 19.   Strauss: "O wärst du mein!" (Lenau), Op. 26, no. 2, mm. 4–11.

Mahler and Pfitzner rarely did so to imitate speech. Reger, however, produced his so-called prose style by this means. An extreme example by Friedrich Klose, from the first song of the *Bruno Lieder*, involves such compound time signatures as $\frac{18}{8}$. His insertion of numerous rests and irregular sequences of time values fragments melody and aids further in suggesting speech (ex. 20).[48]

Example 20.   Klose: *Fünf-Gesänge*, no. 1 (Bruno), mm. 22–26.

Late romantics were, of course, also intimately aware of the fact that a singer's ability to approximate speech declines as he leaves his speaking register and approaches the extremes of his range. Strauss and Pfitzner assigned to a singer's speaking register parlando passages that bear important text, even in the "lyrical" lied, where conservative critics thought it out of place (ex. 21).

Example 21.   Pfitzner: "Leierkasten" (Busse), Op. 15, no. 1, mm. 8–12.

Wolf was a master of making speechlike vocal lines psychologically vivid. His music speaks more eloquently on the subject than do the comments of critic Hermann Bahr and Michael Georg Conrad, leader of the naturalistic movement in German literature. "Man sagt mir, deine Mutter woll' es nicht" from the *Italian Songbook* presents an excellent illustration. The poem concerns a girl who is filled with anxiety because her lover's mother disapproves of her. She tries to pluck up courage to tell her lover to defy his mother.

Man sagt mir, deine Mutter woll' es nicht;	I am told that your mother does not wish you to come to me, so
So bleibe weg, mein Schatz, tu' ihr den willen.	stay away, my love, and do her bidding. No, dearest! Do not
Ach Liebster, nein! tu' ihr den Willen nicht	obey her, come to me secretly in defiance of her! No, my beloved!
Besuch' mich doch, tu's ihr zum Trotz, im Stillen!	Do not listen to her, but in defiance of her come more often
Nein, mein Geliebter, folg' ihr nimmermehr,	than before! Pay no heed to her, whatever she may say; defy her,
Tu's ihr zum Trotz, komm öfter als bisher!	my love, and come to me every day!⁴⁹
Nein, höre nicht auf sie, was sie auch sage;	
Tu's ihr zum Trotz, mein Lieb, komm alle Tage!	

Wolf captures the psychological overtones in his characterization—the girl's agitation, her temporary indecision, her vacillation, her growing courage, and finally her fixed determination. The syncopations in example 22a help to convey the girl's initial hesitation. Her first attempt to induce her lover to disobey his mother is timid. She falters while saying "tu' ihr den Willen nicht" ("do not obey her"). Wolf's melody falls on the key word *nicht* (not). And he instructs the performer to sing the phrase softly (ex. 22b). Although the girl seems more determined on her second attempt by uttering the defiant "tu's ihr zum Trotz," (defy her), she still falters, adding cautiously: "im Stillen." A sudden change of dynamics from forte to piano paints her loss of courage. The dynamic marking of *piano* also graphically depicts *Stillen* (ex. 22c).

Example 22. Wolf: "Man sagt mir" (Heyse), (a) mm. 3–4; (b) mm. 6–7; (c) mm. 8–9; (d) mm. 12–13; (e) mm. 16–20.

She becomes bolder with each successive attempt and is sufficiently inspired in her third attempt to say: "tu's ihr zum Trotz." Wolf represents her growing courage by setting the first three words to notes of higher pitch. But his descending vocal inflection on the key word *Trotz* (defy) shows that the girl's courage has again slackened (ex. 22d). With her courage finally at its height she announces loudly: "tu's ihr zum Trotz, mein Lieb, komm' alle Tage"—with firm emphasis on *Trotz* and *alle* (ex. 22e). This song, a fine example of musical characterization, illustrates how Wolf sets repeated verbal phrases differently to reflect the particular shade of meaning each phrase acquires as a result of its changing position in the poetic context.

Although such naturalistic writing was an important element in vocal music during the entire period of late romanticism, it was intensively cultivated only to about 1910. Avant-garde composers like Schoenberg had earlier reacted against the style. Mahler, who apparently never favored it, expressed strong distaste for declamation in an interview with Wolf's biographer Ernst Decsey: "[Mahler] answered [my questions] furiously. . . . 'I demand a theme, development of the theme, thematic manipulation, song, not *de-cla-ma-tion!'* and with each syllable he hit the back of his hand in his palm. I had the feeling he was about to explode."[50]

chapter five

Naturalistic Description and the
Reaction It Provoked

Having drawn lifelike characters, lied composers sought to
place them in true-to-life settings. They strove to create an illusion of reality by
painting a scene in the piano part with a palette of descriptive music. Late
romantics believed that they could suggest scenery by means of the piano.

Audiences of the time delighted in musical illustration. Wolf commented
with chagrin on his listeners' unrestrained imagination: "They search for operatic scenes in my lyrical productions and every one screams: too bad for the piece,
it would certainly have been something if it had been an opera." Yet Wolf
himself imagined "realistic settings for his songs. In *Gesang Weylas* [he visu-
alized] the goddess of Orplid sitting on a reef in the moonlight with a harp in
her arms. In the second Coptic song [he saw] a feast of wise men from all
countries—merry, high spirited sounds."[1] And Pfitzner, in "Sie haben heut'
Abend Gesellschaft" (Op. 4, no. 2), sought to evoke the distant sound of a party
with this instruction to the pianist: "In order to create the impression that music
from the house is being heard in the street through the closed window . . . play
the music for the right hand much softer than that for the left hand."[2] Performance directions from fin-de-siècle lied composers show their fascination with
verisimilitude. Richard Trunk wrote "very fragrant" in "Nachtigallen" (Op. 21,
no. 2). Reger specified "threateningly" above a passage that pictures a threatening hammer in "Wehe" (Op. 62, no. 1). Pfitzner indicated *schlank* (lithe) over a
passage in "Wandl' ich in dem Morgentau" (Op. 33, no. 4) that images a little
fish in the millbrook.

Early nineteenth-century composers were also attracted by musical imagery.
But they took their idea for illustrating a text from late eighteenth-century
melodrama, of which it was a principal feature, and applied it to the lied. Alfred
Einstein believed that "the romantic lied is unthinkable without its predecessor,
the early melodrama." Later composers like Berlioz and Wagner intensified the
procedure. By the eighties and nineties musicians were so captivated by the
pictorial in music that they interpreted the music of their own period (and of
others) in terms of description. Einstein generalized that "a Romantic is unable
to make abstract music." In the words of Strauss: "There is no such thing as
abstract music, if music is good, it means something and then it is program

music." This fascination with precise representation led some late romantics to overstep the boundaries of good judgment. The final scene of *Götterdämmerung*, describing the destruction of Valhalla, was made more vivid "by the addition of pistol shots and a pair of thunder machines behind the stage which almost drowned out the orchestra." Helm quoted the telegram the conductor sent to Wagner directly after the performance. "First performance of *Götterdämmerung* just concluded. Magnificent success. Siegfried's death and closing scene created a shattering effect."[3]

Late romantics heatedly discussed musical description, creating more confusion than coherence. The majority of nineteenth-century musicians fiercely repudiated program music. Yet some lied composers, even while disparaging program music, wrote their own examples. In the instrumental postlude of "Epiphanias," Wolf, through descriptive leitmotives, pictured the departure of the three kings in their search for the Christ child, adding this program: "Here each one walks off alone to his own characteristic rhythm." Twelve bars later he specified: "Here they meet to continue their journey together." Yet later Wolf wrote: "I hate all programs. . . . I rely only on the suggestive power of music."[4] In truth, fin-de-siècle composers wrote descriptive music of one kind or another during at least one phase of their development. They were as eager to experiment with one kind of descriptive music as they later were to reject the kind that had previously attracted them. Of the various kinds, the one called Naturalistic Description came under the severest attack.

Late romantics used two kinds of Naturalistic Description frequently in the lied: imitation and association. Both often occur in combination, even in the setting for a single line of poetry. The imitation of sounds in the environment, probably the oldest kind of musical description, is the most commonly encountered. Lied composers adopted a limited number of musical devices to represent the limitless variety of extramusical sounds. Wolf, for instance, used a trill to imitate a bird in "Karwoche," a bee in "Der Knabe und das Immlein," the murmur of a brook in "Heimweh," and the hiss of a snake in "Verschling der Abgrund." Composers occasionally introduced imitation into the voice part, primarily for humorous effects. To reproduce a drum roll in "Trommellied," Paul Graener directed the singer to execute a long, sustained roll ("Drrr"). Example 23 shows how various composers copied the sounds of animals, those of a cat, a mouse, and a jackass.

Because exact imitation of nonmusical sounds is difficult to create, especially with a piano, late romantics regarded the task of creating convincing examples as a test of ingenuity. "I consider it the greatest triumph of musical technique," Strauss stated, "to describe the sound an object yields." He demonstrated his point, we are told, by touching a knife to a fork. "Do you see" Strauss said, "they make a sound; a great skill is required to render in music such soft sounds so that the listener is not left in doubt as to the composer's intentions. This is my purpose."[5] *Verisimilitude* was the aim of the late romantic composer in his desire

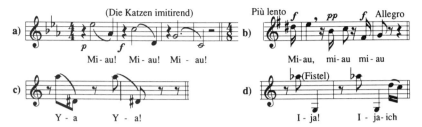

Example 23.　(a) Plüddemann: "Die Katzen und der Hausherr" (Lichtwer), mm. 1–4; (b) Reger: "Zwei Mäuschen" (Boetilz), Op. 76, no. 48, mm. 36–37; (c) Wolf: "Lied des transferierten Zettel" (Shakespeare/Bernhoff), mm. 15–16; (d) Mahler: "Lob des hohen Verstandes" (*Des Knaben Wunderhorn*), mm. 82–83.

to represent extramusical sounds vividly. *Objectivity,* another important word, refers to the wish of fin-de-siècle composers, influenced by naturalism, to render only the *objective* impression of the poetry they set.

Early romantics might imitate musical instruments by writing the kind of music associated with their sound. Mere suggestion was scarcely enough for late romantics, who sought vivid imitation. Julius Bittner marked a piano passage in "Ausblick" with horn figurations, *quasi corni.* Reger instructed the pianist in "Der verliebte Jäger" (Op. 76, no. 13) to "imitate a horn as realistically as possible." Plüddemann went still further. He instructed the pianist to imitate the sound of a horn, its echo, and timpani, in "Der wilde Jäger" (1883), trumpets and harps in "Dantes Traum," and the effect of a full orchestra in "Der Taucher." Wolf took delight in imitative description. On hearing an Aeolian harp for the first time, he remarked: "Look, I've *never* heard an Aeolian harp and yet I divined it just so, exactly as the Aeolian harp there sounds; so it is in my song. That is most remarkable."[6] For Mahler, who aspired to imitate musical instruments faithfully, it was a logical step to progress from the piano song to the orchestral lied.

Sometimes the fondness of late romantics for imitation overwhelmed their better judgment. Even outstanding composers occasionally marred a song's structure by thrusting imitative passages into it. The result may be little more than a series of sound effects, as is the imitation by Strauss of a storm, with its clap of thunder and crack of lightning (ex. 24).

The better lieder, however, are rarely crowded with imitative effects, even when the opportunity for description exists in texts. Wolf eschewed imitation where it was too obvious or would destroy a song's atmosphere, as a crowing rooster would have done in "Das verlassene Mägdlein." He generally sought to weave the fabric of an entire song from one imitative motive: an Aeolian harp in "An eine Aeolsharfe," the wind in "Lied vom Winde," and a galloping horse in "Der Gärtner."

Strauss, too, followed this practice. Although many songs are rich in imitative description, the majority are not. His sketch books show that he exercised

Example 24. Strauss: "Von den Sieben Zechbrüdern" (Uhland), Op. 47, no. 5, mm. 148–150.

care in producing his effects. He sometimes sketched the effect, or designated the one he planned to use, as he did in the manuscript of "Hochzeitlich Lied" (Op. 37, no. 6), where he wrote the word *glocken* (bells) above the left hand of the piano part.[7] But remarkable examples of imitation occur in his orchestral songs. "Nächtlicher Gang" (Op. 44, no. 2) has many—the flutter of flags in a storm at midnight, the hoot of a great owl, the snarling of dogs, and rattling fear. Strauss simulated sounds seldom heard in piano songs of other composers: the breaking of stones ("Das Lied des Steinklopfers," Op. 49, no. 4), the bellowing of a little ox ("Die heiligen drei Könige," Op. 56, no. 6), and the beating of a human heart ("Hymnus," Op. 33, no. 3).

Although we have seen that Reger embraced New German music after his move to Munich, he showed less interest in musical illustration than Wolf and Strauss, even in those songs (Op. 51 to Op. 75) that are rich in other kinds of musical description. Yet he fashioned imitations with alacrity, weaving extended passages from one effect into ostinato figures. He impressively utilized the descriptive potentialities of rhythm to represent the blow of a smith's hammer in "Schmied Schmerz," Op. 51, no. 6, and "Wehe," Op. 62, no. 1, and the heavy beat of hooves in "Gute Nacht," Op. 55, no. 13, and "Pflügerin Sorge," Op. 62, no. 15.

Mahler's attitude underwent basic change as he matured. He foreshadowed the shift away from the aesthetics of naturalism that was later to affect music in general. Although he occasionally used imitation in early songs, he later gave up portraying words for the sheer delight of imitating sounds. The mature Mahler used imitation less as objective representation, more as symbolic suggestion. The cowbells in the Sixth Symphony do not decorate a pastoral scene, but symbolize lonely isolation.

Pfitzner's early songs, like the ballad "Herr Oluf," Op. 12 (1891), contain fine examples of imitation. Amusing and ingenious examples also occur in his orchestral songs, which will be discussed in Chapter 12. Imitations in his piano lieder are equally deft. The melody he used in "Sonst" (Op. 15, no. 4) to mimic a musical clock is not his own, but as he explained in a footnote in the song, "one played by a musical toy I heard in my childhood and that was written down from memory. When set in motion this toy would play a little melody from which the eight measures above are a direct quotation." In later years, Pfitzner wrote vehement essays against musical illustration. His great love of the German countryside, especially as pictured in Josef von Eichendorff's poetry, continued to inspire musical description. But instead of imitating nature's sounds, Pfitzner sought to reflect her inner realm. He shaded rather than delineated imagery, blurring, for example, the sound of bells instead of painting it vividly.

Association involves even more intricate descriptive procedures. Though of great variety, these procedures share a common element: the composer seeks to associate musical figures with key words so as to represent them strongly. Late romantics created a large number of associations. Some are simple, even naive; others are personal, subtle, and recondite, requiring explanation. The simplest kinds first: words are interpreted in their denotative sense. *Long* is merely set to a long time value (as is *lange* in Wolf's "Wir haben beide lange Zeit geschwiegen") and *softly* and *loud* are contrasted (as in Pfitzner's "Singt mein Schatz wie ein Fink," Op. 33, no. 5, by underscoring each word with its equivalent dynamic sign. Strauss's representation of *singing* ("Die heiligen drei Könige") by a complex coloratura associated with virtuoso singing and Pfitzner's depiction, by a long sustained call of "I call" ("Stimme der Sehnsucht" [Op. 19, no. 1]) illustrates the denotative method of association. Sometimes composers, delighted to discover good examples, emphasized denotative words to the point where they were lifted out of context. In "Hat gesagt-bleibt's nicht dabei" (Op. 36, no. 3), for example, Strauss engages in a delightful musical romp on the numbers *one, two,* and, particularly, *three.*

Most association, however, occurs through the connotations of words. The procedure of late romantics is the familiar one used by Italian madrigalists and baroque composers: to relate visualized with musical motion. Thus the crackling sound of fire and the splash of water are not imitated, but their undulating movements are associated with undulating melody. In this way, Strauss pictured *wandering* in the voice part of "Winterliebe" (Op. 48, no. 5) with a long, twisted melisma (mm. 32–35) that suggests the track. Most late romantics associated music with visualized motion. The windlike rush of thought in "Lied des Verfolgten im Turm" and the swimming of fish in "Des Antonius . . . Fischpredigt" are Mahlerian examples. Strauss depicted motion more often than his outstanding contemporaries, devising many unusual images. In "Hab' ich Euch denn je geraten" (Op. 67, no. 5), he created the impression of nets being cast into the sea with a descending rush of thirty-seconds in the piano part (mm. 12–13).

Repeatedly, composers depicted words that implied cessation of motion: *rest, silence,* and *death.* Pfitzner momentarily stopped the flow of his music after the word *end* in the phrase "es geht mit mir zu Ende" (my end is nearing,

"Hussens Kerker," Op. 32, no. 1). Strauss and Reger, respectively, painted *Totenreich* (death's realm; "Rückleben," Op. 47, no. 3) and *Totenschlafen* (death's sleep; "Der Alte," Op. 55, no. 15) with soft, sustained chords.

Late romantics frequently rendered words of direction (*up* and *down*) and their connotations, such as sky, star, and light (see *Licht* in ex. 1c) for "up." Strauss associated words connoting direction most often. In his middle years he differed from most of his contemporaries by setting such words in wide leaps that brought them into sharp relief. He evidently exercised care in planning these associations. In a draft found among his manuscripts for the song "Nachts in der Kajüte," Strauss sketched a number of single measures, labeling one with high chords "heaven" and another, with low chords, "sea." Wolf and Mahler, in contrast, seemed often to have deliberately avoided illustrating the denotative meaning of words of direction (ex. 25).

Some associations made with *ascent* and *descent* are among the recondite kinds mentioned above. Wolf linked traits of personality with ascending and descending melody in his opera *Der Corregidor*: "The motive of . . . Lukas (*notabene*), a rustic native, is an ascending melodic line, whereas that of the Corregidor, a decadent nobleman, descends. The characteristic traits of these motives have just occurred to me. Are they not remarkably appropriate?" The identification made by nineteenth-century composers of the concept of landscape with the sound of horns is one. In the piano parts of their lieder, composers from Beethoven and Schubert to Strauss wrote music that suggested horns where the text concerned forests or landscapes.[8]

A special type of association—that of contiguity—occurs when a carefully declaimed vocal passage is repeated immediately in the piano part. The listener, hearing the piano part, may recall the words with such clarity that he gets the impression that they are being "spoken" by the piano. Strauss created such an effect (see brackets) in "Gefunden" (ex. 26).

Lied composers sometimes used a kind of pictorialism that resembles "ocular" music, but mainly for humorous purposes. They occasionally aped the madrigalist's practice of depicting words such as *nero* with black noteheads and *bianco* with white ones. Courvoisier naively portrayed African Pygmies in

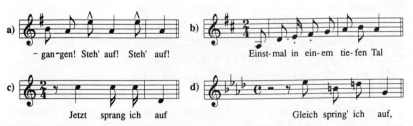

Example 25. Mahler: (a) "Frühlingsmorgen" (Leander), mm. 13–14; (b) "Lob des hohen Verstandes" (*Des Knaben Wunderhorn*), mm. 9–11; Wolf: (c) "Zur Warnung" (Moerike), mm. 44–45; (d) "Schon streckt' ich aus" (Heyse), mm. 7–8.

Example 26.   Strauss: "Gefunden" (Goethe), Op. 56, no. 1, mm. 12–16.

"Grosse Reise" (Op. 28, vol. 4, no. 5) with black noteheads. Wolf brought the words *a long sausage* in "Der Tambour" into special prominence, not only by drawing notes across the staff in the shape of a sausage but by setting the passage to the highest pitches in the song's voice part. And in "Ich und Du" (Op. 11, no. 1) Pfitzner pictured in the piano part (mm. 28–31) two drops running down a leaf, joining, and falling off.

Strauss produced exquisite examples of ocular music by means of melismas. His picture of *flames* ("Amor," Op. 68, no. 5) through jagged melismas in the voice part resembles a flame's fluctuating contour. Other late romantics occasionally also came close to ocular music in their representation of words connoting direction, as did Reger for the phrase "Nun steh' ich über Grat und Kluft" (now I stand above a ridge and ravine) in "Der Alte" (Op. 55, no. 15). In measures 1–3, Reger portrayed a ridge (*Grat*) in the vocal line and a ravine (*Kluft*) in the piano part.

Naturalistic Description provoked waves of criticism. Its proponents considered examples from Berlioz, Wagner, and Strauss as archetypes of modern music. Its antagonists disdained all four kinds of illustrative music, program music in particular, claiming that it gave music a secondary role. Echoes of this disdain reverberated throughout the century, from Schumann's censure of Berlioz's program for *Symphonie fantastique* to vitriolic attacks on the "programs" of Strauss and Mahler (fig. 6).

Wagner was a cardinal figure in arguments concerning Naturalistic Description, owing to his theory of music drama. He had assigned a secondary role to music in *Opera and Drama* (1851). "The error in opera consisted of this: a means of expression—the music—had been made the objective while the end itself—the drama—became the means." The drama in Wagner's radical *Gesamtkunstwerk* (total artwork) is supreme and the other arts—music, the dance, scene-painting—fuse to comment on its progress. Wagner's early *Ring* operas abandon clear-cut musical forms in favor of naturalistic speechlike vocal lines immersed in a sea of "endless" descriptive music.

Wagner's radical contribution unleashed furious debate. Hanslick deplored

Figure 6. R. Wilke, "Parody on Descriptive Music": "At my F major paraphrase the listener must have the impression that a pale lady is passing a lilac-colored glove tremblingly over his neck" (original title: "Tonmalerei" [Tone painting], from *Simplizissimus*)

the concept of music having a secondary role in service of drama. He argued in *Von musikalisch-Schönen* (The beautiful in music; 1854) that "the listener . . . experiences music as a sounding image of the great movements in the universe." Hanslick's thesis, observes Carl Dahlhaus, "hides metaphysical implications. . . . By 'dissolving' itself from functions, texts, and programs, pure instrumental music can appear as an image of the 'absolute.'" Nietzsche's criticism of Wagner the theorist is similar. "Music is not a medium of the drama . . . The nature of things resounds from music; drama merely reproduces their appearances."[9]

The lied did not escape criticism. Angry exchanges during the fin de siècle created more heat than light. Weingartner interpreted Mauke's suggestion that the singer change his costume according to the mood of each song (see Chapter 2) as a plea to provide scenery for lieder. Specific objections, too, were leveled. "Through misunderstanding, [Wolf and Strauss] were trying to adapt Wagner's musico-dramatic reforms to the lied," Niemann challenged, and thus: "They were guilty of confusing the theatre with the concert hall."[10] Theatricalisms had been inserted into the lied.

The more basic objection, of course, was that the practice gave the music of the lied a secondary role in service to the poetry. Though conceived for performance in the home, Wolf's "Epiphanias," mentioned above, nevertheless gives music a secondary role: to describe visual action. The postlude converts pure music into program music, a procedure many late romantics scorned. "Music is the art . . . as Schopenhauer expressed it, of idea and not of shadow. Only withered naturalism dares to subject her to coarse objectivity" because it concentrates only on "life's surface" and thereby completely ignores the world within, the poet Ernst Ludwig Schellenberg stated. Schellenberg, a Schopenhauerean, presented clear-headed criticism of Naturalistic Description in the lied: "The practice whereby lied composers illustrate . . . each mention of birds with trills and runs" draws undue attention to the individual word of a poem.[11] In such a process, composers consider the poem only in its smallest parts, as separate words and phrases. We might call this analytic description, since it is concerned primarily with details. This process, Schellenberg professed, produced songs of discrete and disconnected units.

In earlier generations, Schellenberg continued, individuals also dismissed Naturalistic Description: "The imitation of thunder in music," Goethe thought, "is inartistic." But he cherished "the musician who could evoke in me the feeling I perceive when I hear thunder." For Goethe, "the greatest and noblest privilege in music is to express through mood the inner core of [things] and without the use of crude external means." Criticism of Naturalistic Description ran throughout the nineteenth century and climaxed in challenges such as Schellenberg's: "Not the word as such is of real significance but the sense of the poem."[12]

Late romantics who disdained the practice of imaging isolated words of a text—an analytic tactic, the essence of Naturalistic Description—favored what we may call a synthetic tactic. Here composers create a musical parallel in mood for a scene or for the poem as a whole. They reject imitation and association entirely, considering the illustration of details such as the imitation of thunder crude and naive. Instead, they aim to express the mood evoked by thunder.

If we look beneath the arguments for and against Naturalistic Description we discover that members of both factions actually shared a fundamental musical aesthetic: the belief that music towers above all the arts because of its supreme powers of expression. This aesthetic derives from Schopenhauer, whose comments have special relevance to the lied. Music "represents the metaphysical of everything that is physical in the world, the thing-in-itself of every phenomenon. . . . Music gives at once heightened significance to every painting, indeed, to every scene of real life and of the world. It certainly does this the more analogous its melody is to the inner spirit of a given phenomenon. This is the reason why one can set a poem to music as a song."[13]

What occurs in great lieder in nineteenth-century aesthetics, to paraphrase Schopenhauer, is that music expresses the inner nature of things while the poetry merely reproduces their outer appearances. Late romantics considered a song a failure if such musico-poetic fusion did not occur. Wolf, Mahler, Strauss, Pfitzner, and others wrote their own texts in valiant attempts to achieve an ideal fusion of words and music. But they rarely set their own texts.

Later in life Wagner also sought to express in music the world within, the inner core of things. His composition of *Tristan* (1859) had brought about a fundamental change in his thinking. *Tristan*—a work for symphony orchestra with added voice parts—gave music, instrumental music, the central role. It denied in every respect the theory he had expounded in *Opera and Drama*. Wagner, a convinced Schopenhauerean, now argued that music was superior to the other arts. He never openly recanted his earlier theory, however.

Late romantics in general, enlightened Wagnerites included, regarded absolute music as supreme in expressiveness. Their view of absolute music was, to say the least, entirely different from ours. Contemporary musical dictionaries reflect the difference. "The great power of [absolute] music," according to Riemann (1908), "lies in the direct emotions which it awakens" and in its "free outpouring of feeling." Riemann ascribed to absolute music "the power to awaken definite associations . . . alone or supported by the other arts—to characterize, to illustrate, to describe." Only "ultra-conservative musicians utterly deny to [absolute] music the power to represent anything." Later dictionaries, like *Grove* (1954) and Riemann-Gurlitt (1967), inspired perhaps by reactions to romanticism, consider representation or illustration in music—analytic or synthetic—to be outside the realm of pure music. "Absolute music is free from extra-musical implications" claims the *Harvard Dictionary of Music* (1969). The *New Grove* (1980) and the *New Harvard* (1986) have not adopted these restrictive definitions.[14]

Late romantics, affirming that music is supreme in expressiveness, hypothesized that each key has the capacity to evoke special moods, traits of personality, types of scenery, and even specific colors. Pfitzner refers to the passage in Meyerbeer's *Les Huguenots* (act 2), where Raoul's bandage is removed so that he sees the sunlight: "Suddenly the bright quality of A major shines forth—four measures of nothing but bright and brilliant A major." Franz Strauss, the composer's son, informed me that his father often wrote the key on the page of a poem he had just read and planned to set to music. The lied composer and aesthetician Hermann Stephani (1877–1960) believed that each key has a particular *Stimmungscharacter*—a special capacity to create mood—as a result of its position in the cycle of fifths. Numerous studies were written during the fin de siècle on the subject. Physicist Hermann von Helmholtz (1821–94) was strongly attracted by the theory. In short, nineteenth-century musicians were as strongly convinced of its truth as later musicians, especially after 1920, question it. Inquiry in the 1950s by physicist Charles Culver, however, lends credence to the theory with respect to stringed instruments: "Different keys may possess definite [extramusical] characteristics . . . [because] each open string of a violin has its own tone of spectrum, and in playing in certain keys, C major, for example, use is made of open strings more often than in executing a passage in such a key as G flat."[15]

Lied composers like Wolf, professing that keys have extramusical connotations, categorically rejected requests by singers to transpose their songs. Schumann had earlier opposed transposition for the same reason. Robert Franz was particularly outspoken: "Expression in my songs depends entirely on the key I have selected for them. After death, I can do nothing to oppose transposed editions. However, as long as I live, I will fight against them with my hands and feet." But Wolf and others were not always consistent in their refusal to allow their songs to be transposed. Further, composers did not identify a particular key with the same characteristics. Stephani considered F-sharp major "abnormally shrill and strident," Berlioz dubbed it "cutting," while D'Indy and Franck thought it characterized "divine Love."[16]

Lied composers of the fin de siècle exploited music's supreme expressiveness in a variety of other ways. The geniuses might link harmonic color so closely with an object's psychological connotations that the music seemed to acquire properties of the object itself. Nearly every time *Sonne* (sun) appears as a key word in his songs, Strauss represents it with a major chord that, in its harmonic context, gives the impression that the music itself is glowing brightly. Strauss brings out the bright color of this simple chord and the word it paints by preceding it with dissonant chords ("Der Arbeitsmann," Op. 39, no. 3; m. 13), with a major chromatic chord ("Breit über mein Haupt," Op. 19, no. 2; m. 9), or by modulating from a minor to a major key on the "color" chord ("Von dunklem Schleier umsponnen," Op. 17, no. 4; m. 6). In "Blindenklage" (Op. 56, no. 2), the phrase *Sonnenhellen Fluren* (sunlit fields) is underlined by a minor chord (m. 24), because the text concerns the blind.

"Grenzen der Menschheit" presents an impressive example of how Wolf gives "heightened significance" to Goethe's philosophic poem without resorting to Naturalistic Description. Goethe here crystallized the two eternal human enterprises, to raise oneself to the stars and to command on earth. When man attempts the first, "nowhere is his foothold secure—he becomes a plaything for the clouds and winds." Wolf evokes the feeling of insecurity, of treading on clouds, by veiling the tonality through a series of augmented chords (mm. 44–48). But for Goethe's next line, "when man stands solidly . . . on firm enduring earth," Wolf immediately reestablishes tonality with reassuring solidity (mm. 55–59). "If a modern composer wishes to suggest *chaos* musically," Wolf once said, "he would never use a [major or minor] triad, but an augmented chord."[17] Late romantics often made use of the predictability of tonality to evoke feelings of certainty and stability and of the temporary suspension of tonality for the reverse. Strauss never permitted *Sonne* to float aimlessly in tempestuous nontonal seas when the word connoted a positive force.

Lied composers exploited music's supreme expressiveness to create a variety of evocative atmospheres: times of day, weather conditions, geographical color, religious and pagan scenes. Often piano preludes, interludes, and postludes were given a special role. Preludes foreshadowed the mood or atmosphere of the opening stanza of a poem. Wolf, and occasionally Mahler, wrote long preludes of this kind. Interludes could serve several purposes: to make smooth transitions of mood from stanza to stanza, for example. Pfitzner and Reger often wrote long transitional interludes. Those of Hermann Zilcher serve to link separate songs of a cycle, as in the sixteen-measure interlude between "Helle Nacht" and "Zuversicht" in the *Dehmel* cycle (Op. 25). For Mahler and Reger the postlude might function as *Ausmalung der Stimmung:* as a continuation and gradual dissipation of the atmosphere of the poem. Mahler appropriately labeled some postludes in pianoforte versions *verklingen* (fading away), as in "Der Schild-wache Nachtlied," or *gänzlich ersterbend* (dying away), as in "Urlicht." The postlude, of course, also could serve a special purpose, to describe a series of events that took place after those recounted in the poem, as in Wolf's "Gutmann und Gutweib" and "Epiphanias."

The views of late romantics that music represents the thing-in-itself of every phenomenon apparently bound their aesthetics to those of the nineteenth century. They echoed earlier nineteenth-century critics with those customary words of censure *crude* and *crass.* Proponents, still considering themselves among the past century's avant-garde, nevertheless delighted to discover brilliant examples of descriptive music. The era following World War I shattered this division in a disavowal not only of naturalism but also of the metaphysical nature of music. The disavowal of naturalism was international: think of the response of Schoenberg (his *Hanging Gardens*), Satie, and the later Stravinsky, among others. At the end of the twentieth century, critics still have little patience with musical illustration. They prefer purely musical to extramusical analyses. They thus often broaden our understanding of a subject. But in so doing they tend to impose modern views on the fin-de-siècle lied and to ignore the aesthetic out of which it grew.

chapter six

The Height of Naturalism in Music:
The Actor and Musician in Collaboration

We now turn to the period of the height of the interest in naturalism, looking as well at the factors involved in naturalism's ultimate dissolution. We saw in Chapter 4 how singers and composers—with the actor as model—shaped their voice parts after the speech inflections of well-recited poetry. Radical late romantics aspired to higher degrees of naturalism in music. They sought direct collaboration of the actor and the musician by means of melodrama, the genre that combines spoken texts with instrumental music.

Lied and melodramas for piano were not envisaged during the fin de siècle as mutually exclusive artistic expressions (as they are today) but as genres that shared common ground. Composers of both accepted a similar challenge: to sharpen naturalism in compositions that lacked scenery, costumes, and action. Their means proved strikingly similar. More important, in achieving their objectives, musicians and actors entered a domain that today is nearly uninhabited, the gray area between speaking and singing. Singers had entered that area with Sprechgesang; actors responded similarly when employing elevated speech. When fin-de-siècle actors performed melodrama, however, they utilized an even more musical kind of recitation, with the consequence that the contour of their recitation resembled the vocal line of a naturalistic lied, especially one rendered in Sprechgesang. The collaboration of actor and musician yielded a singular artistic product: it produced the high point of verbal intelligibility, the ultimate expression in music of naturalism.

The curious fact is that Engelbert Humperdinck (1854–1921), composer of music for fairy tales, was the first late romantic to revive melodrama in order to sharpen naturalism. At the time, his contribution seemed inevitable, for many musicians were seeking this objective. "Our modern opera is taking a path that must lead to melodrama. The dominant endeavor of our time, which no one can escape, is to bring reality to the stage. One must find a form that is suitable to express this trend. In my opinion, melodrama is that form."[1] Rousseau had created melodrama in 1770 partly to heighten naturalism in music. But after sporadic cultivation it fell into relative disuse until the close of the nineteenth century, when it had a brilliant revival.[2]

Humperdinck fused recitation and music for another reason: to deal with texts more suitable for speaking than for singing. As he explained: "Everything that does not fall under the concept of melody—and this involves a great number of texts that do not have lyrical feeling but rather an abstract or intellectual basis—should remain unsung. Such [passages] include everything in which music has a subordinate role." Accordingly, Hans Sommer (1837–1922) differentiated texts in his opera *Waldschratt* (1912) by assigning spoken text to actors rather than singers. Cosima Wagner once entertained the idea of having Beckmesser, in *Die Meistersinger,* performed by a comedian who had never been on the operatic stage.[3] Many late romantics specified passages in their operas that should be spoken. Weingartner exploited the naturalistic possibilities of recitation in a unique fashion. In his *Musik zu Goethes Faust* (Op. 43, 1908), he distinguished spirits from humans by having the spirits sing their parts and the real people to speak theirs.

Humperdinck's bold venture *Die Königskinder* (1897) was far more radical. The composer actually specified the inflection, pitch, and accentuation actors should employ in reciting the text. "This is the first time the attempt is being made to apply Wagnerian principles to melodrama. In accordance with these principles the exact inflections of the declamation have been designated by a notation that I have devised." He thought that the kind of elevated speech Wagner created in passages of his music dramas was the kind the ancient Greeks had used to perform their plays. The Greek drama, for Wagner as well as for Humperdinck, epitomized the acme of dramatic perfection. For Humperdinck, *Königskinder* represented its modern counterpart: "It appears to me that the close union of the spoken word and orchestral melody uncovers possibilities for new and original forms of expression. . . . Should it succeed, then we shall have a genre that has some similarity to the melodramatic recitation of the old Greek theater."[4]

Humperdinck may seem to have modeled his elevated speech after the grandiloquent style of actors of the time. Actually, his notation calls for a kind of recitation that is even more musical than the grandiloquent style. To indicate (spoken) pitch, he replaced the oval heads of conventional musical notation with *x*'s (ex. 27a). "The *Sprechnoten* (♩) that are applied in melodramatic passages," he explained in the introduction to his score, "are used for the purpose of indicating the rhythm and inflection of intensified speech (melody of the spoken verse) and for bringing these [passages] in agreement with the accompanying music. The usual type of notation (♩) is applied to lied passages." The composer thus entered deeply into that domain between speech and singing.

Königskinder is revolutionary in another sense: music and text are more extensively combined than in any earlier melodrama. Although the genre had been proclaimed "the most modern of all that is modern" in the late eighteenth century, early nineteenth-century composers continued to adhere to the predominant strict classicistic principles of composition. These dictate that the two

Example 27. Humperdinck: (a) *Die Königskinder* (Bernstein-Porges), p. 4, mm. 3–4 (orchestral score, 1897); (b) "Maiahnung" (Leiffmann), mm. 4–6.

arts of melodrama, music and literature, remain autonomous. Goethe warned in his *Proserpina* that confusion would result if the arts were intermingled: the music should function only to cement together blocks of dialogue.[5] Eighteenth- and early nineteenth-century composers—Rousseau, Benda, Mozart, Beethoven and Mendelssohn—agreed in principle. But as classicism waned, composers began to blend the music and the literature of melodrama, first only in restricted passages, later in extensive ones. Humperdinck coined the term "bound melodrama" (*gebundenes Melodram*) to describe the new style. It may be applied to any composition in which spoken text is to be recited in precise rhythm against a musical background.

The premiere of *Königskinder* (January 23, 1897) bewildered its audiences. Critics objected to Humperdinck's requirement that the actor recite in rhythm and pitch. They argued that only a musical actor could realize Humperdinck's Sprechnoten. The composer contended that his Sprechnoten were only signs for "relative pitch, for the raising and lowering of the voice." They permitted the actor the freedom to exercise his art. He did, however, admit that "only an actor with musical training could fill all his requirements." Max von Schillings thought that *Königskinder* failed at its first performance because "its style was too novel and the period of rehearsals too short." The fiasco induced the shy composer to withdraw the work and later to revise it as an opera, which, incidentally, had been his original plan.[6] Nevertheless, he sought in 1898 again to link poetic recitation and music via melodramatic recitation, but this time in the lied, in "Maiahnung" (ex. 27b).

The furious debate on *Königskinder* enveloped melodrama as a whole. The violence of the disagreement is evident in this pitifully disparaging comment that appeared in the *Allgemeine Musik-Zeitung:* "The melodrama . . . is preponderantly a miscarriage, a desolate primeval forest so dark that not even the smallest ray of spiritual sunshine can penetrate it."[7]

The adverse criticism destroyed Humperdinck's radical experiment, but the controversy nonetheless had positive results. Subsequent attempts—outside of opera—to fuse recitation and music met with success beyond expectation. Champions of this artistic union—among them von Possart—made these triumphs possible. As director [*Generalintendant*] of the Munich Court Opera, von Possart had endorsed the premiere of *Königskinder,* and he requested Strauss, Schillings and others to compose melodrama.

Strauss's *Enoch Arden,* for actor and piano—completed February 26, a month after the premiere of *Königskinder*—reversed the negative commentary on melodrama. Criticism of *Königskinder* had not deterred Strauss. Its brilliant premiere, in which it was performed by Strauss and von Possart, on March 24, 1897, was followed by performances throughout Germany, in London, and even in Sandown, on the Isle of Wight (where Tennyson, the poem's author, had died). Strauss's letters detail the unflagging enthusiasm of his audiences. *Enoch Arden's* remarkable success contributed substantially to Strauss's prestige. He sought other actors, like Emil Tschirch, for further presentations, and composed a second melodrama, dedicated to von Possart, *Das Schloss am Meere* (1899).[8] And the triumph scored by Schillings's *Hexenlied* in 1902 superseded even Strauss's victory.

Such critics as Norman Del Mar express surprise at the extraordinary demand during the fin de siècle for "so unrewarding and problematic a medium" as melodrama. Its immense success reminds us "of the actual differentials which separate the [late] Romantic period from our own as well as of the persistent illusions that these differentials do not exist."[9] Two of these differentials deserve our attention now: the late-romantic predilection for recitation and the "curious" style in which fin-de-siècle melodramas were performed.

Audiences throughout the nineteenth century fancied recitation of poetry at concerts. Some examples during the fin de siècle were imaginative: for instance, in performances of the *Schöne Müllerin,* Amalie Joachim recited the *Müller* poems that Schubert had not set to music. Interest in recitation at concerts underscores the vital role played by language in German music in the nineteenth century. Recitations with musical background were also in great favor at social gatherings in homes, societies, and public concerts. Books and articles on the subject appeared in good number. Publishers printed fliers advertising lists of recently published *Deklamationen mit Klavierbegleitung* (declamation with piano accompaniment). Strauss's publisher of *Enoch Arden,* Forberg of Leipzig, wisely included such a flier with a copy of the melodrama. Unknown composers like Ferdinand Hummel, Richard Kügele, and Gustav Lewin composed such musical recitatives, hoping for quick recognition.[10] This latest rage became an important feature of cabaret entertainment, the Überbrettl (as it was known in

Berlin) and the Elf Scharfrichter (the Munich version). In melodrama, the musical public could combine in one artistic experience its liking for language, often recited to perfection, with its love for music. Today, there are few performances of melodrama in Germany or anywhere else, while recitations of poetry at concerts have ceased.

Late romantics developed various kinds of recitations with music. Forberg's flier provides a curious example: "Friedrich [*sic*] Chopin, Fünf Dichtungen" (five poems), an arrangement by Richard Burmeister of five poems by K. Ujejski to be recited to five pieces by Chopin—the "funeral march from the B minor Sonata and four Mazurkas." Steinitzer mentions another forgotten, related diversion: *gesprochene Lieder* (spoken songs): poems that were read over background music at social gatherings. Decades earlier (in 1856), the adagio from Mozart's Quintet, K.V. 516, served as the background for a recitation (fig. 7). Spoken songs included the recitation of lied texts with their piano accompaniment. Steinitzer explains the preference thus: in gesprochene Lieder "every syllable of a lied text finally can be understood," an objective nearly all singers seek but few achieve.[11]

The spectacular success of *Das Hexenlied* and *Enoch Arden* resulted not only from the liking of late romantics for recitation but also from their style of performance. "Melodrama has undeniably received fresh impetus in the recent past as a result of gifted artists such as Wüllner and von Possart." One understands why *Das Hexenlied* of Schillings was so successful after hearing Wüllner's extraordinary rendition. "The deep effect produced by *Das Hexenlied* . . . pleads more for melodrama than do all the theories against it."[12] Its success stimulated translation and publication of its German text in English, French, and Russian.

A fascinating recording of *Hexenlied,* performed by Wüllner under the direction of the composer, illustrates the difference between late-romantic and modern performance of melodrama.[13] Although recorded late, in 1933—Wüllner was then just short of his seventy-fifth birthday—Schillings and Wüllner provided a stylistically accurate late-romantic rendition, for few performers understood the style more intimately than they. The intensity of Wüllner's reading is astonishing. His emotions range from calm to violent, even hysterical. For today's listeners his performance may, at times, sound extravagant and even eccentric.

Scored for speaker and piano or orchestra, *Das Hexenlied* (The tale of the witch) is not the children's story its title suggests but a complex miniature drama with sensual and deep psychological elements. The poet Ernst von Wildenbruch (1845–1900)—who revised the original poem especially for Schillings—cast these elements into the form of a fable about the last confession of an aged monk, Medardus.[14] Regarded as the "holiest of all" in his cloister, Medardus's confession shocked his brethren. As a young priest, he was called to save the soul of a girl due to be burned the next morning for witchcraft. The terrified young "witch" filled Medardus with compassion. He easily fell prey to

Dritte

ABEND-UNTERHALTUNG

der

Gesellschaft der Musikfreunde

des österreichischen Kaiserstaates

Dienstag, den 11. März 1856, Abends 7 Uhr,

im Gesellschafts-Saale.

~ ~

ERSTE ABTHEILUNG.

1. **Trio** in B-dur (Nr. 11) für Pianoforte, Clarinette und Violoncell von **L. v. Beethoven.**

2. **Lieder:** a) Das erste Veilchen, von **Mendelssohn.**
   b) Auf dem Wasser zu singen, von **Franz Schubert.**

3. **Das Waldvöglein,** Lied für Sopran mit Waldhorn- und Forte-piano-Begleitung, von **Franz Lachner.**

4. **Duett** für Sopran und Tenor aus der Oper: „Jessonda". von **L. v. Spohr.**

ZWEITE ABTHEILUNG.

5. a) **Adagio** aus dem Streichquintette in G-moll, von **Mozart.**
   b) **Declamation** eines auf dieses Adagio Bezug habenden Gedichtes, von **Franz von Braunau.**

6. **Bass-Arie** aus der Oper: „Figaros Hochzeit", von **Mozart.**

7. **„Kindliche Bitte",** Lied, vorgetragen von 12 Sopranstimmen mit Begleitung der Phisharmonika, von **G. Preyer.**

8. **„Grossmutter und Enkelin",** Duett für Alt und Sopran, von **Meyerbeer.**

9. **„Waldlied,"** Männerchor von **Abt.**

---

*Die vierte Abend-Unterhaltung wird nicht am 18. März, sondern erst **Dienstag den 1. April** d. J. stattfinden.*

Figure 7. Two Programs with Recitation: (a) Adagio from Mozart Quintet: March 11, 1856; (b) Melodrama with orchestra Proch: March 27, 1866 (Archive of the Gesellschaft der Musikfreunde, Vienna)

K. K. Hof- Operntheater.

Dienstag den 27. März 1866,

Abends 7 Uhr,

zum Vortheile des Bürgerspitalfondes,

unter der Leitung des k. k. Hof-Opern-Kapellmeisters Herrn

Heinrich Proch,

musikalisch-deklamatorische

AKADEMIE.

Programm.

Erste Abtheilung:

1. (Auf vielseitiges Verlangen.) **Ouverture** zur Oper: „Tannhäuser", von Richard Wagner, ausgeführt von der Kapelle des k. k. Hofoperntheaters.

2. **„Das Blümlein"**, Lied von Proch, gesungen von Fräulein **Marie Rabatinsky**, k. k. Hofopernsängerin.

3. (neu) **Der Christbaum.** Gedicht von Josef Weil, mit melodramatischer Orchesterbegleitung von Proch, gesprochen von Fräulein **Friederike Bognár**, k. k. Hofschauspielerin.

4. **Serenade und Allegro giojoso,** für Pianoforte mit Orchesterbegleitung von Felix Mendelssohn-Bartholdy, vorgetragen von Herrn **Josef Rubinstein.**

5. **Adelaide** von Beethoven, gesungen von Herrn **G. Roger.**

Zweite Abtheilung:

6. (neu) **Fest-Ouverture** für das Konzert zur Eröffnung der englischen Industrie-Ausstellung von 1862, a) **Triumf-Marsch,** b) **Religiöser Marsch,** c) **Geschwind-Marsch,** d) **englisches Volkslied,** componirt von Giacomo Meyerbeer, ausgeführt von der Kapelle des k. k. Hofoperntheaters.

7. **Bollero** aus der Oper: „Die sicilianische Vesper", von Verdi, gesungen von Frau **Emille Kainz-Prause**, k. k. Hofopernsängerin.

8. **Duo** für zwei Harfen, über Motive aus der Oper: „Trovatore", componirt von Herrn J. Dubez, vorgetragen von Demselben und seiner Schwester Fräulein **Anna Dubez.**

9. **Ungarische Lieder,** gesungen von Fräulein **Marie Rabatinsky.**

10. (neu) **Ma belle,** französische Chansonnette, nach der Melodie des Mabel-Walzer, von D. Godfrey, gesungen von Herrn **G. Roger.**

In Berücksichtigung des wohlthätigen Zweckes wurde vom hohen k. k. Oberstkämmereramte das Theater zu dieser Akademie überlassen, und die Mitwirkung der Mitglieder der beiden Hoftheater gestattet, so wie auch in gleicher Rücksicht des Zweckes die Direktion des Harmonie-Theaters die Mitwirkung des Herrn Roger gestattete, und sämmtliche obbenannte Herren und Damen ihre Mitwirkung bereitwilligst übernommen haben.

her seduction. Guilt-ridden, Medardus was plagued for the rest of his life by hearing in his inner ear the sensuous song the girl had sung to him.

Wüllner frequently recites in what we have identified as intensified or elevated speech. The ecstatic effect produced is eminently appropriate for the poem's erotic subject, especially for the girl's seductive song (m. 50 and mm. 95 ff.). Wüllner, however—proceeding deeper into the area between speaking and singing than Kainz and Moissi did in their recitation of "Prometheus"—not only applies portamentos to key words, sustains their vowels quantitatively, and speaks on actual pitches but sometimes, curiously enough, actually sings passages such as the one quoted in example 28. Wüllner's reading of the weirdly climactic line "from amid the roaring pyre the girl began to sing" is especially bizarre, because he, too, suddenly begins to sing. Wüllner confines his use of elevated speech to passages in which the text is emotional or in some way connotes music. He applies elevated speech to bound melodramatic passages, and tends to recite in natural speech texts that are unaccompanied by music.

The use of highly inflected speech was certainly not an exclusive trait of Wüllner's style: "This time the performer was Dr. Wüllner who spoke well and *naturally* and did not sing the entire poem throughout as does Ernst von Possart" (emphasis mine), a critic wrote. Emil Tschirch, who performed *Enoch Arden* with Strauss, mentions that Strauss found his recitation "more natural than Possart's." Apparently von Possart's style of recitation was even further removed from "natural" speech than that of Wüllner and Tschirch. We may, however, conclude from the advice Wilhelm Kienzl offered actors in his book on declamation that highly inflected speech was an intrinsic ingredient of melodramatic recitation during the fin de siècle: "The reciter should guard against one special error—that of letting himself be bound too closely to speechlike pitches. Through half-sung, half-spoken tones that many reciters employ . . . speech becomes music. The listener must put aside this unusual aural impression of the spoken word as much as possible. We must hope for musically trained reciters." That Kienzl's comment reflects the prevailing taste rather than his personal

Example 28.   Schillings: *Das Hexenlied* (Wildenbruch), mm. 189–191.

preference is clear from this contemporary English judgment: "The difficulty of modulating the voice judiciously in music of this description [melodrama], is, indeed, almost insuperable. The general temptation is to let it glide, insensibly, into some note sounded by the orchestra, in which case the effect produced resembles that of a Recitative sung hideously out of tune."[15] As stressed, the vocal training that actors received during the fin de siècle contributed considerably to the musical character of their delivery: it helped produce that now-extinct style of recitation.

A brief examination of two modern performances of *Enoch Arden* reveals the vast difference between late-romantic and modern performance of melodrama. The review in the *New York Times* of Claire Bloom's 1990 performances of *Enoch Arden* suggests that actors today would probably receive severe censure if they performed in the styles of von Possart, Wüllner, or Bispham. Bloom's performance, claimed the critic, "was more attractive in . . . [one] respect alone, than the famous recording of Claude Rains and Glenn Gould." She recited "with minimum of interpretative comment." The critic, however, complained that "here and there, as the verse reached some height of falsified feeling, she could not resist histrionic overkill." Although Rains's recitation was more emotive than Bloom's, he steered clear of the extraordinary fin-de-siècle style. As a post-Victorian, Rains (1889–1967) understood that style but applied only a touch of its intensity in his delivery, and only to climactic passages in which music and text are heard simultaneously. For our critic, that touch was too much. It signified *burlesque* of "the work's counterfeit emotions."[16]

Bloom's delivery was less emotive than Rains's. She related events as the experiences of others, not her own, as had Wüllner. Nor was she able, as were fin-de-siècle actors, to fill the hall with the sound of her voice. She projected through a microphone. Yet the critic deplored the fact that "Strauss's vacuous accompaniment threatened to blanket even her amplified voice." Her vocal timbre, too, differed from that of late-romantic actors, who were trained to place and project their voices in a manner similar to singers. And of course she never attempted elevated speech, nor sought to bridge the transition between the spoken and sung word by reciting on musical pitches. Her delivery followed the tenets of good modern recitation.

The *Times* critic registers the popular distaste for melodrama in general: "It is not easy to understand why Richard Strauss at the artistically mature age of 33 should have felt impelled to set Tennyson's narrative poem . . . as a melodrama . . . a piece that most devout biographers brush past in embarrassment." (Yet Tennyson's poem was enormously successful in England. Twelve translations appeared in Germany from 1867 to 1914, including fine examples by Max Mendheim, Adolf Strodtmann, and Friedrich Wilhelm Weber.) Our critic's choice of phrases: "counterfeit emotions," "histrionic overkill," and "falsified feelings," indicates his dislike of fin-de-siècle performance style. Finally, he applauds Bloom because she "kept her composure," but criticizes "the rubbery extravagance of Gould's pianism," even though an elastic tempo was the hallmark of late-romantic performance in general and of melodrama in particular. The critic's injunction seems to be: render late-romantic melodrama if you must, but not in late-romantic style.

My discussion of the late-romantic style of performance should prepare us to understand my earlier assertion that melodrama and lied shared important common elements during the fin de siècle. We recall that singers no less than actors applied theatrical techniques in lied and melodrama performance: character delineation, facial pantomime, gesture, and that extreme form of late romantic "overkill," graphic representation of words. Singers sometimes employed these with extravagance, and so, too, did Wüllner, as both singer and reciter. He graphically represented the words *schluchzen und weinen:* he was actually sobbing in the climactic passage of *Hexenlied,* where Medardus confesses he heard the girl "sobbing and weeping" as he fled from her.

Abundant evidence of the intense rendering by fin-de-siècle singers and actors includes visual testimony, like the photograph of singer David Bispham, also an eminently successful reciter (see fig. 5). Even spectators responded emotionally, by crying during moving passages. Wüllner's "recitation of the last song of *Ilias* moved me so much each time he recited it," the composer and accompanist Hermann Zilcher (1881–1948) acknowledged, "that I was forced to face away from the public while [accompanying him] because I was crying."[17]

Actors and singers alike applied elements of their arts to attain emotive high points in performance. Both entered deeply into that gray area between speech and singing. And most important, both developed chiseled enunciation: crisply rolled *r*'s and explosively enunciated consonants to aid verbal intelligibility and thus convey emotive high points in poetry with great clarity. Actors, of course, achieved greater verbal intelligibility than singers. Even the best singers found it necessary to distribute texts as aids at concerts. In consequence melodrama, for zealous late romantics, came to represent the ultimate expression of naturalism in music. This explains the unprecedented phenomenon discussed in Chapter 4: the exaltation of Wüllner, "the singer without a voice," called the greatest living interpreter of the lieder by Brahms, Weingartner, and other outstanding musicians.

Even the ideal setting for melodrama during the fin de siècle expresses a taste that is now out of fashion. Schillings's plan for a performance of *Hexenlied* in Heidelberg (1903) was to conceal both conductor and orchestra from view, according to the Wagnerian ideal at Bayreuth. Only the speaker, von Possart, was to be visible, while the music was to emanate from a mystic cavern. Schillings's comment is significant: "With a covered orchestra [*Hexenlied*] will finally produce its ultimate effect."[18] With the exception of Bayreuth, performance with the orchestra covered is today a thing of the past.

Lied and melodrama shared further common elements in performance. Johanna von Rauchenberger, Strauss's sister, told me that when Strauss performed his two melodramas with von Possart, he accompanied at the piano in a free and improvisatory manner, drawing upon experience gained from accompanying his lieder. Such experience had given Strauss, and the artists performing melodrama or lied, a thorough mastery of the similar problems involved in performing both genres. Each performer could adjust his pace to that of the other in passages in which one or the other wished to hesitate or accelerate. Accordingly, Strauss did not in *Enoch Arden* provide rhythmic note values for the speaker in those passages in which he sought the closest correlation between words and music. He left only vague hints in the published score of his free manner of performance: key words were underlined to indicate they should be recited on the main beats of the bar. Strauss also marked specific bars of the music that might be repeated—but "only if absolutely necessary"—to bring speaker and pianist into proper coordination.

The *Hexenlied* recording elucidates how late romantics resolved the perplexing problem of correlating spoken words with orchestral background. No problem exists in passages where the composer provides time values for the words (see ex. 28). But difficulties do arise in passages in which words are placed above the music without precise rhythmic indications. Schillings adopted two solutions. He allowed the music to dominate in the passage in which the witch entreats Medardus to flee with her (ex. 29, the escape scene). The excited but steady pace of the music produces a sense of urgency that is remarkably appropriate. We perceive that Medardus is falling captive to the girl's mesmeric seduction. Here Wüllner adjusted his pace to Schillings's pressing tempo by synchronizing accented syllables with the accented beats of the measure. Metric poetry, of course, facilitates such precise coordination of text and music. This is why Schillings, as we shall see, considered verse easier than prose to compose as lied and melodrama.

In a passage in which the text dominates—the passage that paints Medardus's growing compassion and passion for the "bewitched" girl (the seduction scene)—Schillings supported all of Wüllner's "rhythmic liberties" by conducting with the elasticity characteristic of late-romantic tempi: with rubatos, holds, and pauses that are not indicated in the score (see Chapter 10).

Example 29.   Schillings: *Das Hexenlied*, mm. 224–227.

Occasionally, Schillings approached almost complete abandonment of metronomic time.

Since actor and musician rarely perform together, the composition of melodrama connoted a somewhat apprehensive adventure even for composers as experienced as Strauss and Schillings. They feared that problems might arise in performance that they had not foreseen in composition. Both composers turned to von Possart for advice. Although Strauss's queries occurred in conference with von Possart as the two worked together in Munich and are lost to us, Schillings's questions, fortunately, are preserved in informative, unpublished letters.

Significant parallels, some subtle, exist between the two genres in the process of composition. Schillings's correspondence reveals what he considers requisites of good melodrama text: like that of the lied, it should be verse rather than prose, which, the composer discovered, "is uncommonly difficult to treat melodramatically." The melodramas of Strauss and Schillings are all set in verse. But verse that is compact and terse, like Goethe's "Der Gott und die Bajadere," Schillings confessed, is as troublesome to compose for as melodrama. Further, ideal melodrama text, also like that of lied, should be colored by a *Grundgedanke*—a basic thought or mood.[19]

Schillings's correspondence yields information also on musical unity, a focal problem of melodrama composition. The music, in following the poem closely, must not become fragmentary—as it often was in such contemporary examples as the setting of Poe's "Raven" by Max Heinrich (1853–1916). Schillings abandoned work on Goethe's "Der Gott und die Bajadere" because he considered the music too fragmentary.

Enoch Arden and *Hexenlied* are unified by recurring motives, skillfully developed to fit the action—a further parallel, incidentally, between melodrama and through-composed lieder that will be evaluated in Chapter 11. Schillings casts *Hexenlied* in the broad musical frame of sonata form, with four large sections: exposition, development, recapitulation, and coda. For *Hexenlied,* an orchestral melodrama, is conspicuous for extensive passages of music. *Enoch Arden* has little continuous music. Schillings inserts three extensive recitations between major sections of the sonata form to avoid injuring the musical structure. This text sets scenes and unfolds narratives. Further, he interrupts the course of his music with many short verbal interjections, which he introduces either in the manner of a recitative—with familiar stereotyped chordal outbursts (ex. 30) —or by placing them directly after unresolved chords that are strong enough to require resolution even after interruption (mm. 116–117). But like Strauss, Schillings sought to link purely verbal and purely musical passages by reintroducing music into the story at moments of suspense and by carefully matching the mood of the music to that of the text. These passages are inserted at psychologically crucial moments: they heighten rather than weaken the drama. They actually integrate music and text.

A final parallel: Strauss and Schillings used similar means in both genres to

Wir haben den Teufel im Kloster zu Gast,
   Medardus ist dem Ver - sucher verfallen, Medardus ringt in des Satans Krallen!
It's the devil himself we have for a
   guest; Medardus is of God forsaken, Medardus writhes in the clutches of Satan!

Example 30.   Schillings: *Das Hexenlied*, mm. 67–69.

sharpen naturalism. With the absence of scenery, costumes, and action, they painted scenes with the aid of descriptive music. Instrumental music serves in melodrama in extensive passages that have no recitation to create mood. Such passages consist of the work's prelude, which in *Hexenlied* depicts the lugubrious cloister milieu, and three shorter ones. And Schillings inserted atmospheric instrumental passages at psychologically crucial moments. Inflamed music bursts forth when Medardus discovers, to his horror, that he desires the girl (m. 181). Another occurs when, after fifty years of penitence, he realizes that he still wishes to consummate that love (m. 378).

Schillings composed extensive passages in which words and music are heard simultaneously in two different ways. Where only the context of the words needs to be understood, he assigns the melody to the instrumental music, allowing the voice to declaim above it with relative intelligibility (see the escape scene, ex. 29). When the listener's attention is meant to be riveted on each word, however, as in the seduction scene, the music provided is no longer attractively lyrical but based on one leitmotive (see the X^1 in ex. 31) that is freely shaped and transformed to underscore nuances of the text.

Lied and melodrama had an especially intimate interrelation for Strauss. He learned to combine words and music in melodrama from the experience gained

sie wandte das Haupt,   auf ihren Knien   Ihr nackter Arm meine
   sie schaute mich an,   kroch sie heran,   Knie' umfing, an
She turned her head,   on her knees she   her naked arms enfolded
   our eyes they met,   crept to my feet,   my knee.

Example 31.   Schillings: *Das Hexenlied*, mm. 175–178.

composing lieder, not opera. Before composing *Enoch Arden* Strauss had completed more than thirty-three cycles of lieder but only one opera, the immature *Guntram* (1892–93). Lied was a forerunner also for Strauss's "experiments" with bold harmony in opera. Recall Willi Schuh's vital observation (in Chapter 1, above) that Strauss "experimented first in the lied with daring harmony" and later cultivated them in his symphonic poems and operas. *Enoch Arden*, for reciter and piano, illuminates not only the differences but also the similarities in composition between lied and melodrama.

Enoch Arden, with a text by Tennyson, translated into German by Adolf Strodtmann (Berlin, 1886), is a sentimental period piece in which innocence is raised to Victorian heights. Caught in the eternal triangle are its three characters: Enoch, Philip Ray, and Annie Lee, first pictured in childhood courtship. Annie eventually marries Enoch, who disappears at sea in a shipwreck. With immense propriety, Philip waits ten years before he asks Annie to marry him. Annie, though destitute, asks for another year, then another month, and then another five months, before she consents. Enoch had been rescued, however, and he returns home after Annie and Philip marry. He decides to live in seclusion rather than to disturb Annie's new happiness. He insists that she be notified of his return only after his death.

Strauss accepted a major challenge in treating Tennyson's poem. The text is long and involved. (The melodrama requires about an hour to perform.) Accordingly, Strauss divided it into two parts. He provided very little continuous music, usually only a page or so following long, unaccompanied narratives without music. These detail the action. They range from short passages of 19 lines to sections of from 85 to 142 lines.

How does Strauss unify the music and create continuity between verse and music? Let us look at his more subtle means first. The music is atmospheric; it always closely matches the mood stirred in the preceding verse, continuing but never interrupting its course. This music will be reintroduced following long blocks of text, at times unobtrusively, at others, dramatically. The music adds credibility to the sentimental text. For instance, the foaming sea provides a pungent Grundgedanke for *Enoch Arden*. It serves as background throughout the work, separating Enoch and Annie in tragedy, but uniting Annie with Philip in happiness.

Recurring motives afford Strauss a more obvious way of achieving musical unity. They are closely related to the text and easy to recall. The motives of the three main characters are presented while the speaker introduces them: "Annie Lee, the prettiest little damsel in the port [motive *U*], Philip Ray, the miller's only son [*V*], and Enoch Arden, a rough sailor's lad [*W*]" (see *U, V*, and *W* in ex. 32a). Other motives include Annie and Enoch's love (see *Y* in ex. 32b), Enoch's departure to sea (see *Q* in ex. 32c), and the stormy sea.

The motives convey the heart of the drama, interpreting actions and even suggesting action yet to come. They reveal Annie's inner thoughts: her wish,

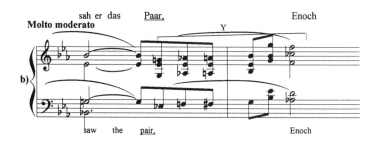

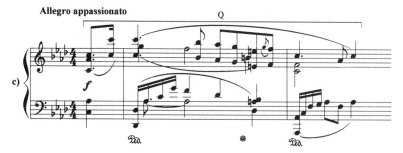

Example 32.   Strauss: *Enoch Arden* (Tennyson/Strodtmann), piano-vocal score, (a) p. 4, mm. 9–13; (b) p. 7, mm. 1–2; (c) p. 8, mm. 9–10.

before she can summon the courage to consent, *finally* to marry Philip. One would expect the passage that Strauss entitled "Annies Traum" (Annie's dream) to be yet another of her fantasies on Enoch's whereabouts. The music, however, a transformation of Philip's motive (ex. 33a), suggests that Philip's proposal is now really uppermost in her mind. Convinced by her dream that Enoch is dead, she calls to Philip, on awakening: "There is no reason why we should not wed." The wedding follows, to Philip's motive, in his key (see piano-vocal score, p. 14). We discover in a later scene that Enoch, shipwrecked on a "golden isle," heard the "pealing of his parish [wedding] bells." Strauss underscores the supernatural experience with Philip's motive, keyed in E major (p. 18). Part 1 of *Enoch Arden* ends with the birth of Philip and Annie's child. Strauss closes this happy scene with the motives of both Philip and Annie, united in E major.

Key symbolism plays an important role in Strauss's treatment of the dominant motives. Enoch's is in "heroic" E-flat major, the key of the hero of Strauss's *Ein Heldenleben* (composed in 1897–98). The motive of Philip, his rival, is in the distantly related E major, while Annie's is in G major. Appropriately, Enoch and Philip are separated musically, as in life, by distant relationship, while Annie is musically, as in life, close to both Enoch and Philip, as are the keys of E flat and E to G major in Strauss's favored tertial key relationships. Although Strauss

Example 33.   Strauss: *Enoch Arden*, piano-vocal score, (a) p. 12, mm. 1–3; (b) p. 21, mm. 5–11.

modulates extensively and to distant keys, he nearly always quotes these motives, especially Enoch's and Philip's, in their characteristic keys. See, for instance, the motive of Enoch (W) in example 33b. Strauss's key for the turbulent
sea is G minor both in the prelude (the musical interlude following the opening
stanza [p. 4]) and in the scene in which Enoch is shipwrecked (pp. 16 and 17).

The musical motives build dramatic tension and climax vividly along with
the action. Yearning to see Annie's "sweet face again" after his silent return
home, Enoch steals one night to Philip and Annie's window and looks at "his
wife no more . . . and all the warmth, the peace, the happiness, and him, that
other, reigning his place." Though tortured, he vows "never to let her know . . .
[and] shatter all the happiness of the hearth." Strauss provides an extended
passage of bound melodrama (pp. 19–23) in which the speaker expresses Enoch's
torment against agitated music developed entirely from the motives of Enoch's
and Annie's love (Y), Enoch's departure (Q), and Enoch's motive (W: see ex.
33b). This tragic scene, the work's most gripping moment, shows Strauss's skill
at developing, transforming, and interlinking motives contrapuntally to underscore a story as it unfolds. *Enoch Arden* might be regarded as a preliminary study
for the great dramas that followed like *Salome* and *Elektra*.

The triumph of *Enoch Arden* was short-lived. The public has long since
turned away from fin-de-siècle melodrama. Strauss himself later scorned melodrama. "I would like to express the strongest apprehension about melodrama of
all kinds (emphasis mine)," Strauss wrote to Hofmannsthal in 1917. "It is the
clumsiest and stupidest art form I know." Although Strauss's anger is being
directed at melodrama in opera, he might have had precisely the same fear of
melodrama in concert while composing *Enoch Arden*, with its vast expanses of
text and little music. Further, Strauss's reasons for composing *Enoch Arden*
probably had more to do with winning von Possart, director at the Munich
opera, to his side than with his interest in the genre. On the "spectacular
triumph," of the premiere, Strauss wrote home: "Possart is now with me heart
and soul."[20] The preponderance of text Strauss assigned the speaker focused
attention on von Possart.

Strauss's second melodrama, *Das Schloss am Meere* (1899)—inspired by collaboration with von Possart—could hardly be more dissimilar from his first.
Although both are descriptive, motivic, and deeply atmospheric, the second is
short and includes much music. The poem, by Ludwig Uhland (1787–1862),
which the speaker recites to piano accompaniment, contains but eight stanzas.
Thus pianist and speaker together evoke the atmosphere, develop the imagery,
and build to the ballad's climax in its final line. Strauss apparently had no fear
about the audience "catching the words" when he composed this bound melodrama for von Possart. Positive experiences while working with von Possart in
concert undoubtedly gave him the necessary assurance.

For late romantics the ultimate expression of naturalism in music was the
collaboration of actor and musician in melodrama. Music had reached a peak of

verbal intelligibility when it was combined with recitation in melodrama. For radicals like Humperdinck, this union represented the height of the influence of language and literature on music. Late-romantic critics had for decades been aware that composers were seeking greater verbal intelligibility in the lied through theatrical declamation. Rudolf Louis was most explicit. He identified a trend in the history of the lied "that is inclined toward the declamatory . . . one in which lyric tonal expression is elevated in naturalistic recitation to a point where the lied veers into melodrama."[21] Louis was referring to one stream in the development of the lied, in which the piano became the principal vehicle for carrying melody and the voice the chief means of conveying the poetry. Melodrama represents the peak of that development, since all musical expression is assigned to instrumental music and verbal expression to the voice.

Early in lied history, aesthetes foresaw an entirely different link with melodrama. As noted, the procedure of illustrating lied *texts* musically had originated in melodrama and later was applied to the lied. Goethe, in his *Proserpina* discussion mentioned above, foresaw that "melodrama will resolve into song as its ultimate expression, and only then achieve complete satisfaction." For Goethe greater lyricism rather than greater verbal intelligibility was the aesthetic objective. The fin de siècle saw the reverse: the lied resolving into melodrama, lyricism into speech.

Humperdinck's revival of melodrama to attain the zenith of naturalism in music proved to be ironic. The highly inflected recitation late-romantic actors applied to his Sprechnoten suggested a style to Schoenberg that reached beyond naturalism to expressionism (see Chapter 9, below). One cannot fail to notice striking similarities between the melodramatic notations of Schoenberg and Humperdinck, although Schoenberg's notation for his Sprechstimme in *Glückliche Hand* (1909–13) and *Pierrot Lunaire* (1912) does differ slightly from Humperdinck's Sprechnoten. Schoenberg placed crosses on the stems of the time values (♪ ♪), instead of using them as note heads. His system facilitates the use of half notes and dotted half notes (♩ ♩.). But the symbols Schoenberg had used earlier for the spoken part of *Gurrelieder* (1900–1901, orchestration, 1911) are exactly the same as those of *Königskinder*. And so, too, were his objectives for their execution. These similarities raise the question, Did Schoenberg have any knowledge of Humperdinck's innovative notation while devising his own? The chances are he did. The heated debates surrounding *Königskinder* and melodrama involved important periodicals, among them the *Neue Musikalische Rundschau* of Prague and the *Allgemeine Musikzeitung* of Berlin. Schoenberg—always interested in musical controversy—must at least have been aware of this verbal barrage. Further, he had the opportunity to hear the melodramatic version of *Königskinder* in Vienna, when it was performed on May 10, 1897, several months after its Munich premiere. *Königskinder,* the composer's son discovered, was performed as melodrama in 130(!) theaters. Incidentally, *Königskinder* received an ideal performance in Frankfurt (?1897), where the esteemed actress and singer Hedwig Schako realized Humperdinck's Sprechnoten splendidly.[22]

The irony is that although Humperdinck revived melodrama to attain a more naturalistic expression in music, the manner in which he and later composers applied it did more to destroy than to intensify naturalism.

chapter seven

Pan-German Nationalism

The military and political triumphs that unified Germany in 1871 incited fierce Pan-German nationalism. Patriots considered the newly formed Second Reich as the beginning of a period of great destiny. Meanwhile, in the Austro-Hungarian Empire the hatred of the German minority for the Hapsburg dynasty deepened, and their dream for unity with the new Reich intensified.

Germans were intoxicated by their country's advances in metallurgy, engineering, steel, chemical, and electronic production: advances that had brought it to a position of technological leadership in Europe. The erection of monuments of leading military and political figures became almost an industry in major German cities. Patriotic literature in verse, novels, and historical studies swamped the literary market.[1]

The victories, however, proved temporary. Discord began to erode Germany's newly acquired unity, as Fritz Stern's penetrating evaluation reveals: "After 1871 many thoughtful Germans were gripped by a mood of mingled pride and disenchantment: pride in the power and unity of the Reich, disenchantment with the culture of the empire. . . . Beneath the crust of prosperous politics the old Germany was disintegrating, pulled apart by modernity—by liberalism, secularism, and industrialism." Germany's rapid industrialization created enormous social and economic upheavals. Magnates of heavy industry, bankers, and stockholders formed cartels that honeycombed the country and stamped out competition. "Get-rich-quick" ventures created economic crises, the worst of which was the stock market crash of 1873.[2]

Germany's rapid modernization alienated many: small businessmen impoverished by great industry, skilled artisans displaced by machines, and peasants crippled by high mortgages. University professors and bureaucrats—long accorded the highest distinction in Germany—were now challenged by a new elite of often crude entrepreneurs. In addition, the politically powerless middle class, joined by romantic intellectuals and radical students, converged to promote conservative policies hostile to modern capitalism. A conservative revolution, passionately nationalist, antimodernist, and racist, was under way, and it persisted into World War I.[3]

Nationalism intensified with the accession of Wilhelm II in 1888. He insisted that his country, its educational system, and its arts were not sufficiently Germanic. The foundation of the Pan-German League, dedicated to *Deutschthum* (ancient German unity) and the publication of Julius Langbehn's *Rembrandt als Erzieher* (Rembrandt as teacher) followed in 1890. This book, "a blurred ideal image of a Volk united behind [its] aristocracy," achieved "immense popularity." Langbehn's "rambling, vague, and often frenzied disquisition on culture was not confined to nationalist and petty bourgeois circles. It elicited a sympathetic response also from [moderates]."[4] Langbehn's book underwent thirty-seven editions in little more than a year, and reached forty-nine by 1909. Langbehn fumed against the "poisons" of modernity: to be precise, repulsive, rapidly growing great cities. He added new chapters, one advocating anti-Semitism as a solution to the nation's woes. Langbehn felt that hope for German oneness lay in the peasantry and in simplicity and nature.

Fin-de-siècle nationalists invested Volk, *Volksthum*, and Deutschthum with mythical and mystic significance: the concepts, they felt, connoted the uncorrupted character of the primeval German. *Volkstümlich*, as in *volkstümliches Lied*—which we translate today simply as "folklike song"—signified mystic qualities expressive of the German soul, which were most apparent in the peasantry.[5]

Such nationalist ideology provided a strong current in fin-de-siècle German art and social thought. It produced *Heimatkunst*, literature that glorified the peasant and the provincial community against modern city life. Simple "countryfolk [became] the repository and exemplars of German nationalism." Even champions of naturalism like Hauptmann, Johannes Schlaf, and Michael Georg Conrad were attracted to Heimatkunst, the art, as Langbehn saw it, that expressed the nation's soul.[6]

The *Jugendbewegung* (youth movement) was deeply affected by völkisch ideology as well. University students were among the most aggressive Pan-German nationalists. They protested against modernity, city life, and the loss of national community. Their strong nationalist focus was antidemocratic, antiliberal, and xenophobic. Heinrich von Treitschke's lectures in the University of Berlin on German greatness stimulated a vast body of students with a national fervor unparalleled in the university's history. In Vienna, the *Burschenschaften*, the student fraternities, marched on Saturday afternoons "singing German national songs, then attacked Slavs, Italians, and especially Jews," according to George Berkley, who reproduces a sketch of an anti-Semitic brawl at the University of Vienna in 1897 in his book *Vienna and Its Jews*. Jews were eventually excluded from most groups to ensure "racial hygiene."[7]

The aims of the Jugendbewegung changed frequently over the course of its relatively short life. During its earliest days (1901–07), the Wandervogel (literally, "birds of passage"), as the movement was popularly known, had no definite organization. Young people sought to escape national "evils" by a flight into nature. There they could "build a culture to contrast with city life from which they were fleeing."[8] Its members, called *Bacchanten*, dressed as traveling artisans and identified themselves with medieval scholars.

The movement lost some of its undisciplined character between 1908 and 1913. It became an important cultural force, with 25,000 members and a monthly publication called *Wandervogel*. Its philosophy expressed the alienation of the romantics. "In his wanderings from lamenting mountains and valleys," wrote Hans Breuer, one of its leaders, "the Wandervogel will gradually find his primeval ties in the holy company of Nature. . . . The tree which was ripped from its native soil will grow new roots. Mankind, who has sprung from the womb of Nature, will gradually find his primeval relatives again . . . and become natural." The Wandervogel sought their roots in nature and in the German peasantry and its songs, which were regarded as a link to a lost German heritage. Trenchantly nationalistic, they "believed that widespread singing of the folk song would lead to a spiritual rebirth of the German people." Breuer specified: "In the Volkslied—the soul of the Germans—there lives the pulse of our entire German history."[9]

The first edition of the *Zupfgeigenhansl*, a collection of folk songs published by Breuer in 1909, was almost immediately exhausted. By 1913 one hundred thousand copies had been sold. The Volkslied became the Wandervogel's beacon. Its popularity sparked numerous anthologies. The folk music specialist Fritz Jöde himself published more than thirty. "That which the Wandervogel is searching for in- and out-of-doors," Breuer wrote, "is written in the Volkslied . . . the most complete expression of the Wandervogel ideal." Indeed, "Nowhere in recent times was the folk song sung so passionately . . . as by the Wandervogel."[10] Simplicity was an important musical goal of the movement, for which the folk song served as model. The Wandervogel sang their songs to plain, unadorned accompaniments. Skillful playing, deemed artificial and sophisticated, was actually frowned upon. The guitar, the standard instrument, was strummed. But simplicity was far from the goal of contemporary musicians. "The existence of a trend toward Volkstümlichkeit seems especially curious when one realizes how far the technique of modern music has developed from the naive—from folklike simplicity," the critic Max Vanessa noted in 1903 in the *Neue musikalische Presse*.

The strongest summons for völkisch ideology in music came from the highest power in the land, the kaiser. Wilhelm II denounced contemporary choral music as not genuinely Germanic—not volkstümlich and too complex. In 1903 he created two commissions of professors and professional musicians to arrange Volkslieder for male chorus. They were urged "not merely to imitate the . . . Volk in their song and thereby to create the folklike character only superficially, but to capture the essential traits of their songs: their directness, truth, and simplicity, and to imprint . . . such a spirit deeply in the music so that the folk would understand and gladly embrace such songs as their own."[11]

The kaiser's proclamation influenced even composers of the concert lied, some of whom sought to initiate reforms during the time of the lied's greatest complexity, when the lied was still zealously cultivated. According to Jöde, who bemoaned the fact in verse, a defenseless public was being overwhelmed:

Mountains of music are being turned out today
symphonies and potpourris
oratorios, operas, operettas, and salon music
and dance music, dance music a flood of it
and lieder, lieder, still more
a deluge
and all for voice and piano.[12]

The Berlin weekly *Die Woche,* responding to the kaiser's battle cry, waged a valiant war against sophistication in the concert lied. The paper's plan of attack was unique: to arouse interest through a contest in the neglected folklike lied (volkstümliches Lied). "The art of making music in the home is all but lost. Today, Hausmusik [music for the home], like the Volkslied, is being suffocated by the fashionable popular song, on the one hand, and the excessive growth of concert life, on the other." The paper urged that Hausmusik again be cultivated "as the fertile soil in which the folk song grows."[13] Its editors hoped to provide models—modern folklike lieder—for the cultivation of "genuinely German" music for the home.

Die Woche offered reasons for the neglect of the folklike lied: composers "do not understand the difficulties involved in writing simple songs. They are actually afraid of being simple for fear of being accused of triviality." The public similarly "has lost its ability to be naive and appreciate the naive." For "everywhere one demands large numbers of performers. . . . The orchestral lied is receiving most of the attention today," instead of the folklike lied. In short, "The music of our time has become overgrown and overcomplicated. It is now caught in its own decline."[14] *Die Woche*'s contest committee hoped to prove that modern volkstümlich songs could be attractive and contemporary, yet simple. Outstanding composers were to provide models for such lieder in a collection to be published by *Die Woche* entitled *Im Volkston: Moderne Preislieder.* Eugen d'Albert, Leo Blech, Humperdinck, Kienzl, Pfitzner, Schillings, Thuille, Siegfried Wagner, and Herman Zumpe were among the contributors.

To stimulate the public to compose folklike songs, *Die Woche* offered thirty prizes of a hundred marks each. The prize songs were to be published in the second volume of *Im Volkston.* The chief traits demanded of these songs were carefully delineated: "They must be folklike and yet cast in a musical idiom that is contemporary. They must be no longer than fifty measures and hitherto unpublished. The melody must be completely vocal, simple enough to be sung upon one hearing, and not dependent in any manner upon the piano part." Contestants were cautioned not to imitate the genuine folk song and thereby to create spurious examples but rather to capture the folk song's spirit. Two songs by Herman Zumpe were presented as models. Professional musicians—Humperdinck, Carl Krebs, Eduard Lassen, Felix Schmidt, and Thuille—acted as judges.

Three additional prizes of three thousand, two thousand, and one thousand marks—considerable sums for the time—were to be awarded to the composers of the three best of the thirty chosen songs. These three would be selected by the public, not professional musicians. Were not the "folk" the best judges of what was folklike? (Such sentiment echoes Wandervogel philosophy and the kaiser's proclamation.) The committee hoped to arouse widespread interest in the contest by involving the public, and the results exceeded even the committee's expectations. The song entries reached 8,859. After the prizes were awarded, *Die Woche* selected an additional thirty songs, lieder deemed outstanding but, for some reason, not in the class of the first thirty. These were published in a third volume, and the public was again invited to select the best, this time from all ninety songs. The same high prizes were offered. A total of 53,915 votes was cast, and more than 120,000 copies of the three favorite songs were sold.

Die Woche may have undertaken the contest simply as a shrewd business venture, but the effect upon the folklike lied cannot be disregarded. "Great artists," the paper proudly announced on February 27, 1904, "who have for a long time neglected the volkstümlich song are now including at least some examples in their recitals or giving complete programs of them."

Nationalist ideology made other positive artistic contributions. Societies and periodicals were founded to study folk art in Germany and Austria. Yet this ideology also evoked intense ethnic hostility. A trend, xenophobic in its overtones, emerged, with dire consequences. Austria provides tragic examples of a paranoia that had considerable musical consequences, visible directly in the lied.

The defeat of Austria by Prussia in 1866 and the *Ausgleich* (the dual monarchy of Austria and Hungary) that followed (1876), provoked Austrian Pan-Germans to attack movements for self-determination by Czechs, Slavs, and other ethnic groups, in the hope of retaining political supremacy.[15] The rise of the radical right exacerbated ethnic hostility. Pan-German students sought to expel Italians from academic institutions in Vienna. They attacked not only the "enemy" without but the one within, the Jews. The right-wing newspapers *Deutsche Volksblatt* and *Deutsche Zeitung* endeavored to eradicate the Jewish *Geist* from Germanic culture. This Pan-German anti-Semitism, which arose in the late 1870s, had a paradoxical character in Austria: Liberal-nationalist Jews (young Mahler among them), followers of Victor Adler and the historian Heinrich Friedjung, had originally allied themselves with Georg von Schönerer as Pan-German adherents. After 1885, however, the nationalist crusade shifted to the extreme right. It "became officially enshrined" in anti-Semitism under Schönerer, one of Hitler's models. Adler's reaction was to found Austria's Social Democrats.[16]

This xenophobia was the "new" anti-Semitism; *anti-Judaism* is Berkley's name for the centuries-old intolerance. Anti-Judaism had "focused almost completely on Jews as a religious group"; conversion often erased that prejudice. "The new dogma insisted that Jews had combined in a conspiracy to achieve domination over Germans." Jews "constituted a moral threat to the German people. . . . Perhaps never before in Europe had a minority risen so fast or gone so far as did the German Jews in the 19th century," writes Fritz Stern. The liberal legislation of the 1850s and 1860s granted full legal rights to Jews, and many achieved eminence. Germany's unification, industrialization, and modernity opened areas for advancement. After 1870 Jews became prominent in banking, business, law, medicine, the arts, and education. Ten percent of Prussian students were Jews, more than seven times their ratio in the general population. Almost half the Viennese medical students were Jews.[17]

Extremists imputed the rise to the "sins" of the fin de siècle—modernity, capitalism, liberal reforms, big-city life. Jews were also accused of "Americanizing" Deutschthum, that is, eroding national unity. These extremists called for abolition of the laws of emancipation, expulsion of Jews from the professions, universities, and civil service, and limits on further immigration.[18]

Pan-German nationalism had a strong effect on the arts. The most successful new operas in Germany in the early 1890s were Italian veristic imports. Nationalists regarded the importation as an invasion and the premiere of Humperdinck's *Hänsel und Gretel* (1893) as a counterattack. In the jingoist language of the time, a critic wrote: "We will never forget how Humperdinck . . . broke the power of the commercial murder operettas[!] and . . . bravely defended German . . . sensibilities and German art." Nationalists considered *Hänsel und Gretel* thoroughly Germanic because they thought it saturated with Volklieder, the intrinsic expression of the German spirit.[19] They argued that Humperdinck had constructed a new genre, a "folk opera," based on Volkslieder. He captivated the hearts of Germans and stimulated their composers to return to their national musical heritage for inspiration. The success of *Hänsel und Gretel* was celebrated not as a musical triumph but as a nationalist victory.

Meanwhile, anti-Semites sought to jeopardize the reputation of artists by calling them Jewish, regardless of whether they were. Pan-German nationalists in the Wagner Verein of Vienna, for instance, endeavored to stop Joseph Schalk from performing songs by the young, avant-garde Wolf by alleging, falsely, that Wolf and Schalk were Jewish. Adolf Bartels, a Heimatkunst extremist, sought likewise to "denigrate" the sophisticated urbanites Thomas and Heinrich Mann by labeling them Jews.[20]

Anti-Semitism also manifested itself more subtly through acrimonious humor. Even those who were not anti-Semitic, like Wolf, took part in the fashionable sport. Wolf once explained, shaking with laughter, that he had intentionally quoted music of two Jewish composers when setting the line "But alas, there come Jews with I.O.U.'s of unpaid debts" in his song "Ritter Kurts Brautfahrt": "I got one theme from Goldmark, it's from *The Queen of Sheba:* the

other is from *Die sieben Todsünden* of Adalbert von Goldschmidt." Goldschmidt
had become Wolf's friend and benefactor during the composer's earliest years.
Wolf could count on him, almost any time, for books and scores, advice and
funds. Goldschmidt, who was well-to-do, was a fine poet and musician. His
generosity "knew no bounds."[21] One need not wonder how he felt upon hearing
his music quoted by Wolf at the point in the text concerning vile moneylenders
of the Middle Ages.

Of course, the tragedy of anti-Semitism in the arts cuts deeper. It has been
underlined by Mahler specialists in particular, but they tend to describe it simply
in terms of the old prejudice such as that experienced by Mendelssohn and
Meyerbeer. Few music historians have noted that Mahler confronted a new
xenophobia. Indeed, the term *anti-Semitism* wasn't even "invented" until 1867.
With the election of Karl Lueger as mayor of Vienna in 1897, anti-Semitic
ideology won its first major victory in Vienna. That very year Mahler had been
appointed head of the Imperial Opera in Vienna. The kaiser, who opposed anti-
Semitism, favored Mahler's appointment. Mayor Lueger soon acted directly
against Mahler. He "did not want the Philharmonic's yearly benefit concert for
the poor of Vienna [January 15, 1899] to be conducted by the 'Jew' Mahler."
Lueger also prevented Schoenberg from teaching in public institutions in
Vienna.[22]

In spite of Mahler's remarkable skill as conductor, reviews by Pan-German
nationalists remained unremittingly negative. Their criticism was undisguisedly
ethnic and often of such crudity as to sound ludicrous today. When Mahler
sought extra brass for greater intensity, a nationalist adversary retorted: "Aryan
trumpets are not loud enough for [Mahler]. Perhaps . . . he should [obtain] the
trumpets of Israel for the opera, the self-same trumpets that the entire Jewish
press has been blasting in praise of 'Mr. Director' with such deafening noise that
the walls of Vienna are beginning to crack!"[23] The vicious campaign eventually
forced Mahler's resignation as director of the Philharmonic concerts in 1901.

Critics during the fin de siècle often evaluated with two different criteria:
ethnic and musical. Even the astute critic Theodor Helm thought that "one
could hardly expect Mahler to possess true German spirit" in conducting Bruckner. *Tristan*, the *Deutsches Volksblatt* reported, "suited Mahler's non-German
temperament, whereas the typically German quality of *Die Meistersinger* and
the *Ring* remained alien to him."[24]

Mahler was severely censured for his volkstümlich songs. Although he was
the first to focus *international* attention on *Des Knaben Wunderhorn,* that great
repository of folk poetry, his settings invariably encountered sharp nationalist
rebukes. Mahler "speaks a musical German," the critic Rudolf Louis wrote, "but
with the accent, inflection, and above all, the gestures of the East, of the ever-so-
eastern Asiatic Jews." The *Deutsche Zeitung* concluded a long assault on Mahler
with this reprimand: "You have given lieder of a popular nature at the Philhar-

monic concerts. Forgive us, O hallowed masters of the German lied, that we even call your songs lieder!"[25]

A common belief during the fin de siècle was that members of ethnic groups transmit their "racial" identity directly into their music. The folk song, the definitive example, accordingly expresses the ethnic soul and spirit (*Geist*) of its people. Herder had conceived of the Volkslied as the true voice of a people. Nietzsche called it "the musical mirror of the world . . . the original melody." Nationalists concluded, therefore, that only ethnic Germans could provide German folk poetry with appropriate Germanic music. Unlike the radical innovations of Wolf and Strauss, those of Mahler—such as his use of parody and irony—were perceived by nationalists as "foreign and Asiatic." Yet little over a generation later, leading composers from Russia to England (including Germany)—Prokofiev, Shostakovich, Hindemith, and Britten—acknowledged their indebtedness to Mahler. Nor did ethnic divisiveness play a role in the widespread Mahler renaissance that occurred after 1960.

Although nationalist ideology exercised a wide appeal during the fin de siècle, extremists soon estranged themselves from their public. Even Lueger denounced Schönerer; after his election as mayor, Lueger no longer advocated radical resolutions. In fact, he made this remarkably revealing confession about anti-Semitism: it is "a very good means of creating a stir to make headway in politics. But when one is at the top, one no longer has use for it. This is a sport for the lower breeds." Nevertheless, Lueger's demagoguery and election made anti-Semitism "both normal and respectable." As Schnitzler sadly disclosed: "It is not possible for a Jew, especially in public life, to ignore the fact that he was a Jew."[26]

The Volkstümlich Song and Its Composers

Swept along by nationalist sentiment, composers wrote collections of volkstümlich songs. This genre has a long and honored history, rooted in the Berlin schools of the late eighteenth century, if not earlier. Völkisch thought and Heimatkunst of the fin de siècle provided new stimuli. Composers responded by using the same titles for cycles, using similar subjects, or drawing poetry from the same collections. Alexander Ritter, Martin Plüddemann, Richard Trunk, and Reger entitled lieder that set folkish poetry *Schlichte Weisen* (Simple airs).[27] Schillings, Ansorge, Joseph Haas, and Kienzl called their cycles *Ernte Lieder* (Harvest songs). The use of texts from *Des Knaben Wunderhorn* presents an unusual example of the nationalist influence. This rich collection of folk poetry, published in 1806 by Arnim and Brentano, remained relatively neglected throughout the nineteenth century, although Mendelssohn, Schumann, Brahms, and Wolf had turned to it occasionally. But after Mahler's masterpieces appeared, so many composers set this poetry that Georg Goehler, lied composer and propagandist for Mahler, concluded: "It has now become fashionable to compose *Wunderhorn Lieder*."[28]

Theodor Streicher began his artistic *Wunderhorn Lieder* while Mahler was still setting his own *Wunderhorn* texts. Mahler evidently heard some of Streicher's songs while they were still in manuscript. "'I should like very much to play compositions of mine,' Streicher told Mahler. 'To what words?' Mahler asked. '*Knaben Wunderhorn*,' Streicher replied. Mahler grunted."[29] Mahler was far from enthusiastic! The styles of the two composers could hardly have been more dissimilar: Streicher's subtle art flows from Wolf, whose lieder Mahler disliked. But *Wunderhorn* texts were set in a variety of styles during the years around 1900, when interest in the volkstümlich was strong.

Folk music was a principal inspiration for young Mahler, the symphonist and the lied composer. His earliest published folkish lied, "Hans und Grethe," was later developed into the scherzo of his First Symphony. Although Reger wrote more volkstümlich songs than Mahler, few contemporaries cultivated the genre as intensively or for so long as did Mahler.

Mahler captured the spirit of the folk song by placing the melody in the voice part, where it commands attention. He aimed at melodies that are simple, clear-cut and diatonic, unlike those of the typical concert lied. Fragments from actual folk songs lie embedded within some of Mahler's songs. Compare, for instance, this phrase from his "Trost im Unglück" (ex. 34a) with the folk song "Husarenliebe" (ex. 34b).

Fritz Egon Pamer discovered other fragments from folk songs in "Der Tamboursg'sell" and "Zu Strassburg auf der Schanz." And he noticed melodic similarities between Mahler's lieder and folk songs with similar titles, "Um schlimme Kinder artig zu machen," "Scheiden und Meiden," and "Revelge."[30] Ernst Klusen concluded that the folk song influenced Mahler's melodic structure, though indirectly. Klusen researched the folk songs of Iglau (now called Jihlava) and its environs, on the border between Bohemia and Moravia, where Mahler had spent nearly all of his first fifteen years. Strong streams of Czech (Bohemian and Moravian) and Germanic folk songs of Silesia, upper Saxony, and northern Bavaria flow through this country. Klusen isolated conspicuous folk-song formulas which are prominent in the Mahler lied in general. In the third song from the *Kindertotenlieder,* for instance, there occurs a configuration that is prominent in a type of Moravian folk song: a melodic curve of two rising conjunct fourths that later descend stepwise via repeated notes to the fifth above the first note in the melody (ex. 35).[31] Klusen discovered several other melodic

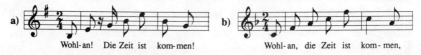

Example 34. (a) Mahler: "Trost im Unglück" (*Des Knaben Wunderhorn*), mm. 13–14; (b) Erk-Böhme: "Husarenliebe" (*Deutscher Liederhort*, 3:281), mm. 1–2.

Example 35.   (a) Mahler: "Wenn dein Mütterlein" (Rückert), mm. 8–9, 12–15; (b) Bartoš: "Národní písně mordavské."

configurations that share family resemblances in Mahler's lieder and Czech and German folk songs.

It is not surprising that Mahler was influenced by the folk song in shaping melody in his folklike lieder. As a child of six, he already knew well over two hundred folk songs. He may have unconsciously developed turns of phrase from these in his folklike lieder. Klusen's evidence supports this possibility. Or some fragment may simply have sprung to mind when he set a text with which it had long been associated. Pamer's research strengthens the second possibility. That folk-song fragments do not seem out of place in the Mahler lied attests to its intrinsic folkishness. Mahler himself acknowledged his debt to the folk songs of his homeland: "The Bohemian music of the land of my childhood has crept into many of my things. This struck me to be true especially of *Fischpredigt*. The national motive which lies embedded in it can be heard in its natural state in the piping of Bohemian [folk] musicians."[32]

Other folkish elements give Mahler's volkstümlich songs the ring of authenticity. Nearly every one of his lieder breathes the distinctive character of a specific category of folk song, such as *Tanzlieder* (dance songs) or *Soldatenlieder* (soldier's songs). Although the folk dance is idealized (as it is in the mazurkas of Chopin), as many as five of the *12 Lieder aus "Des Knaben Wunderhorn"* are Tanzlieder.[33] Dancelike passages appear in three other lieder in this collection. "Hans und Grethe" is saturated with the spirit of the Ländler (folk dance), as its leaps (see *X*, ex. 36) bear witness. Reminiscent, too, is the rustic, robust figure that falls heavily on the first beat (*Y*). It appears even in the voice part (mm. 38 and 39) where it splits the word *Ringel* into two distinct syllables. And the clash of a tonic drone with dominant harmony (mm. 2 and 4) suggests clumsy dissonances of village music. The refrain "Juche! Juche!" (not shown) adds folkish flavoring.

The Soldatenlied kindled in Mahler several fiery examples: "Zu Strassburg auf der Schanz," "Der Tamboursg'sell," and "Revelge." Military bands marched frequently through the streets of Vienna and Berlin. Rampant nationalism renewed enthusiasm for Soldatenlieder, long a favorite type of folk song. Mahler's own liking for military music goes back to his early youth; he is said to have

Example 36.   Mahler: "Hans und Grethe" (Mahler), mm. 53–58.

hidden himself in a barrack just to hear trumpet calls. The mature Mahler also found military music fascinating. The vigorous tramping rhythm of his Soldatenlieder is irresistible: short, clipped, dotted figures with staccatos (♫♩ ♫♩) or with forceful repeated-note patterns. Their pulse is even more alive than that of their "models," as a comparison of the folk song "Le Deserteur" with his own composition (on the same text) shows (ex. 37). Mahler's rhythmic directions, *Im gemessenem Marschtempo* (in strict march tempo), *äusserst rhythmisch* (extremely rhythmic), and *streng im takt* (with rigorous pulse), make explicit his aim for a crisp and spirited accent. Structurally, the Soldatenlieder, the early ones especially, tend to be the most folklike of Mahler's volkstümlich songs. Recurring melodic figures (such as the five-note group which closes nearly every phrase of "Tamboursg'sell" [♩ ♩ ♩ ♩ | ♩ ▬]) articulate their simple design.

Mahler's folkish verse displays unusual sensitivity to the poetry of the Volkslied. His early verse, the three songs for Josephine Poisl and the cantata *Das Klangende Lied,* both of 1880, present impressive examples. The text of the *Gesellen* songs provides a singular problem. Mahler claimed to have written the words. Nevertheless, the first stanza of "Wenn mein Schatz Hochzeit macht" (When my love weds) appears in a *Knaben Wunderhorn* poem.[34] And the second stanza from the same song, which begins "Blümlein blau, verdorre nicht," occurs in the same *Wunderhorn* poem and in several Volkslieder. The symbolic "Blümlein blau" (little blue flower) turns up in the first and fourth stanzas of another folk lyric, "Weder Glück noch Stern," that Mahler had set earlier (ca.

Example 37.   (a) Mahler: "Zu Strassburg auf der Schanz" (*Des Knaben Wunderhorn*), mm. 5–6; (b) Erk-Böhme: "Le Deserteur" (*Deutscher Liederhort,* 3:261).

1876). It reappears, fused with Mahler's own words, in his *Gesellen* text (1883–84). Apparently, the little blue flower that eventually must fade remained a favored symbol with Mahler for years. The joining of folk verse with Mahler's poetry resembles the similar fusion of melodic formulas from folk songs with Mahler's original melodies. Mahler interwove elements of folk poetry with his own verse so skillfully that the two seem artistically homogeneous.

Mahler's settings of texts heighten their folkishness. His critics (Helm, for instance) were quick to censure Mahler's declamation.[35] (We have seen that even Wolf's declamation in his folklike songs aroused criticism.) Obdurate New German theorists censured "inept" declamation and jigging rhythm even in volkstümlich songs. They overlooked the fact that jigging rhythm—an attribute of the Volkslied—lends the volkstümlich song a distinctive primitive charm. Folklike musical gestures, dance, and marchlike figures flood Mahler's melodic style, causing him occasionally to accent some words "incorrectly." However, this style of composition, stirred by his great love for the Volkslied, inspired Mahler to create songs that are distinct from the great mass of contemporaneous concert lieder.

Reger's late style was also fundamentally influenced by the Volkslied. His earlier lieder, in contrast, are rich in elements of the "literary lied style" Wolf had cultivated, a style then in high vogue. After 1903, however, Reger felt a need for change. "At one time, I thought that I must outdo Hugo Wolf," Reger confessed. "Today I believe that no one should adopt the style of another and develop it. Everyone should say what he has to say in his own manner."[36]

The immediate reason Reger composed *Schlichte Weisen* is linked to the *Woche* contest. One morning his wife placed a folk poem, "Waldeinsamkeit," before him and encouraged him to compete for the prize. Reger's entry did not win. Today, however, "Waldeinsamkeit" is celebrated as one of his best known and most successful folkish expressions, while the *Woche*'s prize songs have all long since fallen into oblivion. "Waldeinsamkeit" spurred Reger to write more volkstümlich songs, such as the *Schlichte Weisen* set: the cycle, as mentioned, that marks his first attempts to create the "genuine" Reger lied.

Reger wrote more folkish lieder in this first cycle from his third period than most late romantics composed in their entire lives. He took nine years (1903–12) to complete the six volumes, the final two of which are *Kinderlieder* (Children's songs). Reger's objective in all six volumes was to write simply and appealingly. Attractive vocal melodies and true accompaniments, the kind that double melody in the voice parts, occur frequently, especially in the Kinderlieder. So, too, do diatonic vocal lines, strophic forms, and rhythmic patterns. There is nevertheless considerable variety in the *Schlichte Weisen*. In addition to lyrical songs and folklike lieder, one finds complex concert songs: virtuoso scherzi and chromatic modulatory essays, where tonality is stretched substantially. Some songs derive from Brahms, others, particularly humorous ones, from Wolf— "Mausfallensprüchlein," for example. Stimmungslieder, declamatory songs, and songs in dialect are among this grand set of sixty. The *Schlichte Weisen* is rich in "hits," several of which, arranged by editors, were collected in commercially profitable editions. "Mariä Wiegenlied" (no. 52), of which no less than sixteen commercial arrangements were made (for zither and accordion, even!), ranks high among favorites. "Waldeinsamkeit" (no. 3) is another success, to which might be added "Du meines Herzens Krönelein" (no. 1), "Wenn die Linde blüht" (no. 4), "Am Brünnele" (no. 9), "Mit Rosen bestreut" (no. 12), "Mein Schätzelein" (no. 14), "In einem Rosengärtelein" (no. 18), "Vorbeimarsch" (no. 30), and "Zum Schlafen" (no. 59). Reger himself arranged several of his most lyrical songs for various purely instrumental combinations.[37]

The music of the Volkslied served as catalyst for other composers who wished to rejuvenate the sophisticated concert lied. Composers of lesser stature—Heinrich Kaspar Schmid (1874–1953) and Walter Courvoisier (1875–1931), for instance—made engaging contributions. Schmid, like Reger, developed a folklike idiom as an antidote to the impassioned lieder he had composed in the 1890s. He sought an intrinsic Bavarian idiom by steeping himself deeply in genuine Bavarian music, avidly collecting old songs, and even setting texts in Bavarian dialect.[38] Along with several sets of Kinderlieder and the *Lieder zur Laute* (Op. 31, 1920), these serve as fine media for Hausmusik.

Courvoisier aimed at a rebirth of the concert lied. He sought a concise, ingenuous folklike style, evident especially in his *Kinderreimen* (Op. 28). He composed collections in which strophic songs, notably absent in his earlier lieder, reappear conspicuously. In addition, he selected poetry that, for the most part, predated the nineteenth century. His *Geistliche Lieder* includes verse by the monk Procopius (1380–1434) and Martin Luther, while the *Lieder auf alte deutsche Gedichte* set poetry dating from the twelfth to the nineteenth centuries, including Minnesinger verse. Courvoisier sought in these lieder to write volkstümlich songs that are more closely rooted in the old Volkslied. Archaic musical touches—modal and melismatic writing, hollow fifths suggesting organum, and linear texture similar to older polyphony—match this old poetry effectively.[39] The Marian songs are fine examples: gentle, placid songs, they are pastel in shade, as is to be expected in settings of texts about Mary. Their texture is hymnlike and the timbre of the piano part organlike. Tonal feeling is blurred by modality and irregular progressions, as in "Marias Traum" (Mary's dream), in which a chantlike *Kyrie eleison* is woven after the words "as if under her heart a tree were growing" (ex. 38). Courvoisier's results, however, did not match his efforts. His volkstümlich songs are in traditional late-romantic style. Musical description abounds (such as the dissonant "grief" seconds [see ﹥ in bars 1 and 2] for Christ's martyrdom); the harmony, permeated with chromatic shifts and archaic touches, is also characteristic of the late romantic.

Critics soon recognized a fundamental incongruity in the "modern" volkstümlich songs. Though nationalism mandated that German composers write

Example 38. Courvoisier: "Marias Traum" (anonymous, 16th century), Op. 27, no. 7, mm. 4–8.

simple (*schlicht*) ethnic songs, the results were just the reverse: complex, emotive, and highly personal. Reviews of Mahler's volkstümlich songs bring the problem into perspective. (The review below is musical rather than ethnic.) The *Börsenzeitung* dubbed Mahler's folkishness "contrived simplicity." Its critics found the disparity between "the style of the texts and the refinement of the orchestration" intolerable. Even Hanslick, often sympathetic, now criticized the "modern" Mahler for "adopting the naïveté[,] . . . [the] simple . . . and somewhat clumsy language of the Volkslied" and providing it with accompaniment that is "far too rich and too subtle."[40]

This aesthetic incongruity—rural, folkish texts given sophisticated urban settings—typifies the volkstümlich songs of the fin de siècle. Apparently, the objectives and the results of the composers were in direct conflict.

Undoubtedly, simplicity was Mahler's intention. Otherwise he would never have impatiently interrupted an analysis of his "Schildwache Nachtlied" with the words: "Oh, dominant be hanged! Approach these things naively as they are meant to be." Folklike simplicity, nevertheless, could not have been Mahler's main purpose or he would not have written volkstümlich songs for large symphony orchestra. His ultimate aim was to leave his personal imprint on songs. "Despite the simplicity and folkishness of ["Rheinlegendchen"]," Mahler disclosed, "the composition is highly individual, especially in the harmonization, which the public will not understand."[41] Mahler's medium for personal expression was the orchestra. The older he grew, the more individual his orchestral treatments of the folklike element became. Especially in later symphonies, he imaginatively reshaped, exaggerated, and even distorted the folklike element.

Reger soon realized that few of his early *Schlichte Weisen* were homophonic in a folklike sense. Several interweave three, four, or even five polyphonic lines: "Du meines Herzens Krönelein" (no. 1), "In einem Rosengärtelein" (no. 18), and "Gottes Segen" (no. 31), for instance. He therefore pursued simplicity more vigorously. "Now I am working on *very, very, easy* choral preludes (Op. 135a), childlike in their *simplicity*" (emphasis mine).[42] The *Zwölf Geistliche Lieder* (Op. 137) and especially the *Fünf neuen Kinderlieder* (Op. 142) clearly show how Reger climbed toward his elusive goal. But even these late songs are not really simple.

In spite of Schmid's aim to write Hausmusik and music for the amateur, his results were also not always on target. His folkish lieder are rich in late-romantic shadings, derivative of Brahms, Wolf, and others. Schmid, however, achieved individuality of another kind in his exotic *Türkisches Liederbuch* (Op. 19), discussed in Chapter 9, and in his Eichendorff lieder (for example, Opp. 23a, 32a and 32b, and 33).

The commission appointed by Kaiser Wilhelm II to publish a collection of the choicest specimens of German folk songs for male chorus dutifully rejected over 7,000 songs as too complex. Nevertheless, it selected clusters of chromatic choral music from opera and concert lieder by Wagner, Liszt, and others. The contest *Die Woche* organized to stir public interest in volkstümlich songs also produced few, if any, of the objectives intended. "About half of all the songs [submitted]," the judges later conceded, "proved to be pure art songs with complex harmony." Even a glance at the three prize songs, however, shows them also to be concert lieder.[43]

In spite of their intentions, late romantics tended to write in a folkish style we may call "complex-simplicity." Strauss confessed: "I took to heart Kaiser Wilhelm's proclamation—compose in a simple folklike manner—and set forth to write many a folklike thing for male chorus. I hoped and believed I could create something truly simple. . . . The things turned out to be so complex that I am happy the Kaiser never heard them. I had, in effect, allowed a rattlesnake to grow into a dragon."[44]

Nationalism evidently did not persuade late romantics to root their music in the Volkslied and thus develop a truly simple folklike idiom. The question arises, Did late romantics really venerate the folk song, as their statements manifest? Facts indicate the opposite. "The Volkslied in its proper sphere is the simple and artless expression of some homely sentiment," wrote Albert Bach, an authority on the ballad. *Grove* (1890) also disparaged the Volkslied as the "rude, spontaneous outcome of native inspiration, the wild indigenous fruit of their own soil."[45]

Composers held similar opinions. Humperdinck—so-called master composer of "folk operas"—considered the genuine old Volkslied "interesting but unattractive." For him, the Volkslied was raw material that needed to be fashioned into art.[46] Reger turned to actual folk poetry for only a half-dozen of his "folkish" *Schlichte Weisen*. He drew the rest from the verse of twenty-six poets, contemporaries for the most part. Mahler freely altered folk verse. He combined stanzas from different poems and, as shown, merged folk verse with his own poetry to make lied texts. Although he saturated many of his songs with the Ländler, he did not want his public to concentrate on this element. He actually suppressed overt reference to the folk dance. "Hans und Grethe" was formerly entitled "Maitanz im Grünen" (May dance on the green). Mahler even changed the performance direction of "Hans und Grethe" from *Zeitmass eines Ländlers* (in Ländler tempo) to *Im gemächlichen Walzertempo*. The direction *gemächlich* (comfortably, with ease) raises the suspicion that Mahler in fact had the Ländler and not a waltz tempo in mind.[47]

A generation earlier Brahms had shown a similar lack of interest in whether the Volkslieder he used were genuine. He turned again and again to the collection of Anton Wilhelm Florentin von Zuccalmaglio (1803–69) for his "ideal" folk songs, even after Ludwig Erk, scholar and authority, asserted that Franz Magnus Böhme's, not Zuccalmaglio's, collection was authentic. Brahms's tart reply is characteristic of the condescending attitude: "Do you find in all Böhme one single bar of music that interests you in the slightest, *yes, that moves you?*" (emphasis mine).[48] Brahms, apparently, was more concerned about the emotive character of a Volkslied than its authenticity. Contrast this attitude with the later view: composers such as Armin Knab, Percy Grainger, and, of course, Bartók and Kodály painstakingly sought only genuine folk songs.

Knab later pointed out that the disparaging attitude of late romantics toward the Volkslied doomed the Kaiserliederbuch to failure. The composers had tried to improve on the folk song by incorporating their own stylistic elements into it. Knab, Jöde, and Walter Hensel challenged the "excessively large number of sick, sweet, and sentimental" folkish songs late romantics composed as "discrediting the concept of the volkstümlich."[49]

Of all reformers, Knab (1881–1951) took the most vigorous steps to disentangle himself from late romanticism and reform the concert lied. The lied, on which he built a lasting reputation in Germany, was Knab's principal stimulus and chief means of effecting his stylistic change. He wrote extensively on the subject, avoiding the now-familiar hollow generalities. "Above all," Knab proclaimed, "the voice part should express the complete essence of the lied," rather than the piano, which, with its rich harmony, dominated the late nineteenth-century lied. "After Wagner, one forgot that the newest harmony sounds pale in only a few decades, while the oldest melodies gain in power even after centuries."[50] The vigor of the lied lies in melody, Knab concluded. He turned to the genuine Volkslied for his model, rather than the sentimental volkstümlich song of the early twentieth century.

Knab's stylistic development discloses a remarkable transition from the late-romantic to the modern lied. Early songs (1903–08), such as "Oh Hell Erwacht" (1905), are intrinsically late romantic: richly colored, subjective concert lieder. His late songs, in contrast, reveal an extraordinary stylistic development. These songs are *Chorlieder* communal music: they represent a complete rejection of the romantic lied.

Knab's ideas on how to reform the lied crystallized slowly. Two major factors were involved. The first was his attraction to poetry of national unity, folk and medieval verse, which he considered the common heritage of *all* Germans. Such poetry stimulated Knab (between 1914 and 1921) to develop a musical language suited to its communal spirit. We recall how right-wing nationalists celebrated folk and medieval art as communal expressions, disparaging the romantics, even Wagner. The German Youth Movement (1921–1933), Knab's second stimulus, impelled him to his aesthetic objective.

Three steps are apparent in Knab's reform of the concert lied. We see the first in several songs from his earliest volume, the *Wunderhorn Lieder* (1904–20): already there are attempts to give melody sovereignty, texture a linear design, and form central attention.[51] More important, these songs show Knab's rejection of the personal poetry of the nineteenth-century lied, poetry too often, in his opinion, concerned with alienation. Knab's *Lautenlieder* (1905–20) move into the second step and herald a stronger disavowal of the late nineteenth-century concept of the lied. These thirty lieder are easier to perform than any of the other volkstümlich songs discussed. Their voice parts and accompaniments (for guitar) are simple enough to be sung and played by nonprofessionals. They thus mirror the musical objectives of the later Wandervogel. Knab now stood close to the Wandervogel's leaders, Fritz Jöde and August Halm. His Chorlieder reveal the final step in Knab's rejection of the late nineteenth-century lied. These folklike choral songs for unison or three-part choir are "the strongest musical expression of the communal spirit," Knab felt.[52] Knab therefore cultivated the Chorlied intensively after 1920. The music of his late years (1933–51) shows increased attention to choral music, the oratorio, and the cantata.

The call of nationalism and the stimulus of the Volkslied had vital artistic consequences for the lied. Criticism of the "inherent weakness" of the concert lied—its lack of easily singable melody, its amorphous form and general complexity—finally saw positive results. Radicals took the extreme step, eventually abandoning the pianoforte song. Choral lieder by Knab and arrangements by Jöde led eventually to the imaginative contributions of Hugo Distler (1908–42). Other avenues were found. They included volkstümlich songs for the amateur, in a style akin to *Gebrauchsmusik* ("utility" music). Composers also wrote pieces for "folk" instruments, *Gitarrenlieder*. Artistic Gitarrenlieder helped bridge the gap that had existed since the early nineteenth century between folk and art music. Schmid, Julius Weismann, and Josef Reiter, among other composers, wrote Gitarrenlieder, though not of the simple kind favored by the Wandervogel. Still others arranged attractive piano lieder, such as the hits of Reger's

Schlichte Weisen, as Gitarrenlieder. The poetry of Hermann Löns was an immediate stimulus for many. Löns inspired numerous popular settings by amateur composers.[53] Such Lautenlieder, as they were frequently called, were not the clumsy, untutored ephemera of the early Wandervogel, but "utility" music of quality.

Nationalism during the fin de siècle, we might conclude, certainly stimulated renewed interest in the volkstümlich song. But whereas the contributions of Mahler, Reger, and other late romantics sustained the inherited tradition, the work of younger radicals helped to bring that tradition to an end.

chapter eight

The Ballad and the Kinderlied

Nationalism during the fin de siècle also inspired the revival of the ballad. Right-wing nationalists, in particular, celebrated the ballad as the most genuine artistic expression of the earliest Germans. Like the folk song, the ballad symbolized Deutschthum because its origins were thought to be communal and its music and language intrinsically Germanic. Further, its glorious tales of heroism aroused pride in the fatherland. The ballad was an ideal genre for the late nineteenth century, the time when, as we have seen, "old Germany was [thought to be] disintegrating, pulled apart by modernity—by liberalism, secularism, and industrialization."

Even Hugo Wolf responded to these stirrings. Attempting to court the nationalists, he set Robert Reinick's "Dem Vaterland." "When the German Kaiser hears it," Wolf contended, "he will make me Imperial Chancellor on the spot. It ends with the words 'Heil dir, heil, du deutsches Land.' Well, one can shout 'Heil dir' for a long time before it really gets into one's marrow in the way it does with my music. How I arrived at this death-or-glory patriotic strain is a riddle to myself."[1]

Martin Plüddemann was superbly qualified in those patriotic times to specialize in the ballad. He had impeccable nationalist credentials as music critic of the right-wing *Deutsche Zeitung*. Called "one of the most German of composers," Plüddemann carefully developed the ballad in nationalistic terms. "I have at least added one dimension to the ballad—the heroic, the intrinsically Germanic in the sense of the masculine, the powerfully valiant, a trait that in Loewe is weakly represented." His patriotic "Ode an die preussische Armee" (1881)—into which he wove the "Hohenfriedberger Marsch"—received an ovation when it was performed in Berlin for the kaiser. Plüddemann dubbed the "Hohenfriedberger" "that magnificent march of marches." Its text, which depicts Frederick the Great as a Roman Caesar, celebrates the military and political triumphs of modern Germany.[2]

The term *ballad* embraces at least eight different genres, including the one I shall discuss, the nineteenth-century art ballad for solo voice and piano.[3] Its subjects include both tales of national heroes and the world of spirits, legends, and fantasy. Traditional narrative ballads served as models for the art ballad, and romanticism strongly influenced nineteenth-century ballad composers. Tales selected were often those cast in gloomy gray, and human beings were repeatedly treated as the victims of supernatural powers. The language of the traditional Germanic ballad is archaic or in dialect, with simple syntax and uniformity of meter, rhythm, and stanzaic organization. The action may be intense and vivid, but its presentation is impersonal. For the ballad in essence is an epic genre. Events are related by a narrator rather than, as in opera or lied, experienced by a protagonist. The ballad is more suggestive than descriptive: details are left to the imagination. Yet late-romantic composers often interweave dramatic and lyric elements into the narrative.

Plüddemann, himself a scholar and composer of the ballad, considered Carl Loewe its creator. Loewe's predecessors, Plüddemann contested, were mere forerunners. Plüddemann's thesis, based on Loewe's works, is that the composer should distinguish lyric from narrative as sharply in music as the poets did in literature. No problem exists in seeking a musical parallel for the lyric in poetry. Lyrical melody, with its intimacy and ardor of feeling, is an ideal counterpart. Lyrical melody, however, is inappropriate in the ballad. It distracts attention from the details of the story. The task of finding a musical counterpart of narration, claimed Plüddemann, is formidable. "All epic . . . translates into [musical] substance that is unyielding." Before Loewe, "composers became tedious the minute they began to narrate."[4] Their chief means was the dull *secco* recitative. Loewe's contribution was his ability to narrate musically: interest actually heightens within Loewe's narrations.

Plüddemann classified the ballad as a genre distinct from the lied, for three general reasons. First, delineation of character dominates the ballad, not the lied. In addition, the lied is characterized by sensuous lyricism, the ballad, by a kind of melody that helps in the narration of dramatic action. Finally, while one mood often pervades an entire lied, mood in the ballad changes with each dramatic situation. The ballad acquires its seriated musical structure, Plüddemann specified, directly from its contrasting moods.

Specialists in the fin de siècle also recognized the ballad as a genre distinct from the lied.[5] Philipp Spitta, for instance, raised the question of whether Schubert's "Erlkönig" is a ballad. "A basic feeling predominates so strongly throughout *Erlkönig* that it draws everything irresistibly down into its depths. That should never occur in a ballad." Schubert's impulse is too lyrical here. Spitta, therefore, concluded that this great song is not a ballad. Commentators unaware of these distinctions often criticized the ballad unfavorably. "Rarely does the musical mood of the ballad," Edward Dannreuther objected, "embrace the entire poem. Almost invariably the stress is laid upon externals of the story rather than upon the lyrical emotion which underlies it. The impression left is that of a partially musical recitation by an actor, not the consistent outpouring of the musician."[6]

Many fin-de-siècle singers—failing also to recognize the ballad as a genre distinct from the lied—neglected to develop the kinds of delivery necessary for the ballad: one for its epic narration, another for its dramatic passages, and a third for its occasional gentler calm lyric passages. "Herr Reichmann sang the [Loewe] ballad 'Heinrich der Vogler' again with the same indifference towards the now epic, the now dramatic tones of the poem," Hugo Wolf wrote during his stint as a music critic. "Whether the narrator or hero speaks is all the same to him." Reichmann also failed to delineate character in the ballad: "One cannot expect Herr Reichmann to characterize the individuals by modulating his voice and by bringing each of them plastically before our eyes. All he had to offer were beautiful sweet tones."[7]

Crisp enunciation and vivid representation of words were other dramatic skills singers were expected to cultivate when interpreting a ballad. But they were not to overstep the limitations on the drama inherent in the ballad. Plüddemann cautioned: "Only in a few passages . . . is it permissible to 'show-off' one's voice' and sing with brilliance and breadth. Such performance is the *rule in opera.*" He explained: "The temperature of the ballad is markedly cooler than that of the drama. . . . Its impassioned accents are more to be suggested than actually realized."[8]

Stylistically, the ballad belongs midway between the lied and the drama. Adolf König summarized its relation to each in 1904: "The ballad differs from the lied by its richer seriated structure. But it lacks the unity and deep sense of feeling provided by melody in the lied. . . . The ballad enjoys the advantage of presenting essentials of plot in striking brevity but without living perceptibility." Ballad "composers must distinctly individualize the persons who speak or act," Albert Bach noted in 1890. The ballad shares this characteristic with music drama but not with the lied. Thus, as Plüddemann so nicely put it, the ballad helps to form a grand crescendo from lied to drama.[9]

Plüddemann's main endeavor as a composer was to translate the ballad's lyric, dramatic, and epic elements into appropriate music. Like Loewe, he illustrated textual imagery in the piano parts. His tone painting, however, is denser than Loewe's. Some passages of his ballads resemble piano reductions of large orchestral scores. Plüddemann commented: "Anyone who does not understand how to play orchestrally should not attempt these piano parts. They are not 'accompaniments' in the old sense, but rather full piano-orchestra scores."[10] Structurally, Plüddemann's ballads resemble those of Loewe. Their form underscores the folkish foundation of the texts.

Plüddemann sets each stanza as a separate musical section when it relates a different aspect of the story. Changes of harmony, key, and time signature sharpen sectional contours, as do fermatas and caesuras. Leitmotives also unify his ballads. "The leitmotive suits the essential nature of the ballad" Plüddemann wrote, "The master Carl Loewe used them in exactly the same manner [as Wagner]. One finds [forerunners of] the leitmotive even in old Zumsteeg. Ballad poetry with its repetition of . . . texts calls for the repetition of similar music. Perhaps the appearance of the leitmotive before R. Wagner—in

Zumsteg and Carl Loewe—may be explained as an inner affinity of the ballad for the true music drama."[11]

Plüddemann's dramatic inclination, however, was stronger than Loewe's. It drew him to Wagner. "Anyone who is unable exactly to reproduce spoken language in music according to Wagner's example should, at very best, never compose ballads," Plüddemann warned. His characterization, also influenced by Wagner, is sculptured and gripping. Plüddemann's greatest achievement lies in his ability to narrate musically, a skill he identified as the *"parlando ballad style."[12] A particularly fine example of this style, according to the composer, occurs in his "Frau Mette," in the dialogue between Bender and Frau Mette.

For ballad subjects, Plüddemann reached back to the sagas, fairy tales, and medieval history. Three giant ballads are the pinnacle of his success: "Des Sängers Fluch" (Uhland, 1885), which is symphonic in conception; "Der Taucher" (Schiller, 1885), particularly effective in tone painting and declamation; and "Der wilde Jäger" (Bürger, 1883), perhaps his best ballad. To his distinction, Plüddemann was the only late romantic to be thoroughly faithful to the intrinsic nature of the traditional ballad.

Wolf, Mahler, and Pfitzner were attracted to the traditional literary ballad in their youth. Mahler imitated it in his sinister tale of fratricide—his cantata *Das klangende Lied* (1878, revised 1898)—in which an envious knight kills his younger brother for a red flower with which he can win the hand of his queen.

The traditional ballad exerted a particularly strong appeal on the young Wolf, as several manuscripts in Vienna City Library attest. "Der Raubschütz" (Lenau, 1876) relates a gory tale told at midnight about a ghost of a murdered gamekeeper. "Der Kehraus" (Eichendorff, ca. 1878) is a *danse macabre*.[13] Loewe stimulated Wolf's enthusiasm for the ballad. Wolf "could sing from memory most [Loewe] ballads . . . he passionately admired" and with "compelling intensity." "Archibald Douglas" "was a particular favorite."[14] Loewe's influence is unmistakable in "Raubschütz" and "Frühlingsglocken" (1876). The atmosphere of Loewe's ballads, though not his style, even pervades a few of Wolf's mature songs: "Nixe Binsefuss" and "Die Geister am Mummelsee." The melody of the singer in "Der Sänger" recalls Loewe, and the great ballads in the *Moerike* cycle are said to have been tributes to him.

In their maturity, however, Mahler and Wolf underwent marked change in feeling toward the ballad. Mahler looked to the future of the ballad, not the past, as did Plüddemann. His first orchestral settings of *Wunderhorn* ballads were so strikingly original that he could find no title for them save the cryptic *Humoresken*. Loewe "would have understood my Humoresques," Mahler thought. "He is the precursor of this kind of writing."[15] Loewe was a stimulus of the mature Mahler ballad.

Although Mahler set a generous number of ballads from *Des Knaben Wunderhorn* magnificently—"Revelge," "Zu Strassburg auf der Schanz," and "Der Tamboursg'sell"—his name is not linked to the ballad as such. Whether one examines the gay "Rheinlegendchen" or the cruel "Das irdische Leben," one encounters lyrical melody. Mahler shunned the series of episodes, each with its own mood, that is the special domain of the ballad. For his songs, including those on ballad texts, he sought a single mood drawn from a poem's depths. Mahler even sets narration lyrically in his ballads. Further, he transformed the objective character of the ballad into subjective expression. "O Leide!" (O grief!), "Weh!" (woe!), and other remonstrances stand out, especially when one realizes these are the composer's own insertions into the folk poetry. Further, Mahler inserts subjective tone painting into his ballads. After setting the first three stanzas of "Der Tamboursg'sell" strophically, he added a somber orchestral interlude, an effusion of Mahlerian anguish, that leads to the ballad's final section. Mahler's concept of the ballad differed remarkably from Loewe's. He distorted the ballad's music, rendered it grotesque through parody, and, as I shall show in Chapter 9, subjected it to symbolist interpretation.

The mature Wolf also converted the ballad into a late-romantic genre. Only "Nixe Binsefuss" and "Der Feuerreiter" (to poems by Moerike) concern fantastic subjects. His other ballads, like "Der Jäger" and "Storchenbotschaft" (also to poems by Moerike), are too lyrical and too far removed from the world of grisly legends and sagas to be traditional Germanic ballads. Unlike the early romantics, who wished to compose with simplicity (as Wolf had done in "Rattenfänger," 1888), Wolf was interested mainly in vivid presentation. In "Geister am Mummelsee," he employs leitmotives and other descriptive techniques at every opportunity the text affords. Wolf's zeal for illustrating sometimes outstripped his better judgment. In his arrangement of "Feuerreiter" for chorus and orchestra one hears sounds of the crowd terrified by fire—merely suggested in the pianoforte here—with the result that suggestion is converted into near reality. In exercising his enormous skill for delineation, Wolf tends to transform the ballad from one in which events are retold into one in which they are actually beheld. Loewe's settings could scarcely be more dissimilar. In Loewe, the ballad's rich imagery remains implicit. Events are related impersonally in parlando ballad style, while the music remains graciously folklike.

Strauss, who similarly transformed the traditional ballad, used its texts for a variety of musical genres: pianoforte songs, melodrama, male choral compositions, and even such Brobdingnagian ventures as *Taillefer* (Op. 52). "Von den sieben Zechbrüdern" (Uhland), Op. 47, no. 5, one of few ballads he set as a pianoforte song, marks the spectacular skill at musical illustration of Strauss the modernist. Ludwig Uhland, esteemed for his imitations of ancient ballads, wrote this long poem about seven revelers who cursed water, having mistaken it for wine. In his wrath at their blasphemy, God turns their forest into thousands of islands drenched as if by the original flood. Strauss's bubbling scherzo offers detailed musical commentary: a twisting canon symbolizes the tipsy drinkers following the leader, prickly dissonances depict a dense thicket, and sounds of springs, rivers, and rain stream over the song, practically moistening its pages.

His fondness for depiction, however, can sometimes become pure sound effect imposed onto a song (see ex. 24). Such copious commentary transforms Uhland's allusions into explicit expositions.

Were minor masters more faithful to the traditional ballad? The songs of Hans Sommer (1837–1922), Josef Reiter (1862–1939), and Emil Mattiesen (1875–1939), though forgotten today, provide instructive answers. Hopes for Sommer ran high in the 1890s, when he was the subject of a good number of positive evaluations. That perceptive critic Fuller Maitland thought that Sommer "bids fair some day to rival Schubert himself." Sommer's selection of texts by contemporary poets is novel: Carmen Sylva (pen name of Queen Elizabeth of Rumania, 1843–1916), Felix Dahn, and Alfred, Lord Tennyson (in translation). His settings, too, are of interest. Melody is assigned to the piano part, which allows Sommer to declaim the voice part in a natural speechlike manner without loss of melodic interest. "Sir Aethelbert I" provides a fine example of this at the passage where the knight, overpowered by the beauty of the "white fairy," cries out: "A kiss on your red mouth is worth a thousand lives." The piano part—marked *schwungvoll* (soaring, full of fire)—gives full lyrical expression to the passion of the moment, while the voice is almost reduced to narration. Nevertheless, the passage affords the singer ample scope for intense expression, with its longer time values and careful vocal registration (ex. 39). Although structural divisions akin to those of the Loewe ballad appear in "Wüstenklänge" and "Die Räuberbrüder" (both Op. 8), Sommer is typically late romantic in his choices of harmony and form: free and fluid. Interestingly enough, Sommer was a professor of mathematics before he began concentrating on music.[16]

Reiter, the most conservative of the three, sought to shape the ballad as a genre distinct from the lied. The finest of his twenty-one ballads, "Edward" (Scottish, trans. Herder), "Der Sänger" (Goethe), and "Des Sängers Fluch" (Uhland), are intrinsically balladlike: rhetorical rather than lyrical. They evince the composer's strong predilection for folklike expression. Nevertheless, Reiter, as a late romantic, could not resist coloring his ballads with Wagner-Liszt harmonies and unifying them with leitmotives. Reiter generated an early and modest following—a Josef Reiter society was founded in 1889. His one-act nationalistic opera, *Der Bundschuh* (1900), met initial success, when it was conducted by Mahler. But by 1937 Max Morold, Reiter's champion, concluded: "His ballads have disappeared and are forgotten."[17]

Although he wrote in a late-romantic style that was then on the wane, Mattiesen was the most forward-looking of the three. His first opus, the ballad "Lenore" (1913), is typical of his work and one of his best ballads. This long song by Gottfried August Bürger (1747–94)—thirty-two stanzas of eight lines each, a prototype of romantic ballad poetry—is filled with the ghastly imagery that many composers (Zumsteeg, Loewe, Liszt) detailed in tone. In his vast setting of forty-five pages, Mattiesen sketches a different musical illustration for practically every line of text: the "trapp, trapp, trapp" of the horses' hooves (ex. 40a),

Example 39. Sommer: "Sir Aethelbert I" (Dahn), Op. 11; mm. 61–65.

the croaking of toads (piano-vocal score, p. 33), gravel and sparks flying about (p. 40), and several references to moonlight (exx. 40b and 40c), each of which is painted with a similar recurring motive (see also pp. 25, 29, 36, 44), which contributes to the ballad's musical unity. Mattiesen's target here as in his other ballads is the creation of a frenzied mood, which betrays the influence of Plüddemann and Wolf. The piano parts in all his ballads are of bravura proportions that approach bombast. Even his advocate Hans Joachim Moser is forced to admit: "Stylistically Mattiesen mixes older and newer idioms somewhat indiscriminately, yes naively."[18] To his credit, Mattiesen conjures up moods that are acrid and harrowing, like those of his ballad poetry.

Neither major nor minor composers of the fin de siècle were attracted by the traditional ballad; the ballads of Sommer, Reiter, and Mattiesen were cut from the same late-romantic cloth as those of Wolf and Strauss. The only real stylistic differences among them result from the artistic individuality of the masters. As expected, the musical profiles of the first three, though evident, are much fainter than those of Wolf and Strauss.

Fin-de-siècle nationalism evidently could not rescue the ballad from neglect. "We have little liking, in our extremely emotional times, for the ballad with its 'epic-objectivity,'" Rudolf Louis asserted. This epic genre, saturated with factual details, is too cool, too lacking in emotional ardor, to attract contemporaries, he explained. Plüddemann equated the late-romantic lack of interest in allusion

Example 40.   Mattiesen: "Lenore" (Bürger), piano-vocal score, (a) p. 20; (b) p. 40; (c) p. 41.

and obscurity with his fellow composers' indifference to the ballad. It "hardly suits our modern taste, which is attracted by the . . . wish vividly to express all thoughts rather than to make them known through conjecture or suggestion."[19] Late romantics found the traditional ballad, which had already been set repeatedly by their predecessors, tired and uninspired. Accordingly, they struck out in new directions. Mahler concentrated on the ballad's inner meaning, its symbolism; Wolf and Strauss conceived it as a vehicle for musical description.

Plüddemann, nevertheless, endeavored to give the ballad renewed life. "Does not this kind of poetry, the oldest and the most Germanic, deserve to be . . . popular when clothed in music?" Many evenings of ballads followed, first in Berlin and later in Graz, where he achieved degrees of success. His small but ardent following of connoisseurs gave a Plüddemann concert in Vienna (March 4, 1894) the same jubilant response that audiences accorded the city's rising star Hugo Wolf at a concert the next month.[20] But even this enthusiastic response did not rescue the ballad from its decline.

Proud of their success with the volkstümlich song, editors of the Berlin weekly *Die Woche* sought to rekindle interest in the ballad through two contests. "Of all kinds of poetry," *Die Woche* announced, "the ballad of late years is cultivated least of all." The same generous prizes were offered again: three thousand, two thousand, and one thousand marks for the best three songs submitted. With only 742 entries, the result was disappointing.[21] Typically late-romantic songs were submitted, some as many as forty pages long. Many of these resemble piano etudes with added voice parts. But at least the subjects submitted were traditional: "Robespierre," prize song by Hans Hermann, enacts a blood-curdling march to the guillotine. "Die Geister von Aenglistal," the second-prize ballad by Heinrich Eckl, tells how the paradise of Aenglistal was transformed into a desolate valley of stone after its gracious spirits were frightened away.

Schoenberg submitted two ballads. "Der verlorene Haufen," in the style of the descriptive ballads mentioned above, is uncharacteristic of his style of the time. Narration in the voice part draws us into a tale that is graphically illustrated by the piano. And surprisingly enough, Schoenberg repeats long musical passages without modification, perhaps to suggest the folkish simplicity characteristic of ballads. "Jane Grey," in contrast, is closer to the typical ballad and deserves applause. The tone is objective, almost one of cool detachment. The narration relates past events rather than present experiences. Even the wails for Jane's death, long melismas, and the poignant postlude in the piano, though packed with feelings, do not depict the emotion of actual experience. Neither of Schoenberg's submissions won a prize. Far from starting a vogue, the contest and its uninspiring prize songs were almost immediately forgotten. And with them, the traditional ballad, also considered uninspiring in the fin de siècle, slipped back into its dark and mysterious past.

Innovation and the Kinderlied

Late romantics who wished to cling to the past were attracted to the ballad. Those who wished to break with it turned to the Kinderlied.

The Kinderlied was cultivated intensively during the early decades of the twentieth century. Composers wrote three distinct kinds of Kinderlieder: for the concert hall, for adults and children to perform together at home, and for performance by children only. The custom was introduced of offering public evenings of children's songs, *Kinderliederabende*. The composer Wilhelm Kienzl (1857–1941) initiated evenings in concert halls in Graz, Vienna, Klagenfurt, and Laibach (Ljubljana), with the best artists, including Marie Gutheil-Schoder and Martha Winternitz-Dorda. Although the picture Kienzl paints seems precious, it was quickly imitated: "I had fashioned the concert hall into a kind of nursery. All kinds of toys were painted in groups around a little Christmas tree I had placed in front of the piano. I sat at the keyboard dressed in a great velvet coat, playing the role of the 'uncle.' The singer, the 'aunt,' sat in a large armchair. A little flock of festively dressed children from six to twelve years old were seated in a half-circle about us. A boy was my page-turner. Beyond this, I introduced a two-step device to achieve intimacy between the podium with the children and the auditorium with the adults."[22]

The folk Kinderlied, an important subcategory of the Volkslied, delighted many. There are collections of these, just as there are collections of folk *Trinklieder* (drinking songs), *Studentenlieder* (student songs), and Soldatenlieder.[23] And as composers imitated the Soldatenlied, for instance, so too did they pattern songs after folk Kinderlieder. Loewe, Schumann, Wilhelm Taubert (1811–91), Carl Reinecke (1824–1910), and Josef Rheinberger (1839–1901) are among the most prolific nineteenth-century composers of Kinderlieder.

The stature of Engelbert Humperdinck, composer of the finest late-romantic Kinderlieder, is curious, even paradoxical. The name of his famous opera, *Hänsel und Gretel*, is better known than his own: he has attracted less scholarly attention than many less important composers.[24] No biography of him was written until 1965, and that book was only the result of the dedication of his son, its author. Yet to his contemporaries Humperdinck was the man who created the so-called folk opera (*Hänsel und Gretel*), stemmed the invasion of Italian verismo opera in Germanic Europe, and, unleashed a storm of controversy with his revolutionary melodrama *Die Königskinder*.

Humperdinck's style is as individual in the lied as in his melodrama and opera. As we have seen, his melodramatic lied "Maiahnung" (see ex. 27b) is unparalleled. Although he showed the influence of Wagner in early songs, "Sonntagsruhe" (?1890–92), and some of his *Junge Lieder* (1898), he did not take the easiest path, which at that time would have been to write Wagnerian and Wolfian lieder. The Wolf influence occurred early in his career. In 1890 Humperdinck, serving as adviser for the music publisher Schott, reviewed manuscripts of Wolf songs and was immediately captivated by them. A year later he confessed that Wolf "has almost killed me with his *Spanish Songs*."[25]

After 1906 Humperdinck veered sharply from Wagner and Wolf: his songs became increasingly more simple. He wished to cultivate the dying art of Hausmusik, to write songs that young children could perform. He composed several on texts by his family: a talented sister, his father, his wife, and his brother-in-law Hermann Wette.

The Kinderlied played a central role in Humperdinck's composition, for it stimulated the creation of *Hänsel und Gretel*. Responding to his sister Adelheid Wette's urgent plea—"Help, help, fast . . . compose something for me that is pretty and really volkstümlich!"—Humperdinck provided four delightful Kinderlieder. Later adding to their number, he reworked them as a *Singspiel* and finally as his famous opera.[26] The early Kinderlied "Rosenringel" (1895–96, Rosmer) is the key to his opera *Die Königskinder*.

Humperdinck wrote ingenuous vocal melodies in his Kinderlieder. His piano parts support rather than draw attention from the voice. They are not bare accompaniments, however. Some are moderately contrapuntal and mildly chromatic. Others develop a central motive artfully. Still others are expressive little tone paintings. Animals are frequently pictured: a lark motive is developed in the piano part of "Die Lerche" (1904, Wette), a buzzing beetle in "Käferlied" (1909, Strassburger), and the "prattle and chatter" of a swallow in "Die Schwalbe" (1901; ex. 41, where thirty-seconds are followed by "hopping" staccato eighth notes). On the whole, Humperdinck's songs are uncomplicated. Early reviewers criticized them for being so simple that anyone could have written them. One smiles at such criticism today, recalling the massive concert lieder, many now forgotten, that Humperdinck's contemporaries were composing.

Humperdinck showed individuality also in his attitude toward his songs. This shy composer did not draw attention to them. He did not use opus numbers and rarely grouped songs in cycles. He composed only three cycles of Kinderlieder: *Junge Lieder* (1898, texts by Moritz Leiffmann), *Dideldumdei* (1909), and *Bunte Welt* (1909), both on texts by Albert Sergel, whose children's poetry provided texts for several composers of Kinderlieder. The attractive *Vier Kinderlieder* (1901) was published as a collection by the publisher, Max Brockhaus, not the composer. Humperdinck composed songs for newspapers, almanacs, and festive occasions or simply as gifts for friends. Many are widely scattered and out of print. Still worse, one third are lost.[27]

Humperdinck was an avid collector and arranger of Kinderlieder. His *Sang und Klang fürs Kinderherz* (1909) presents forty-five charming songs, mostly Volkslieder or quasi-Volkslieder, along with works by Mozart, Weber, and himself. This beautifully illustrated collection sold several hundred thousand copies and prompted another successful collection in 1911. Humperdinck's love for the folksong also inspired volkstümlich songs. "Am Rhein," one of his most successful, published in *Die Woche*, was commissioned for an exhibition in

Example 41. Humperdinck: "Die Schwalbe" (Dieffenbach), mm. 34–38.

Düsseldorf. "Rosmarin" (1903), another triumph, appeared in *Die Woche*'s special edition. Some are in his native Swabian dialect.[28] Indelibly linked to the folksong, Humperdinck served on his kaiser's commission for the *Volksliederbuch für Männerchor* and as judge in *Die Woche* contest.

After 1900 composers turned to the Kinderlied to achieve the simplicity they had failed to reach in the volkstümlich song. But instead of creating simple songs, many—Reger, for instance—wrote complex, personal lieder. A similar fate apparently awaited composers who cultivated the Kinderlied in an attempt to reform the concert lied. Only radical reformers achieved complete success. They condensed the lied in length and breadth and distilled its components. Suggestion replaced description as disdain for tone painting grew. A thin-lined piano part supplanted the rich canvas of the late nineteenth-century lied. Some radicals went further, dispensing entirely with the piano part and concentrating their ideas in the vocal line. They sought the home or school for performance rather than the concert hall. Further, they composed songs in the idiom of Gebrauchsmusik (utility music), the kind known as Hausmusik. Their songs fit the concept of communal music: songs designated for groups to sing in unison.

Two phases are apparent in the development of the Kinderlied. In the first, important traits of the concert lied persisted, though reduced in strength: descriptive piano parts, chromatic harmony, and subtly declaimed voice parts. Blissful innocence was affected. Such Kinderlieder, concert songs in miniature, were designated for performance by adults. Composers of the second phase (which overlapped the first) succeeded in creating truly simple songs. They limited technical difficulties and placed strong limitations on expressive details. These songs were intended for performance by and for children. Many of them are quite artistic, however.

Composers of lesser stature made considerable contributions to both phases. Warm and widespread recognition greeted their efforts. Leo Blech (1871–1958), whose Kinderlieder fall into the first phase, developed the style he had learned from his teacher, Humperdinck, into a more advanced harmonic language. An outstanding conductor, Blech mastered comic and folklike expression in his lieder and in several attractive operas: *Das war ich* (1902), *Alpenkönig und Menschenfeind* (1903), and *Versiegelt* (1908). Blech's six volumes of Kinderlieder, the most successful of his songs, were admired in the United States, as well as in Germany.[29] Their gracious simplicity is deceptive. Many, like "Der Traum" (Op. 24, no. 4), are tricky, delicate scherzi filled with musical descriptions in both piano and voice parts. Others sound like extracts from *Hänsel und Gretel*: "Kindergebet" (Op. 24, no. 7), for example. Several, like "Wiegenlied" (Op. 28, no. 6), sparkle with ninth chords, touches of "impressionism." These are concert lieder in miniature "to be sung to children big and small," as the subtitle of the opus suggests.

The *Kleine Lieder zu Kinderreimen* (Op. 28) of Walter Courvoisier, songs for the adult who enjoys "the innocence of childhood and wishes again to be young,"

Figure 8. Courvoisier, Manuscript of "Das grosse Loch" (Münchner Stadbibliothek/ Musikbibliothek; reprinted with permission of Annemarie Fabricus)

is a huge set of fifty-two songs in four volumes.[30] Their charm lies in humor, in various kinds of musical description: the ocular music in "Grosse Reise" (discussed in Chapter 5) and the open fifths that portray the big hole in Gretel's shoe ("Das grosse Loch," vol. 3, no. 11) through which "one can see all ten. Who will close the hole?" (see fig. 8, mm. 5–11.) Altered chords, sudden dissonances, and

other chromatic devices of late-romantic music create further imagery to delight the listener. The texts of the *Kleine Lieder* were carefully selected from folk poetry, particularly from *Des Knaben Wunderhorn,* and from contemporary poets like Richard Dehmel; his wife, Paula Dehmel; Albert Sergel; and Gustav Falke.

The *Fragmente eines Federspiels* (Op. 7) of Walter Braunfels (1882–1954) also falls into the first phase of the movement. Like Courvoisier, Braunfels traces his roots to Munich, to the New Germans. But Braunfels soon developed a neo-classical, linear contrapuntal style within his late-romantic idiom. He etched one-lined accompaniments for either the right or left hand (or both) of the piano part (see no. 2, "Der Gimpel," or no. 7, "Der Wiedehopf"). This line follows the vocal melody, embellishing it occasionally. Simple harmonic support is its underpinning, yet many songs present challenges for even the professional performer. Several of the *Fragmente* are only a page long. Their scoring for voice and piano or small orchestra is also characteristic of their sophistication. Braunfels, who composed songs throughout his creative life, from Op. 1, *Sechs Gesänge,* to the incomplete *Trauer-Tanz und Werbelieder,* Op. 65 (manuscript, 1947), published ten cycles of lieder. His opera *Die Vögel* (1920) was one of the most frequently performed German operas between 1920 and 1925. But Braunfels's fate, like that of Blech, was to have his rising fame cut short by a Nazi ban. After 1945 he never regained favor.[31]

The *Fünfzehn kleine Lieder* (Op. 37) of Hermann Zilcher, tiny concert songs based on fables by Hey-Specter, mix traits of late-romantic and contemporary music in unequal proportion.[32] On the one hand, Zilcher sought economy of texture, one-line descriptive piano parts with simple harmonic support. The piano simply sings along with melody in the voice, as in "Abend" (no. 15), or sketches a miniature tone painting, as in "Wo sind die Blumen hin?" (no. 14), in which a falling, ostinato-like figure paints the image of snowflakes. Such musical imagery is often more suggestive than detailed. A kind of sugary late romanticism permeates the songs in this collection, however, as it does most Kinderlieder of the fin de siècle.

The *Zehn Kinderlieder* (Op. 44) of Richard Trunk (1879–1968), delightful characterizations written for expert performers, remind one of Blech's children's songs. Chromatic chords sparkle throughout. "Die Gänse" (The geese; no. 2) is rhythmically attractive in persistent offbeats that first upset the pulse and later create an appropriate waddling movement—all accomplished in a single page. The songs are meant to be direct and unaffected. But, as just suggested, "simplicity," in this fine composer's only cycle of Kinderlieder, is achieved for the most part through late-romantic techniques.

Few late romantics were as dedicated to the Volkslied and to children's music as Heinrich Kaspar Schmid. One of his earliest publications—Op. 3, "Eine Sonatine (im Volkston)"—was written for children to perform. So, too, are these Kinderlieder: Op. 14, *Zwei Weihnachtsgesänge,* for a choir of girls or boys; Op. 22, "Ein Weihnachtslied," for four-part children's choir; and Op. 25, *Sieben dreistimmige Jugendlieder.* "The music [Op. 25] may, at first glance, astonish the reader by its plainness," Schmid's advocate Hermann Roth cautions. "This is really Hausmusik for the amateur."[33] Actually, Schmid's Op. 25 is far from plain and simple. Neither is *Ringelreihen,* Op. 15 (1907–08), Schmid's most important Kinderlieder, with twenty-one songs. Descriptive tone painting is abundant in *Ringelreihen.* Subtle through-composed lieder are frequent, yet simple strophic songs crop up impressively. "Nüsse knacken" (no. 2) and "Aus Feld und Wiese" (no. 3) each take only a page and are provided with uncomplicated accompaniment. Today Schmid's strides toward simplicity, like those of the composers just discussed, seem like tiny steps. Yet his efforts appear significant when his songs are compared with the impassioned lieder of the 1890s. We are again reminded of the courage it took in those days to write even moderately simple music, for fear of being called amateurish.

Joseph Haas (1879–1860) and Armin Knab developed the Kinderlied far beyond those just mentioned. Once regarded as one of the foremost German composers, Haas found his work widely performed and published during his day. Although he wrote significant large-scale works, his mastery lay in smaller forms, the lied in particular.[34]

Kinderlieder for adults implied a contradiction in terms for Haas. In a lecture Haas clearly distinguished the genuine Kinderlied from the familiar late-romantic variety.[35] Melody should be concentrated in the voice part and be simple enough for children to sing. It should sound complete and meaningful even without piano accompaniment, which must be devoid of tone painting or contrapuntal and harmonic sophistication. The song should resemble a draftsman's sketch rather than a rich canvas. Only strophic form is acceptable. Above all, sentimental sweetness must be rejected in verse and music alike. Rejected, too, is the romantic concept of the child's life as unspoiled and pure.

Haas slowly developed an idiom suitable for his Kinderlieder. His earliest songs, especially Op. 1, *Drei Lieder* (1904), in their iridescent chromaticism, reflect the style of his teacher, Reger. *Vier Lieder* (Op. 5), particularly "In der Frühe," is folklike in the style of Reger's *Schlichte Weisen*. In 1911 Haas entered a new musical world with *Rum bidi bum* (Op. 33), based on amiable children's poetry by Hoffmann von Fallersleben (1798–1874). This is Gebrauchsmusik for children, for practical use in school. (Haas developed the lied as Gebrauchsmusik before the term was in general use.)[36] Technical difficulties are avoided. The songs are tonal and strophic; they may be sung by a soloist, in unison, or by a two-part children's choir. The piano part is simple, always doubling the vocal melody.

The *Schelmenlieder* (Roguish songs) provide further development of the Kinderlied. The piano part, as in "Ein hartgesottnes Eilein" (A little hard-boiled egg), is no longer simply a harmonic background for melody but rather a two-part texture of equal importance to the voice. Each line is individual and simple. Exact repetition is confined essentially to the voice part, as is appropriate for children's music. Once again, the voice part may be sung by one child or by a group. These prankish children's songs have considerable charm, with a good deal of humor in the music and the text. "Ein hartgesottnes Eilein"—which begins with a blithe four-bar introduction—concerns a baby goose who has just pecked its way out of a little hard-boiled egg and struts boldly in boots to annoy a snail with seven children. The timbre of this three part piece is stunning: the bottom line rumbles in the piano's lowest register (mm. 8–12) against a second melody, for the high voices of children, combined with a tricksy third part in the piano. Here the cord that had linked twentieth-century Kinderlieder to romantic lieder is effectively severed.[37] Haas developed ever-greater lyricism in the

Kinderlied, lyricism of a popular variety, for which instrumental accompaniment seems unnecessary. His voice parts are conceived for a group, the essence of communal music.

In addition to Kinderlieder, Haas wrote religious songs for voice and organ and traditional pianoforte songs. Although his lieder show great variety, two styles recur frequently: a folklike idiom, expressed in his volkstümlich, humorous, and children's songs, and a devotional one. Though no revolutionary, he searched intensively for paths out of late romanticism, not via atonal expression but through folkish simplicity. *Optimistic* is the word that best describes Haas's music. It is saturated with humor. "I am no pessimist," he once told me. "For me, everything must start with joy."

Knab purged the Kinderlied of late-romantic complexity with the same vigor that he had used in purifying the volkstümlich song. Even *Kinderlieder* (1906–22), the first of three large cycles, consisting of twenty-three songs, is simpler than most early cycles by his contemporaries. Based mainly on folk verse (*Des Knaben Wunderhorn*) and poems by Dehmel and Hugo Lang, the collection falls into three groups. The first (nos. 1–6) are nearly all a single page, diatonic, and composed of simple four-bar phrases. Piano parts function only to support the voice. The second are Tanzlieder, songs meant to be danced and sung by children. "Ziehs naufi," a duet for boy and girl to sing in alternation, contains eight bars of song and eight bars of dance. The piano parts in general consist of only two linear lines. Here and there tiny dissonances, major seventh chords, and unexpected turns of phrase stiffen the music's naive folkishness. The final group (nos. 12–23), which fits the late-romantic idiom more clearly, shows that even Knab's results were not always consistent with his aims. These songs are not for the child performer, as their chromaticism (nos. 15, 19, 20, and 21), modality (nos. 13, 18, and 22), and accompaniment (rich in four-part writing and musical description) show.

Knab's *Neue Kinderlieder* (1929) break completely with late-romantic tradition. The first eight are Tanzlieder and the final eight the simplest Kinderlieder. The accompaniment of all sixteen consists of only two or three lines, one of which usually doubles the voice. Most are in strophic form. The *Alte Kinderreime* (1931) represent Knab's ultimate reform of the Kinderlied. Components of the concert lied are thoroughly distilled throughout. Vocal melody is in the spirit of the genuine folk Kinderlied. "Ammenuhr" is built on just four pitches, but it is made sophisticated by dissonance and engaging changes of time signature. A thin-lined instrumental sketch supplants the rich piano part of the late nineteenth-century concert lied (ex. 42). These songs may be performed in a variety of ways: as solo songs, unison choral lieder, or part songs with string, wind (piano), or no accompaniment. Knab's objective is akin to Carl Orff's epoch-making contribution, *Schulmusik* (1930–33). With two exceptions, these songs may be sung without piano accompaniment.

Bestimmt

Bu - ko von Halberstadt, | bring doch meinem | Kind wat! Was | soll ich ihm denn | brin- gen?
Geige

Example 42. Knab: *Alte Kinderreime* (*Schöne alte Kinderreime*), no. 1, mm. 1–6. (Copyright © 1932 B. Schott's Soehne, Mainz. Reprinted with permission from European American Music.)

My study of the Kinderlied draws attention to a whole body of charming but almost forgotten songs, some of which certainly would enrich current lied repertory. More important, we can see the remarkable transformation of the Kinderlied from a genre conceived by late romantics for soloists to one that is now regarded as communal group music. This transformation reflects the reaction of the modern world to the stress on self-expression of the romantic composer. In gradual transition, the hesitant steps of conservatives were measured against the vigorous strides of radicals. The Kinderlied thus provides an important link between late-romantic and contemporary music, one that has long been neglected.

chapter nine

The Twilight of Late Romanticism

The late-romantic period culminated in artistic richness. But like fall foliage, the variety of expressions glowed brightly and faded quickly. Wolf commented in 1894: "How short is the life of artistic styles today! Hardly has naturalism appeared when it seems to be dying and symbolism enters. Now even symbolism is beginning to be overtaken. Mascagni's *Verismo*—*Cavalleria* surfaced and sank—then *Bajazzo* [*I Pagliacci*], then the fairy-tales in *Hannele* and Humperdinck's *Hänsel und Gretel*. . . . It's plain that everything in the public eye today lasts for a short time and suddenly disappears."[1] In the fin de siècle, symbolism, impressionism, orientalism, decadence, art nouveau, and expressionism each appeared and left an imprint on the lied.

Symbolism enjoyed greater authority during the fin de siècle than any of the other avant-garde styles noted above, although its importance today is often overlooked. There are two main reasons for its current obscurity. In the first place, the definition of symbolism is somewhat problematic because its adherents disputed endlessly, grouping and regrouping themselves into ephemeral cliques. Family resemblances of thought, nevertheless, emerged. Second, symbolism fell under a cloud after World War I until its renaissance in the late 1960s. During these decades, symbolism, as Alastair Mackintosh quipped, "was not even well enough known to be dismissed."[2] This lack of interest accounts for many misconceptions about fin-de-siècle music.

The rise of symbolism to prominence at the turn of the century occurred during conflicts between the artistic old and new guards. Masters of the avant-garde like Stephane Mallarmé, Mahler, August Strindberg, Stefan George, and Schoenberg condemned naturalism as pseudo-positivist art. They deemed its objective—to render the world of appearances faithfully—shallow and devoid of aesthetic value. They themselves focused on life's hidden core—the mysteries of existence, spiritual concerns, the dark recesses of the mind—rather than on life's periphery, the sphere of naturalism. They opened new areas of artistic endeavor in all directions.

The influence of symbolism on the lied was crucial. Its adherents engendered a new lied aesthetic. It was Mahler who broke the ground for this new aesthetic, Schoenberg and others who completed the work. Mahler's *Kindertotenlieder*, on poems by Friedrich Rückert, brings our discussion of this new aesthetic into focus.

In the 428 poems he called *Kindertotenlieder*, Rückert recorded his experiences during the illness and subsequent death of his children, Luise (1830–33) and his beloved Ernst (1829–34).[3] "Nun will die Sonne," written on the morning after the death of a child, seems to be a typical expression of mourning. It contrasts Rückert's grief with the unconcerned world about him:

Nun will die Sonne so hell aufgehen,	Now the sun will rise as brightly,
Als sei kein Unglück die Nacht geschehen.	As if the night had brought no grief.
Das Unglück geschah auch mir allein.	The grief was also mine alone,
Die Sonne, sie schneinet allgemein.	The sun shines for everyone.
Du musst die Nacht nicht in dir verschrenken	You must not merge the night within you,
Musst sie ins ewige Licht versenken!	But submerge it in eternal light!
Ein Lämpchen erlosch in meinem Zelt,	A little lamp went out in my tent,
Heil sei dem Freudenlicht der Welt!	Hail to the joyful light of the world!

The poem is much more than a maudlin nineteenth-century expression of mourning. Hidden meanings and puzzles abound. What, for instance, do lines 5 and 6 signify—to merge night in eternal light? Mahler's song draws special attention to the enigma by setting line 6 twice. His second setting is an ecstatic climax, a melisma that peaks on the highest note in the voice part of the song. A remarkable development (mm. 52–67) of the motive associated with *Nacht* (night), when death occurred, follows (see *M* in ex. 43a). Next Mahler links puzzles of his own to those of Rückert. Shimmering glockenspiel *pointillisme*, heard three times, in groups of two (m. 64), is one such puzzle. Another is his merging of the ideas of death and life in one motive. He later sets motive *M*— which earlier had underscored *death* (*Nacht*)—to *life*, in the line "joyful *light* of the world." (*Light*—*Licht* in *Freudenlicht*, see *M* in ex. 43b—signifies life for poet and composer, we shall see.) Equally perplexing is Mahler's key word in the closing line of this song of mourning: *Freudenlicht* (joyful light).

Literal meaning recedes further into the background in the mystic second poem.

Nun seh' ich wohl, warum so dunkle Flammen	Now I can see why you flashed at me
Ihr sprühtet mir in manchem Augenblicke,	Such darkly glowing flames in many twinkles of an eye,

O Augen, gleichsam um in einem Blicke	O eyes, as if you compressed
Zu drängen eure ganze Macht zusammen.	All your power into one glance.

Dort ahnt' ich nicht, weil Nebel mich umschwammen, — Alas, I had no presentment, 5

Gewoben vom verblendenden Geschicke, — Enshrouded in mist woven from blinding fate,

Dass sich der Strahl bereits zur Heimkehr schicke — That the ray was already preparing to return

Dorthin, von wannen alle Strahlen stammen. — To that realm whence all rays stem.

Ihr wolltet mir mit eurem Leuchten sagen: — You chose to tell me with your shimmer:

Wir möchten nah dir immer bleiben gerne, — We would gladly stay near you always. 10

Doch ist uns das vom Schicksal abgeschlagen. — But fate has denied us this wish.

Sieh' recht uns an! denn bald sind wir dir ferne. — Behold us now! for soon we'll be far from you.

Was dir noch Augen sind in diesen Tagen, — What to you in these days are only eyes,

In künfti'gen Nächten sind es dir nur Sterne. — Will to you in future nights, be only stars.

Example 43. Mahler: (a) "Nun will die Sonn'" (Rückert), mm. 12–15; (b) "Nun will die Sonn'," mm. 76–77; (c) "In diesem Wetter" (Rückert), mm. 119–120.

Here Rückert's cryptic symbolism is clarified. "Now I can see why . . . Such darkly glowing flames" are revelatory lines reminiscent of the biblical "through a glass, darkly" (I Cor. 13:12). They imply, "I have perceived reality (until now) only in part." Beyond the dark flames lies a greater reality—inner reality. For Rückert, "eyes" are rife with hidden meaning: light, enlightenment, light of the soul, and most important, light of inner reality. The children's eyes suggest their impending death. The thought "I see" (*seh' ich,* l. 1), with its allusion to eyes, recurs in this poem in varying contexts and connotations: eyes "spray," emit "sparks" (*Ihr sprühtet*), and "twinkle" (*Augenblicke*); there are "glances" (*Blicke*), "rays" (*Strahlen*), "light" (*Leuchten*), and "stars" (*Sterne*). Mahler underscores the crucial symbol of the eyes with a most pregnant musical idea, which he states at the beginning of the song (see *P* in ex. 44a) with the revelatory line, "Now I see" (ex. 44b).[4] He remolds the idea plastically in the instrumental and vocal music, each time *eyes* or one of its symbols is suggested (ex. 44c). Mahler gives additional emphasis to eyes by setting "O Augen!" twice (l. 3) and adding an exclamation point (ex. 44d).

To Mahler, the mystical essence of the *Kindertotenlieder*—what lies beyond the dark flames?—is focused in two couplets of the second poem. Both reveal the significance of the children's fate. The first couplet (ll. 7 and 8) expresses a central concept of Mahler's mature thought: life as eternal renewal—the ray of light never fades. The second couplet affirms panpsychism: humans, plants, and the cosmos all have consciousness. "What to you in these days are only eyes / Will to you in future nights, be only stars." The crucial symbol "eyes" now connotes "stars." For these key couplets, Mahler takes pains to develop motive *P* ("Now I see") into a soaring, moving vocal line (mm. 29–36 and 61–67), a passage that climaxes on high F, the highest vocal pitch heard so far in the cycle.

Mahler, no less than Rückert, was eminently aware that mysteries of existence are revealed in mystic thought in privileged moments—"in manchem *Augenblicke*" (in many twinkles of an *eye*), and again: "in einem *Blicke*" (in one glance). In such moments it is "as if you compressed / *all* your power into one glance" (italics mine). Mahler took special trouble in setting line 4: we find it sketched no fewer than nine times in the manuscript draft in the Pierpont Morgan Library.

The second song thus clarifies two puzzles raised in the first song: why Mahler merged the concepts of death and life in one motive and why he introduced glockenspiel pointillisme. The pointillisme symbolizes life's eternal renewal, the mystic essence of *Kindertotenlieder*. The children's real fate, revealed in this song, was not simply to die but to be part of life's process of eternal renewal, and the glockenspiel often symbolizes eternity when used as a bell, as the Mahler specialist Constantin Floros notes.[5]

Mahler's sketch for "Nun will die Sonn'" indicates that the song was conceived of in terms of its symbolism from its inception. Edward Reilly's com-

Example 44. Mahler: "Nun seh' ich wohl" (Rückert), (a) mm. 1–2; (b) mm. 5–6; (c) m. 28; (d) mm. 11–13.

ments on the manuscript are revealing: "In measures 13 to 15, in addition to Rückert's text *die Nacht gescheh'n* [l. 2], Mahler wrote in ink the words *dem Freudenlicht der Welt* [l. 8]. And in the following four measures Mahler has again included material related to this portion of the final stanza: two bars in pencil, setting *Heil* [l. 8] in a form not ultimately used, and two bars in ink with *dem Freudenlicht* again (*der Welt* is inadvertently omitted) in a form virtually identical with the last three bars of the voice line in the printed song. Though there is no indication of scoring, the word *Glöcklein* is found where the high D's first appear in measure 20." The sketch "indicates that Mahler was already thinking of the ending of the song or sensed a possible ending implicit in the beginning."[6]

The final song, "In diesem Wetter," firmly unifies the cycle's structure and its symbolism through cyclical repetition of motives from the first song. Three examples: (1) The salient eighth-note rhythmic figures (see the *R*'s in ex. 43a) recur subtly in the final song in the tortuous guilt-ridden line: "I would never have sent the children out in such a storm." Here these figures—all derived from *Unglück* (grief; see ex. 43a)—are distorted through jagged intervals, expanded (ex. 45a), and quoted in the vocal line (ex. 45b). (2) More significant, the glockenspiel *pointillisme*, connoting eternal light rekindling life, returns directly before the finale's closing section, marked *Wie ein Wiegenlied* (like a lullaby; mm. 93–100). (3) Most important: motive *M* (see exx. 43a and 43b)—which had been linked in the initial song first to death then to life (joyful light)—reappears, recast as accompaniment for the entire closing *lullaby*, thus suggesting life's eternal renewal (see *I* in ex. 43c).[7]

Mahler specialists are increasingly recognizing the importance of symbolism to Mahler's aesthetics. Donald Mitchell presents the provocative argument that the symbolism of *Kindertotenlieder* and *Das Lied von der Erde* provides these works with their broad structure, their "organizing frame." Their first and final movements "frame both cycles" because they function in both works as mainstays or buttresses, enclosing the inner songs. The finales serve also as denouements for the works' symbolism. Mahler presents puzzles—symbolist puzzles—in the opening movements that he resolves in the finales.[8] In so doing, Mitchell concludes, Mahler ties the work's symbolism to its structure.

Mitchell's example of how Mahler fuses symbolism and structure in *Das Lied von der Erde* is subtle. "Although death is established as a presence in the first movement," the finale makes evident the reason for its presence. "The rite of death has to be enacted: the protagonist . . . has to die, and death be celebrated, before rebirth, renewal, the cycle of life, may be experienced." This occurs in "Abschied." "*Das Lied* would make no sense . . . without . . . the symphony's *dénouement*." Mahler ties the work's thematic material to its symbolism thus: the motive—A, G, E, and C—expressing "desperate protest" in the first movement (see ex. 46a), serves in "Abschied" in reverse order—E, G, and A (ex. 46b)—both as its serene coda and as its final chord of the added sixth—C, E, G, and A (ex. 46c). "The very last bars of *Das Lied* return us to its very first. There could not be a clearer symbolic enactment of the life-cycle itself, the circular process of life, death and renewal."[9] In increasing numbers specialists recognize the importance in Mahler's art of its "inner" symbolist message.

Example 45. Mahler: "In diesem Wetter," (a) mm. 9–10; (b) m. 19.

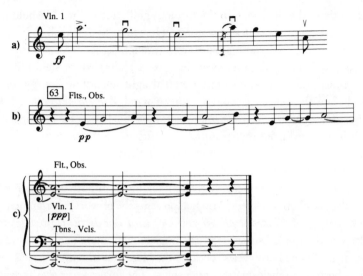

Example 46. Mahler: "Das Trinklied vom Jammer der Erde" (Bethge), (a) mm. 5–9; "Abschied" (Bethge), (b) mm. 499–504; (c) mm. 570–572.

One may, therefore, now advance the thesis that Mahler's symbolism is akin to that of his contemporaries, the French symbolist poets. Although his art and theirs differed in many ways, they all shared important objectives.

The French symbolists held that our world of appearances—the phenomenal or representational world, as Kant and Schopenhauer termed it—is not the only existence. Symbolists sensed a higher existence, a hidden reality, knowable only by the "privileged" (artists of genius), who were privileged because they could illuminate what lies beyond the veil: an inner reality. But the symbolists agreed that artists of genius penetrated the veil only in an ecstatic state, an *état d'âme*. Charles Baudelaire (1821–64) was their prophet, Paul Verlaine, Stephane Mallarmé, and Arthur Rimbaud their high priests; Wagner and, to some extent, Edgar Allan Poe were recognized as seers—and all were perceived as being endowed with a mystical power of clairvoyance.

Mahler too recognized a higher existence beyond the representational world. "The only true reality on earth is soul. . . . What we call reality is no more than a formula, a shadow with no substance—And you must not, please, take this for a poetic metaphor." His own creativity, Mahler believed, sprang from that hidden world: "My need to express myself, symphonically, begins at the threshold 'to the other world,' where the mystical rules, the world in which things are no longer separated by *time and space*" (emphasis mine). Accordingly, Mahler wrote boldly on the title page of his manuscript: "I have created ['Lied des Verfolgten im Thurme'] through the pain of the hidden (metaphysical) world."[10]

Symbolist poets equated outer reality with a poem's literal meaning and inner reality with its essence. They conveyed essence—inner meaning—through symbols. For them, symbols implied anything that in privileged moments opened the depths of life. Fables, legends, myths, and allegories were of particular importance, since they embodied eternal truths and acted as bridges between outer and inner reality. The poets' symbols, however, were often recondite and personal: dead leaves for Poe and Verlaine, fauns and nymphs for Mallarmé. These symbols served, nevertheless, as "catalysts" to evoke the invisible world, to conjure up in sound, image, or feeling, the veritable face of the universe.

Mahler's *Kindertotenlieder* is filled with such inner meaning and recondite symbols. Earlier, Mahler had struggled to convey the inner meaning of his symphonies with programs, which created heated rather than enlightened responses.[11] Mahler turned to fables, legends, and old folk poetry—which he might alter—to illuminate hidden meanings. "Sankt Antonius Fischpredigt," he explained, is not just a droll tale of the hapless saint, who, finding his church deserted, preaches to the fish; it is a commentary on "life's futility." For Mahler, "Verspätung" (Delay), the story of the child who died of starvation while waiting for its mother to bake bread, concerns not only famine but the artist's lot: recognition often comes too late. Accordingly, he changed its wording and title to "Das irdische Leben" (Earthly life) to indicate this inner meaning.[12]

Suggestion provides symbolists with the ultimate key to hidden reality. French symbolists used words more for what they evoked than for what they meant. This is precisely what Mahler did, as this crucial insight from Dika Newlin indicates: Mahler "takes the word completely out of the intellective realm into a world of symbolic-musical expression. . . . The text-word . . . always has more value as a symbol, as an outlet for the ultimate content of the music, than as the conveyor of an immediate and practical meaning."[13]

French symbolists sought to imbue their poetry with the suggestiveness they held to be the privilege of music. "Music meant above all a suggestive indefiniteness of vague emotive states favorable to the birth and . . . rebirth of the poetic experience." They identified music as the crown of the arts. "To take everything back from music" that poetry had lost to it was Mallarmé's declared ambition.[14]

Mahler luxuriated in music's supreme power to suggest. For him, music deepens and widens meaning in poetry. "You can express [in lieder] so much more in the music than the words directly say." Further, "Music expresses [nature's] essence better than any other art or science." His Third Symphony—which is "of all Nature—tells secrets so profound that we can imagine them only in dreams." For French symbolists no less than for Mahler dreams, the unconscious, inspiration, and imagination represent "mystic bridges" between the seen and the unseen.[15]

In the end, nevertheless, ambiguity persists. For the aim of French symbolists, as Hertz so nicely summarized it, was to create "an aura of subtle mystery and expressive ambiguity, an introspective style that suggests rather than defines." Mahler's symbolist objective was similar. His alteration of the poetry at the close of "Abschied"—his change of *I* to *he*—for instance, gives rise to an ambiguity not found in Hans Bethge's original poem. It results in what Mitchell calls a "textual muddle."

[Bethge]	[Bethge]
Ich stieg vom Pferd und reichte ihm den Trunk	I alighted from my horse and handed him the drink
Des Abschieds dar. Ich fragte ihn, wohin	Of farewell. I asked him where
Und auch warum er reisen wolle. Er	He was going, and also why. He
Sprach mit umflorter Stimme: Du mein Freund,	Spoke with a veiled voice: "Ah! my friend,
Mir war das Glück in dieser Welt nicht hold.	Fortune was not kind to me in this world!"
[Mahler]	[Mahler]
Er stieg vom Pferd und reichte ihm den Trunk des Abschieds dar.	*He* alighted from his horse and handed him the drink of farewell.
Er fragte ihn, wohin *er* führe	*He* asked him where he is going,
Und auch warum es müsste sein.	And also why it had to be.
Er sprach, seine Stimme war umflort:	He spoke, his voice was veiled:
Du, mein Freund,	"Ah! my friend—
Mir war auf dieser Welt das Glück nicht hold!	Fortune was not kind to me in this world!"

Who arrived, who was waiting, who is departing? In short, which friend is which? Critics pondering the questions are in sharp disagreement. Yet one detail seems certain. The "textual muddle" that Mahler created was no accident. Mahler was a sophisticated intellectual, no naive poetaster, a fine versifier, fully aware that his alteration throws a shadow over the text. The shadow occurs precisely at the point in "Abschied" where the protagonist dies and life's eternal renewal is perceived. Mitchell and Hermann Danuser both perceive the existence in "Abschied" of a hidden or *inner* "drama" (Mitchell), an *inner* "program" (Danuser), a message, we might add, that is as mysterious as it is elusive.[16]

How does one account for similarities in the thought of Mahler and the French symbolists? French symbolist aesthetic seemed totally new when Jean Moréas (1856–1910) published his *Manifeste du symbolisme* in 1886. It wasn't. Baudelaire had laid the foundations a generation earlier. Its literary style, however, was anticipated in France and Germany even earlier. Lilian Furst's imaginative study "reveals the extent to which the *Frühromantik* [German romantics at the turn of the eighteenth century] and French symbolism are linked as counterparts." Fundamental contributions of Rückert and Moerike followed. Moerike, as has been demonstrated by the perceptive literary scholars Jack Stein and Walter Höllerer, shifted "the center of gravity . . . away from literal meaning towards the more subtle lyric aspects to a degree that is true of no other German poet until Hugo von Hofmannsthal and Stefan George at the turn of the century, whose works clearly come under the influence of the French symbolists."[17]

Symbolism surfaced repeatedly in the nineteenth century, stimulated by four currents that affected artistic deliberation throughout the century: 1) the oneness of the universe (monism); 2) mysticism and the doctrine of correspondences; 3) art as a symbol of hidden reality; and 4) music as the crown of the arts.

The oneness of the universe. Traceable back through history to the ancient Greeks, this theory is fundamental in the philosophy of Johann Fichte (1762–1814), Friedrich von Schelling (1775–1854), Georg Hegel (1770–1831), and Schopenhauer, who sought to convert the transcendental idealism of Immanuel Kant (1724–1804) into a purer idealism. In spite of strong differences in their thought, Fichte, Schelling, and Hegel conceived of a supraindividual consciousness, a universal oneness. The astounding regard in which Hegel, for instance, was held—for having developed one of the most grandiose philosophies of the universe ever posited—lent an impressive urgency, certainly in central Europe, to the premise that the world of appearances, outer reality, is actually one with the vast cosmic order. Though maddeningly complex, the main concept of Hegel's idealist philosophy filtered into the nineteenth-century mainstream, albeit in greatly simplified versions.

Mysticism and the doctrine of correspondences. Most important to this thought is the work of Emanuel Swedenborg (1688–1772), engineer, scholar, and scientist. Swedenborg held that our material world "corresponds" to the spiritual world through symbols he called Hieroglyphics.[18] He fused monism and mysticism by affirming that immaterial substance works in a common world of spirit and matter. Such occult theory soon replaced the eighteenth-century belief that art is elegant diversion with a new concept: art reveals the mysteries of existence.

Art as a symbol of hidden reality. German idealist philosophers from Fichte to Nietzsche agreed that art is a symbol or reflection of hidden reality. Schelling believed that works of artistic genius are clear revelations of the absolute; Hegel recognized art as among the highest expressions of it. German idealists gave prominence to the concept that artistic genius is privileged. To Schopenhauer, "the essential and the permanent of all phenomena of the world become visual art, poetry or music."[19]

Music as the crown of the arts. One of the oldest concepts in philosophy, this theory was salient in nineteenth-century aesthetics. Schelling conceived music as the archetypal rhythm of nature. For Schopenhauer, music ranked as "the supreme art, the soul of the universe"—and also for Nietzsche: "Music may correctly be termed as a repetition and recast of the world: the copy of primal unity."[20]

Mahler's thought sprang from these ideas. Central in his thought was idealist philosophy of Schopenhauer, of Rudolf Hermann Lotze (1817–81), of Eduard von Hartmann (1842–1906), and, in particular, of Gustav Theodor Fechner (1801–87), who developed a theory of panpsychism. Fechner's belief that the entire cosmos is animate became of central importance to Mahler. Fechner and Rückert became complementary exponents of Mahler's mystical "feelings" about existence. "Remarkable how much Fechner feels and beholds like Rückert; they are two kindred souls, and one side of my being is bound to them as the third. How few know anything of them both."[21]

The first two currents, in particular, had an enormous impact on nineteenth-century arts and ultimately on symbolism. They entered artistic life early in the century. Byron affirmed monism in his poem *Childe Harold's Progress:* "Are not the mountains, waves, and sky, a part of me and my soul, as I am of them?" E. T. A. Hoffmann spoke of mystic symbols that reveal marvels when the beholder is in an ecstatic state. "In that state of delirium that precedes sleep, particularly when I have been saturated with music, I perceive an accord between colors, sound, and perfumes." Hoffmann, and certainly Swedenborg, influenced Baudelaire's "law" of correspondences, the essence of French symbolist philosophy.[22] This doctrine, which Baudelaire expressed in his famous poem "Correspondences," links matter (phenomena) and idea (inner reality) in one vast and endless reciprocal interrelation. In addition, the Theosophical Society (1875), founded in the United States by Helene Blavatsky, gave ancient occultist tradition and Swedenborg's theories renewed impetus in the fin de siècle. The influence of occultist theory persisted from Goethe, Hoffmann, Balzac, and Baudelaire to Mahler, Strindberg, Schoenberg, and his followers in the twentieth century.

Literary figures gave primacy to music as crown of the arts long before the symbolists. Wilhelm Heinrich Wackenroder, Novalis, Tieck, Jean Paul, Hoffmann, and Thomas Carlyle believed that music expressed the unutterable: that it was the original language of nature. By the end of the century, the concept was firmly embedded in Western European thought. Paul Valéry affirmed: "Any [French] literary history of the late nineteenth century that contains no reference to music would be useless, a history worse than incomplete."[23]

These currents merged in the fin de siècle in a river rich in symbolist expression. Symbolism had achieved authority in Europe, the United States, and even in Asia, in literature, art, and music. Unconventional experiments by symbolist poets with rhyme, rhythm, and syntax produced the most radical alteration of French poetry: vers libre. The symbolist contribution finally gave the naturalism of Flaubert, Zola and the Parnassian poets the coup de grace.

Though the symbolist aesthetic has been studied in art and literature, music historians have until the 1980s neglected it. French symbolists, however, explored the role of music intensely, particularly in Wagner. For Mallarmé, Wagner's theater became "a temple and the spectacle a ceremony in which the masses participate in a sacred rite." Eulogies for Wagner in France climaxed in the publication of the journal *Revue Wagnérienne* (1885–88), a showcase for French symbolist theories.[24]

Symbolist aesthetic in music—evident early in our century in Schoenberg, as we shall see—was anticipated not only by Wagner and Mahler, but by Wolf and others. As mentioned, Wolf discerned Moerike's symbolism almost a century before the literary specialists. "Und steht Ihr früh am Morgen auf," "Ganymed," and "In der frühe" provide fine examples.

The suggestiveness of tonality helped evoke the three cosmic realms—the terrestrial, celestial, and the spiritual—in "Und steht ihr früh am Morgen auf." There, Wolf suggested the rising from one realm to the next through tertial modulations. The song's initial picture of the beloved rising early on a fresh, peaceful Sunday morning is conveyed by a tranquil four-bar phrase, set firmly in E major (ex. 47a). For the poem's celestial image, the shining sun, the music ascends tertially to A flat (ex. 47b). Reference to the angels later prompts another tertial ascent of the same phrase to the song's "highest" key: C major (ex. 47c). Since the poem's next scene is on earth (the beloved attracting all mankind to mass), the music descends to the "earthly" key of E major, held by a gravitational pedal on low E (ex. 47d).

Significantly, the keys Wolf selected form a cycle: E, A flat, C, and E. And the cycle (circle or ellipse), having no beginning or ending, has always been accepted as a symbol of oneness. Whether in mythology, alchemy, theology, dreams, or even Renaissance musical notation, the cycle stands for perfection, wholeness. In geometry, it signifies the whole made up of separate parts; in biology, the continuity of terrestrial life; in astronomy, the continuous revolution of the planets. Its implications in the psychology of Jung are profound. Wolf's choice, consciously and subconsciously, of keys that are major thirds apart enables him musically to symbolize the cycle. His suggestion of the three realms by "one" phrase evokes the symbolist concept of monism.

"Ganymed," set to Goethe's great pantheistic hymn, provides a subtle example of tertial modulations at the service of symbolism. The song's initial fragrant phrase, firmly in D major, suggests the splendors of our earth. But here the soaring up over the clouds "to Thy bosom, all-loving Father" at the song's close, proceeds from D, F sharp, and B flat to *high* D major. D major, low and high, is *both* the terrestrial and the spiritual key: magnificent musical symbolism for the pantheistic union of God and nature. Although Wolf's setting of "Ganymed" inevitably invites comparison with Schubert's, Eric Sams discerned an essential difference: "Wolf has perceived more of the deeper significance of the poem. His song is all symbol."[25]

"In der Frühe" discloses Wolf's use of tertial modulations for a diametrically

Example 47. Wolf: "Und steht Ihr früh am Morgen auf" (Heyse), (a) m. 2; (b) m. 6; (c) m. 10 (voice part omitted); (d) m. 16 (voice part omitted).

opposed purpose. Critics and singers who concentrate on the work's obvious imagery—darkness and breaking of day as seen by an insomniac—miss the work's symbolism, brilliantly conveyed by poet and composer.

Kein Schlaf noch kühlt das Auge mir,	Sleep has not yet cooled my eyes
Dort gehet schon der Tag herfür	Day just dawns
An meinem Kammerfenster.	before my chamber window.
Es wühlet mein verstörter Sinn	My troubled spirit
Noch zwischen Zweifeln her und hin	still tortured by doubt and fear 5
Und schaffet Nachtgespenster.	creates nightmares.
—Ängste, quäle	—Alarm, torment
Dich nicht länger, meine Seele!	yourself no more my soul!
Freu dich! schon sind da und dorten	Rejoice! already hither and yon
Morgenglocken wach geworden.	Morning bells have wakened. 10

What is disturbing the protagonist's sleep? The poem is vague. The protagonist tries to reassure himself: "Alarm, torment / yourself no more my soul!" Is the sought-after comfort ever attained? Moerike enshrouds the answer in a haze. He intentionally isolates and thereby stresses the words *Ängste, quäle* (l. 7)—the initial words of the supposed statement of solace.[26] Further, the poem's imagery is deeply suggestive. The image of darkness seems to connote pain while that of day signifies comfort. Yet the poem's closing lines leave the question unanswered. For Moerike, disregarding literal meaning, brought ambiguities into prominence to a degree unprecedented in German romantic poetry.

Wolf gives the images of darkness and daybreak a double meaning. His thick instrumental scoring in the dark reaches of the piano (see ex. 48a) suggests murky twilight and the pain of sleeplessness. The "brightening" passage evokes not only daybreak but the feeling of a torment gradually eased (ex. 48c). Wolf gives greater importance to the poem's deeper connotations. In the first place, the intensity of the central motive (ex. 48a), throbbing feverishly at first and comforting at the song's close, is suggestive of more than mere temporal change. Second, Wolf's vocal line for "My troubled spirit still tortured by doubts" (ex. 48d) is disturbingly twisted, miles from naturalistic speechlike declamation. And the voice part of "Day just dawns" (and still no relief) is filled with all the frustration these words can convey (ex. 48b). Wolf soothes the feverish spasms into peaceful pulsations at the song's close. But this time he molds the tertial keys (mm. 11–16) into an incomplete or broken cycle: E, G, B flat, and D—a musical parallel of the shadow Moerike cast in the poem's conclusion.

"In der Frühe" had further implications for Wolf. He interpreted the protagonist's anguish as a religious experience: the contrite sinner seeking comfort. His feverish development of the central motive (see ex. 48a) suggests supplication for spiritual relief. Wolf—always scrupulous about the sequence of his songs within his cycles—placed "In der Frühe" among other religious lieder, "Seufzer" and "Wo find' ich Trost?" Both are undisguised appeals for divine intervention. "Wo find' ich Trost?" concerns a night of spiritual torment. It closes with the familiar question: "Watchman, watchman, is night soon spent? What shall save me from Death and Sin?" The subject of the remorseful sinner appealed to Wolf, from the early "Ergebung" (1881) to his masterful treatments in *Spanish* (Sacred) *Songs* (1889–90).[27] These songs all concern a solitary person facing eternal forces, who pleads to God for comfort and pardon.

The rise of symbolism to prominence in Germany and Austria occurred during a time of crisis, first in poetry and later in music. By the 1890s, Jeffrey Adams notes, "the classical-romantic lyric model" of German poetry was perceived as having been "diluted by decades of epigonal abuse." Arno Holz (1863–1929), outstanding exponent of naturalism, sought to invigorate the old poetry with new life. Stefan George (1868–1933), however, responded with "one of the most vehement attacks on naturalism to emerge from the turn-of-the-century literary debate." George sought a highly intellectual and spiritual art of mystery to contrast with fin-de-siècle life, which, he charged, lacked aesthetic value. Poetry must be devoid of political and social concern, particularly of *der menge Stempel:* "trite expressions . . . drained of common resonance, flattened by popu-

Example 48.   Wolf: "In der Frühe" (Moerike), (a) m. 1; (b) m. 3; (c) mm. 11–16; (d) mm. 6–9.

lar use." George admired Verlaine, Mallarmé, and, above all, Baudelaire. Nurtured by French symbolists, with whom he studied while in Paris, George reinvigorated German poetry with symbolic language.[28]

The crisis in music involved Schoenberg in the break with tradition I discussed in Chapter 1. "Collaboration" with George, within the symbolist camp, provided the ultimate stimulus for Schoenberg's modernist breakthrough in *The Book of Hanging Gardens* (1908–09). Here the scene is a distant realm, where antiquity and timelessness coexist. A narrator tells of a lovers' union in a paradisal garden and of the garden's dissolution as the lovers part. Different levels of consciousness are evoked through rich and sophisticated language. Meaning, even that of the garden, is equivocal. "George," Carl E. Schorske states, "sets up a tension . . . between the socially ordered nature of the garden" and "the eruptive passion of an initiate to love." For Malcolm MacDonald, the garden is an "an objective correlative . . . at first a paradise, later alien and uninvolved." For Lawrence Kramer, "the garden-world itself, supposedly a paradise, is as ambivalent as the love that it sanctions." Hertz suggests: "The subtle, indirect yet undeniable association between garden and lover is a symbolist technique. . . . The garden . . . becomes one with the act of love."[29] The garden has been personified. In the first poem, with the love as yet unrealized, the garden is a place where "soft voices mourn . . . little brooks lament." In the ninth, a "short kiss" is "a raindrop on parched desert." I too see the garden as the externalization of stages of the love affair. For *Hanging Gardens,* George selected stanzas of metric symmetry, typical of the lyric poetry of the early part of the century, and infused them with symbolist aesthetics. His symbolist poetry in strict form served as a remarkable foil for Schoenberg.

Schoenberg's *Hanging Gardens* signifies a new way of joining words and music in the lied. The composer condemned in 1912 as "most banal" the "convention" that composers must "do justice to the words of the poet . . . that the music . . . must run exactly parallel to them." Music expresses "innermost essence," he argued, "denied to poetry, an art still bound to subject matter." Schoenberg discovered earlier that though he "had absolutely no idea" of the poetry of several well-known songs by Schubert, "it appeared that . . . I had grasped the content, the real content, perhaps even more profoundly" through the music.[30]

For Schoenberg, "external agreement between music and texts as shown in declamation, tempo, and tonality, had little to do with inner meaning; that is equivalent to the elementary imitation of nature embodied in the copying of a picture." He rejected pictorial representation in the lieder of *Hanging Gardens:* "The assumption that . . . music must summon up images of one sort or another . . . is as widespread as only the false and banal can be." For George no less than Schoenberg, imagery in the poetry evokes emotions, not pictures. Like the French symbolists, notes Ulrich K. Goldsmith, George "insisted that the full intent of the poet is realized when his words create the suggested mood of a poem—a *Seelenzustand* or *état d'âme*—in the listener or reader."[31]

The atonal network of *Hanging Gardens* is, indeed, equivocal. Further, Schoenberg's interweaving of asymmetric melodic structure and flexible rhythm within the atonal network creates an ambiguity no earlier composer had achieved. It draws attention from George's symmetrical stanzas while serving as a remarkable parallel to "the spiritual labyrinth through which George's narrator wanders."[32]

In *Hanging Gardens* Schoenberg achieved his long-sought-after fusion of the arts of the lied "on a higher plane." In his next major works, *Erwartung* (Op. 17, 1909) and *Die Glückliche Hand* (Op. 18, 1910–13), he plunged into expressionism. Our inner world became his artistic concern, as this extraordinary comment suggests: "Art is the cry of distress uttered by those who experience at firsthand the fate of mankind[,] . . . [who] often close their eyes, in order to perceive things incommunicable by the senses, to envision within themselves the process that only seems to be in the world outside. The world revolves within—inside them; what bursts out is merely the echo—the work of art!" Schoenberg was disillusioned, as were many fin-de-siècle intellectuals, with the failure of science and positivism to focus on life's spiritual core. Lured by metaphysical and mystic pursuits, he planned a symphony "inspired by the program symphonies of Mahler . . . a truly cosmic [conception] . . . the largest symphony ever written." Strindberg, not Mahler, ultimately opened deep spiritual paths for Schoenberg, as well as for Berg, Webern, and Zemlinsky. Strindberg focused attention on Swedenborg's mysticism, which Balzac had reintroduced in his novel *Séraphita*. The consequence was a projected *Séraphita* oratorio. Strindberg's autobiographic fragment "Jacob Wrestling," however, inspired a major Schoenberg project, the oratorio *Die Jacobleiter*. Yet Schoenberg left all these prospects unfinished, save his four orchestral songs (Op. 22). Evidently the years of uncompleted works (1912–17) to his first serial essays (ca. 1923), were for Schoenberg a time of inner vision.[33]

Symbolism influenced the fin-de-siècle lied more than our discussion has as yet indicated. Confused music critics applied the impressionist label to lieder that express symbolist aesthetics. Let us look first at the mystic allusions of Wolf's "Nachtzauber" (1887). The poem, by Eichendorff, on the oneness of humans with nature, conceives music as the original melody of nature. "Out of blossoms . . . young limbs, white arms, red lips sprout. . . . From the mountain descending softly, primal songs awaken." Wolf's contribution is not a tone painting of nature at night but an evocation of our mystic oneness with Nature. His strong atmospheric chromatics, shifting tonality, and blurred feeling of key—tied in the piano part to a delicate pattern of arabesques—remind many critics of procedures that Debussy later favored. Accordingly, they quickly identified Wolf's "experiment" as "foreshadows of Debussyan impressionism." Strauss covers "Leises Lied" (Op. 39, no. 1) of 1898 with a light veil of mystery. The symbolist poem by the rebellious Dehmel tells of a lone figure in a lovers' garden in gray night. Starlight shimmers in a fountain, like his beloved's eyes. But now, far off, she has become a part of nature. Night's magic fuses her eyes and the stars, a union similar to that of "eyes and stars" in *Kindertotenlieder*. Strauss set these mystic allusions to passages of hazy tritones, which stand out prominently from Strauss's more familiar chromatic context, prompting further references on the part of the critics to Debussy and impressionism.[34]

Conrad Ansorge's settings of symbolist verse by George brought poet and composer into active correspondence on their common aesthetic. George recognized Ansorge's success in Op. 14 (1899) in creating appropriate music for his symbolist verse. In reviewing "Meine weissen Ara" and other songs of Op. 14, however, critics identified Ansorge's results—his light patches of color, moments of silence, blurring pedal effects, and occasional vagueness of tonality—as the "earliest examples of impressionism in Germany." Ansorge resented the label: "You would render me the greatest kindness," he requested a critic, "if you would scratch the phrase 'its impressionist shape.'" Although Ansorge continued to reject the label, he was, nevertheless, celebrated, even in his obituary, as an impressionist.[35]

Music critics, influencing some composers, applied the impressionist label not only to songs with "shimmering" effects but even to the poetry. Some traced Debussy's impressionist roots to his early settings of Verlaine and his close association with the Verlaine family. The *Harvard Dictionary of Music* (1969) states that "the refined poetry of Verlaine, Baudelaire, and Mallarmé"—and impressionist painting—was the genesis of Debussy's impressionist style. But Verlaine, Baudelaire, and Mallarmé were leading symbolists, not impressionists. Because Richard Trunk considered Verlaine an impressionist, this fine lied composer identified his first Verlaine songs, in conversation with me, as the beginning of his impressionist period.

Further, music critics ignored Debussy's dislike of Monet and impressionism to draw parallels between the composer's *Cathédrale engloutie* (1910) and Monet's Rouen Cathedral paintings (ca. 1894), hailing Debussy as the Monet of music and concluding that impressionist painting was the source of Debussy's style. "The paintings of the French Impressionists . . . suggested to Debussy a new type of music," states the *Harvard Dictionary of Music*. Debussy "wished to transfer his sense-impression directly from his own sensibilities to the listener. . . . He wanted a more convincing *realism*" (emphasis mine).[36]

Critics also failed to recognize that the mystic element in symbolist verse served lied composers as the initial spur for their luminescent musical effects. Composers intuitively sought such poetry, which yielded verse of inner experience where least expected, in the poetry of the late eighteenth century. One of Pfitzner's most imposing songs, "An den Mond" (Op. 18, 1906), on the Goethe text, touches on the union of man and Nature. A wanderer sees the moon as a friendly eye and the rustling of nature as his own song. A descending whole-tone scale—the foundation for the song—serves as musical symbolism for the mysterious union. It permeates the voice part and each strand of the linear piano part. Special pedal effects further blur the song's contour and heighten its mystery. Pfitzner's intention was to show how "nature and soul fuse." Critics, however, applied the *impressionist* label quickly.

Spurious labeling had another source. Before World War I *impressionism* signified avant-garde ventures. "Every great artist is an impressionist," Schoenberg declared. His "cultivated reaction to the subtlest stimuli reveals to him *the unheard of, the new*" (emphasis mine). The modern impressionist vision of nature concentrates on nature's depths, not its surface. Its practitioners consider the early nineteenth-century focus on buttercups and daisies naive. Joseph Marx thus stated that his lieder about nature, in contrast to early nineteenth-century lieder, suggest "all vistas of nature as states of the soul," a view akin to the aesthetics of impressionist painting.[37]

But impressionists did not paint "the states of the soul." Impressionists took their easels out-of-doors to paint nature as they perceived it. They aimed to capture momentary impressions of ever-changing nature, in different lights at different times of day. This leads to our central problem: impressionism occurred a generation later in music (ca. 1890–1920) than in art (ca. 1860–86). The reason often given for the delay—the "ubiquitous time-lag" of music—does not resolve this problem.[38] As mentioned, the 1890s was the decade when avant-garde artists and poets were abandoning naturalism. Debussy, no less avant-garde, was not about to adopt the very aesthetic contemporary artists and poets were discarding as out-of-date.

Debussy rejected the impressionist aesthetic categorically. Its "naturalist" foundation offended him. "Music is not intended to reproduce Nature more or less exactly," as the impressionists had done, "but to receive the mysterious accord that exists between Nature and the imagination." Idealist philosophy that conceives of music as the archetypal rhythm of nature echoes throughout Debussy's thought. "Music is a mysterious form of mathematics whose elements are derived from the infinite."[39] Debussy attended Mallarmé's Tuesday-evening symbolist gatherings enthusiastically, set Mallarmé's symbolist verse superbly, and selected the great symbolist play, Maeterlinck's *Pelléas et Mélisande*, after long search, as libretto for his opera.

Another major flaw exists in the notion of a musical impressionism. Although critics linked luminescent musical effects with impressionist painting, they often described the results in terms of symbolist aesthetics. Even the astute Schoenberg depicted the impressionist composer as one who is "attracted by what is soft, hardly audible, therefore mysterious. . . . His curiosity is provoked to taste the unknown . . . [to] find the unheard of." But as we have seen, exploration into the unknown, the unheard of, the mysterious, has more to do with life's mysterious inner core than with the aesthetic of Monet. Such problems prompted widespread reexamination of whether Debussy was stimulated by impressionist or symbolist aesthetics.[40]

The impressionist label creates a special problem when it is applied to German music. Pursuit of luminescent effects in fin-de-siècle France—following its defeat in the Franco-Prussian War of 1870–71 and decades of German musical hegemony—implied Gallic revolt against Teutonic (Wagner and

Faksimile nach dem nicht veröffentlichten Originalmanuskript.

Figure 9. Ritter, Facsimile of unpublished manuscript of "Noch eine Nachtigall?" (from S. Hausegger, *Alexander Ritter*)

Brahms) heaviness. But as Schoenberg observed: "Similar things were being written at the same time," independent of the French. Lied composers, in a tendency to lighten texture, were also creating musical luminescent effects, giving melody and its supporting bass less definition while at the same time searching for new ways to veil tonality. Examples before 1900 are evident not only in Wolf but in works of lesser-known composers—Alexander Ritter, Arnold Mendelssohn, Humperdinck, Kienzl, and Thuille. Ritter (?1833–96), remembered today mainly for converting young Strauss to the avant-garde, was among the first Germans to create shimmering effects in the lied (see "Noch eine Nachtigall?" fig. 9). As might be expected, he was identified as the "father of German impressionism."[41]

Musical luminescence attracted scores of lied composers after 1900. They employed a variety of scales: exotic, modal, and whole tone; pentatonic and tritone figures; unresolved dissonance; and chords with added seconds and fourths, as well as gliding parallel chords. They also sought feathery instrumental timbre for orchestral songs: using the glass harmonica (Schillings's *Glockenlieder*) and antique cymbals (Franz Schreker's *Zwei lyrische Gesänge*). Special pedal effects for the piano were introduced by Zilcher and Pfitzner.[42]

The mysterious "Aeolsharfe" (Op. 75, no. 11, 1903), delicate and pointillistic, is a fine example of Reger's response to this influence. Contrary to the opinion, held in particular outside Germany, that Reger's music always had a "very thick texture" and "an unsatisfying restlessness that often seems to go nowhere in particular," "Aeolsharfe" (ex. 49a) is lightly colored by what critics called "enigmatic" harmony. It lends symbolist mystery to the music of the aeolian harp, which the poet Hermann Lingg called the eternal "melody of the stars." Reger thought this innovative lied "one of the best I have composed."[43]

Debussy's influence in Germany occurred later than one might expect. Even Schoenberg, who wrote passages similar to Debussy's in his *Pelleas und Melisande* (1902–03), indicated that he first heard Debussy's music three or four years later. The response of Rudi Stephan (1887–1915), who is hardly known today, is typical of many younger lied composers. He abandoned his earlier idol, Wolf, for the new rage, Debussy. Although critics called the radiant harmony of his *Liebeszauber* (1911, rev. 1913) impressionist, with its chromatically altered augmented chords, the work—a descriptive tone poem for baritone and large orchestra with tumultuous instrumental outbursts—still reflects earlier Germanic influence.[44] "Pappel im Strahl" (July 30, 1913), however—lighter in texture than any lied yet discussed—reveals Debussy's strong imprint. The poem, distinctly symbolist, paints leaves falling from poplar trees as a personification of love. "She trembles a thousand times, yet entangled in dream. . . . The kisses glide, like sparks in a breeze." A recurring motive, a tritone in thirds, is harmonized by misty augmented chords (ex. 49b). Quartel movement adds its own luster. But Stephan dispels the mist, here and there, with firm cadences in the piano part.

Joseph Haas's remarks to me provide a fine concluding appraisal of Debussy influence in Germany: "We in Germany all went through an impressionist phase, even Reger. Since I always listened to the latest that was being written, I was, for a while, influenced by the liquefaction of sound, the joy in expressive

Example 49. (a) Reger: "Aeolsharfe" (Lingg), Op. 75, no. 11, mm. 1–2; (b) Stephan: "Pappel im Strahl" (Schandrel), mm. 18–21; (c) Haas: "Graue Tage" (Flaischlen), Op. 48, no. 1, mm. 12–16.

timbre, without much thought of thematic backbone. My *Flaischlenlieder* [of 1918] show the influence, but even here there is no fully grown impressionism. My liking is for more linear timbre, for music shaped in motives and themes, not for a free flow of sound. Years later, I warned my pupils: 'Don't lose yourself in pure sound. One becomes mannered. Too much pure sound is spineless [*knochenlos*].'"

Haas's comment rings true for many German composers. Debussy's influence, though prominent, was brief, most apparent between 1910 and 1920. Even then Germans tended to focus their phosphorescent harmony into firmer cadences, preferring more muscular structuring in the piano part. Only "Graue

Tage" of Haas's *Flaischlenlieder* (Op. 48) contains that "liquefaction of sound." Patches of light color, weak pulsations, cloudy seconds, and augmented fourths suggest the opening words of the Cäsar Flaischlen poem: "All threads cut . . . empty existence . . . dead space" (ex. 49c). The airy shapelessness of the song's first half is distilled at its close in a passage firmly in A major, where the text mentions "flashes" of life. Haas, Stephan, and others soon abandoned their brief captivation for airy sonority. Stephan turned to expressionism. But World War I destroyed this promising composer, along with other young contemporaries in the arts.

The lure of the East, evident in the 1860s, climaxed in the fin de siècle. It inspired a wealth of lieder on ancient Chinese poetry in German translation, enriching the fin-de-siècle lied. Mahler's great *Das Lied von der Erde* (1911) did not initiate the vogue for Chinoiserie. Nor did Hans Bethge's *Die chinesische Flöte* (1907), which had inspired Mahler. Bethge's paraphrases of the Chinese poetry, an immediate success, underwent ten printings in little over a decade. Yet it had its antecedents in such works as Hans Heilmann's *Chinesische Lyrik* (1905), the first of a fourteen(!)-volume publication entitled *Die Fruchtschale, Eine Sammlung*. Othmar Schoeck also expressed the new rage before Bethge and Mahler. "Recently (June, 1907) I have become half Chinese . . . totally captivated by the little book of Chinese poems I just discovered [*Schi-King*, by Li-Tai-Po]. . . . I know at most only a dozen poems in our complete literature that can be compared to these Chinese lyrics." By the way, Schoeck concluded his song "In der Herberge" (Op. 7, no. 3, 1907) with the same Chinese melody that Puccini was later to use in his *Turandot* (1924): "Moo-Lee-Wah." Marx's "Ein junger Dichter denkt an die Geliebte" (1909, on a text by Sao-han) and Hubert Pataky's *Chinesische Lieder* and *Vier Chinesische Lieder* (Op. 4, 1910, and Op. 5, on Bethge's translations), also predate the Mahler premiere.[45]

The appeal of ancient Chinese poetry persisted into the 1920s: Julius Weismann (1879–1950), *Drei Lieder aus dem Chinesischen* (Op. 52, 1913) and *Drei Lieder aus dem Chinesischen* (Op. 55, 1915); Walter Braunfels, *Drei chinesische Gesänge* (Op. 19, 1914); and Julius Bittner (1874–1939), *Sechs Lieder von der unglücklichen Liebe der edlen Dame Pang Tschi Yü* (1922) are some examples. Though forgotten today, Bittner's *Sechs Lieder* were well reviewed. In the cycle he tells the story of Pang Tschi Yü (32–16 B.C.), who was loved but soon abandoned by the emperor. "Would you throw this fan away as heedlessly as you abandoned me?" she wrote on the fan she presented him. With great courage, Pang, renouncing her womanliness in the fifth song, rides into battle with the men. Tragedy deepens in the final song, in which Pang bids all earthly things farewell, expiring on a star in a kind of Tristanesque transfiguration still cherished by the musical public. Critics prized, in particular, Bittner's picture of the moonrise (in the fourth song): a harmonic blur of whole tones that becomes bright E major at the passage where the moon breaks through the clouds. One critic identified Bittner's effect as "exotic atonal imagery."[46]

Chinoiserie such as Bittner's was often identified as impressionist, being lightly colored and richly chromatic, with passages of floating tonality. It is spiced with familiar clichés of exotic music: pentatonic, modal, and whole tone scales; monophonic writing; quartel harmony, open fifths, and exotic instrumental timbres. Such flavoring, one might quip today, produced a dish familiar to the Central European palate, a kind of Wienerschnitzel chinesischer Art. The stimulus of ancient Chinese poetry, however, ran deeper: it "illuminated the sadness and enigmas of existence," Bethge thought, "with a stream of symbols" expressive of the fin-de-siècle state of mind.[47]

The fascination with Japanese art was stimulated by the World Exhibition in London (1862). But ancient Japanese subjects proved less of a magnet for fin-de-siècle lied composers. Noteworthy, however, is Marx's richly colored "Japanisches Regenlied" (1909), one of his most successful songs, a deeply atmospheric and melodious Stimmungslied, sprinkled with the pentatonic. Yet the *Japanische Lieder,* Op. 45 (1908), of Felix Weingartner are of an entirely different flavor from the songs discussed. Each of Weingartner's nine songs is built on an exotic scale, which the composer printed directly under the song's title. Each scale creates a special musical color, as does the one quoted below for "Am heiligen See" (At the holy lake, ex. 50). These are not touches of exotic color strewn on rich late-romantic harmony, as in Puccini and others. Rather they reveal that Weingartner, like many contemporaries (Debussy, for instance), was in search of new modes of expression, new ways of blurring tonal feeling. In the monophonic passage for piano below, Weingartner met more success than in the tonal one that follows. For his public, such monophony characterized Eastern music. But although the innovative passages of these songs once sounded modern, the cycle today is unquestionably late romantic. Weingartner's trips to Japan had stimulated these experiments in Eastern effects. Though Weingartner is hardly known today as a composer, some of his lieder were very popular. "Liebesfeier" (1891) resounded from the studios of nearly every singer during the fin de siècle.[48]

Poetry of the Middle East, particularly that of the Persian Hafis (see Chapter 1), embodies another aspect of the rage for the exotic. Central Europeans have long been enchanted by Hafis's ribald poetry, his racy verse on wine, song, and tireless love. Goethe's adaptations of some of the poems in the *Westöslicher Divan* attracted Schumann and Wolf. Strauss's *Gesänge des Orients* (Op. 77, 1928), which sets five of Hafis's poems in their German translations by Bethge, attempts to match the poetry's intoxication with musical ebullience. The music's excessive exuberance, however, tends to give the cycle a shapelessness that may account for its infrequent performance.

In contrast, Theodor Streicher's *25 Hafislieder* (1907–08) are refined songs, some of which would certainly enrich concert repertory today. They advance Wolf's chromaticism with quickly shifting keys and painstakingly careful declamation, as illustrated in example 18. To Schoeck's *Zwölf Hafis-Lieder* (Op. 33)

Example 50. Weingartner: "Am heiligen See" (Ohotsuno Ozi), Op. 45, no. 1, mm. 10–19.

and Feliz Woyrsch's *Drei perisische Lieder* (Op. 6), one might add other exotica: the *Türkisches Liederbuch* of Heinrich Kaspar Schmid (Op. 19), on poetry of Assim Agha Gül-hanendé, translated by B. Schulze-Smidt; Kurdish and Malayan songs of Friedrich Klose (Op. 3); Indian songs by Georg Goehler and Julius Weismann; and Zemlinsky's *Lyrische Symphonie* (Op. 18), consisting of seven songs for soprano, baritone, and orchestra, on poetry of Rabindranath Tagore.

Art nouveau (*Jugendstil*) was so popular at the turn of the century that it was called the "1900 style." "In the midst of . . . fin de siècle mood, people were striving energetically to attain a renaissance, a new form-language, an Art Nouveau, and a new *Jugend* [youth], with all the wealth of symbolism contained in these words."[49] Art nouveau is actually an offshoot of symbolism. Its visual artists, hostile to reality, aimed to suggest rather than to represent. Floral symbols and two-dimensional planes are important in both styles. But Jugendstil is profusely ornamented, its symbols profiled in more abstract decorative lines.

Luxuriant, swirling lines in two-dimensional planes are distinguishing features of Jugendstil. The style, however, is erotic in a procreative way. Its eroticism is often subtle and sublimated. Roots, buds, shoots, and trees, swirling, twisted, and interlaced, reveal life force. Stalks eclipsing their flowers, spermlike whiplash, and serpentine contours suggest the masculine element. Water, waves, egg shapes are female symbols; art nouveau also features well-rounded women in seductive poses. Indeed, women eclipsed men in the attention of artists. Female nudes, society women, and females of fantasy were painted with long voluptuous tresses floating among sinuous floral decorations that themselves exude eroticism.[50] Analyses of musical Jugendstil, however, generally ignore this procreative element. And although the style blossomed throughout Western Europe and America—in painting, poster illumination, book illustration, tapestry, woodcuts, sculpture, interior design, and architecture, all evident in criticism—musical Jugendstil, however, elicited only passing comments early in our century.[51]

The influence of Jugendstil on the German musical scene is, nevertheless, visually evident in printed music and concert programs. After 1900, sheet music of lieder was frequently decorated with Jugendstil motives. Alban Berg, himself a gifted artist, designed a Jugendstil cover for the first edition of his *Four Songs* (Op. 2). "Schoenberg [was] very pleased with my title pages . . . in the soft, plantlike style of the Art Nouveau of 1900," Berg confided to Anton Webern. Concert programs were for years decorated with these graceful lines, not only in Germany and Austria but in New York, at Carnegie Hall. Jugendstil motives were visually evident in the performance of the lied, as this 1901 review of a concert given by Magda and Franz Henri von Dulong indicates: "Frau Magda projected a strong image of [Jugendstil] with her hair styled à la Botticelli and the slim pre-Raphaelite line [of her gown]."[52]

Elements of Jugendstil are evident also in lied texts. *Das Lied von der Erde* provides examples, particularly in the revisions Mahler made of the poetry. He inserted Jugend not only into the text but even into the titles of some movements. Bethge's "Der Pavillon aus Porzellan" became "Von der Jugend," and the unidentified "friends" in Bethge's text became "youths" in Mahler's. Jugendstil motives are particularly evident in the fourth song, "Von der Schönheit" (Of beauty), which Bethge had prosaically entitled "Am Ufer" (On the bank). First, there is the alliterative series of floral symbols connoting burgeoning spring: *Blüten, Blumen, Blätter,* and *Büschen* (buds, blossoms, blades, and bushes). In addition, the song is filled with imagery of rippling water, swaying grass, flowers, and slender limbs of girls. Most prominent, however, is the procreative juvenescent scene of boys on horseback cantering around the girls. Mahler greatly expanded Bethge's verse—into which Bethge had himself introduced Jugendstil motives—to make this scene central in "Von der Schönheit."[53]

In the final song, "Abschied," Mahler combined Bethge's words "Menschen gehn heimwärts" (People go homeward) with two lines of his own, extracted from a poem written in 1884—lines he revised and into which he inserted Jugend: "Die müden Menschen geh'n heimwärts, / Um im Schlaf vergess'nes Glück / Und Jugend neu zu lernen!" Mahler's final verbal change, which closes *Das Lied,* is decisive. Instead of Bethge's: "The earth is everywhere the same, / and the white clouds are eternal," Mahler wrote: "Everywhere the dear earth awakens / in spring and grows green again! / Everywhere and forever distant blue. / Forever . . . forever."[54] In so doing, he intersects the procreative ideology of Jugendstil with his symbolist concept of life as eternal renewal.

Mahler undoubtedly understood Jugendstil ideology in visual art. His close friends Carl Moll, Gustav Klimt, Alfred Roller, and Kolo Moser had founded the Viennese branch of the movement, known as the Secession. When Mahler expressed his "exorbitant desire to know all that was to be known . . . about pure painting and the ability to judge it," Alma Mahler tells us, "Moll, Klimt, and Moser disputed the right to be his teacher." And when Mahler was asked to conduct at a Secessionist celebration, "he made the occasion a labor of love." Further, Mahler had the title page of his Rückert lieder printed in "Secessionist" typeface. And the Mahlers used a Secessionist monograph on their stationery.[55]

The revival of interest in Jugendstil in the 1960s provoked far-reaching discussion, both popular and scholarly, about every aspect of the movement, even music.[56] Vigorous debate ensued on the question of whether there was a musical Jugendstil. The evidence has not as yet affirmed the existence of musical Jugendstil, although provocative issues, as will be noted, were raised recently. For some early advocates, Mahler was the ideal candidate; for others, Strauss seemed more likely, though Debussy and young Schoenberg top several lists as nominees. Disagreement was stronger on which specific works exemplify musical Jugendstil, becoming most contentious on these fundamental issues: When was the period of musical Jugendstil and what are its specific musical attributes?

Earlier inquiry defines musical Jugendstil in terms of its most prominent element in the visual arts: swirling decorative line. Current inquiry challenges this definition. Dahlhaus, for instance, argues that line in Jugendstil painting is not equivalent to line in music. He contends that Jugendstil in art had its genesis in Wagner. Jugendstil arose from Wagner's flowing suspension of time, "strömenden Zeitenthobenheit." Time in Wagner's later dramas seems fluid, yet "it does not progress . . . it has no goal." Dahlhaus concludes that "the paradox of a suspension of time that flows . . . inspired the flowing line of Jugendstil art." This flowing suspension of time suggested Jugendstil style to artists, not composers, however. For Dahlhaus denies the existence of musical Jugendstil.[57]

Walter Frisch, also, holds that music was "a force behind the aesthetic of Jugendstil, especially in the movement's tendency towards abstract design. . . . . Instrumental music had [long] been valued for its 'absoluteness,' its lack of referentiality." However Frisch, unlike Dahlhaus, affirms the existence of musical Jugendstil, providing engaging examples of how artists like Wassily Kandinsky took "music as a model for [Jugendstil] abstraction. . . . Specific colors . . . are said to produce certain effects on the viewer much like those produced by music. Thus [quoting Kandinsky], 'keen lemon-yellow hurts the eye in time as a prolonged and shrill trumpet-tone the ear.'" This color-sound synaesthesia is one of several crucial examples Frisch cites to show that Jugendstil artists incorporate elements from their sister arts in their compositions.[58] Contemporary poets, Frisch adds, quoting Dehmel, incorporate "painterly and musical effects."

He provides this musical example of sound-color synaesthesia from the song "Erwartung" (Schoenberg): "As a corollary to the poem's color play, Schoenberg creates a distinctive five-note 'color' chord." In an apparent nod to Dahlhaus, Frisch notes that Schoenberg created a "sense of goallessness" to mirror "goalless modifying phrases" in Dehmel's poem.[59]

But synaesthesia—crucial in Frisch's analysis of Jugendstil—is fundamental also in symbolism. This is evident in Baudelaire's doctrine of correspondences and his remark: "What would be truly surprising would be to find that sound *could not* suggest color, that colors could not evoke the idea of a melody, and that sound and color were *unsuitable* for translation of ideas, seeing that things have always found their expression through a system of reciprocal analogy ever since the day when God uttered the world like a complex and indivisible statement."[60] Far from being an exclusive element of Jugendstil, synaesthesia was deeply embedded also in late-romantic aesthetics, certainly in symbolism. Examples are engaging and abundant: the "mouth organ" of liquor casks in Huysmans's "A Rebours" (1884), contrived by the eccentric Des Esseintes, who "would imbibe a drop here, another there [holding that] dry curaçao was like a clarinet. . . . Then, to complete the orchestra, comes kirsch blowing a wild trumpet blast; gin and whiskey, deafening the palate with their harsh outbursts of cornets and trombones." For Kandinsky: "light blue is like a flute, a darker blue a cello, a still darker the marvelous double bass." Kandinsky also experimented with *Der gelbe Klang* (the Yellow Timbre). Scriabin's "Prometheus" blends changing colors, projected by a *clavier a lumières,* with instrumental sounds; Rimbaud aimed to invest vowels with visual color. Such eccentric synaesthesia were actually attempted in the "perfume" concerts discussed earlier, where perfumes appropriate for certain lieder were wafted through the air while the songs were performed.[61] Can one decide from these examples which are specifically Jugendstil synaesthesia?

Other problems in affirming musical Jugendstil exist. Dahlhaus and Frisch, who hardly touch on symbolism, situate music as the genesis of Jugendstil. But French symbolists considered music, Wagner in particular, as the genesis of symbolism. And they, too, regarded the suspension of time as the essence of symbolist aesthetics. Evidently symbolism is closely linked with Jugendstil. Art historians like Alastair Mackintosh regard Jugendstil as "both the natural child of symbolism . . . and a reaction against it." Yet recent studies of musical Jugendstil ignore symbolism entirely or treat it as a shadowy substance somewhere in the background. Dahlhaus only alludes to symbolism in his discussion of musical Jugendstil. And though Frisch states, "French symbolism [is] a movement in many ways closely allied to Jugendstil," he provides no elucidation.[62] Although the cloud of uninterest that hovered over symbolism and Jugendstil lifted in the 1960s, apparently it still shrouds musical discussions concerning their connection.

Have Dahlhaus, Frisch, and others specified attributes unique to musical

Jugendstil or ground shared in common by symbolism and Jugendstil? If distinctions between the two styles are not as clearly drawn in music as in art, then it would seem that we are really considering Jugendstil partly in terms of symbolism. A further problem exists with the notion of musical Jugendstil, to wit, the dearth of statements by composers expressing their intentions to create Jugendstil in music. Dahlhaus adds still other problems in his denial of musical Jugendstil: "The term Jugendstil though serviceable for characterizing some traits, proves worthless as a means of capturing in a nutshell the newness of music about 1900. . . . It is hard to imagine a category linking the primacy of 'sonority' (meaning the fusion of harmony and instrumentation) in fin de siècle music and the bold outlines of Jugendstil."[63]

These discussions of musical Jugendstil indicate a positive change from the time when musicologists considered investigation into links among the arts as an inconsequential pursuit. Although serious problems in affirming musical Jugendstil remain, the initial steps have been taken by Frisch and others and even by Dahlhaus, who, despite his denial of musical Jugendstil, challenges us indirectly to further study with his provocative theory about Wagner's inspiration of artistic Jugendstil. As well, Jarocinski, Hertz, and others are exploring musical symbolism. Hertz notes the essential symbolist contribution: it "freed" the poet "from the necessity to describe reality." And he adds fundamental links between literary and musical symbolism, while indicating two basic features of symbolism: a marked "hostility to periodic differentiation" and "a kind of open-ended evocation of meanings . . . achieved by assembling unresolved actions and questions [and] conflicting blocks of images in the text. Tonal ambiguity in music parallels this literary tendency."[64] Mahler's rejection of Naturalistic Description, heightened by the comments and compositions of Schoenberg and others, reveals that these composers sought in music to "suggest" life's inner core rather than to depict life's surface. And examples presented above from *Kindertotenlieder* and *Das Lied* show how music and poetry converged to express symbolism. Problems nevertheless remain. For instance, ambiguity in music and hostility to periodic differentiation—prominent indeed in the fin de siècle— were not tied to symbolism alone, as I shall show in the next chapters.

The failure of science and positivism to focus on life's inner core evoked two final revolts of fin-de-siècle intellectuals against naturalism: decadence and expressionism. Although they involved the lied only peripherally, both are of great importance historically, for they show late romanticism in its final decay.

Decadents were passionately antinaturalistic, unconcerned with social problems, morality, or truth to nature. "There is nothing good and nothing evil. There is only art," is how Robert Hitchens expressed decadent ideology in *The Green Carnation* (1895). Decadents wished to stir the senses, to catch every exquisite passion, to explore the evil side of experience. They delighted in the strange, the morbid, and the degenerate. They "took subtle joy in playing with fire and calling it sin, scourging themselves for unholy delight, and tasting bitter-sweet actions potent with remorse." Ernest Dawson expressed the ideology aptly: "I cry for madder music and for stronger wine."[65]

The femme fatale, prime symbol of decadence, attracted widespread attention in the fin de siècle: she appeared in Jean Delville's *The Idol of Perversity* (1891), Franz von Stuck's *Sensuality* (1891), Edvard Munch's *Vampire* (1893), Fernand Khnopff's *The Caress* (1896), and Frank Wedekind's dramas. Strindberg spared woman no sympathy: "Since the first woman contracted with the devil, shall not her daughters do the same?"[66] The theme found its climax in Salome, depicted by Gustave Moreau, Mallarmé, Huysmans, Beardsley, Klimt, and, of course, Oscar Wilde, whose play was searingly set in opera by Strauss.

Strauss's "Frühlingsfeier" (Op. 56, no. 5), on a text by Heinrich Heine, is a remarkable expression in the lied of decadence, close in style and time of composition to *Salome*. It celebrates the Greek festival of spring. A procession of lamenting women carry an effigy of the slain Adonis. Mourning ends at dawn when the image is "thrown into the sea . . . with joyful anticipation of Adonis' return . . . next spring."[67] Heine's poem, all turbulence, omits the festival's joyful conclusion. Passages of dissonant chromaticism depict bare-breasted maenads, excited by the image of slain Adonis: "By the glimmer of torches, they search here and there in the woods, . . . crying, laughing, sobbing, and screaming, 'Adonis! Adonis!'" An interlude of folklike lyricism represents the "wondrous beauty of youthful Adonis." "Frühlingsfeier," one of Strauss's most tempestuous lieder, ends in frenzy to the words "his blood colored the flowers red" and to hysterical screams of "Adonis."

The excesses of decadence expose romanticism in decay. For decadence and romanticism are actually opposite sides of the same coin. Both express insatiable desire to escape the monotony of daily life, the shackles of decorum. But whereas romantics turned to dreams and fantasy, decadents protested with petulance, eccentricity, and perversity. Decadence glowed an intense purple in the nineties, but the new century saw it fade. An outraged public, seeking to silence this revolt against society, imprisoned Wilde, who later died a penitent Catholic in France. Beardsley, Huysmans, and Verlaine also renounced decadent excesses for a while by converting to Catholicism.

Expressionists, on the other hand, pierced the outer shell of reality to penetrate life's inner core. Their antagonism to naturalism surpassed even that of the symbolists and the Jugendstil artists. "The basic intention of expressionism is to shatter reality, to go to the very roots of things until they are no longer individually or sensually colored," the German poet Gottfried Benn (1886–1956) announced. Because externalities hinder penetration, expressionists shut out the outer world. They gave artistic shape to inner, often subconscious states. Repressed anxiety, torment, and conflict were discharged directly into a style, spawned by a fascination for the grotesque, for art of macabre content. Hermann Bahr, an eyewitness, described expressionism's essence: "Never yet has any period been so shaken by horror, by such fear of death. . . . Never has man been more insignificant. Never has he felt so nervous. . . . Man cries out for his soul. . . . And art cries with him. . . . She cries for the spirit: that is expressionism."[68]

The roots of expressionism reach back to Wagner, to passages in his characterization—of Kundry (*Parsifal*), for instance—that probe subconscious states. Mahler and Strauss, who raised the threshold of inner torment to higher levels, could distort musical line with the fervor of expressionists. Unforgettable examples occur in Strauss's *Elektra* and Mahler's symphonies: consider, for example, his distortion of the Ländler in his Ninth.

The lied also played a vital role in the path toward expressionism. Wide leaps of great intensity in the vocal lines of Mahler ("Das irdische Leben") and Strauss ("Lied an meinen Sohn"; see ex. 1a) show expressionism in formulative stages. Outstanding and lesser known composers alike sought not only music but texts of unrelieved tension. Among little-known lieder, Reger's "Sehnsucht" (Op. 70, no. 9) deserves passing attention. The poem, by Ludwig Jacobowski, expresses endless torture: "reopened wounds that cut deeper and wider." Reger's short lied of nineteen bars—a continuous climax that begins forte and culminates triple forte—parallels the poem's turbulence. A veiled and quickly shifting tonality mirrors the poem's bitter fate. Pianist and singer alike reflect anguish never relieved. The piano part, orchestrally conceived, thunders in climactic passages that the singer is directed to perform "con tutta la forza."

But Mahler, Strauss, and Reger were expressionism's forerunners. They restricted the expression of extreme musical tension. Expressionists, in contrast, emancipated dissonance and embraced atonality to sustain tension at highest levels throughout entire works. Expressionism surfaced in German music in Schoenberg, and in art in Kokoshka and Kandinsky at the close of the twentieth century's first decade.[69] Schoenberg's *Pierrot Lunaire*, a paramount example, conjures up strange images with its feverish atonal atmosphere and its Sprechstimme recitation. Such recitation repudiates traditional singing and naturalism in speech inflection. Amazingly, Schoenberg actually permitted reciters to render his Sprechstimme notation with the greatest freedom, provided they fully realized his primary intention: creation of a hallucinatory atmosphere.[70]

Expressionism underwent two stages of development. In its first stage, it encapsulated the peak of late-romantic subjectivity driven to frenzy. As I shall show in Chapters 10 and 11, its adherents, like all late romantics, shaped the musical elements of rhythm, form, and tonality freely. In the second stage, however—called "abstract expressionism"—its adherents sought to rein in excessive musical liberty.[71] The war had interceded. Objectives changed. The aim now was, to paraphrase Gertrude Stein, to "kill Romanticism dead."

Expressionists aspired to revitalize art, the human race, and its institutions. "The industrial materialism which raised its head in the last decade [of the nineteenth century] like a giant in all countries of Europe is tearing itself to pieces in blind bestiality," lamented Gerrit Engelke, poet of the war years. "I hope . . . a new life may arise out of the ruins of Europe."[72] Absolute forms in music and nonobjectivity in visual art became governing principles as Schoenberg entered his twelve-tone era and Kandinsky his "architectural period." Expressionists, in their response to the new artistic goal, shaped subconscious states abstractly. And they spurned romantic individualism. "Each man is no longer individual, bound to duty, ethics, society, family," Kasimir Edschmid (1890–1966), a theorist of expressionism, stated. "Through his art he becomes nothing but the most exalted and the most powerful: *he becomes Man*."[73]

part three

The Unifying Aesthetic

Expressive Aesthetics in Performance

In Part II of this book, "The Disparate Aesthetic," I looked at the fin-de-siècle lied as an amalgam of divergent styles. The violent conflicts that often arose among adherents of these styles tend to conceal the fact that late romantics shared fundamental ideas. In the chapters that follow, I shall focus on these shared principles. Expressive aesthetics, discussed in Chapter 3, is a pillar of late-romantic thought, but to what extent was it actually accepted during the fin de siècle? The concert scene provides an ideal site in which to begin study of this question.

Expressive aesthetics met wide public approval in lied performance. Expressive performance, for instance, encouraged the singer to stress feelings, sometimes to an excessively introspective degree. "Have you cried while studying this song?" Julius Stockhausen asked one of his pupils. "Cried . . . why?" she replied. "I have had enough," Stockhausen rejoined. "You will not sing this song, at least not with me."[1] Even a more recent singer like Julia Culp confessed to me in an interview: "I was often near tears in some songs! I felt them so deeply."

Audiences revered the expressive performances of singers who identified themselves closely with the emotional experiences expressed in lieder. Ludwig Wüllner, perhaps the most admired singer, "aspires to bind life and the lied as closely as possible. He creates the impression that he is not now just about to sing an ingratiating song but . . . that he finds himself in such a spiritual mood [*Seelenstimmung*] that he must straightaway sing this particular song." Many singers believed that they could do justice to a particular song only when moved to sing it. Indeed, some performers affected an air of deep inspiration before singing. The stimulus of the moment was so important to Wüllner and Raimund von Zur Mühlen that they might suddenly perform a lied that was not on the program. Feodor Chaliapin carried the belief in the mood of the moment to an extreme. "Chaliapin does not follow any set printed program. He sings whatever the mood prompts him." Booklets with English texts instead of programs were distributed at his concerts. "Each song was announced by its number immediately before it was sung, as if the singer were obeying the whim of the moment."[2]

The press encouraged the display of emotion in lied performance—as long as the results were artistic. Critics praised stirring performance extravagantly with such phrases as "mit hinreissend leidenschaftlichem Ausdruck" (with over-powering impassioned expression). And audiences responded uninhibitedly. Natalie Bauer-Lechner "saw the way men wept and youths embraced each other" during an ovation for Mahler's Second Symphony. "No milder word than fever can be used to describe the violent enthusiasm of [French audiences] of the late eighteen-eighties and early eighteen-nineties. . . . Lekeu fainted after the prelude of *Tristan* at Bayreuth and had to be carried out of the theatre. Such was . . . the state of delirium in which people listened to music."[3]

Lied composition, too, was often a deeply emotional experience for the late romantic: "Often enough the tears rolled down my cheeks as I wrote," Wolf confessed. Mahler told Guido Adler that when composing his *Kindertotenlieder:* "I placed myself in the situation that a child of mine had died." Mahler perceived that "only when I experience am I a tone-poet—and only when I am a tone-poet do I experience."[4] This close identification of art and life, already apparent among early romantics, is fundamentally different from the attitude of their classicist predecessors, as is evident in Goethe's famous remark to Eckermann: "The romantic is sick, the classical is healthy."

Gesture is another important element that characterized expressive perfor-mance. I refer not to the histrionic gesturing already discussed but to the kind signifying inner agitation: the heaving of the breast, swaying of the body, or impassioned clasping of hands. The press encouraged singers to cultivate facial pantomime as well: "Wüllner's facial pantomime constitutes a true work of art. . . . Preference for powerfully impassioned expression is a characteristic of his performance."[5] Eyewitnesses whom I have interviewed, musicians who knew the fin-de-siècle style intimately (Elena Gerhardt, Julia Culp, August Schmid-Lindner), believed that artistic singers categorically rejected gesture in lied performance. But careful analysis of reviews reveals that disapproval was registered only when gesturing was in poor taste—as is evident in this review, which contrasts David Bispham with the usual run of singers of 1907: "He understands thoroughly the value of facial expression. . . . No such ranting posturing as we too frequently see."[6] Subtle gesture was regarded as an intrinsic element of lied interpretation. "Why should a concert singer stand . . . with hands folded in front of him or stiffly at his side?" a critic wrote, affirming Bispham's right to gesture. Bispham placed limits on his gesturing, as is evident in his polite censure of Wüllner, who "goes a little too far . . . and resorts to means which it were not wholly unreasonable, perhaps, to regard as beyond the legitimate art of song—the bowing of the head as if in prayer, and the impas-sioned clasping of the hands upon the breast."[7] Restrictions on gesturing appar-ently were flexible, for, as we have seen, Wüllner was considered the paradigm of the interpretative artist.

Of course, artistic singers during the fin de siècle also used purely vocal means—beauty of tone, warmth of vocal color—to awaken emotional response.

Many went farther. They differentiated key words and phrases through a kaleidoscope of vocal shadings, for gloom, joy, tumult, tenderness, jealousy, and grief.

In addition to reviews, phonograph recordings from the fin de siècle show
that expressive performance was indeed a mannered art. Singers tended to
emphasize emotive words through sobs, audible breathing, slurs, portamenti,
and tremolos. Evidently, the portamento was a great favorite, though vocal
teachers cautioned against its too-generous application: "It should be reserved
for moments when feeling runs high."[8] Mahler, Strauss, Schillings, Reger,
Marx, and their contemporaries nevertheless called for the portamento often in
vocal and instrumental music—and not only when feeling ran high.

Composers provided the singer ample opportunity to infuse emotive words
with feelings. The melisma was one such means (see ex. 51). Mahler often used
melismas for this purpose. In "Es sungen drei Engel," he further stressed *bit-
terlich!* by means of slurs, accentuation, and the performance direction "Die mit >
bezeichneten Noten sehr herausgestossen" (ex. 52).[9] Wolf also highlighted emotive words but in an entirely different manner: he underscored them with
pungent harmony.

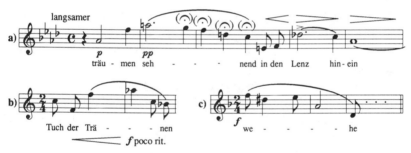

Example 51.   (a) Heinrich Kaspar Schmid: "Des Apfelbaumes Frühlingstraum" (A. Ritter),
Op. 9, no. 4, mm. 28–31; (b) Joseph Marx: "Tuch der Tränen" (Wertheimer), vol. 2, no. 12, mm.
9–10; (c) Knab: "Was ist denn mir so wehe" (Eichendorff), mm. 16–18.

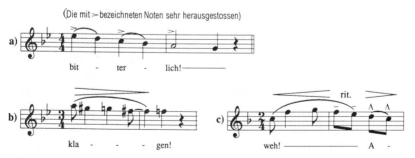

Example 52.   Mahler: (a) "Es sungen drei Engel" (*Des Knaben Wunderhorn*), mm. 51–52;
(b) "Erinnerung" (Leander), mm. 32–33; (c) "Scheiden und Meiden" (*Des Knaben Wunderhorn*), mm. 75–76.

Further, singers tended to fill their performance with changes of tempo and *Luftpausen* (breath pauses) not indicated in the score, even in songs that early romantics had rendered strictly in time. They avoided metronomic pulsations in such lieder as Schubert's "Wohin" and "Erlkönig" by inserting retards, accelerandos, and holds at will. Felix Weingartner contended that often in passages "where a gradual animation or gentle and delicate slowing-off is required . . . a violent spasmodic *accelerando* or *ritenuto* was made."[10]

Agogic stress, the slight lengthening of note values, was another means by which musicians intensified expression. Recordings show that outstanding singers applied these devices extravagantly.[11] The Luftpause, used to heighten expression, "would be inserted, particularly in the case of *crescendo,* immediately followed by a *piano,* as if the music were sprinkled with fermatas." Mahler called for ten pauses in the piano version of his short song "Urlicht" and sixteen pauses in the orchestral. Musicians liberally inserted these pauses into dynamic passages. Frederick Niecks deplored the fact that outstanding pianists played "even-rhythmed reiterations" unevenly, to "obviate monotony."[12] Singers adopted uneven pulsation to underscore poetic or impassioned moments or to enunciate with speechlike clarity.

Rhythm was particularly important in expressive aesthetics. Late-romantic composers and performers made rhythm subservient to expression. They realized their objectives by creating ever-new shadings of tempo and by broadening adagios to an unprecedented degree.

We can see this in these performance directions for tempo: "Very restless and impassioned" (Wolf's "Bitt ihn o Mutter"); "lost in reverie" (Mahler's "Wo die Schönen Trompeten blasen"); "in a haughty vernal tone" (Strauss's "Herr Lenz"); "lugubrious" (Reger's "Friedhofsgang"); and "as in narration" (Pfitzner's "Schön Suschen"). Such directions indicate more about a song's emotional content than about its pulse. When traditional tempo indications do occur, composers often linked them to words indicating expression. Two examples from Wolf: "Slowly and painfully" ("Seufzer") and "Slowly and with innermost feeling" ("Neue Liebe"). Such directions disclose how intimately mood (expression) and motion (tempo) were linked in the mind of the late romantic. Indeed, they were interdependent even during lied composition. Tempo was often determined by the mood of the poem being set. The association, explicit in Joseph Marx's comment, "Every mood has its own tempo," provides one explanation of why so many changes of tempo occur in the late-romantic lied—to mirror changes of mood in the poetry.[13]

Late romantics insisted that tempo must reflect the changing emotional content of a piece. "Tempo," Mahler asserted, "can never remain completely unvaried even for two successive [measures]. Metronome markings are inadequate—indeed, almost worthless, because the tempo must be varied even two measures [after an indication] if one wishes to avoid playing a work like an organ grinder." Although their views in composition were often diametrically opposed, Strauss called Mahler "one of the few [musicians] . . . who understands tempo modification."[14]

The ways composers directed changes of tempo through verbal instructions is noteworthy, at least from their abundance. More interesting, however, is how they effected such changes in the actual notation. Wolf and Mahler, for instance, used different procedures. To broaden the pulse Wolf might introduce various kinds of syncopation, as in "An den Schlaf." Here he resorts increasingly to longer time values, passing in effect from $\frac{2}{2}$ to $\frac{4}{2}$ to $\frac{3}{2}$ in the final bars while fading into a kind of Tristanesque transfiguration (ex. 53a). Wolf's changes of note value served to slacken and hasten tempo in "Schmerzliche Wonne." Here he suddenly switches from a rapid pulse of six, heard throughout the song, to four, then to a broad two, petering out in bars 6 and 7 to an uncertain unit of one—on the bar's weak beat (ex. 53b). A sudden return at the song's close to its original movement in six produces an unexpected burst of renewed energy.

Mahler modified tempo through changes of time signature. In "Der Schild-wache Nachtlied," he replaced here and there the regular $\frac{6}{4}$ measures with three measures of four beats each. These inserted bars of $\frac{4}{4}$ add an unexpected extra pulse that falls on the rests, creating the effect of fermatas. Measures 4 through 9 could easily have been notated conventionally, with fermatas and breath pauses

Example 53. Wolf: (a) "An den Schlaf" (Moerike), mm. 28–34; (b) "Schmerzliche Wonne" (Geibel), mm. 84–92.

(ex. 54b). Mahler's solution is superior: it indicates the precise length of each "hold" while keeping the beat pulsing regularly during the tempo modification, thus avoiding the possibility of dead halts on fermatas. Such explicit rhythmic notation bears testimony to Mahler's assertion: "In order that no misunderstandings be possible in matters of rhythm, I racked my brains to write out all the details with the greatest exactness. . . . Everything is indicated through the note-values and the rests, even the tiniest minutiae."[15]

Measured tempo-modifications, as these unconventional methods might be called, indicate the exact degree to which tempo is to be slackened or hastened. The concept is ingenious: the effect of free rhythm is produced by means that are rhythmically strict. Verbal instructions, in contrast, permit the performer to determine the degree to which pulse may be modified.

Late romantics, extremists in expressive performance, proceeded beyond such flexible tempi to near-freedom from the tyranny of the bar line. Franz Kullak notes that musicians tried to blur the beat in some works to achieve "complete abandonment of metronomic time." Niecks adds that they played "not two bars of the same length, nor within the bars, two beats alike." Mahler, the conductor Robert Heger informed me, "conducted passages of the *Tristan* prelude in a recitative-like manner that seemed to have no tempo and he played the piano parts of his lieder in a considerably freer style than he generally conducted his orchestral works." Reger "accompanied not only his own lieder freely, but also the works of other composers," according to Schmid-Lindner. Brahms's friend George Henschel accompanied the songs he sang with "the air of an improvisation," a critic noted. "It is as if, in absolute mastery of his art, he could let go, could free himself from all restraint, could let his fancy wander at will."[16]

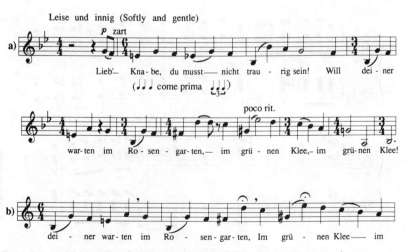

Example 54.   Mahler: "Der Schildwache Nachtlied" (*Des Knaben Wunderhorn*), mm. 15–25, (a) Mahler's score; (b) conventional notation.

Some composers labored to inscribe in actual notation a liquid rhythmic flow, unhampered by any regularity of pulsation. Joseph Marx sought this kind of rhythm in "Nocturne" through multiple time signatures, performance directions, and the kind of rhythmic configurations assigned to the pianist (ex. 55). When rendered with due license these permit performers to approximate "free rhythm." Mahler introduced thirty-six(!) measured tempo modifications into "Um Mitternacht" to establish seemingly indeterminate rhythm. He achieved the peak of pulselessness—a tempo dominated by expression—in "Abschied," the finale of *Das Lied*. His remarkable comment to Bruno Walter—which Mitchell quotes three different times in his study—is worth quoting again here: "Have you any idea how this is to be conducted? I haven't."[17]

The elemental, ironclad discipline of the march fascinated the same late romantics who sought the greatest freedom of tempi, Mahler, for example. Its strict pulse and that of the dance is heard in lieder of many late romantics. Composers rarely sustained the pulse throughout an entire lied, however. Characteristically, they followed passages of inflexible tread with others of supple

Example 55. Marx: "Nocturne" (Hartleben), mm. 1–2.

motion. The ultimate example is again Mahler's "Abschied," in which sections of the strictest and freest tempi alternate.

The march, as noted, serves symbolic purposes. Its main function in the fin-de-siècle lied, however, is as a means of expression. The refined but pert pace of Wolf's "Sie blasen zum Abmarsch" is no less stirring than the muscular stride that closes his second "Coptisches Lied." It generates excitement. The fire and fury of Mahler's "Revelge" almost sweeps audiences into active participation.

Late romantics, intent on saturating performance with expression, assigned the adagio a commanding role. The adagio, the heart of late-romantic tempi, has long been regarded as the most expressive. Recall C. P. E. Bach's description of the "tenderness of the adagio," Mozart's reference to its expressiveness, and his father's statement about its "paroxysms." Early romantics like Johann Hummel lauded the adagio's "singing, expressive, and melting style." Paganini's adagio "does not allow the eye to remain dry."[18]

Late romantics phrased the adagio in a long-breathed manner that, to borrow Wagner's words, "tends towards infinite expansion"—one in which "languor of feeling grows into ecstasy." They fused spacious tempi with expansive singing lines and, in the process, stretched them almost to the breaking point. Kullak deplored that "slow tempi are being dragged in a most painful manner." Weingartner singled out the Wagnerites at Bayreuth as those inclined to "drag . . . and draw-out tempi."[19] The older Brahms and his followers also tended to overdo adagios. Brahms's "'Unbewegte laue Luft' (Op. 57, no. 8) could never be taken slowly enough to suit the master." Elena Gerhardt, in an interview with me, insisted that Arthur Nikisch "played the piano parts of some song by Brahms surprisingly slow, insisting that Brahms, himself had paced them in this manner." Since Gerhardt, in her earlier years, was herself inclined "to elongate tempi" one can imagine how broad those of Brahms and Nikisch must have been.[20] I might mention, in conclusion, the once well-known objective of late romantic singers: to sustain unusually wide-arched phrases in slow tempi, seemingly effortlessly, with one breath ("Mainacht," of Brahms).

Timbre and dynamics, as one might expect, also served late romantics as major elements of expression. These composers, like their contemporaries in painting, were colorists, fascinated by the emotional qualities of tone color. They created a truly opulent instrumental palette for the lied. One example is Reger's airy and delicate pastel coloring of a bird in flight expressed in the exploration of the extreme upper register of the keyboard (ex. 56). Stimulated by Liszt's keyboard music, late romantics sought still brighter tints, especially in songs of the early twentieth century. Since the keyboard was extended from six to more than seven octaves when the modern piano emerged after the mid-century, the passages in examples 56, 57a, and 58 were either unplayable in Schubert's day or were of much paler color.[21]

Timbre in the late-romantic lied is characterized by striking changes of register from bar to bar or even within the same measure (ex. 57a), along with

Example 56. Reger: "All'mein Gedanken" (Dahn), Op. 75, no. 9, mm. 12–14 (voice part omitted).

tiny patches of color over several octaves that shade into one another (ex. 57b). These examples only hint at the richness of keyboard timbres, so important in evoking the mercurial moods that characterize the romantic lied. Special pedaling effects range from veils of luminous haze to steely percussive clashes. Most interesting is Wolf's descent into murky depths in "Die Geister am Mummelsee," a reflection of the attraction for late romantics of dark timbre (ex. 58).

Vocal timbre had a special attraction for fin-de-siècle composers. Strauss conceived Op. 10 "definitely for tenor" and Op. 15 "for alto." Pfitzner entitled Op. 6 *Sechs Lieder für hohen Bariton* (Six lieder for high baritone, 1888–89). "Naturally the sculptor must sing bass," is Wolf's instruction for his Michelangelo songs.[22] Reger designated *An die Hoffnung* (Op. 124) for alto and many other songs for voices of specific timbre, as did these younger lesser-known colorists: Schoeck, Zilcher, Trunk, Haas, and Joseph Marx. Before 1830 composers rarely left such instructions; they simply wrote: "lied for voice and piano."

Example 57. (a) Reger: "Ruhe" (Evers), Op. 62, no. 3; mm. 1–2; (b) Wolf: "Wer tat deinem Füsslein weh?" (Geibel), mm. 27–28.

Example 58. Wolf: "Die Geister am Mummelsee" (Moerike), mm. 1–2 (voice part omitted).

They were more interested in line, that is, melody, than in color. Nor did they object when a song composed for one kind of singer was sung by another with an entirely different kind of voice. The day of the professional lieder singer who mastered subtleties of timbre lay in the future.

One savors vicariously a late-romantic predilection for dark color in Paul Bekker's enthusiasm for the "unique timbre" of the baritone—"duskier [than the tenor] . . . imbued with supra-human power, and infused with a mood that is doleful and tragic."23 The dark timbre of Wagnerian singers had a singular appeal. They produced their shade by singing with the larynx in a low position. Friedrich Schmitt, a founder of the German school of singing, introduced Wagner to this vocal technique, hoping that it would produce the hue Wagner had long sought for *Der fliegende Holländer*. "At the passage: *Die düstre Glut, die ich fühle*, Wagner exclaimed: 'darker, still darker!' In response, Schmitt screamed [at Julius Hey, his pupil]: 'you botched the low larynx position.'"24 Hey evidently failed to fulfill the technique's main requisite—to maintain the larynx always in its low position, even when proceeding into an upper register. When correctly produced, the color was much to Wagner's liking. Hey later explained the advantages of this technique, called *Tiefgriff der Stimme*, in his *Gesangs-Unterricht:* it enables the singer to produce the darkest and most voluminous sound with minimum effort. This deep-throated timbre became an ideal for fin-de-siècle singers, from the highly dramatic soprano down to the bass. Actors applied the technique assiduously to acquire rich speaking voices and to help articulation. Singers who were unable to produce the timbre naturally darkened their voices artificially to approximate it. The technique fascinated even Brahmsites like Stockhausen. But Stockhausen taught his students the dangerous method of forcing the larynx down with a finger to achieve the Tiefgriff der Stimme. Singers who overemphasized darkness and volume produced a quality Lilli Lehmann named *röhren* (stove-pipe) singing.25

German romanticism arose in part from a fascination with darkness, mysterious night, evident in the shadowy legend of the Flying Dutchman, the dark canvases of Caspar David Friedrich, and the specter worlds of E. T. A. Hoffmann and Novalis (in "Hymnen an die Nacht"). Dimly lit atmospheric rooms later became the rage of Wilhelmian and Victorian decor. Poetry of night also beguiled such late romantics as Pfitzner, Reger, and especially Mahler. For them, Wagner's deep feeling for the crepuscular—his dark stage effects, his personification of night in *Tristan und Isolde*—was crucial.26

When Wolf hailed his "Erstes Liebeslied eines Mädchen" as "of so striking a character, and of such intensity, that it would lacerate the nervous system of a block of marble," he was expressing a typically late-romantic objective: to create music of great intensity.27 Some composers of the fin de siècle reached for extremes of expression that seem beyond the capacity of performers and their instruments: Tchaikovsky's sudden change from *pppppp* to *ff*, for instance, or Mahler's insistence on a *fffff* pizzicato.28

Masters of the late-romantic lied also broke through conventional limitations on expression. Mahler did so with these instructions: *schreiend* (screaming; "Der Tamboursg'sell, orchestral version), *wild* ("Revelge"), *mit Erschütterung* and *mit ausbrechendem Schmerz* (convulsively, breaking out in pain; *Kindertotenlieder,* the first and third song, respectively). His objective—to breathe the fiery presence of electrifying performance into his written scores—prompted Mahler repeatedly to replace one mark of expression with another, as his manuscripts demonstrate. Differences between printed versions are frequent as well.[29]

Reger also ignores conventional limitations on expression. Dynamics cover an especially wide range in his songs, stretching from *pppp* to *ffff.* Climaxes of triple forte thunder in 20 percent of his songs. Even the singer is given heroic assignments, as in "Ritter rät dem Knappen dies" (Op. 70, no. 3), where the instruction reads: *ff* "con tutta la forza." In some songs, like "Wehe" (Op. 62, no. 1), Reger deliberately rejects traditional limits: "Becoming continually faster and faster in a demoniacal vein."

Among lesser masters, Joseph Marx aimed at an excitation of feelings that surpassed many. He marked a passage in triple forte in "Toskanischer Frühling" (1908) with the superlative *höchst ausdrucksvoll* (with utmost expression). Emotion surges throughout "Im Maien" (1908) and climaxes at *ffff* in a piano part that approaches orchestral power and opulence (ex. 59). With the piano's damper pedals depressed and all strings resounding, the sonority becomes so expansive it creates the impression that all the registers are resounding simultaneously. Marx descends from such towering heights within eight bars through a kaleidoscope of shadings: *fff, ff, f, mf, mp, p, pp* to *ppp.*

Fierce climaxes mark Schoenberg's early published songs. "Dank" (Op. 1, no. 1) storms to triple forte and later ascends through a molto crescendo to *ffff.* No less than seven other pianoforte lieder from these years fulminate at triple forte. These were the years when Armin Knab composed most of his *Mombert-Lieder*

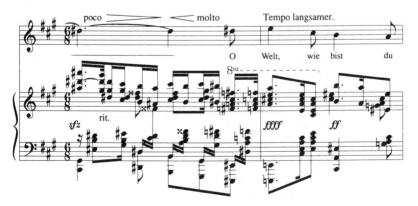

Example 59.   Marx: "Im Maien" (Rodenberg), mm. 103–104.

(1905–08), massive songs of feverish intensity which Oskar Lang accurately called dithyrambic hymns.[30]

For several reasons one might question the use of extreme dynamics in the lied, especially today, when we have many singers with lighter—lyric and spinto—voices. At the turn of the century, however, volume and weight were important requisites even for lied singers. Many lied singers were Wagnerians. Ferdinand Jäger, Heldentenor of Bayreuth, was among the first important performers of Wolf's lieder. Other Wagnerians who sang lieder include Franz Betz (Bayreuth's first Wotan), Anton van Rooy, Theodor Reichmann, Eugen Gura, Karl Scheidemann, and Anton Sistermans. Their sound in dramatic songs was stentorian, especially in comparison with that heard today.[31]

Further, dynamic signs, as lied performers would acknowledge, are far from precise indications of volume and weight. The same sign may be interpreted differently in different songs. As the experienced accompanist Gerald Moore points out: "The forte in *Nachtigall* by Brahms is lighter and more singing than the heavy ponderous forte of [his] *Der Schmid*."[32] Additionally, a *ff* may not sound any louder even if the composer writes *ffff* because many singers are unable to sing triple or quadruple forte. Their performances may be thoroughly impressive, nevertheless, if they build intense climaxes. In actual practice, extreme dynamics serve more of a psychological function—to associate excitement with the music—than the practical purpose of indicating precise degrees of loudness.

The five lied masters, in actual practice, were relatively circumspect in their use of dynamics. They specified extreme dynamics mainly in their lieder composed at the turn of the century. Most of Wolf's were written between 1892 and 1901; Mahler's, also between 1892 and 1901; Strauss's, between 1898 and 1905; Reger's, between 1900 and 1903. Pfitzner's period was more extensive: from 1885 to 1907. Even Schoenberg wrote most of his dynamically intense lieder between 1897 and 1907.

Although Wolf's dynamic range is broad—it extends from *pppp* to *fff*—one rarely finds these extremes in a single song. The crescendo of *ppp* to *fff* (in "Neue Liebe") occurs in only 1 percent of his lieder. And in only 5 percent does Wolf proceed, even gradually, from *pp* to *fff*.[33] Although *fff* seems to be his dynamic pinnacle, Wolf reaches this peak in less than 10 percent of his songs. His limits in individual songs are usually *pp* to *ff*.

Dynamics are more restricted in Strauss's songs than in those of any other master of the late-romantic lied. Although they stretch from *ppp* to *fff* in "Lied an meinem Sohn" (Op. 39, no. 5), these extremes are infrequently encountered, even in dramatic songs. Triple fortes appear so seldom as to be uncharacteristic. They are scarce even in his orchestral songs, where one might expect them to abound. The few examples occur in dramatic songs composed in 1898.[34] Even *ff* > *pp* is rarely found. Strauss also showed economy with soft dynamics.

Triple piano occurs in only 10 percent of his lieder. Examples are restricted to songs that end or fade into silence, an effect of which he was fond.

The most remarkable aspect of expression in the late-romantic lied is not its fierce climax but its incredible refinement. Nuance was of paramount interest to late romantics. Detailed indications and subtle distinctions abound in their lieder. Gentle swelling and ebbing of dynamics imparts the impression that their songs are alive—that they breathe, sigh, and pulsate.

Wolf calculated expression with meticulous precision. The pianist is required to diminish from *pp* to *ppp*, sometimes on one beat, as in "Auf eine Christblume I," measure 71. The closing bars of "Schon strekt' ich aus im Bett die müden Glieder" alternate *pp* and *ppp* from one measure to the next. The two-beat motive in "Dereinst, dereinst, Gedanke mein" is altered in almost each of its thirty statements. Example 60 is especially richly nuanced. At times, Wolf reaches for the impossible: see, for instance, his direction for a crescendo in the piano part of example 61. The voice part, in contrast, usually has few detailed indications. That of "Prometheus" has only 12, while more than 130 appear in the piano part.

Wolf sought startling effects, especially in the final bars of many songs. But here again extremes are avoided. Only 7 percent thunder at *fff* and 17 percent at *ff*. Just 10 percent terminate with sudden changes of intensity or with unexpected sforzandi. Few conclude with mezzo-forte or forte (2 percent) or simply with

Example 60.   Wolf: "Du sagst mir" (Heyse), mm. 15–17 (voice part omitted).

Example 61.   Wolf: "Tretet ein, hoher Krieger" (Keller), m. 24.

piano (4 percent). On the other hand, 60 percent close with such verbal indications as "fading away," "almost inaudible" or "like a breath."

Reger's fancy for refined expression grew into a craving for the nuance, especially in the lieder of his maturity, where he sought to outdo Wolf. Some distinctions are so subtle as to be tenuous. The number of indications in some is astonishing. Each bar of "Verklärung" (Op. 55, no. 6) has at least five different kinds of signs. And Reger used many expressive adjectives. Their total number in bar 8 exceeds twenty! (See ex. 62.) Reger also was fond of concluding songs in whispers. About 40 percent end with a triple piano. He followed conventional limitations on expression in early songs, in which Italian terms outnumber those in German. The impassioned songs of his middle years show the reverse.

Strauss applied dynamic shading with a sparing hand. Far fewer indications occur in his Stimmungslieder, his most popular songs, than in those of Wolf, Mahler, and Reger. He often sustains one mood with a single symbol for extensive passages. The early "Ständchen" (Op. 17, no. 2) has 47 bars of pianissimo and 32 measures of piano. "Leises Lied" (Op. 39, no. 1) is almost entirely pianissimo. Nuance is rare even in songs of his maturity: "Wiegenlied" (Op. 41, no. 1), "Waldseligkeit" (Op. 49, no. 1), and "Gefunden" (Op. 56, no. 1). Pastel coloring characterizes most of Strauss's late lieder (Opp. 67 and 68), the dynamic "Lied der Frauen" (Op. 68, no. 6), excepted, of course. Such pastel shading is preeminent also in the bittersweet songs of Strauss's last years.

Although Strauss gave few directions as to dynamics, he did not expect singers to restrict themselves to those found in written notation. As an experienced accompanist, he understood the preference of late-romantic performers for nuance. He encouraged esteemed singers to introduce subtle shadings where appropriate, as Elena Gerhardt, Julia Culp, and others who performed with Strauss at the keyboard informed me.

Certainly the fire burns with more fury and more frequently in the *Pfitznerlied* than in the *Strausslied*. Thundering fortes appear in the voice part of

Example 62.   Reger: "Verklärung" (Itzerott), Op. 55, no. 6, m. 8.

impassioned songs Pfitzner composed throughout his career.[35] Nevertheless, in a large number of his songs, he was sparing in his use of marks of expression. He shaded dynamics only occasionally. Like Strauss, he sustained the same general dynamic level for long stretches in his Stimmungslieder and even in dramatic songs. In "In Danzig" (Op. 22, no. 1), for instance, a *pp* is maintained for sixteen bars.

Fin-de-siècle singers, as recordings reveal, expended painstaking efforts to express nuances. Lilli Lehmann created subtle diminuendos within a single measure, as well as striking changes from forte to hushed stillness in Schubert's "Du bist die Ruh'" (1907). Recordings of Schubert's "Ständchen" by Johanna Gadski (1908), Paul Reimers (1914), and Julia Culp (1915) are rich in dynamic refinement. After World War I this practice continued: listen, for example, to Friedrich Brodensen's recording of Schubert's "Sei mir gegrüsst" (ca. 1923). Editors, too, were attracted by the practice. They inserted dynamic shadings into their editions of Schubert's songs.[36]

Wolf showed no sympathy for singers who introduced "refinements" not indicated in his scores. His detailed instructions were meant to serve as a rein on "creative" interpretation, which he abhorred. Consequently, "an engagement to sing Wolf's songs [with the composer at the piano] was not to be lightly undertaken. He paid no regard at all to the presence of an audience. If his artistic feelings . . . were outraged . . . he would rebuke the singer audibly even during a public performance." He read publishers' proofs with exacting care, refusing to compromise on any attempts to eliminate detail.[37]

A refinement in expression adored by late romantics was a fade into silence at the close of a song. The music thus seemed to vanish into the infinite, making even applause inappropriate. Wolf, Strauss, and Reger, as illustrated, prized the hushed conclusion. So did Mahler. More than 60 percent of his songs end with *pp* or even softer dynamics. Late-romantic composers did not invent this gentle expression: examples occur throughout the nineteenth century. But they brought the effect to a peak, although in so doing, they risked some negative consequences. Less adept singers who sought to meet the challenge fooled the audience—through skillful facial expressions and gestures—into believing that they were producing decrescendi that faded into nothingness when their voices were actually silent.[38] Late romantics had brought their excessive concentration on expression to a reductio ad absurdum.

When did expressive aesthetics begin to influence lied performance? Monike Hunnius throws light on this question in her comparison of Julius Stockhausen (1826–1906) and Raimund von Zur Mühlen (1854–1931). She considered the more expressive performer the more modern. Thus, although Stockhausen "sustained a transfigured and radiant atmosphere in every song . . . Mühlen deeply affected the souls of his listeners by transporting them into the world of his songs, vigorously and forcefully, so that it seemed to them he was singing about their own joys and sorrows." That commanding authority Felix

Weingartner also equated modern performance with fervor. But for Weingartner, Ludwig Wüllner was the "master of the art of interpretation." Wüllner "reflects his deep inner agitation not only upon his face but also upon those of his listeners." Brahms, Gerhardt, and Culp, as Chapter 4 indicated, agreed that Wüllner was the most expressive and thus the most modern interpreter of lieder. Stockhausen, in contrast, represented the more reserved earlier style. Even the conservative critic Eduard Hanslick considered Stockhausen a bit "cool." He wished Stockhausen would display "more power and fire" in his performance.[39] Before 1830 performers were guided by the aesthetic identified above as pragmatic. Their aim was to please patron and public. Fin-de-siècle performers like Wüllner and Zur Mühlen, however, expected audiences to adjust to their sentiment.

We may conclude that expressive performance reached a peak during the fin de siècle. Leopold von Sonnleithner, Schubert's friend, is again our witness. He censures the "new" style of around 1860 as "extravagant display of emotion." The young singer brimming with health "sings of desperate love with such violence that . . . we fear she may burst into hysteria." Sonnleithner warns the singer to "avoid all those strong effects with which performers today offend the sensitive listener: the shrill shriek of joy or of pain." In earlier days, "many singers sang lieder by Mozart, Schubert, and other masters with telling effect, and without reaching for those means which belong to the musical drama. Such singers are active even today, but their number is small." Though Stockhausen "is unable to escape prevailing taste, he comes closest to that unaffected noble, naive conception, which Schubert himself desired." Sonnleithner objected also to another aspect of the new style of performing lieder—that of singing songs from memory. This permits "the freest play of facial pantomime and gesticulation." Histrionics are difficult to execute when singers perform while holding the music.[40]

When did the elastic tempo favored by late romantics begin to influence lied performance? Not at the beginning of the nineteenth century. Performance then was governed by classicist principles of moderation, balance, and control. Tempo was strict. The degree of tempo modification, Hummel instructed, was to be "almost imperceptible," with such passages carefully marked and limited mainly to "songlike" ones. Schubert "indicated exactly where he wanted a *ritardando* or *accelerando*. . . . He would not tolerate the slightest arbitrariness or the least deviation in tempo."[41] By mid-century, however, "the principle of maintaining a uniform tempo [had] almost been unlearned," Carl Czerny deplored. Liszt, and particularly Wagner, widened the breach considerably between conservatives and radicals. In 1869 Wagner stung musicians favoring uniformity of tempo as "eunuchs of classical chastity" who feared expression. He forcefully enunciated these three principles, destined to characterize the late-romantic praxis: 1) tempo modification be accepted as a sine qua non; 2) sections of sharply contrasting tempo be linked "unobtrusively"; and 3) singing be regarded as the essential way of selecting correct tempo.[42]

The "temperance league," as Wagner called conservatives, eventually lost all ground. By 1883 a journalist observed that Liszt's ideas on tempo, so controversial in 1853, "are today . . . acknowledged as correct." Even Brahms, in his later years, agreed. The conductor Fritz Steinbach (1855–1916), whom Brahms had praised, interpreted Brahms's *Variations on a Theme by Haydn* (Op. 56a) with continual modifications of tempo and even with passages in free rhythm. The concept of tempo modification evidently had run full course, from Hummel's "almost imperceptible" (1828) to Kullak's clearly "perceptible" (1898). Kullak stipulated that composers indicate rallentandos "only where they are most important and significant. . . . Aside from such passages, there are many others in which a perceptible ritardando not only can create a beautiful effect, but actually seems to be a requirement of the music."[43]

The fin de siècle saw the peak in performance of expressive aesthetics. This point contradicts authorities who contend that the fin de siècle marks the beginning of modern music. Lied performance during that period provides little evidence of a fundamental change of style. To the contrary, as we see in this chapter, established styles of performance reached their climax during that period, and the mores of concert life showed no significant change. Study of the cult of personality and the creative performance will corroborate this view.

Expressive aesthetics centered on the artist as creator, as noted in Chapter 3, emphasized consciousness of self. Performers responding to this aesthetic expressed their individuality in every aspect of performance, including their bearing on the concert stage. "There exists no greater praise for an artist today [1904]," Arthur Laser observed, "than that he possess 'individuality.'" Artists posed grandiloquently to convey the impression of unmistakable inspiration. Listeners who with needless murmur or applause dared to distract singers like Wüllner or Zur Mühlen "were often cut by a lethal glance."[44] And audiences encouraged a cult of personality.

Composers responded to this aesthetic in different ways. As accompanist of his own lieder, Strauss provides an unparalleled example. Alfred Orel is our witness: "As I turned to the first lied, Strauss spoke softly to me: 'You need not look at the music, because I don't play it as written.' I learned an art of accompaniment . . . *that has since disappeared.* . . . The printed notes served only as cues for the composer. . . . Strauss doubled the bass line and enriched chords countless times. But he also observed the printed score closely, for instance, in playing 'Morgen.' In 'Cäcili,' however, one could hear the rushing sound of a full orchestra" (emphasis mine). While the singer acknowledged applause, Strauss played "excerpts from his operas that formed a transition to the next lied. . . . He played the famous closing duet from *Rosenkavalier* softly before beginning 'Du meines Herzens Krönelein.'" These were musically closely related to the song in question. Pfitzner sometimes also accompanied songs in this manner, improvising musical links between them.[45] And as mentioned in Chapter 3, composers expressed consciousness of self also by writing autobiographical music.

"Creative interpretation"—*Schöpferische Interpretation*—also makes evident that the ideal lied performance during the fin de siècle was entirely different from the kind we now prize. Today we expect performers to follow the composer's intentions carefully. Late romantics, however, expected the performer "to plunge deeply into the spirit of the work and, to some degree, rebuild it anew," as Arthur Nikisch explains.[46] They considered the performer a *Neuschöpfer*, a creative artist. The printed page, for the Neuschöpfer, was but a sketch of a work. The degree to which outstanding performers "re-created"—recomposed—passages of masterworks, with the approval of the composers, is almost forgotten today. The accompanist Coenraad V. Bos presents a striking example:

> During the rehearsal [of Brahms's *Vier ernste Gesänge*] von Zur Mühlen told me he could not sing the final phrase of St. Paul's words . . . as Brahms had marked them: *diminuendo* and *piano*. . . . The words *die Liebe ist die grössteste unter ihnen,* which are repeated by Brahms, demanded an effect of cumulative power—not anti-climactic reflection. . . . So [Zur Mühlen] instructed me: "When you approach the ending of the fourth song . . . make an intensification of the tone at the reiteration of these words [and] continue the *crescendo* after I have finished singing, to the close of the piano postlude, ending triple *forte*."[47]

With creative interpretation singers sought to illuminate subtleties composers had overlooked in their settings. Zur Mühlen's extreme license indicates the degree to which such freedom was tolerated.

Wagner, who favored such performance, charged that without the interpreter's imagination the score remains forever "soulless pen music—nothing more." During the fin de siècle, even master composers tolerated performance liberty. The older Brahms actually sanctioned Zur Mühlen's license. He told George Henschel that a "thinking, sensible singer may, without hesitation, change a note which . . . is for the time being out of his compass . . . *provided the declamation remains correct and the accentuation does not suffer.*" Strauss approved of Elena Gerhardt's change of the word order in "Traum durch die Dämmerung" (Op. 29, no. 1) from "blaues, mildes Licht" to "mildes, blaues Licht." It enabled her to produce a more effective decrescendo. Strauss even adopted her suggestion in the printed version of the song. Reger "allowed singers any license," according to Schmid-Lindner, "that could be justified."[48]

Critics favored the artist who made changes in tempo, dynamics, and even notation, as long as the performance was artistic. Even the resolute Theodor Helm concluded: "Although Alice Barbi took liberties in singing . . . passages [from Schubert's "Wohin"] . . . the purely subjective effect of her performance was irresistible."[49]

The pendulum of taste soon began to swing in the opposite direction. "Whence this aversion to maintaining a uniform tempo for any length of time?" Weingartner questioned angrily. To restrain performers from taking liberties, composers resorted more and more to measured tempo modifications. The year 1900 marks a dramatic rise in their application. Strauss and Mahler had been attracted earlier by the technique: sixteen tempo indications occur in Strauss's "Epheu," Op. 22, no. 3 (1888), alone. Though Mahler used the technique sparingly in early lieder, it occurs abundantly in his later songs. Reger's keen interest in tempo modification is evident especially in Op. 51 (1900), while Pfitzner's interest started in 1904, after his Op. 15. A score of lesser masters followed suit. The time signatures involved in the changes were not always conventional. After 1900 quintuple time—rare in 1888—and less usual signatures began to appear frequently in the lied.[50]

Interest in changes of time signature signified a revival of "additive rhythm," which had been long absent from western Europe. In one of the ironies of music history, modern composers—Stravinsky, Bartók, and others—employed additive rhythms for a diametrically opposed reason: to regenerate rhythm by saturating it with irresistible power. Mahler, ultra-late romantic, seems, in the rhythmic abstract in example 63, to have had precisely this objective. The passage appears rhythmically ebullient, with irregular accents, like a piece of modern music. Nothing could be farther from the truth. Mahler's intentions in this passage were not to energize but to enervate rhythm.

Few streams are as dissimilar as the modern and the late romantic, the modern a raging torrent, the late romantic after World War I drained and exhausted. The two rhythmic streams flowed side by side through the first generation of the twentieth century, separate and isolated. Small wonder, when one was fed by aged late romanticism and the other by a newly born contemporary idiom. A glance at Franz Schreker's Walt Whitman songs, *Von Ewigen Leben* (pianoforte version, 1923, orchestra version, 1927), suggests the insularity. After rehearsal number 140 (orchestral version), this sequence of time signatures appears: $\frac{3}{4}$, $\frac{3}{8}$, C, $\frac{2}{4}$, $\frac{9}{16}$, $\frac{3}{4}$, $\frac{5}{4}$, and C. Though the sequence is reminiscent of Bartók's *Mikrokosmos* (1926–37), the two works are worlds apart. Schreker, once a young radical, had become a conservative. Here additive rhythm loosens rather than strengthens rhythmic bonds. The number of composers of Schreker's orientation, in 1927 and even thereafter, is surprisingly large. Few produced anything enduring, however. Their view had become worn and moribund, further evidence of the demise of late romanticism.

As the fin de siècle saw the peak in performance of expressive aesthetics, the

Example 63. Mahler: "Urlicht" (*Des Knaben Wunderhorn*), mm. 8–13.

years following World War I witnessed its decline. Discriminating singers began to react against its excesses—the practice of emphasizing emotive words through sobs, slurs, tremolos, and especially portamenti. Julia Culp refused to sing a sweeping portamento near the beginning of Strauss's "Freundliche Vision" even though Strauss requested her to do so. Gerhard Hüsch responded similarly to Richard Trunk's appeal for a "tiny *gefühls* (expressive) portamento" in one of Trunk's songs.[51]

Reaction to creative interpretation also became apparent: "The impression given by performance of this kind," Weingartner protested, "was that . . . [the performer] wanted to divert the attention of the audience from the music to himself." Pfitzner objected that performers wished "under all circumstances to render the music differently from the way it was written. . . . If a passage is composed in one way, they purposely will perform it in another way."[52]

Reaction to the cult of personality started earlier, but at first with little effect. Singers expressed the worst aspect of the cult in their condescending attitude toward the accompanist, who was regarded as little more than a skilled servant and expected to follow their liberties—even to transpose a lied at sight! Bos designated the accompanist's inferior rank as the "role of self-abnegation." Zur Mühlen complimented Bos only when his "playing of Schubert's [*Die schöne Müllerin*] was at all times . . . in accord with my instructions."[53] Wolf, nevertheless, sought to elevate the role of accompanist by entitling his lieder "songs for voice and piano." Conrad Ansorge gave an instruction in uppercase type on the title page of Op. 14 (1900): "WITH REFERENCE TO THE PIANO PARTS, THE FOLLOWING IS EMPHASIZED; THE PIANIST MUST NOT 'MURMUR' WHILE THE VOCALIST IS SINGING AND SUDDENLY PLAY 'LOUD' WHEN HE IS SILENT. THIS OUTMODED CUSTOM MUST BE DROPPED BECAUSE THE *GESÄNGE* IN THIS VOLUME ARE FOR VOICE *AND* PIANO." Wilhelm Altmann noted in 1901: "Recently it has become a custom to select [well-known] artists as accompanists," giving them greater respect thereby. But Chaliapin still ruled the concert stage baronially as late as the 1920s. He often began a song "with an imperious wave of the hand to his accompanist."[54] He, however, was one of the last of the great personalities. After World War I outstanding accompanists like Raucheisen, Bos, and Gerald Moore were consulted on programming and interpretation and found their way into conservatories as teachers and coaches.

The predilection for darkness discussed above is another late-romantic element in sharp contrast with modern color preferences—for airy rooms brightened by picture windows by day and fluorescent light by night and for audio equipment emphasizing high frequencies. Vocal instruction currently in favor trains students to focus on the uvula to produce light-colored brilliance. This preference came as a reaction to the low-larynx technique, which sacrificed brilliance for darkness and volume. The consequence is that today one rarely hears low-larynx sonority even in works where it is appropriate. Gerhard

Hüsch, in an interview, thought the technique and its dark timbre were already forgotten by the 1940s.[55]

After World War I modern musicians, especially in southern Europe, began to rebel against phrasing that "tends towards infinite expansion." Strauss elucidates the point: "It is probable that the pulse of the present generation beats faster than it did in the age of the post-chaise. . . . The younger generation and the Latin peoples rebel against Richard Wagner's 'languors,' obviously incapable of making themselves at home in the emotional and spiritual atmosphere of an earlier age." Predecessors of late romantics also did not share the tendency to overdo the slower tempi. As recently as 1869 Wagner complained that "none of our conductors are courageous enough to take an adagio [in a truly slow] manner." Today, especially in the United States, adagios of late-romantic works are rarely heard in their characteristic long-breathed and animated fashion.[56]

For the late romantic, the "element of feeling" was the foundation of musical art. Rhythm was subservient to it. Mahler perceived: "Whether the overall tempo is a degree faster or slower often depends on the mood of the conductor."[57] Bartók refused to rely on the mood of the performer; he timed the movements of his music to the second. Stravinsky stated the truth for the modern musician: "Rhythm and motion, not the element of feeling, are the foundation of musical art." Modern musicians assign rhythm a primary role, not a secondary role at the service of expression. This reversal is not a mere shift of emphasis but a complete change of thought regarding the role of rhythm.

Lied performance was directly affected. Hermann Prey "insisted again and again" in his master class at the Schubertiade (1992), concerning the interpretation of "Erlkönig": "Sing in rhythm. Even when you change your character you must never change the rhythm. Rhythm is like a block. This piece lives or dies by the rhythm." To maintain tempo, Prey urged students to clap. Recordings of "Erlkönig" made after World War II show that modern performers—Kirsten Flagstad, Dietrich Fischer-Dieskau, and Prey—in telling performances, also treated rhythm as a foundation. Two readings by Fischer-Dieskau with Gerald Moore at the piano are particularly revealing. The later version (1969–72) is rhythmically more strict. The obvious retard Moore inserted (measures 85–86) in the earlier rendition (ca. 1952–54) is barely noticeable in the later reading.[58]

However, none of these earlier performers—Lilli Lehmann (1848–1929), David Bispham (1857–1921), Johanna Gadski (1872–1932), and Sophie Braslau (1892–1935)—treat rhythm "like a block" in their recordings of "Erlkönig." On the contrary, they all treat rhythm elastically in renditions that are intrinsic examples of the late-romantic praxis.[59] And so, too, does Johannes Messchaert (1857–1922), in another fine document of that praxis, a publication he entitled *Eine Gesangstunde* (A vocal lesson). The student is instructed in performance of "Erlkönig" to introduce changes of tone color, dynamics, tempo, and declamation. Liszt's piano-solo transcription of "Erlkönig" provides an early example of the style in question.[60]

Why did late romantics fill the lied with such agogics? The main reason is not the infuriating custom whereby singers simply take liberties with tempo. Nor is it that singers identified the lied as a quasi-solo genre, with interpretative freedom vouchsafed to them. In truth, they considered the lied a personal and intimate musical genre. They were thus guided primarily by the pulse of their inner rhythms rather than by a fixed measure of time imposed from without. Such a performance style, expressing all the changes of mood a singer experienced in interpreting a song, is governed by expressive aesthetics. It characterizes the late-romantic praxis.

chapter eleven

Structural Principles and the
Common Aesthetic

Late romantics, despite their fierce conflicts on aesthetics, were motivated by similar concerns in structuring lieder. When one delves beneath the lied's physiognomy (where diversity is most evident) to an examination of its tissues, remarkable similarities appear. Minor and major composers alike aimed at unity and integration, both in fashioning single lieder and in grouping them into cycles. The formal contribution of these composers represents the culmination of a century's development of the lied, from songs that were noteworthy for their structural clarity to those that are outstanding for their structural ambiguity. After reaching a high point in formal fluidity, however, the majority of late romantics, even radicals like Strauss and Reger, were unwilling to proceed further, to stamp out the old entirely and build a new tradition, as did Schoenberg. As sketched in Chapter 2, they returned to the roots of the lied, the old tradition, to give the Modern Lied new meaning.

The movement toward unity and integration initiated by Beethoven had far-reaching consequences, even in the late-romantic period.[1] According to Michael Raucheisen, singers gave entire programs of songs on the same subject, for example, *Blumenlieder* or *Liebeslieder* (songs about flowers or about love). Critics undertook the campaign discussed in Chapter 2 to unify concert programs. Lied composers wrote sets rather than individual songs. "Don't compose scattered sheets," Joseph Haas informed me that he advised his students. "If you write a song today and another next week, you will have a pile of disconnected things. The result will be confusion. The cycle is your only means of unifying separate songs." Early romantics, in contrast, preferred writing single songs to cycles. Present knowledge is that Schubert conceived only two sets among more than six hundred lieder. Research may require revision of this conclusion.[2]

Late romantics unified songs within collections in several ways—by poet (Wolf's *Moerike-Lieder*) or by subject (Reger's *Schlichte Weisen*). Many composers characteristically aimed also at "äussere Geschlossenheit und innere Zusammenhang," external unity and inner coherence. They selected texts similar in subject and mood, either by a single poet (Mahler's *Kindertotenlieder*) or by several (Courvoisier's *Geistliche Lieder*). Haas consolidated his *Lieder des Glücks* through "the spiritual ideal of *Glück* (luck, fortune) that permeates all its poetry."

Wolf's large songbooks, each framed around the work of one poet, are carefully unified collections rather than compilations of diversified styles of poetry and music. Wolf frequently rearranged the sequence of songs in his volumes to achieve outer unity and inner coherence. "Ein Ständchen Euch zu bringen" from the *Italian Songbook,* originally song number sixteen, was changed to the fourteenth, and back to the sixteenth, before he finally decided that its best position was number twenty-two.[3] The giant *Moerike* set begins with a hymn of hope ("Der Genesene an die Hoffnung") and concludes with a farewell ("Abschied"). Moreover, Wolf sought a characteristic musical atmosphere for each volume. Distinctive performance directions appear in each. *Gequält* (tormented) is common in the *Spanish* (Sacred) *Songs,* though not in the *Italian Songbook,* where *innig* (fervent), *ruhig* (tranquil), and *sanft* (gentle) are frequent. Although chromatics abound in *Goethe* and *Moerike* lieder, they are relatively infrequent in *Eichendorff* songs, especially in the voice parts. In spite of Wolf's habit of setting poetry while in a white heat, he generally had selected nearly all his texts for songbooks well in advance of their composition.

Wolf's mature procedure of composing songbooks around one poet descended from Schumann. His first set (1878) is on a favorite poet of Schumann's, Heinrich Heine. Wolf planned cycles on Heine and on other Schumann poets: one each on Adalbert von Chamisso (1877), Hoffmann von Fallersleben (1878), and Eichendorff (an *In der Fremde* cycle, 1881). But Wolf set only a relatively small number of Schumann's poets successfully. Songs on texts by Robert Reinick—the two *Wiegenlieder* (1882), for example—are among his best. Young Wolf paid little attention to Goethe and Moerike. We do see Loewe's influence, but mainly in Wolf's ballads. Surprisingly enough, the influence of Wagner during Wolf's early years is least apparent in his songs.[4] Schumann remained Wolf's formulative authority in the lied.

Pfitzner also learned from Schumann how to unify separate lieder in his cycles. He elucidated his favored plan in discussing his cantata *Von deutscher Seele:* "The thought of binding together separate lieder [of a cycle] through musical transitions was not new to me. . . . I had conceived this idea from study of the songs of Robert Schumann. His *Eichendorff Lieder [Liederkreis]* (Op. 39) first made the necessity evident to me of not allowing the threads connecting the individual songs ever to break." Pfitzner saw Schumann's great success in Op. 39 in these terms: "The unparalleled intensity of the mood" from each separate song persisted even during pauses between the songs, despite "their drastic brevity." Schumann had created "uninterrupted unity" in the cycle.[5] Although Pfitzner sustained mood from one number to the next in this cantata through instrumental transitions, he abjured such links in his lieder. Pfitzner felt that mood ought to link one song to the next, as it did in his settings, particularly of Eichendorff. Pfitzner's mature cycles thus are not collections of disparate lieder but groups of songs with inner unity.

Because late romantics regarded the cycle as indivisible, several composers disapproved of extracting songs from cycles for separate performance. Pfitzner specified on the first page of his *Alte Weisen* (Op. 33): "These eight songs as a whole have an intimate connection and should only be performed together and in the proper order." Mahler's direction for *Kindertotenlieder* is similar: "These five songs were conceived as an inseparable whole and should be performed without pause." He went further in behalf of cyclic unity. "The continuity of the [*Kindertotenlieder*] must be sustained and not interrupted by disturbances such as applause at the end of each number." The pause between songs is an integral part of the cycle. It permits the atmosphere of one song to run uninterruptedly into another. Occasionally the length of a pause was specified. Conrad Ansorge wanted the pause between the second and third songs of *Waller im Schnee* (Op. 14) to be longer than any other within the group. Franz Schreker stated that "Das Gras," the second song of his *Zwei lyrische Gesänge,* "should be sung directly after the preceding one with nearly no pause between them." Mahler prescribed "a pause of no less than five minutes" between the first and second movements of his Second Symphony.

Late romantics achieved cycle unity in other ways. The "pedal tone" of the fourteenth song of Zilcher's *Fünfzehn kleine Lieder* (Op. 37), the composer instructed, should "be sustained into the next song." Heinrich Kaspar Schmid joined the five songs of his *Der Pilger* (Op. 33) similarly. Cycle unity was, of course, also achieved thematically, by beginning and ending the set with the same music, as in Schumann's *Frauenliebe und Leben.* Zilcher's *Dehmel Zyklus* (Op. 25) and his *Aus dem Hohenlied Salomonis* (Op. 38) are fin-de-siècle examples. Better known, of course, is Mahler's *Kindertotenlieder,* in which the second and final songs are thematically interlinked. Another integrating device was to build two or more songs on the same motive, as Wolf did with his two "Peregrina" songs and with "Der Knabe und das Immlein" and "Ein Stündlein wohl vor Tag." Haas's *Kuckuckslieder* (Op. 37) are unified by a cuckoo-call in the piano part of each song. Hans Sommer adapted the Wagnerian leitmotive system to his lied cycles. Ansorge sought still closer union in *Amaranths Waldeslieder.* He quotes music from the second song and words and music from the first song as the opening and closing, respectively, of the final song (the fifth). Ansorge conceived his *Vigilien* in one movement of separate sections rather than as a group of independent songs. His song cycles are among the tightest structures in the late-romantic lied.

Instrumental transitions serve as another means of linking separate songs within cycles, like those between "Helle Nacht" and "Zuversicht" in Zilcher's *Dehmel Zyklus.* While accompanying at Liederabende, as noted in Chapter 10, Strauss and Pfitzner improvised transitions between the songs. Perhaps Beethoven's *An die ferne Geliebte* was the model for this kind of integration. Fin-de-siècle composers, however, rarely joined separate songs of a cycle with transitions. Zilcher offered the choice of performing "Musikantengruss," "Abendlandschaft," and "Der Einsiedler" of his *Eichendorff* cycle, Op. 60, either interlinked with transitions or as separate songs.

In their quest for unity and integration, late romantics disparaged the old tradition and its lied structures—strophic, varied strophic, and sectional forms—as seriated and thoroughly antiquated. In practice, however, they observed tradition more than is generally assumed.

Strophic and Varied Strophic Forms

Strophic form—one of the simplest of song structures—is ideally suited to folk and lyric poetry. Tradition decrees that composers of folk or art songs set but one stanza of a metrical poem to a vocal melody.[6] In art songs, a simple accompaniment provides harmony to support the melody's contour and strengthen its cadences. The resulting unit—here called a strophe—may be repeated for each subsequent stanza in the poem.

Strophic songs are agglomerates of "separate and independent" strophes, separate because the strophes are never joined, independent because any strophe may in performance be omitted. They illustrate symmetry in music, since each strophe is the same shape. They also epitomize seriation, through repetition and addition: strophe, pause, strophe, pause. As such, the strophic form parallels seriation in Doric architecture: column, space, column, space.[7]

This neat and orderly form played a prominent role in late eighteenth-century monumental collections of folk songs like the *Blumenlese* (1782) and the *Mildheimliches Liederbuch* (1799). Strophic form was cultivated less and less by successive generations of nineteenth-century composers, least of all at the century's close. Mahler was outspoken: "Loewe . . . cannot free himself from the old [strophic] form. . . . You will no longer find [exact] repetition in my songs . . . precisely because within music there lies the law of perpetual growth, continual development—just as in the world. . . . This development must be one of progress, otherwise it is worthless."[8] Late romantics disparaged strophic form as "movement without progress"—the music leads nowhere! It always returns to its beginning.

The decline of strophic form during the century stimulated increased interest in its offshoot: varied strophic form, a kind of variation in which the melody and/or accompaniment is modified to reflect changes in the poetry. Early romantics generally varied the strophic procedure in moderation. Although late romantics, following tradition, sometimes did likewise, they tended to vary strophes freely with respect to length and contour, so lavishly, at times, that the underlying strophic design is disguised. A strophe may be varied by omitting phrases, by presenting others in a different order, or by developing a motive from an earlier strophe in a later one. Late romantics often did not hesitate to alter a poem's organization to adapt it to their musical plan.

Wolf, like most late romantics, set folkish poetry in traditional designs, though, in his later years, rarely in strict strophic form.[9] In "Ein Stündlein wohl vor Tag," a swallow, before dawn, softly confides to a girl that her lover is unfaithful. Moerike intensifies the poem's mood as it reaches its painful climax in the final (third) stanza. Wolf's setting parallels both the poem's folk-song style and its intensification of mood, the first by strophic repetition of two simple phrases, the second by the setting of each of three strophes a half tone higher—proceeding from G minor to A flat to A minor. Further, he directs that the second strophe be sung "with intensified expression" and the final one "painfully." Wolf's bow to strophic design may be traditional, but the manner in which he produces continuous flow to climax is far from conventional. Robert Franz, in contrast, set the same poem as a simple folkish song in AA'A form.

Wolf generally modified voice parts more than piano parts in his varied strophic songs. Alterations range from slight changes in certain lieder to complete recomposition in others. In the freest kinds, strophic repetition is readily apparent only in the piano part, his objective being to avoid "movement without progress." Wolf linked strophes so smoothly that the listener often is unaware that a strophe is over and its varied repetition under way, as in the fiery "Erstes Liebeslied eines Mädchen." The remarkable erotic poem by Moerike, pastor of Cleversulzbach (Württemberg), likens a young girl's first experience of love to a snake that shoots into the heart, where it twists, burrows, and torments its owner. The poem's naïveté is expressed not only through its youth-oriented subject, but through its agitation and irregular verse, all of which Wolf sustains musically. The voice part, short impassioned outbursts, is spun over a strophic design in the piano part. Continuous movement toward the climax is ensured, despite the traditional form in the piano part. For the song's eight strophes are each in different keys, attainable only by chromatic or enharmonic means. The keys are A, C sharp, E flat, E, A flat, C, D flat, and A. Further, the strophes are linked by smooth modulations and by the voice part, which overlaps some of them. Some strophes are varied harmonically; in one instance (mm. 7 to 14), Wolf presents only the second half of the strophe. The listener's attention, as a consequence, is not focused on the song's formal outline but on its forward movement. "*Erstes Liebeslied eines Mädchen,*" Wolf exclaimed, "is by far the best thing that I have done up to now [1888]. Compared with this song everything earlier was child's play."[10]

Mahler also fused tradition and fin-de-siècle modernity in volkstümlich song. But Mahler's means differ radically from Wolf's. "Um schlimme Kinder artig zu machen" is a brilliant example from his early maturity. The *Knaben Wunderhorn* poem on which the song is based consists of four symmetrical stanzas of four lines each, the kind of song that lends itself readily to strophic settings. Mahler's structure seems to mirror the poem's rustic simplicity perfectly. Closer examination, however, indicates that the structure is irregular. Mahler shaped the poem's four symmetrical stanzas as two asymmetrical musical strophes: A (mm. 1–19) and A' (mm. 20–38). Each strophe is composed of two smaller segments of irregular length: A = a + b; segment *a* is nine measures long (mm. 4–12), while *b* is seven measures (mm. 13–19). Further, the segments are tonally dissimilar: *a* is in the tonic major, *b* in the relative minor. Still further, Mahler altered the poem to fit his musical design. To accommodate the larger *a* segments, he expanded the poem's first stanza by repeating and adding words, borrowing two lines from the second stanza, and inserting his own refrain: *ku-ku-kuk!* Further, the piano solos also are of irregular length: three bars each—the prelude (mm. 1–3), interlude (mm. 20–22), and postlude (mm. 39–41). And so, too, are the vocal strophes, fifteen measures apiece (mm. 4–18, 23–37). A final point, striking indeed, that indicates how Mahler fused fin-de-siècle modernity with tradition: the two irregular vocal strophes appear to be periods of traditional length, sixteen measure each (mm. 4–19 and 23–38), because Mahler added a measure to each in the piano part (m. 19 and m. 38) to create the semblance of folkish convention.

As one might expect, the most conservative of Mahler's published varied strophic songs are his earliest. "Phantasie" is as strict as any by the early romantics. "Serenade" and "Hans und Grethe" are only slightly modified, although the latter is already a gem of originality. Mahler applies a means of varying strophic form that he favored in his maturity: the insertion of instrumental interludes of irregular length between strophes. Mahler inserted four interludes of greatly differing lengths into the third strophe of "Lob des hohen Verstandes." These bring each interlude into prominence, since each appears unexpectedly and is constructed from striking motives. Such treatment of varied strophic form provides his mature songs with the fluidity associated with through-composed lieder.

The older Mahler continued to mix fin-de-siècle modernism and tradition in volkstümlich song. He might, in varied strophic designs, greatly modify one phrase within a strophe while hardly touching another, as in "Verlor'ne Müh'." Its first strophe is built on five phrases and so, too, are the remaining strophes. Though Mahler hardly touches the first phrase in each strophic repetition, the third phrase reappears each time in a different key. By varying the first phrase least of all, Mahler reaffirms the song's basic traditional design.

The mature composer varied strophes in other interesting ways: by changing the order of the phrases within them, altering the length of some phrases but not others, or occasionally omitting one phrase entirely. Nearly every strophe of "Des Antonius von Padua Fischpredigt" begins with the same folkish phrase (see exx. 64a, 64b, and 64c), but Mahler omits the first phrase in the fourth strophe, starting instead with a modified version of the second phrase (see X^2 in ex. 64d. Bracket X presents the second phrase in its original version; X^1 and X^2 show its modifications).

As mentioned, all but two songs of Strauss's first published cycle, Op. 10, are strophic. "Zueignung" is the strictest, yet even here surging movement in the

Example 64. Mahler: "Des Antonius von Padua Fischpredigt" (*Des Knaben Wunderhorn*), (a) mm. 9–16; (b) mm. 29–32; (c) mm. 64–67, 72–75; (d) mm. 109–112.

third strophe produces formal flexibility and effective climax. Such structure, nevertheless, is in remarkable contrast to the composer's mature songs, which Ernest Newman had censured as "absolutely formless." In maturity, Strauss sought continuous movement unimpeded by the partitions of traditional forms, even when writing varied strophic songs. His strophes, like Mahler's, differ greatly in length and shape. Yet he modified some so liberally that only the first bar or the initial motive resembles the corresponding segment of the original strophe. Strauss's liking for formal fluidity is evident even in the early "Nur Mut!" (Op. 17, no. 5). Only the opening bars of the first, second, and third strophes are similar (see brackets *a, b,* and *c* in example 65). Each begins in a different key, the first in E-flat major, the second in G major and the third in E minor. Interludes linking the strophes, too, are irregularly shaped: the first is four bars, the second a half-bar, and the third one-and-a-half bars. The song's five-bar prelude returns as a postlude, expanded into seven bars.

Most interesting, Strauss resorted to the vigor of sonata form—statement, development, and recapitulation—to impart to varied strophic form a feeling of perpetual growth: movement to climax. "Ich trage meine Minne" (Op. 32, no. 1) of 1896 is in monothematic sonata form. The theme, graciously lyrical (one of the composer's most attractive) is presented in the first strophe, developed in the second, and recapitulated in the third. This typically Straussian theme consists of short phrases, melodic fragments, separated one from the other by rests.

Example 65.   Strauss: "Nur Mut!" (Schack), Op. 17, no. 5, (a) mm. 6–7; (b) mm. 18–19; (c) mm. 27–28.

Strauss extracts motive X of example 66 from the theme and presents it in the piano part of the first strophe (mm. 9–10) to bridge the separate vocal phrases. Agitation in the piano part—produced by syncopation and change of mode (m. 19)—initiates the development. Here Strauss compresses motive X into a tightly knit modulatory sequence that he builds to the song's climax at the close of the second strophe. The passage is a master stroke, a free stretto based on X, which produces climax rather than the slackening of movement inherent in strophic repetition. Strauss introduced the principle of development in many songs, even in his earliest published lieder, such as "Allerseelen" (Op. 10, no. 8).

Wolf, Mahler, and Pfitzner also extracted thematic material from an initial strophe for development in a central one. Pfitzner's "Sie haben heut' Abend Gesellschaft," Op. 4, no. 2 (1888–89), for example, resembles sonata form even more than Strauss's song. The poem, by Heine, depicts an anguished figure standing in darkness below a closed, brightly lit window, listening to party music heard faintly from within. The party's hostess is his former lover. Pfitzner's corner strophes (the first and final strophes), like Strauss's, are statement and recapitulation sections. But Pfitzner presents two principal ideas that contrast thematically and tonally.[11] A six-bar instrumental prelude (mm. 1–6), the initial exposition, takes the form of a long melodic line that encloses the song's two main themes, from which motives X and Y are drawn (exx. 67a and 67b). Both motives are combined, transformed, broken into fragments, and compressed into sequences in the central strophe, the development. Initial development has already occurred in the exposition's repetition (mm. 7 ff.). Pfitzner weaves both motives throughout the song and brings them to climax in its closing bars. Example 67c shows X, occurring rhythmically on different parts of the beat, in imitation of and in combination with Y. Motive X is transformed no less than twenty times; Y is treated similarly.

Mahler's *Das Lied von der Erde*—long acknowledged as an anomaly: the lied cycle as symphony—is not the first example even by Mahler of a lied in sonata form. The four strophes of "Nun will die Sonne," from *Kindertotenlieder*, an

Example 66.   Strauss: "Ich trage meine Minne" (Henckell), Op. 32, no. 1, mm. 32–35.

Example 67.   Pfitzner: "Sie haben heut' Abend Gesellschaft" (Heine), Op. 4, no. 2, (a) m. 1; (b) m. 5; (c) mm. 25–26.

earlier example, function as exposition, restatement, development, and reprise. Donald Mitchell energetically pursues this analysis. A cardinal motive from its first strophe (m. 14; see *M* in ex. 43a) undergoes "vigorous and substantial *orchestral* development" in the third strophe (mm. 58 ff.), investing this strophe with the function of both development section and climax. Mitchell sees this strophe in "almost identical relationship" to the third strophe of "Das Trinklied vom Jammer der Erde" (mm. 203–325) of *Das Lied*.[12] But what remarkable stylistic development "Das Trinklied" represents!

Das Lied has endured decades of debate as to whether it is a symphony or lied cycle, debate which Hermann Danuser, Mitchell, and Stephen Hefling continue. Danuser identifies its four grand sections as comprising exposition, varied repetition, development, and reprise, while Mitchell designates them strophes I through IV. But Danuser's reference to its "symphonic strophe" and Mitchell's comment that *Das Lied*'s "two 'drinking' songs . . . frame the symphony's first part" indicate their acknowledgment that *Das Lied* fuses elements of both genres.[13] In truth, one cannot discuss the work without reference to the fusion in question. Argument arises mainly from differences of emphasis.

Can one resolve the question of whether *Das Lied* is symphony or song cycle? If we take the premise that the lied is vocal, lyrical, homophonic, and cast into traditional song forms and that the symphony is instrumental, governed by structures and techniques of instrumental music, we conclude that Mahler's contribution is unprecedented: he converted lied cycle into symphony. A review of nineteenth-century lied history, however, yields a different conclusion. The lied was already evolving toward the ever-greater structural refinement associated with instrumental music. Strauss, Pfitzner, Mahler, and Wolf utilized development to free lied forms of unyielding repetition. Mahler, master of the orchestral song, attained the ultimate expression of this refinement. (*Kindertotenlieder* exemplifies a penultimate step.) *Das Lied* represents the peak of this evolution.

Sectional Forms

Sectional forms are of great variety and importance in nineteenth-century lieder. Repetition and contrast are inherent in all sectional forms except, of course, binary (AB). The most common is ternary form, the so-called standard song pattern: statement, contrast, repetition (ABA). Repetition and contrast are, of course, intrinsic also in bar (AAB) form, rondo designs (like ABACABA), and such patterns as ABABA and ABCBA.

Conversational poetry provides abundant illustrations of how repetition and contrast serve as essential elements in the union of words and music. When a lied composer uses the same musical section for the same speaker and different sections for different speakers, a kind of rondo form can result, as in "Nachtzügler," the second of Max von Schillings's *Glockenlieder* (Songs of bells, Op. 22). Here the cathedral spirit asks whether all of the bell's rays have returned so that the bell can resound brilliantly. Three rays are still missing. Each, in turn, is questioned and scolded for late arrival. The repeated interrogation, accompanied by the different answers, yields this ABACADA rondo scheme.

Sectional forms serve as intimate companions also for volkstümlich lieder. Wolf's outstanding "Fussreise" provides an interesting example. Though Moerike cast his folkish poem into highly irregular verse, Wolf created the folkish effect, as custom dictates, by shaping the irregular verse into a traditional musical form. He repeated the first vigorous musical section as the final one. The consequence is a rousing Wanderlied in ternary scheme.

Repetition and contrast were cardinal elements for early romantics seeking to compose lieder with clear-cut formal designs. Balanced repetition—statement, contrast, and restatement—exemplifies a major formal ideal followed and advanced by late romantics. Let us look at some of the inimitable ways in which they treated this ideal

Repetition. Mahler's verdict—that "each repetition is already a lie. A work of art must evolve perpetually, like life"—reminds us that late romantics, certainly Mahler, eschewed exact repetition.[14] Yet not only strophic but sectional songs employ repetition, to achieve the seemingly incompatible: convergence of tradition and fin-de-siècle modernism. Wolf's procedure in sectional as in strophic songs was to spin a freely ordered voice part over a relatively stricter design in the piano part. While the piano part of "Im Frühling" states this modified sectional form as AA'BA and codetta, its vocal melody, continually reshaped, creates the impression the song is through-composed. Strauss and Pfitzner had similar objectives but used different means: they introduced stricter forms in the voice part and diversified forms in the piano. This enabled Strauss to interpret the poetry freely in ever-changing multicolored harmony and Pfitzner to give greater prominence to traditional form in folkish songs like "Gretel" (Op. 11, no. 5) and "Unter der Linden" (Op. 24, no. 1), since the voice part usually attracts more attention in performance.

According to custom, late romantics set each refrain to the same music but in inimitable ways. They would often modify the music to reflect the particular shade of meaning the refrain would acquire in its new poetic context. Even the conservative Pfitzner treated refrains in this manner, as in "Zugvogel" (Op. 6, no. 3), where an exhausted migratory bird's struggle to reach land is retold in the refrain: "Nur matt noch regt er die Schwingen breit / Und das Land und die Rast noch so weit, so weit." The refrains gradually reveal that the bird is losing its battle for life. In one, Pfitzner underscores (mm. 32–33) "und das Land und die Rast noch so weit, so weit" (and land and rest still so far), while the final refrain highlights (m. 54) *matt* (exhausted) and places greatest emphasis (mm. 59–60) on *so weit, so weit* (so far, so far). Dramatic pauses inserted during the refrain's course make it resemble the exhausted gasps of the migratory bird, too tired to reach its destination.[15]

Strauss subjects the refrain of "Für funfzehn Pfennige" (Op. 36, no. 2) to ten distinctly different transformations, creating formal unity through the diversity while underscoring the poem's humor. Mahler's grim "Das irdische Leben" presents an unforgettable example. Although the child's pleas—"give me bread else I shall die"—are similarly set, we hear the child's implorations become frantic in the course of the song. The serrated melodic profile of the first statement (ex. 68a) is, in the final unanswered plea, jagged (ex. 68b). Mahler's treatment of the final line, "The child lay dead in the coffin" (ex. 68c), mercilessly accents the poem's grim implications.

Treatment by late romantics of balanced repetition provides other striking examples of the way they merged tradition with fin-de-siècle modernism. They bowed to tradition by beginning a song's corner sections with the same or similar music. They modified the final section increasingly as it approached its ending, however, so that the concluding bars of the corner sections bear little resemblance to each other. The initial effect, as the repetition begins, is of a lied in ternary form. The ultimate impression, however, is of a free-form song.

Strauss wrote many engaging songs in this form. He preferred corner sections of unequal length. In "Wozu noch Mädchen" (Op. 19, no. 1), he restates only five of the eleven bars of the initial section as its closing section. Lengths are reversed in "Und dann nicht mehr" (1929, Op. 87, no. 3, in the complete edition),

Example 68. Mahler: "Das irdische Leben" (*Des Knaben Wunderhorn*), (a) mm. 11–14; (b) mm. 79–82; (c) mm. 119–123.

where the shorter first section (nine bars) is "balanced" by the longer concluding section of fourteen bars.

Balanced repetition may occur in the piano part alone, when a song's prelude returns as its postlude. Late romantics, even Strauss in his maturity, when he veered furthest from convention, composed many examples. In so doing, however, he shifted the unit of balance from greater to lesser prominence, a shift that in architecture parallels double and single stress. In double stress, "two sides [of a cathedral] jut out or carry flanking towers." In single stress, "the sides subordinate, [yield] stress to the center, which may or may not jut out."[16] Double stress, like ternary form, brings the flanking corner sections into prominence. Single stress shifts attention from the sides—the preludes and postludes—to the main body.

Late romantics displayed individuality in their treatment of balanced repetition. They preferred psychological to actual balance. Unlike their classicist predecessors, who applied balanced repetition to achieve symmetry, late romantics aimed at asymmetry, a fundamental aspect of all late-romantic aesthetics, as evident in musical phraseology, discussed below, as in their art and interior design.[17]

Contrast. Late romantics created contrast in an entirely different manner from their baroque and classical predecessors, who preferred to juxtapose dissimilar material for this purpose. Late romantics characteristically used similar music, developing ideas from a previous section to make the contrasting one. Our example, Wolf's "Nimmersatte Liebe"—in ABA′ ternary form—seems to have strongly divergent music for its B section. Closer examination, however, reveals that the composer created contrast here with similar music and, in so doing, integrated text and music intimately. Moerike elaborates on love's splendors in the second stanza of this humorous poem, "Insatiable Love." Wolf does likewise in setting this stanza as section B. Its rhythm, however, is derived from the motive to which *die Lieb'* (love) is set in the song's opening measure (see *X* in ex. 69a). Wolf shapes this motive in rhythmic imitation between voice and piano parts to create the impression that both parts are breathlessly uttering *die lieb'* over and over again, with "panting" rests (ex. 69b).

Mahler administered contrast similarly, though again his objectives could hardly be more remote from Wolf's. He placed the disparate scenes of "Lied des Verfolgten im Turm"—a prisoner in dark dungeon and his sweetheart in sunny fields—in sharp contrast: solemn A sections for the prisoner and sunny B sections for the fields. Yet each is constructed largely from the same music. The first (mm. 11–13) and final (mm. 23–25) phrases of section B are slightly modified versions of the music sung by the prisoner (mm. 7–8). Further, motives from section A form most of the tissue of the B sections, as examples 70a (the prisoner) and 70b (the maiden) indicate.

Late romantics tended to soften contrast even when they sought the strongest kinds. The first of Mahler's *Lieder eines fahrenden Gesellen* paints in ternary form the melancholy Wayfarer (section A), his joy in nature (section B), and his return to melancholia (section A'). Mahler weakens the contrast between sections A and B by reintroducing the "wedding motive" from A into section B (mm. 55–56). In so doing, he reveals not only the source of the Wayfarer's sorrow—his beloved's marriage to another—but the implication that the Wayfarer's pleasure in nature is, consequently, alloyed. Contrast in "Lied des verfolgten im Turm" is similar. Although the beloved is free, the implication—divulged again only in the music—is that her joy in nature is saddened by thoughts of her lover in the dungeon.

Late romantics, we might conclude, imparted new meaning to repetition; for them it is continuous progression rather than a return to the beginning simply to recommence. And they conferred upon contrast the impression of the "old" appearing as "new," by shaping preexistent material to sound like fresh, contrasting sections. Composers like Mahler may have softened contrast, but they deepened its implications through subtle craft. They assigned to contrast the role of expressing a poem's unstated, implied, or symbolic connotations.

Example 69. Wolf: "Nimmersatte Liebe" (Moerike), (a) m. 5; (b) mm. 21–22.

Example 70. Mahler: "Lied des Verfolgten im Turm" (*Des Knaben Wunderhorn*), (a) mm. 1–2; (b) mm. 39–41.

Phraseology. Irregular phraseology is at the core of fin-de-siècle lieder. The impression of structural orderliness, that is, eight-measure units with strict antecedent and consequent phrase organization, does, however, occur, especially to underscore folkish effect in volkstümlich songs. Wolf sought this effect in setting passages of Moerike's folkish "Fussreise." Poet, however, thwarted composer with irregular verses, especially in one passage: the text (ll. 16–18) contains only three lines of the same length. Wolf needed a fourth. Instead of following the old custom of repeating or inserting words to realize his objective, Wolf introduced the "missing" phrase into the piano part (see *a'*, ex. 71) to complete the first of the two melodic sequences.[18]

The late-romantic approach to structure, as suggested by "Fussreise," was thoroughly unlike that of lied composers of around 1800. The earlier composers primarily structured vocal melody. But the late romantics shaped voice and instrumental parts individually, creating the effect of structural dialogue, as did Mahler in "Urlicht": he extended a four- into a five-bar phrase by interpolating motive *X* (see ex. 74, m. 54) into the instrumental music.

Though late romantics gave some phrases of volkstümlich song symmetry,

Example 71. Wolf: "Fussreise" (Moerike), mm. 47–54.

they organized a great many asymmetrically. Units of three, five, six, and ten measures occur in Wolf's "Fussreise," despite its undeniable folkishness. Mahler, Strauss, and Schoenberg went beyond Wolf, in whose lieder four-measure phrases turn up with surprising frequency. They actually favored asymmetric order. Irregular phraseology permeates Mahler's volkstümlich songs. "Wo die schönen Trompeten blasen," for instance, has nine-, eleven-, and thirteen-bar phrases. Its first vocal melody could have been two balanced four-measure units had Mahler not disdained such convention. Instead he created a nine-measure unit by repeating one bar (m. 27), the motive setting *leise*.

In his youth Reger was especially fond of asymmetric phraseology despite his admiration for Brahms. Indeed, this predilection even carried over to his later years, when he exerted every effort to simplify his style. Hugo Riemann apparently had no enduring influence on Reger when he induced his students, Reger among them, to construct strict periods. Gerd Sievers relates this interesting point: "A strong dependence on Riemann's system of phrasing is found in Reger's early works only, and not always even in these. . . . Reger considered himself bound to his teacher only while his student." Though one finds four- and eight-bar units in his mature lieder, Reger preferred asymmetric patterns of five, nine, ten, and eleven measures. Such phraseology is at the core of Reger's style and occurs even in his folkish *Schlichte Weisen* and Kinderlieder. Nor does the asymmetry arise from the kinds of poetry he set. Irregular phraseology is also a chief characteristic of Reger's instrumental music. He even repeated rhythmic patterns and ostinatos asymmetrically. His objective in instrumental and vocal music alike was for continuity of movement. In the lied, Reger would overlap phrases in the piano and voice parts or within the piano part itself or dovetail the close of one phrase with the beginning of another. The result is a thick, interlaced texture without clear-cut units.[19]

Through-Composed Structures

Late romantics considered *Durchkomponiert* (through-composed) structures ideal media for integrating music and poetry in the closest union.[20] Composers are not obliged to use a preexistent musical form for through-composed songs. On the contrary, they may devise a special design for each poem. The requirement to provide new music for each change of thought or mood in verse permits composers to evolve musical ideas that change "perpetually, like life itself": Mahler's musical ideal. This latitude, one might assume, would encourage late romantics to invent great varieties of through-composed structures, lavishly free in shape. In fact, their general practice, certainly that of the masters, was the reverse. As a consequence, broad formal categories emerge. We might examine four of these and their subtypes, from stricter to freer shapes: sectional, episodic, motivic, and free configurations.[21]

Through-composed sectional structures. Form in this category is derived from nonrecurring large sections (unlike those described in sectional forms, above). Three subtypes are prominent. In one, sections contrast with each other with respect to length, key, texture, mood, or subject. German analysts identify this subtype as *Kontrastformen.* Our example, Wolf's farcical "Zur Warnung," has three strongly contrasting units. Section A (and its instrumental prelude) is tonally blurred, whispered, and rhythmically weak because the text concerns an inebriate who just awakened after a night of revelry. The voice enters with the appropriate instruction: "hoarse and hollow." Section B, squarely in A minor, is a humorous epistle, in which our reveler suddenly summons the muse for verse. He abruptly dismisses her, however, explaining in a recitative (section C) that no one should call upon the gods when he has a hangover.

In a second subtype, sections—articulated by cadences, caesuras, or more elusive divisions—are not in sharp contrast, in fact, some may be unified by similar material. Our example, Wolf's "An die Geliebte," in four sections, is a masterpiece of poetic and musical union. Structurally, the song is congruent with Moerike's poem, a Petrarchan sonnet: an octave of two quatrains and a sestet of two tercets. Wolf's first two sections set the sonnet's octave. A syncopated figure from the first section flows into the second, unifying the two quatrains within the octave. Chordal tremolos, comprising the third and fourth sections, link the two tercets within the sestet. Wolf even parallels (mm. 23–24) the dash Moerike inserts into the final tercet to divide it in half. At that point, chordal tremolos become repeated-note chords. Though sections are carefully outlined, Wolf's inner organization—the pervading syncopation and unifying motives (see bars 14 and 20)—creates for songs like "An die Geliebte" a feeling of continuous movement, a dramatic continuity.[22]

Sections in the third subtype, the freest of the three, function like steps rising to climax. Here the listener's attention is focused on emotive rather than on structural elements. These are called *Steigerungsformen* (forms in gradation).[23] Drive to climax is the unifying element. The steps are produced musically by changes of note value, tempo, and/or dynamics. Faster time values and increase in dynamics are common features. In Reger's "Der König bei der Krönung" (Op. 70, no. 2), in two sections, the basic rhythm of the first section (♪ ♫♫) is replaced in the second by thirty-seconds. Reger underscores the increase in rhythmic activity with a corresponding increase in dynamics ($pp < ff$). Examples occur in Reger's most dramatic songs, Op. 51 and Op. 75.

Episodic structures are built from small divisions rather than sections. Though episodes may be short, they can serve well as constructive elements when skillfully chiseled and set into rows. Two kinds are easily apparent: those with and those without motivic interrelations. The first, more tightly organized, kind is illustrated by Wolf's delightful "Elfenlied." Here each of Moerike's wisplike images is musically paralleled with a new delicate, sparkling motive. Each fresh motive is spun into an episode. New episodes are constantly introduced. Wolf prevents these episodes from becoming disconnected by overlapping older with newer motives as the interlinked chain of *X, Y,* and *Z* in example 72 demonstrates.

The second kind of episode—chains of discrete, motivically unrelated episodes—occurs oftener in theory than in works by master composers, who preferred tighter order, even for illustrative lieder. Songs constructed in part from dissimilar episodes do occur, however. Strauss wrote several. "Himmelsboten"

Example 72. Wolf: "Elfenlied" (Moerike), (a) mm. 21–22; (b) mm. 41–42.

(Op. 32, no. 5), which Ernest Newman condemned as melodic and harmonic nonsense, is one (see Chapter 1). Strauss set the first three of the poem's six stanzas as disjunct episodes. After measure 37, however, Strauss restates in broad passages some earlier episodes to achieve stylistic integrity. Dissimilar episodes follow each other in rapid succession also in "Herr Lenz" (Op. 37, no. 5) and other songs. But here, too, as in other songs, Strauss restates motives from earlier episodes.

Motivic development. This category comprises songs built entirely on one or two motives. Although many late romantics attempted to construct entire songs from single motives, few succeeded the way Wolf did. He unified lied structure tightly through motivic development, while intimately integrating music and text. His ingenious solutions become models. Two related but different subtypes serve as illustrations. In the first and most compact kind, a basic motivic gestalt is discernible throughout the song. Here Wolf applies techniques of development associated with eighteenth-century instrumental music. In the second, less compact, type the motive is "transformed" like that of a symphonic poem or a leitmotive in Wagnerian music drama. Some transformations seem so free that their relation to the original motive may not be immediately discernible.

Wolf's "Mein Liebster ist so klein," with its tightly knit motivic development, is an example of the first kind. The basic motive X ($\overset{x}{\square}$) serves to image the "tiny" lover. The motive pulsates anew in nearly all of the song's sixty-eight measures by means of several devices, for instance: intervallic expansion (m. 17), embellishment (m. 31), and inversion and rhythmic augmentation (m. 46).

"Abschied" illustrates Wolf's fabulous skill in paralleling with a single motive (X) the numerous circumstances of Moerike's satire on the critics. The song begins as an unwelcome stranger bursts into a young man's room one evening (ex. 73a), proclaiming: "The honor is mine, your critic, sir, to be!" He raises a lantern high enough to cast the shadow of the young man's face on the wall, which he examines unflatteringly. Here motive X (introduced in example 73a) undergoes two transformations. The first suggests the young man's growing irritation, for the motive is treated climactically as a rising sequence of augmented arpeggios (ex. 73b). The second, following this climax—a sequence of augmented chords—suggests further irritation. This time the motive is in diminution (ex. 73c). Upon his honor, the young man cannot recall the critic's other censures. A clever fragmentation of the motive (ex. 73d) captures the situation's irony. When the intruder finally decides to leave, the young man, as was customary, lights his way to the stairs. An impish trick (ex. 73e) forms in the young man's mind—to give the critic a little kick, "good humoredly," of course, on his backside. "Oh, was that a clattering, stumbling tumble!" (ex. 73f) as the intruder crashed down the steps. "Never have I seen a man descend steps so fast," the young man sings and dances jubilantly to the final transformation (ex. 73g), a gay waltz, altogether ingenious.

Example 73. Wolf: "Abschied" (Moerike), (a) mm. 1–5; (b) mm. 28–31; (c) mm. 32–33; (d) mm. 62–63; (e) m. 70; (f) mm. 78–79; (g) mm. 100–103.

Free configurations. Lieder in this category comprise the freest of through-composed structures, the kind once regarded as most characteristically late romantic. These structures are not unified by distinct sections, episodes, or motives. In some, musical form seems to depend almost entirely on the poetry for coherence. Although the structures may be of several kinds, two basic types serve as illustrations: *Ausdruckskonstante* forms and digressive rambling forms. We turn for both to Reger, who contributed characteristic examples of each.

Ausdruckskonstante forms sustain one invariable element of expression, be it a dynamic marking or a persistent note value, mood, or texture. Songs of this kind are of great variety and, in Reger, are cast in different forms. They include Stimmungslieder like "Traum durch die Dämmerung" (Op. 35, no. 3). Their piano parts—structurally of great importance—often consist of stock accompaniment figures of seemingly endless variety.[24] They all, however, tend to sustain mood derived from the poetry. "Trost" (Op. 15, no. 10) and "Leichtsinniger Rat" (Op. 15, no. 8) are through-composed examples. The first song is almost entirely in half notes and the second in sixteenths.

Songs of the second kind, digressive rambling forms, make musical sense mainly in connection with the poetry.[25] Reger's occasional examples occur mainly in humorous songs from Op. 55 to Op. 75. The musical "point" of each is derived from the humor in the text. Musical ideas thus follow each other almost rhapsodically. Harmonic movement is in constant flux. Short musical "mosaics" change frequently. Relatively long units (phrases) may occur in some lieder, but even these are irregular in shape and dissolve into fragments. Such free through-composed structures, the farthest removed from purely musical design, include "Wir Zwei" (Op. 62, no. 5), "Darum" (Op. 75, no. 15), and "Spatz und Spätzin" (Op. 88, no. 4).

Formal Ambiguity

Late romantics did not regard strophic and sectional forms as exclusive from or independent of through-composed structures. For one can actually arrange fin-de-siècle lieder along continuums that show a gradual shading from either strophic or sectional forms into through-composed structures. Borderline examples accordingly may have elements of more than one category. Deviants are difficult to classify for another reason: late romantics sometimes altered inherited lied structures beyond recognition. The temptation in musical analysis is to create further formal categories, a snare that obscures a major aim of late romantics. Their objective was not so much to construct new formal confines as to blur older ones imaginatively. Formal ambiguity, the consequence of such treatment of structure, is not the essence of symbolism alone, as some specialists argue (see Chapter 9); it saturates the fin-de-siècle lied.

Mahler's "Urlicht" (ex. 74) demonstrates formal ambiguity brilliantly. As the

analysis below indicates, its structure is so protean that "Urlicht" can be classified as any of the three basic lied categories: varied strophic, sectional, or
through-composed. I shall examine "Urlicht" as a four-unit structure: unit 1
(mm. 1–14), "O Röschen rot!"—a festive chorale, hymnlike, and thus of reassuring character—is mainly instrumental. Unit 2 (mm. 15–35) brings the voice into
prominence and speaks of the great torment of the human condition. The two
units—of strongly contrasting mood, mode, and timbre—are clear-cut, separated by caesuras, and conclude with full cadences. Units 3 and 4 are more
smoothly linked. Unit 3 (mm. 36–49) involves the gentle passage "da kam ich
auf einen breiten Weg." Unit 4 (mm. 50–68) underscores the tense "Ach nein!
ich liess mich nicht abweisen!" but concludes with music of delicate fervor.

Sectional Form

1. ABCB′ form. Since units 1, 2, and 3 (A, B, and C) present different music,
each is labeled with a different letter. Units 2 and 4, being musically similar, are
designated B and B′. The beginning of unit 4 (mm. 50–51) is an embellished
variation of the first phrase of unit 2 (mm. 15–16). The closing measures of these
two units, measures 23 ff. and 59 ff., respectively, are even more similar.

2. Ternary form: introduction, ABA′ form. Unit 1, being mainly instrumental, creates the effect of a prelude, an introduction. Units 2, 3, and 4, the main
part of the song, fall into cyclical (ABA′) form, owing to the similarity of units 2
and 4 (see 1, above).

3. Binary form: AB | A′B′ form. Closer examination reveals that unit 3 is a
development of two ideas drawn from unit 1: a harmonic progression and a
rhythmic motive. The chords of the harmonic progression set "O Röschen rot!"
(submediant, dominant, and tonic in D-flat major); they serve also as the
harmonic basis of the entire third unit. The harmonic similarity is concealed in
three ways: a) the chords (of unit 3) are heavily woven with melodic figuration;
b) the second and third chords—measures 44 and 50—respectively, are chromatically altered. (The second chord, consisting of A, C sharp, and E, is the
submediant of the parallel tonic, C-sharp minor, and the third chord—C sharp,
E sharp, G sharp, and B—is a tonic seventh of that key.) And c) the third chord
links units 3 and 4. The rhythmic motive noted: a rising third that sets "O
Röschen rot!" recurs in dimunition in nearly every bar of unit 3 (prominent
especially in the orchestral score). Since this unit develops ideas drawn from unit
1, the two are identified here as A and A′.

Varied Strophic Form

4. AA′ form. "Urlicht" may be divided into two large parts: units 1 and 2
(Part I) and units 3 and 4 (Part II). The two are separated by cadence, caesura,

Example 74.   Mahler: "Urlicht" (*Des Knaben Wunderhorn*).

continued

lie - ber möcht' ich im Him - mel sein!
there - fore were I in heav - en fain!

p espress.

pp

molto espr.

rit.

ritenuto

ppp morendo

(Unit 3)
Etwas bewegter. Somewhat livelier.

Da kam ich auf ei - nen brei - ten
Then come I up - on a broad, fair

pp

Weg,
way,

p espress.

pp

da kam ein En - ge - lein und wollt' mich ab - a -
there came an an - gel and would turn mich ab - a -

(sempre *ppp*)

(Unit 4)
a tempo
passionately,
con portamento · espress. leidenschaftlich, aber zart · but delicately.
ritenuto

wei - sen. · Ach nein, ich ließ mich nicht ab -
side me. · Ah no, I would not turned a -

wei - sen, ach nein, ich ließ mich nicht ab - sen! · zart tenderly Ich
side be, Ah no, I would not turned a - side be! · I

drängend urgently · very fervently, · mit steigerndem Ausdruck
sehr leidenschaftlich, aber zart. · but delicately. · with increasing expression

bin — von Gott, und will · wie - der zu Gott! Der lie - be Gott, der
am — of God, and a - gain would to God! For lov - ing God, for

espr. molto · cresc.

-4-

continued

and change of tempo. The analysis undertaken above in 3 (AB | A′B′) suggests this classification for "Urlicht," a freely modified strophic form:

A | A′
ab a′b′

Through-Composed (Sectional)

5. ABC form. Fritz Egon Pamer, in his excellent study of Mahler's lieder, analyzes "Urlicht" as a tripartite structure: "The first part [units 1 and 2] is chorale-like. The second part [unit 3] is somewhat animated, yet very delicate. The third part [unit 4] rises to a great climax and finally dies away gently in the character of the beginning of the song. Complete freedom prevails within the individual parts."[26]

6. ABA¹ | CB¹A² form. This analysis divides "Urlicht" into two parts, owing to the major division in measure 35 mentioned in 4 above. "O Röschen rot!" (mm. 1–2) serves as the song's brief introduction. Parts I (mm. 3–35) and II (mm. 36–68) are each divisible into three hazy smaller segments. Part I: similar material (mm. 3–14 and mm. 27–35) is labeled A and A¹ respectively; the dissimilar mid-segment thus is designated B (mm. 15–26). Part II: though the opening passage (mm. 36–49) is based on "O Röschen rot!" (see 3, above), Mahler treats this passage quite differently, so that it may be identified as C. The

remainder of Part II—as noted in 1, above—presents B[1] (mm. 50–58), sequential development and variation of the opening phrase of B (mm. 15–17), and A[2], a modified restatement of much of A[1] (Part I).

The fact that "Urlicht" can be analyzed as varied strophic, sectional, and through-composed forms, and in several other ways (not shown), certainly illustrates the formal ambiguity which invades Mahler's mature works (look at *Das Lied*, his song cycle-symphony). Danuser, Mitchell, and Bailey give different lengths even to the principal sections of its various movements. As Mitchell observes: "The more fluid and complex Mahler's forms become, the more difficult it is to measure [them] with complete certainty."[27]

In their youth Schoenberg and Reger endorsed formal fluidity in the lied, yet in maturity they both rebelled against the very excesses that, as young composers, they had developed. In short, both confronted the same challenge but with different consequences. Schoenberg, who suspended tonality in *The Book of Hanging Gardens,* faced a special problem: to find substitutes for the musical order tonality imparts. Hence he explored new paths. (Of course, the tone row, his end product, lay in the future.) Reger, too, sought new ways—by revitalizing older lied concepts, for instance. He was the first outstanding late romantic to meet this challenge in the lied in this manner. That the two met the same challenge differently—Schoenberg through dodecaphony, Reger by anticipating neoclassicism—a brief comparison in the lied of their attitudes toward that challenge provides an instructive conclusion for this chapter.

Though formal ambiguity is evident in Schoenberg's earliest published lieder (Op. 1 to Op. 3, 1898–1903), their design is less iconoclastic than those of Reger. Schoenberg imparted a sense of structural balance in some ("Erwartung," "Waldsonne," and "Die Aufgeregten") by recalling the song's opening measures as a kind of da capo or by restating their initial bars as an instrumental postlude ("Georg von Frundsberg"). He repeated passages, even sections, within the body of a lied, particularly in his ballads of Op. 12. But like Wolf and Strauss, he preferred to modify repeated passages, to reshape them asymmetrically ("Freihold"), or to alter their texture freely ("Erhebung").

Schoenberg's concept of form advanced considerably after 1903. During his transitional years, he sought innovative designs that went beyond mere dependence on inherited lied structures. Strophic form, for instance, is treated as instrumental variation in "Traumleben," "Verlassen," and "Lockung." Structural balance occurs only in a small number of lieder ("Traumleben" and "Alles"). Instead, Schoenberg focused increasingly on tight construction wrought by techniques of development. Constructive motives play an ever increasing role. These are developed through diminution, augmentation, and inversion into a tight web in "Ghasel" (1904), "Jane Grey" (1907), and especially "Ich darf nicht dankend" (1904). Schoenberg's predilection for such composition is foreshadowed in "Wie Georg von Frundsberg von sich selber sang," in "Verlassen" (both of 1903), and even in "Abschied" (Op. 1). In spite of its seemingly puffy construction, "Abschied"'s opening eight-note figure undergoes rigorous development throughout the song.

Although traces of traditional lied structures—ternary and strophic forms—are found in some of its separate songs, *Hanging Gardens* is "architectonically . . . entirely new," as Egon Wellesz asserted. "Although the atonal composer was not explicitly serial," Wolfgang Stroh perceives, "he did work as if he were implicitly using rows, as he moved towards freedom from tonal bonds." In *Hanging Gardens,* short figures (intervallic units and pitch patterns)—Lessem identified four such basic "cells"—become musical building blocks. In Song 14 two basic figures are introduced immediately in the first bar, then developed in a variety of ways—for instance, through octave displacement, which tightly unifies the piano part.[28]

The intervallic unit became for the mature Schoenberg a point of departure. The point for the late romantics, in contrast, was the expansive theme, presented immediately and later broken into motives (units). Schoenberg also used poetry innovatively as a structural "crutch" for the music. Song 14 provides examples. He treated key words pointillistically as independent single units. "The words are not connected in terms of their sense, but are rather combined in a kind of additive logic, first to produce larger units and finally to produce the total form."[29] In treating individual words as independent units, an approach akin to that of later serial composers, Schoenberg was to become entirely different from traditional lied composers, for whom sense and meaning of a poem was the primary factor in setting and structuring a lied.

Reger, radical in youth, blurred the contour of inherited forms almost into a haze on the few occasions he applied them. His varied strophic forms are more freely modified even than those of Wolf, Mahler, Strauss, and certainly Pfitzner. A conservative example first: "Mein Herz" (Op. 43, no. 7) in three strophes. Though the opening measures of the second and third strophes are moderately varied—more in the piano than in the voice part—the remaining measures are increasingly modified so that their closing bars are hardly similar. The second and third strophes are half the length of the first. Specialists have coined the term *strophic-through-composed* for such structures.[30] In Reger's freely modified lieder, only the opening chords of the different strophes are similar. In some, like "Flieder" (Op. 35, no. 4), even this similarity is disguised, for Reger modified the harmony and applied melodic figuration to the chords.

In maturity, Reger saw the error of his radical ventures and his allegiance to New German aesthetics. He determined to proceed no further in blurring form but to aim for the converse: simplicity and formal clarity. "Nowadays much too little attention is paid to architecture in music. This gives Brahms superiority in our times. . . . The Liszt-Strauss trend has influenced a generation of young musicians. They disguise their lack of know-how of pure musical architecture by writing hazy poetic thoughts." For the mature Reger, "Form is a bind only for him who does not command it." Strict forms begin to appear in Op. 76, the

Schlichte Weisen. Some are sharply contoured in strophic form. "Das iuwer min engel walte!" establishes Reger as among the first late romantics to write a strict strophic song later in life. He sharply contoured even some varied strophic songs with fermatas, breath pauses, or rests to delineate the strophes and he would alter the stanzaic order of a poem so that he could set it strophically. He might also alter strophes as abstractly as if he were writing absolute music. For instance, he dissolved the eighth-note pattern of the first strophe of "Schlecht' Wetter" (no. 7) into sixteenths in the second strophe, creating a figural mutation common in instrumental variation.[31]

Schlichte Weisen represents the composer's first attempts to create the "genuine" Reger lied. He realized his objectives only in some of the songs. Others still demonstrate extreme structural fluidity.[32] Reger persisted further along his new path toward simplicity. All but two (nos. 2 and 11) of the twelve songs of Op. 137 (*Zwölf geistliche Lieder*) are in strict strophic form. As mentioned, Reger composed more strophic songs in one opus than did Wolf, Mahler, Strauss, and Pfitzner in all of their lieder. Harmony, in these songs, tends primarily to underscore form rather than evoke radiant color. This change of style was indeed remarkable for a composer who, before 1903, wrote songs that were even more fluid than those of Wolf and Strauss.

Several of Reger's immediate contemporaries also changed style in maturity: Hugo Kaun, Paul Graener, Haas, Knab, and others began to strengthen musical architecture in the lied and to cultivate strict form.

The older Pfitzner reacted similarly. Although characteristic features of the traditional lied—carefully crafted form, gentle cantabile, and stress on mood— persist throughout Pfitzner's period of creativity, the late songs evince greater clarity of design than those of his middle years, especially some of the *Alte Weisen* (Op. 33; 1923) and Opp. 40 and 41 of 1931. Examples in relatively strict form include the slightly varied ternary, "Mir glänzen die Augen" (no. 1) and "Du milchjunger Knabe" (no. 2); "Singt mein schatz wie ein Fink" (no. 5), in AB | A'B'; and especially the scarcely altered strophic "Ich fürcht nit Gespenster" (no. 2) from Op. 33. Strophic form in "Wenn sich Liebes" (Op. 40, no. 2), from his final years of song composition, is even stricter. Its form is less modified even than those of Op. 2.

Pfitzner experimented cautiously in his late years with elements of contemporary musical styles. (His late years began with the cantata *Von deutscher Seele*, 1921, and more lieder, Opp. 29–40.) Dissonance, rhythmic refinements, greater simplicity, and ever-more linearity ("Wanderers Nachtlied," Op. 40, no. 5) are important features. "Das Alter" (Op. 41, no. 3), with its two polyphonic lines over a rhythmic ostinato, is sparse to the point of austerity. Other songs contain passages of polychordal harmony ("Abbitte," Op. 29, no. 1) and tonality stretched to the breaking point ("Eingelegte Ruder," Op. 32, no. 3). Yet these late songs are still subjective. Some of the songs on the topic of aging are autobiographical. Some are still as richly colored as the earlier ones. The lighthearted and enchanting *Keller Lieder*, "Alte Weisen" in particular, is the most accessible of Pfitzner's song cycles. Though Pfitzner set some forty poets, Eichendorff—also a conservative, captivated by a longing for the past—personified the German soul as Pfitzner conceived it and remained the composer's greatest inspiration throughout life.[33]

Late romantics, as stressed, opposed the dissolution of tradition. Even radical late romantics like Strauss, who prepared the way for the breach, fiercely opposed the final break when they realized what Schoenberg's innovations signified. Their advances, in contrast, were followed by retreats into tradition, from which they might launch new advances. Tradition always remained for them the nurturing soil from which their radical ideas sprouted.

chapter twelve

Late-Romantic Expansiveness

Late romantics, obsessed with size, developed the century's most imposing instrumental ensembles, threatening, in the process, to drown the public in a flood of sound. All their efforts—even those of nationalists, who vainly sought to cultivate folkish simplicity—aimed at expansiveness. As we have seen, although the kaiser's commission rejected over 7,000 folksongs as too complex, it selected clusters of chromatic choral pieces by Liszt, Wagner, and others. Efforts of the Berlin weekly *Die Woche* to stimulate interest in volks-tümlich song, we also recall, were equally embarrassing. Master composers like Mahler and Strauss fared no better with folkish simplicity. They gave rural folkish text sophisticated urban settings. Even Reger, in his final attempts in simplicity, his *Fünf neue Kinderlieder* (Five new songs for children), Op. 142 (ex. 75), did not really achieve this objective.

Hugo Riemann justifiably complained: "It is a sign of our times to nurture all kinds of extravagances: complexity of notation, complexity in performance, enlargement of orchestral forces, the piling up of twisted and bewildering confused melodic lines and of entangled and tightly welded harmony that, if possible, refer expressively to poetry and painting of the most modern and most extravagant kind." Ernest Newman showered his invective directly on the Strauss lied: "pounds upon pounds of notes from which we can hardly squeeze a half-ounce of feeling."[1]

Late romantics expanded piano-solo passages in the lied—preludes, interludes, and postludes, an idea that had been introduced by early romantics, Schumann in particular—into monumental proportions. Wolf's piano solos are generally longer than those of his predecessors; immediate followers like Joseph Marx wrote even longer ones. "Im Maien" has a prelude of twenty-nine measures. "Toskanner Sommer" begins with a twenty-measure prelude; "Barcarolle" contains a twenty-six-measure interlude. These solos, Marx believed, express the poetry's breadth and depth: "I have realized in detail that which Wolf has only hinted at."[2] Expansive piano solos function in much the same way that orchestral interludes do in music dramas. Certainly the long transition (sixteen measures) between "Heller Nacht" and "Zuversicht" in Zilcher's *Dehmel* lieder is analogous to an orchestral transition between scenes of a music drama.

Late romantics expanded the lied in breadth too. Terminology coined by

Example 75.   Reger: "Wiegenlied" (G. Stein), Op. 142, no. 1, mm. 21–24.

critics—*symphonic lied style, orchestrally conceived lieder*—compellingly conveys the late-romantic inclination for profusiveness. So too does Plüddemann's forceful pronouncement, mentioned earlier, that anyone who cannot play orchestrally should not attempt the piano parts of his ballads.

The temptation to thicken harmony with ever-more melodic figuration plagued the late romantics. Wolf was tormented by his "crazy habit of always adding new counterpoints." Strauss generalized: "Satan has cursed us Germans by giving us counterpoint in our cradles."[3] His sensuous multivoiced polyphony, steeped in chromatic harmony, is apparent in his songs and orchestral music. Density is also conspicuous in Pfitzner's lieder and orchestral scores. After 1904 he tended increasingly to favor heavily woven linear texture; the purely vertical element of his harmony retreated into the background. Most of his collection *92stes Sonett* (1909; see ex. 76) comprises four (voice and piano) horizontal strands. Although Pfitzner rarely sustains this kind of writing in four parts, three-part linear composition occurs often.

Reger's polyphony has long been celebrated as multivoiced. Textures of three and four parts characterize even the earliest songs. In his maturity, Reger offered textures of five and six parts in which each contrapuntal line showed individuality, which surpass not only his early efforts but also those of contemporaries

Example 76.   Pfitzner: "92stes Sonett" (Petrarch/Förster), Op. 24, no. 3, mm. 3–4.

(see ex. 77). Such density, common in songs for voice and organ, appears only occasionally in the piano lied. It represents the ultimate of the German late-romantic craze for profusiveness.

Strauss, Pfitzner, and especially Mahler developed a special kind of polyphony, unlike the polyphony of the eighteenth century. They preferred sharply contrasting melodies. "The old contrapuntal practices . . . of discovering a melody that combines with another do not interest me," Strauss stated. "I consider an accomplishment the skill of successfully combining two mutually antagonistic themes." For Mahler, the noisy bustle at a folk festival, an organ grinder, military music, and a male chorus occurring simultaneously achieve true polyphony: "Themes must come from entirely different directions and . . . must be completely different from each other, rhythmically and melodically, otherwise one has just many-voiced homophony."[4] Contrapuntal texture, apparent especially in *Kindertotenlieder,* reaches its zenith in *Das Lied von der Erde.* Bach became Mahler's model and the Bach *Gesellschaft*—he owned a copy— was practically his Bible.

Bach was also Reger's model. He scored his *Zwölf geistliche Lieder* (Op. 137) in the manner of Bach chorales. Interweaving lines in the piano part play a subordinate role in Reger's volkstümlich songs, however. The upper line often doubles the vocal melody throughout as, for instance, in the first eight songs of the *Schlichte Weisen.* Further, Reger's polyphony is strongly influenced by New German chromaticism. Early Reger specialists immediately perceived that his "harmony commands melody and rhythm as his most important means of expression."[5]

Harmony certainly functioned as a dominant element in the late-romantic lied; it colors key words and expresses their essence. One might generalize that late romantics—despite their growing attention to linear texture—often drenched polyphony in harmony. Saint-Saens, Reger, and Ludwig Thuille,

Example 77.   Reger: "Wenn in bangen, trüben Stunden" (Novalis), mm. 1–3.

among others, wrote textbooks on harmony. Saint-Saens gave harmony greater importance than melody in the preface to his treatise *Harmonie et melodie* (1885), though decades later (1923) he changed his mind. Enrichment of harmony and veiled tonality reached its peak in the fin de siècle, providing further examples of late-romantic expansiveness.

Late romantics were impelled by their inclination for opulence toward the orchestral song, the genre in which they were able to expand the lied to its utmost. Polyphonic interweaving became richer, descriptive imagery sharper, instrumental solo passages symphonic. The potential for expressiveness through subtleties of orchestral timbres permitted higher levels of intensity and finer delicate shadings. In short, the orchestral song enabled the lied composer to achieve the ultimate in luxuriant sound.

Few early nineteenth-century composers in Germany and Austria would have imagined that the orchestral song, then a lifeless limb of the lied, was destined to grow into a strong branch. They considered the lied, a favorite in the home, too delicate for the weight of the orchestra and too intimate for large concert halls. The concert aria, then in great vogue, permitted no competitor. In France, however, songs with orchestral accompaniment had an early history, beginning around 1834–35 with songs by Berlioz ("La Captive," for example), romances—a genre for voice and pianoforte or orchestra that the French adored—and orchestrations of Schubert lieder in French translation. Resistance to the orchestral lied in Austria and Germany persisted even in the 1860s, when Berlioz, Liszt, Ferdinand Hiller, and Brahms orchestrated Schubert songs. But Brahms and Hiller did so to oblige their mutual enterprising friend Julius Stockhausen, who had heard orchestrated songs of Schubert's in Paris and wanted other orchestral songs to sing. Brahms, fearing that solo voice and orchestra would balance poorly, withdrew two of his five orchestrations. Curiously enough, the solo voice part of these two Brahms songs was actually sung by a male choir in unison upon several occasions. Liszt, always a pioneer, held a minority view on the question of balance: "The instrumental web [of the orchestral song] brings the voice graciously into prominence." He planned to orchestrate "several other pretty things," having had happy results conducting his own orchestral songs.[6]

In spite of the meager attention it received, the orchestral lied sprouted two healthy branches: songs conceived originally for voice and orchestra and instrumentations of preexisting pianoforte songs. In the years around 1900, hardly a week passed without performances of each. Most late romantics, certainly our five masters, cultivated the genre. Conductors orchestrated pianoforte songs, especially those of Schubert, for symphony concert. Felix Mottl's transcriptions of Wagner's *Wesendonck-Lieder* are heard so much more often than Wagner's keyboard versions that many believe the orchestral scores to be Wagner's original conceptions. Orchestral songs were heard even at watering-places (spas) as popular diversions. The sudden rage for orchestral songs put them well ahead of their erstwhile rival—the concert aria, which "completely died out."[7]

Composer Joseph Haas honors the concert-reform movement for making the climate favorable for the orchestral song. The reformers "vehemently opposed mixed programs, those at which a piano was rolled on stage during a symphony concert in order to perform pianoforte songs." Concert reformers found only a few genres for solo voice suitable for performance at symphony concerts. The orchestral lied was the most important of these. According to Karl Bleyle, another composer then active, "Many conductors . . . for reasons of program unity, required or preferred the orchestral lied. When a well-endowed society, and there were many in Germany at the time, wished to give an evening of works by a modern composer—consisting of, for example, a work for orchestra, one for chorus and orchestra, and lieder—the objective was to avoid the necessity of using a piano. Such an occasion called for a composer to orchestrate a lied he had originally conceived for voice and piano."[8]

Mahler's contributions to the orchestral lied are of the first magnitude. His earliest lied conceptions—intimate lyrical expression for voice and piano— were in subsequent works broadened into orchestral songs, then movements of symphonies, and finally into *Das Lied von der Erde,* his loftiest expansion. Here song absorbs symphony or, more accurately stated, song cycle and symphony fuse. Mahler's fascination for the expressive potential of the orchestra began with the *Wayfarer* cycle, his first orchestral songs, and continued to his last years. All but Mahler's early fourteen songs and one late example, "Liebst du um Schönheit," were orchestrated by the composer. With boundless imagination, Mahler expanded the pianoforte song to grandiose proportions.

In addition to weaving vast orchestral fabrics, Mahler also spun delicate chamber-music textures, such as his *Kindertotenlieder.* This unique masterpiece was not an opposition to late-romantic practice but rather its full embodiment. For Mahler was not the first romantic to conceive of the lied as chamber music. Wolf, among others, had done so earlier, and for much smaller groups of instruments, and thus sustained the intimacy of the lied. Wagner's even earlier "Träume" calls for only thirteen players. Nor was Mahler affected by the financial problems involved in assembling large orchestral forces that troubled later composers. Typical late-romantic practice was to continue earlier nineteenth-century predilection for the grandiose, that is, the colossal music drama, on the one hand, and the intimate and the pianoforte lied, on the other. Wagner's *Siegfried Idyll,* composed concurrently with the monumental *Ring* cycle, and Mahler's *Adagietto* (for harp and strings), conceived in the midst of his Fifth Symphony for large orchestra, are further examples. In fin-de-siècle fashion, Mahler thus followed his *Kindertotenlieder* with monumental orchestral peaks.

The orchestral song opened a new world for Mahler, which he colored in hues so individual and profound that he had no ready title for his early essays save the cryptic *Humoresken*. Although Mahler felt a kinship in the *Humoresken* for the Loewe ballad, he thought Loewe "didn't achieve the utmost in it. He settled for the piano, whereas a large-scale composition that plumbs the depths of the subject unconditionally demands the orchestra."[9]

Mahler strove for orchestral timbres even in his early *Lieder und Gesänge*, composed for voice and piano. The pianist is required to play one figure in "Zu Strassburg auf der Schanz" "like a shawn" and another, surprisingly enough, in imitation of a muted drum. The composer explains in a footnote: "The pianist is to imitate the sound of a muted drum by playing all these low trills with the aid of a pedal." Mahler even made an orchestral sketch of the opening of this song.[10] In "Phantasie," the pianist is directed to imitate a harp. Perhaps because he aspired to still greater verisimilitude, the composer suggested, again in a footnote: "If possible, the accompaniment of this song should be played by a harp." "Serenade" bears another puzzling direction: "With the accompaniment of wind instruments." "Serenade," like "Phantasie," is transitional in Mahler's evolution from pianoforte to orchestral song.

Mahler's conception of the orchestral lied differed from that of Wolf, Strauss, Pfitzner, and Reger. They recognized the lied as comprising three separate genres: the pianoforte lied, its orchestrated version, and songs conceived originally for orchestra. Mahler did not. The *Wayfarer* songs raise more questions than they answer. The earliest surviving manuscript (undated), though in piano-vocal score, bears the cryptic instruction "with orchestral accompaniment." Was there an earlier purely piano-vocal version? Donald Mitchell cites an early (around 1891–95) manuscript of this cycle in orchestral, not piano-vocal, score that differs substantially from the published version. When it was finally published in 1897, the cycle appeared in two similar but not identical versions, one for piano and one for orchestra. The two versions may have germinated simultaneously in the composer's mind. If so we have a compositional technique unlike those of our other composers. Mahler apparently used several compositional procedures, some, perhaps, at different stages of his development. Many of his songs were probably conceived first for voice and piano and then orchestrated: "Des Antonius von Padua Fischpredigt" is an interesting example. Others were originally conceived as orchestral songs: "O Mensch! gib acht," as the fourth movement of the Third Symphony. "Es sungen drei Engel" was transcribed by the composer for voice and keyboard from a choral setting, the fifth movement of his Third Symphony. However, after around 1892, Stephen Hefling indicates, "Mahler clearly conceived his songs . . . *either* [for] piano or orchestra." Mahler's orchestral songs, we might therefore conclude, are not simple transcriptions but often fresh "recompositions" of the piano versions.[11]

Comparison of the piano and orchestral versions of various lieder indicates that Mahler heightened expression in the orchestral lied. He tended to mark orchestral lieder with more extreme dynamics than pianoforte songs. Of course, selection of dynamics is often governed by problems of instrumental balance, yet a piano or forte in keyboard versions frequently appears in orchestral scores as a *pp* or *ff*. Mahler utilized to the utmost the great expressive potential of the orchestra in his orchestral lieder. In "Urlicht," bar 49, the piano version is simply marked *pp* >, while in the orchestral version, the indication for this bar reads *ppppp* (see the first-violin part). The conclusion of "Der Schildwache Nachtlied" in the piano version carries the instruction "fading away" but in the orchestral version it is "diminish to total inaudibility."

Mahler's orchestral lieder contain the widest possible range of dynamic shading. Their expression is characterized by a continual flow of fluctuating dynamics. Even single notes are frequently subjected to changing dynamics. Crescendi and decrescendi occur with great frequency and to great dramatic effect. Crescendi are often scored in overlapping series so that as one instrument or group reaches its peak another begins an ascent. In Mahler's pianoforte songs, however, overlapping crescendi and radically changing dynamics are rare: one dynamic mark may serve for an entire phrase. Though sudden radical changes, such as the *fff* > *ppp* in the woodwinds in the last bar of "Revelge," appear infrequently, their presence in orchestral lieder indicates Mahler's affinity for the emotionally charged. Such commands serve a psychological purpose—to heighten the music's inner excitement.

Mahler's orchestral lieder also contain fine distinctions of intensity. Nuance is of the greatest importance. Signs for subtle changes outnumber by far indications in his pianoforte songs. They are applied in great detail and are assigned not merely to individual phrases but to individual notes. "Rheinlegendchen" provides an unusual example even for Mahler (see ex. 78). The composer calls for subtle nuance not only for each beat but even for each half-beat, a requirement that is not suggested in the piano version, where such performance is, of course, impossible. Mahler carefully shaded entire choirs of instruments—even individual instrumental lines within these choirs. Among string ensembles, for instance, he might modify dynamics of some instruments while instructing the others to continue playing at an unaltered level, as evident in example 79a. Of course, the fine shading he introduced into the second-violin part—in the corresponding bar of the piano version (ex. 79b)—provides no hint of this subtlety. In contrast, nuances in piano parts are usually assigned to the entire piano texture. Mahler's development of the orchestral lied shows one unremitting objective: ever-greater precision in the notation of subtleties and refinements of expression, a search he undertook with rhythmic subtleties as well.

Strauss wrote orchestral songs throughout his long life, completing his first at age thirteen and his final ones, *Vier letzte Lieder*, at eighty-four. This legacy of forty-one mature songs includes fifteen originally conceived for orchestra and twenty-six arrangements of pianoforte songs.[12] Strauss first orchestrated his pianoforte songs to provide Pauline de Ahna, later his wife, with an opportunity to sing at symphony concerts. "Pauline," he lamented to his parents, "has very

Example 78.   Mahler: "Rheinlegendchen" (*Des Knaben Wunderhorn*), mm. 57–60.

Example 79.   Mahler: "Wenn mein Schatz" (Mahler), mm. 22–25, (a) orchestral version; (b) piano verson.

little to sing." Richard attracted widespread attention in 1895 as a conductor in Budapest, Berlin, and Leipzig, and the next year in Amsterdam, Barcelona, Brussels, London, and Paris—but not Pauline, the "incomparable singer of his songs."[13]

Pauline, however, triumphed in her first symphony concert, singing four of Strauss's most attractive pianoforte songs in orchestral versions: "Cäcilie" (Op. 27, no. 2), "Morgen" (Op. 27, no. 4), "Liebeshymnus" (Op. 32, no. 3), and "Das Rosenband" (Op. 36, no. 1). "Sensation for Paris," Strauss wrote: "Pauline had to encore 'Morgen' . . . by stormy request." The press confirmed Richard's enthusiastic reports home. New York: "Morgen" "made such an overpowering sensation. It had to be repeated forthwith. 'Cäcilie,' sung with passionate feeling . . . also won distinction of imperative recognition."[14] The couple made conquest after conquest.

Strauss's songs were not just vehicles for Pauline's appearances, they had a personal meaning for the couple. "Cäcilie" was composed a day before their wedding. "Meinem Kinde" (Op. 37, no. 3), "Wiegenlied" (Op. 41, no. 1), and "Muttertändelei" (Op. 43, no. 2) were orchestrated in 1900 as a "motherly group," the first having been composed two months before the birth of their son, Franz. Strauss referred to the three as "Pauline's orchestral songs." Critics praised the songs' personal meaning: "I cannot speak too highly of Madame Strauss's rendering of her husband's songs," a critic wrote from London. "She was perhaps more successful in the motherly group."[15]

Later in Strauss's life, the soprano Viorica Ursuleac inspired orchestrations of other pianoforte songs. Strauss not only scored "Zueignung" (Op. 10, no. 1) for her but, in highest tribute, he inserted a new line of text and music at its conclusion: "You wonderful Helene, for this my thanks!" The printed music is dedicated "For Viorica."[16] Strauss scored other pianoforte songs for another reason: to attract public attention to them. "Having quite by accident played through my . . . Op. 68 again," he remarked, "I am surprised that they are sung so rarely. I will orchestrate them now."[17] The symphony concert hall was an ideal place to draw public attention not only to Pauline but also to his neglected lieder.

Strauss's attraction to the orchestral lied ran deep. Some early keyboard songs were, in a sense, conceived partly in terms of orchestral timbres. When Strauss accompanied "Cäcilie" at the piano, Alfred Orel recalls that he "could hear the rushing sound of a full orchestra."[18] Strauss loved luxuriant sound. He dazzled his listeners with his uncanny skill as an orchestrator, calling for a generous number of instruments in most of his orchestral songs. Some songs, however, show consummate skill with the lightest kinds of coloring. With a single exception, the orchestra in "Wiegenlied" never rises above a pianissimo, yet the numerous dynamic shadings that are created with orchestral timbres are staggering. Strings are divided, subdivided, grouped, and regrouped into as many as eighteen strands. These are woven into a web so distinct that one imagines it can almost be touched. The orchestral web is even lighter than the gauzy piano version. In "Waldseligkeit" (Op. 49, no. 1), another tour de force, one feels the living presence of the German forest. Here strings—dark and sonorous and divided into ten and eleven parts—produce a sense of spatial depth. The bass clarinet and harmonium add resonance and extramusical sound as well: a buzzing breathiness suggestive of a forest breeze. "Frühlingsfeier" (Op. 56, no. 5)—which pictures maenads chasing Adonis with hysterical laughter, crying, and sobbing—is sharpened through orchestration into shocking naturalism: violin glissandi evoke the blood of the dying Adonis spurting forth to redden the flowers. Strauss's orchestral songs often sharpen the imagery and deepen the mood of the pianoforte versions.

Nevertheless, when Strauss orchestrated his pianoforte songs, he did not attempt to notate dynamic nuance, as did Mahler. In general, Strauss sought in orchestral song the equivalent of the dynamics used in his keyboard versions. Even though differences in dynamics may be found between the versions, they serve mainly to achieve proper balance between voice and orchestra. For with respect to shading, most of his orchestral songs seem to be transcriptions or adaptions of keyboard songs. Nor did Strauss often change instructions for expression in orchestrating piano songs. On the contrary, he generally wrote the identical instructions, few though they were, in both versions. In short, he did not seek to pin down each nuance but rather left the search for subtleties to the performer.

Some of the changes Strauss introduced in his orchestrations of pianoforte songs resulted from practical experience gained as conductor and accompanist. He inserted an additional bar or two in preludes for orchestral songs ("Muttertändelei," "Ich liebe dich," and "Amor") that are not required in their piano versions, owing to the more intimate ensemble procedures. He extended postludes of other songs ("Ruhe, meine Seele!" and "Frühlingsfeier"), where the orchestra would require more time than the piano to achieve an appropriate conclusion. Experience also prompted Strauss to permit the singer greater opportunity to broaden key phrases in orchestral songs (see ex. 80a). Changes of key, too, were determined by practical considerations. "Meinem Kinde" is heard in G flat rather than in the original G, which produces a more colorful orchestral result. Strauss also simplified vocal writing and improved upon declamation in orchestrating pianoforte versions (exx. 80b and 80c). "Liebeshymnus," for example, is transposed down a third to avoid a high B flat for the singer. Finally, Strauss's experienced eye is evident in the masterful balance achieved between singer and orchestra. "I perceive that the manuscript of my *Lied der Frauen* [Op. 68, no. 6] is orchestrated much too thickly," he wrote to Clemens Krauss, who conducted it. "Please be good enough . . . to bracket . . . all wind or brass parts you consider dispensable! Remarkable, how much in need of revision one finds one's own compositions, a few years later."[19]

One discovers valuable hints on the performance of the pianoforte lieder from a study of their orchestrations. For instance, we realize how unusually delicate Strauss intended the piano accompaniment of "Meinem Kinde" to be. His scoring is for solos, string quartet, and bass. And though the piano parts of "Muttertändelei" and "Das Rosenband" are sheer and marked by similar dynamics, one discerns from the instrumentation that the piano part of "Muttertändelei" is probably intended to be played with a still lighter touch than that of "Das Rosenband." Strauss's orchestral scoring is even more translucent: twenty-two strings and no basses in "Muttertändelei" while "Das Rosenband" calls for four basses and a slightly larger complement of higher strings.

The reason Wolf orchestrated his pianoforte songs remains obscure. Ernst Decsey speculates that the main reason was his strong dramatic impulse and his passion for verisimilitude. "Everything that Wolf composes has an inclination towards the theater. . . . The scenic surrounding is half of the ring that embraces the actor, the orchestra is the other half." If the orchestra is really half of the ring, why did Wolf not conceive a single song originally for orchestra? Our four other

Example 80.   Strauss: (a) "Ich Liebe Dich" (Liliencron), Op. 37, no. 2; (aa) piano version, mm. 43–45; (bb) orchestral version, mm. 45–48; (b) "Des Dichters Abendgang" (Uhland), Op. 47, no. 2; (cc) piano version, mm. 60–61; (dd) orchestral version, mm. 60–61; (c) "Zueignung" (Gilm), Op. 10, no. 1; (ee) piano version, mm. 25–26; (ff) orchestral version, mm. 25–27.

masters did. Decsey bolsters his argument by noting: "As we can see, the orchestrations follow immediately after the lieder were composed." But the orchestrations of Wolf's songs were rarely immediate afterthoughts. Some were composed from one to eight years after the songs were composed. Even Frank Walker is uncertain of the immediate reason for the orchestrations. He conjectures that Wolf orchestrated his songs "perhaps as the result of hearing some of them played on the organ at the Good Friday concert."[20] Although there may be a connection between that concert and Wolf's scoring of "Seufzer" and "Karwoche" a month later, the link does not provide the complete picture.

The immediate reason is simply that Wolf wanted orchestral music of his own that could be performed at symphony concerts. His early orchestral venture, the symphonic poem *Penthesilea* (1883–85), was a distressing failure in its first performance (1886). His delightful "Christnacht," "Elfenlied" (both for soloists, chorus, and orchestra), and a group of orchestral songs mark his return in May 1889 to orchestral media. Wolf was overjoyed to learn the next year that Felix Weingartner wished to conduct some of his orchestral songs. Eight recently completed lieder were ready and waiting. In addition, Wolf planned not only to score "Prometheus" immediately but even to travel to Munich to hand Weingartner the manuscript.[21] This possibility spurred Wolf to write to the choral conductor Emil Kauffmann: "Would it be possible for you to include in your orchestral concerts lieder of mine for orchestra? I have just orchestrated 'Denk' es o Seele!'" And Wolf asked friends to intercede with other conductors. Hugo Faisst did so with Herman Zumpe. "Your magnificent suggestion," Wolf wrote to Zumpe, "to present a quantity of my orchestrated songs this coming year" delighted him.[22] The new demand at symphony concerts for orchestral lieder evidently attracted Wolf.

Wolf was no man of the world, no public figure like Mahler and Strauss. On the contrary, he was temperamentally unsuited for life as a conductor. Nor did he display a native gift for orchestration. *Penthesilea*, he later admitted, was "dreadfully overlarded." Despite his judgment that "Er ist's" was "sparklingly scored," the publisher, Breitkopf and Härtel, eliminated many of his wind parts. He fiercely rejected criticism of his songs on purely musical grounds, but he sought advice on their orchestration. "He not only listened as I commented on the heavy scoring," Weingartner observed with surprise, "but accepted my individual suggestions almost with childlike thanks."[23] That Wolf profited from this advice is evident. His second version of "Mignon" (1893) is less heavily scored than his first attempt (1890).

Nevertheless, it would be a mistake to conclude that all or most of his orchestral music is unrewarding. Some are graciously colored, as is the *Italian Serenade*. Several are for chamber music: "Gesang Weylas," for harp, horn, and clarinet; "Auf ein altes Bild," for two each of oboes, clarinets, and bassoons; and "Harfenspieler II" and "Seufzer," both for five solo winds and strings. Such instrumentation was exceptional in the 1890s, when many composers sought mass effects. Only the smallest number of Wolf's lieder call for a large orchestra.[24]

Wolf's orchestral songs, in the main, are not recompositions but transcriptions of his pianoforte songs. The minor changes he introduced result in large part from his "crazy habit" of adding more contrapuntal lines. This superb pictorialist did not concentrate on musical description in his orchestral songs. "Der Rattenfänger," however, is an exception: it brilliantly depicts a multitude of rats, mice, and weasels hopping, scurrying, and streaking madly about, enchanted by the ratcatcher's magic song. (In the piano song there are but a few of these pictorial effects.) In general, Wolf sought to intensify mood and to enrich color while translating keyboard into orchestral timbres. In "Harfenspieler III" an undulating line in the strings and winds whips up a telling climax at the song's close.

Wolf went directly to Moerike, the poet whose name is indelibly linked to his own, for the first of more than two dozen orchestrations of pianoforte songs.[25] He added to the earliest group of sacred songs—"Seufzer," "Auf ein altes Bild," and "Schlafendes Jesuskind"—six more on spiritual subjects. The nine form an inner unity for Wolf.[26] From the *Goethe-Lieder*, he quite naturally drew on the three *Harfenlieder*—which form an entity in themselves—and "Prometheus" and "Mignon" ("Kennst du das Land?"), which Wolf always thought too cramped by the limitations of the piano. He transcribed none of the Italian or *Eichendorff* lieder, and only four from his Spanish set, for a special reason: he wished to insert them into his opera *Der Corregidor*. Two others were intended for his never-completed opera, *Manuel Venegas*.

The orchestral lied is a neglected but nevertheless important genre in Pfitzner's oeuvre. The composer scored twenty-three of his pianoforte lieder, besides composing four especially for orchestra.[27] With few exceptions (like "Lethe," 1926), Pfitzner preferred small instrumental groups in his lieder orchestrations and larger ones for songs conceived directly for orchestra. Some orchestrations, like "Frieden" (Op. 5, no. 1)—for two flutes, harp, solo violin, and violas—are sheer and transparent. Others—"Es glänzt so schön die sinkende Sonne" (Op. 4, no. 1), for instance, are singularly colored, for three bassoons, contrabassoon, and strings. Pfitzner's lieder conceived for orchestra are storehouses of imaginative orchestral effects.

Young Pfitzner was engrossed by orchestral music and conducting, like Mahler and Strauss, and became outstanding in both. Thus Pfitzner scored lieder for the world of his immediate experience. Since he held his most important position as conductor in Strasbourg (1908–16), it is no surprise that in these years, "the orchestral song attracted him specially."[28] His orchestrations of six songs by Schumann and two by Loewe, and his composition of the stirring wartime orchestral ballads "Der Trompeter" and "Klage," stem from this period.

Pfitzner orchestrated his pianoforte songs on a favorite subject, nature. In so doing, he preferred to suggest mood rather than to detail imagery. The roar of a mighty river, the rustle of a deep forest are evocations of nature that resound throughout his pianoforte songs, and they are suggested by arpeggios, low tones, or low chords, which the composer directs the pianist to blur with excessive pedal. In their orchestral versions such evocations become atmospheric tone paintings. In the grand ode "An den Mond" (Op. 18) subterranean tones of contrabassoons, bassoons, tuba, and timpani; soft reverberation of three trombones; and gusty harp arpeggios suggest the profundity of nature. Pfitzner deepens suggestiveness substantially with the addition of a grand piano, to be played "with much pedal."

Pfitzner orchestrated other keyboard songs, however, for a diametrically opposed reason: to sharpen their imagery. These songs display his supreme command of orchestral sonority. The harp, an important instrument within them, depicts in "Sonst" (Op. 15, no. 4) Cupid's arrow in flight by means of a glissando played "with strips of paper between the strings." Touches of harp pointillisme enable the auditor almost to see falling apple blossoms in "Es fällt ein Stern herunter" (Op. 4, no. 3). Pfitzner plunges deeper into pictorialism in songs conceived originally for orchestra like "Der Trompeter" (Op. 25, no. 1), a patriotic song of the war years (1915–16). In this gruesome glorification of war, a trumpeter stands on an icy knoll in the Elbe, heroically blasting a victory march as the thundering river's ice shatters and sucks him under. Pfitzner's orchestra allows us to experience the ice splitting, a comrade's leap to safety, the trumpeter's heroic gesture, and the eerie silence that follows.

Humorous effects are also achieved orchestrally. The humor is at its height in the preposterous "Die Heinzelmännchen" (Op. 14). The vivid elements include the yawning of the lazy people of Cologne, suggested by glissandi on trombones and strings; the citizens' snoring, depicted by sustained low tones of bass clarinets, bassoons, and contrabassoons; and the pouring of peas on the floor to trip and catch the elves, represented by short col-legno strokes of the stringed instruments and side-drum rolls, but with a slack drumskin. The various tasks of the *Heinzelmännchen* in the tailor shop in themselves offer a chance for an array of unusual orchestral effects: stringed instruments playing sul ponticello and col legno behind the bridge and yet another harp glissando played with strips of paper between the strings.

Specialists have long argued, John Williamson most recently, that Pfitzner abjured naturalistic description in his pianoforte lied. He did so in the majority of his lieder and in his critical essays. Further, orchestral timbre, in the greater number of his orchestral songs, enriches the lyricism of the original piano versions, deepening sentiment and heightening mood. Nevertheless, as illustrated above, New German aesthetics (naturalistic description) affected even Pfitzner.

Reger's interest in orchestral songs arose in 1901, when, as we have seen, he joined the musical mainstream as an avant-garde New German. He studied orchestral scores, made four-hand piano transcriptions of excerpts from Wagner's operas, and orchestrated pianoforte songs of Schubert, Brahms, and himself. Most important, he sought and acquired a new means of livelihood, as conductor of the outstanding court orchestra at Meiningen.[29] There he composed orchestral music, mixing hues and colors on an opulent orchestral palette.

His first orchestral song, "An die Hoffnung" (Op. 124; 1912), reveals Reger's newly won command of the orchestra. One critic applauded its "resplendent romantic-impressionism," another's verdict was that the song "succeeds, above all, through . . . the wonderful treatment of the orchestra."[30] At its premiere Reger presented, in addition, four pianoforte songs of Schubert that he had just orchestrated. He offered more orchestrated songs of Schubert, Brahms, and others at future Meiningen programs, and at a later concert (1913), he arranged four more of his own pianoforte songs. Although his position at Meiningen came to a close in 1914, Reger's experience there stimulated his interest in the orchestral song. He immersed himself deeper into the genre, composing a second song for orchestra, "Hymnus der Liebe" (Op. 136; 1914). His interest in the genre persisted until his sudden death, in 1916.

In his last years Reger scored twelve more of his pianoforte songs. This ripe harvest reflects the work of an experienced composer, a veteran of conducting, orchestrating, and, alas, wrangling with profit-oriented publishers, visible in his letters to the publisher Simrock. These letters reveal why Reger selected the particular songs he did. Since arrangements of pianoforte songs "are not a very marketable item," Reger selected those that "lend themselves absolutely" to orchestral media and are "always sung." The popular "Mariä Wiegenlied" was an easy choice. So, too, was "Aeolsharfe," "one of my best songs," which "the public will understand in one hearing." "Mein Traum," one of Reger's "most attractive songs," was another.[31] In short, Reger's selections were of his most lyrical, expressive, and easily accessible pianoforte songs. He rejected songs made up exclusively of pianistic figurations.

Reger arranged his pianoforte songs for small orchestra. Experience taught him to avoid his earlier heavy scoring. In contrast, his orchestrations of Brahms and Schubert songs reveal a light hand. Reger gave much thought to their marketability as well. The instrumentation is "technically so simple that any orchestra can play them at sight," he wrote to his publisher. Further, he chose only the "most practical keys," and called for instruments common in most small orchestras, unlike Max Schillings, who asked for a glass harmonica (*Glockenlieder*, Op. 22), Strauss, basset horns ("Das Tal" and "Der Einsame"), and Mahler, oboe d'amore ("Um Mitternacht"). And most attractive for publishers, the songs may be performed with or "without the voice" and thus serve as ideal pieces for diversion at spas and watering places.[32]

Reger made no major structural alterations in the orchestrations of his keyboard songs. He wished to be faithful to the originals, simply to shade them more delicately. Strings are often divided, playing harmonics or high silky tones, while the horn is muted, and the timpani murmur softly in the background. Typical pianistic figurations, found occasionally in the pianoforte songs, were effectively translated into orchestral timbres. Though little more than diversions, these songs are truly attractive.

Expansiveness in the lied, demonstrated in the orchestral song, was indeed widespread during the fin de siècle. That this genre could serve one composer (Reger) as attractive diversion and another (Mahler) as medium for expressive profundity shows its remarkable adaptability. Of course, a variety of reasons drew composers to the genre. As a consequence, they converted the lied from a "monochrome" pianistic genre into a "multichrome" orchestral one.

Yet not all late romantics were blinded by the orchestral lied's Brobdingnagian size. Rudolf Louis challenged this and other weaknesses: "An orchestral accompaniment represents a danger for a purely lyrical text, especially for simpler kinds. There arises . . . disturbing incongruity between the intimate content of the text and demands for intensity made today upon [orchestral] media. Further, the temptation now is to lay more stress upon superficialities such as illustrative tone-painting, pure sound effects and the like . . . than is consistent with the nature of purely lyrical text."³³

Other critics, we recall, had censured expansiveness in the lied with these terms: *symphonic lied style, orchestrally conceived piano parts*. And in this context, Schoenberg's comments on his *Chamber Symphony, No. 1* (Op. 9) of 1906 are crucial. "The length of my earlier compositions was one of the features that linked me with the style of my predecessors, Bruckner, Mahler, and Strauss. . . . I had become tired . . . of writing music of such length. . . . Much of this length in my own works was the result of a desire, common to all of my predecessors and contemporaries, to express every character and mood in a broad manner. . . . My desire to condense . . . gradually changed my style of composition."³⁴

Alban Berg certainly rejected expansiveness in favor of brevity with his *Fünf Orchesterlieder nach Ansichtskartentexten von Peter Altenberg*, Op. 4 (1912)—those "aphoristic" lieder on texts by Peter Altenberg.³⁵ One song has just eleven bars. Earlier, rare examples of short lieder include the *Dehmel Sprüche* (1903) of Theodor Streicher, of which "Leitspruch" is only four measures, and Conrad Ansorge's epigrammatic cycle *Urworte* (Op. 19; 1904). One might add later examples by Joseph Haas (from the *Christuslieder*, Op. 74), Paul Graener, and even Strauss—his curious "Xenion" (Op. 131), a setting from Goethe's *Der West-östlicher Divan* that is only six bars long. Schoenberg's *Sechs kleine Klavier-Stücke*, Op. 19 (1911)—which reject the "drawn-out," the excessively copious in music—were prophetic of the future trend in lieder but were widely ignored. Reaction against expansiveness during the fin de siècle was, indeed, restrained.

After World War I, however, late-romantic expansiveness all but disappeared, and not only for aesthetic reasons. Financial restrictions were to make reaction against large works inevitable, as the cost of assembling large orchestras became prohibitive. The orchestral lied became a victim of this change.

The dominant aesthetic of the fin de siècle was the end product of a century's development. Late romantics favored the inherited standard of interpretation identified as "expressive aesthetics"—an art of self-expression that stressed feeling, creative interpretation, and a cult of personality. Accordingly, they accepted mores of concert life that are different from those that would be acceptable in the postwar world. Fin-de-siècle composers achieved an equally remarkable feat. They fused modernity and tradition, permeating old lied forms with the late-romantic inclination for perpetual growth, continual development. Further, they developed to its height the romantic century's predilection for expansiveness. We may, therefore, affirm that fin-de-siècle musicians considered tradition a revered heritage, which they built upon, giving performance and lied structure the century's freest expression. In their endeavor to preserve tradition, late romantics restrained the radicals who sought to destroy that tradition. The restraint occurred not just in music but in political, social, and economic spheres as well.

The crossover into modernity certainly did not occur before World War I, therefore. It was the war and its vast devastation that brought fundamental changes. The postwar world rejected a return to the status quo ante. The totality of the devastation freed thwarted prewar innovations, producing the elemental changes I have mentioned: the fall of monarchies and the rise in the West of democracies and in the East of communism. Innovations in music proved no less thoroughgoing. A reversal of ideas was under way that affected all aspects of music: performance, composition, even theories concerning its nature. Stravinsky, Schoenberg, and Hindemith, inheriting the scepter of modernity, successfully supplanted fin-de-siècle aesthetics with those of neoclassicism and serialism. Music did not navigate a lone, isolated course; it crossed over into modernity along with the Western world—after the war.

The decline of the old was, however, more gradual than generally recognized. Just as Arno Mayer argues that "the World War of 1939–1945 was umbilically tied to the Great War of 1914–1918," since "forces of perseverance recovered sufficiently to aggravate Europe's general crisis, sponsor fascism and contribute to the resumption of total war" (an extreme, but provocative theory), so might we claim that late romantics persevered in music aesthetic in Weimar Germany by absorbing elements of modernity into their art.[36] We have seen that Strauss's Weimar lieder, for example, certainly absorbed elements of modernity. Yet these and his final distinguished expression in the lied, the *Four Last Songs*, reveal that his aesthetics, in the final analysis, was essentially late romantic. Timothy Jackson advances an interesting theory that indirectly confirms this point. He postulates that Strauss had intended to include "Ruhe, meine Seele!"—composed in 1894 and orchestrated 1948—among the *Four Last Songs*, to form a unified cycle of five. The five songs, he notes, form a stylistic unity, even though "Ruhe, meine Seele!" is separated from the others by more than fifty years.[37]

Strauss's return late in life to the lied—when it was of minor importance in the modern world—is further evidence of his conservative nostalgia for things past. This yearning reminds one also of the past significance of the lied, when it served all leading composers fundamentally—Wolf as his main musical interest, Strauss for radical experiments, Mahler as a source for his ingenious scherzos, and Schoenberg as the final stimulus for his break with tradition (*Das Buch der hängenden Gärten*). We are reminded, too, of the abundant yield of this small form. It reflected dominant trends, even social aspirations that unified fin-de-siècle Germans. Small wonder that so many subjects, styles, and moods—even our concept of the period—find in the lied an ideal mirror of the fin de siècle.

Notes

Unless otherwise noted, all translations from the German are my own.

Prologue

1. Mayer, *Persistence*, 6, 4, challenges the old thesis that the modern age was ushered in by the 1890s: "For too long historians . . . have been far more preoccupied with forces of innovation and the making of the new society than with the forces of inertia and resistance that slowed the waning of the old order." Karl Beckson also identifies the fin de siècle (in England) as the end of the old order. See *London in the 1890s: A Cultural History* (New York, 1993). Modris Eksteins, in *Rites of Spring: The Great War and the Birth of the Modern Age* (Boston, 1989), traces the political, social, and aesthetic roots of modernism to World War I. The shattering of old traditions absorbed novelists. A brilliant example, of course, is Thomas Mann's *Der Zauberberg* (The Magic Mountain). The theme served as primary subject also in Jean Renoir's classic film *Grand Illusion*.

2. *Grove* (1909) has impressive articles on Strauss and Wolf but no entry for Schoenberg. Riemann's *Musik-Lexikon* (1909) provides respectable entries for Strauss and Wolf but only eight lines (largely a work list) for Schoenberg. However, Riemann (1916) includes a lengthier Schoenberg entry (thirty-seven lines), affirming that although Schoenberg's recent works have engendered protest, there is "no denying that he possesses talent." See John Irving's interesting article "Schoenberg in the News: The London Performances of 1912–1914," *Music Review* 48 (1988): 52–70.

3. The works performed at the Skandalkonzert were: Anton Webern, *Six Pieces for Orchestra*; Alexander von Zemlinsky, *Four Orchestral Songs after Poems by Maeterlinck*; Schoenberg, *Chamber Symphony, Op. 9*; Alban Berg, *Two Orchestral Songs on Picture Postcard Texts by Peter Altenberg*; and Mahler, *Kindertotenlieder*. "The shouting and bawling" stopped the concert before the songs by Mahler could be performed: see Stuckenschmidt, *Schoenberg*, 184–187.

4. Del Mar, *Strauss*, 3:475. Recent articles by Bryan Gilliam, Lewis Lockwood in *Richard Strauss: New Perspectives on the Composer and His Work*, ed. Bryan Gilliam (Durham, N.C., 1992), and by Leon Botstein in *Richard Strauss and His World*, ed. Bryan Gilliam (Princeton, 1992), present contrary views of Strauss's late style. Decades earlier Curt Sachs held similar views on Strauss as a modernist in the Weimar years.

5. Donal Henahan, "The Vanishing Lieder Ritual," *New York Times*, April 3, 1988: "As the audience for song recitals has diminished, the traditional ceremonies can no longer be taken for granted" (sec. 2, 29). See also Will Crutchfield, "Singing Recitals Is No Way to Make a Living," *New York Times*, April 6, 1986, sec. 2, 23 ff. Even outstanding singers of lieder cannot succeed financially unless they supplement their income by performing opera and other vocal works. See Bernard Holland, "An Artist's Legacy: The Song Recital," *New York Times*, February 17, 1992: "Singers are the notoriously difficult ticket to sell. Were it not for the partial service that recordings perform, a great literature would be erased from the consciousness of an entire generation" (C-16).

Chapter 1: Innovation

1. See Stern, *Gold*, 181; Mayer, *Persistence*, 45; and Karl Erich Born, "Structural Changes in German Social and Economic Development at the End of the Nineteenth Century," in *Imperial Germany*, ed. James J. Sheehan, 17. I wish to thank historians John Weiss and Ruth Zerner for helpful suggestions on Wilhelmian Germany.

2. Barbara W. Tuchman, *The Proud Tower* (New York, 1966), 416, 455.

3. Quoted in Walker, *Wolf*, 270. Unlike Wolf, Strauss, and other moderns—all staunch New Germans—Mahler challenged the movement's "pedantry" for scorning the Italians, the French (except for Berlioz), the Slavs, and, in particular, the "arch-enemy," Brahms. See Mahler and Strauss, *Correspondence*, 117, including the important remarks there of Herta Blaukopf.

4. Louis, *Gegenwart*, 212 and 214 ff.

5. The full name of the *Kunstwart* critic is not given: see F. G., "Wolf und Keller," *Der Kunstwart* 24 (1911): 59; Edmund von Fryhold, "Die Technik der musikalischen Deklamation," *Die Musik* 4 (1905): 3–16, 115–134, and 147–164; Decsey, *Wolf*, 2:146 ff.; Steinitzer, *Strauss*, 159.

6. Niemann, *Gegenwart*, 190–191. This widely read book underwent twenty editions.

7. Niemann, *Gegenwart*, 190–191; Louis, *Gegenwart*, 200.

8. Gutmann, *Erinnerungen*, 99.

9. Helm, "Wiener Musikleben," 275. On page 276 Helm names the singer, Marianne Brandt, but not the critic: it was Wilhelm Frey, of the *Neues Wiener Tagblatt*.

10. Wolf's comment about the "Der Feuerreiter" is in Wolf, *Kaufmann*, 121–122; translated in Walker, *Wolf*, 333. Singers whom Helm mentions in "Wiener Musikleben" include such luminaries as Alice Barbi, Eugen Gura, and Johannes Messchaert; quote on 276.

11. Wolf's ascendancy was acknowledged in many articles by younger contemporaries. In *Courvoisier*, Kroyer notes that Wolf exercised "an overwhelming influence upon his generation" (34). And Edgar Istel specifies: "Wolf songs . . . quickly became the fashion" ("Thuille" 467).

12. For Reger's comment on Brahms, see Reger, *Meister*, 31. Further information about Brahms's influence on Reger can be found in Wehmeyer, *Auseinandersetzung*, 53–54; Wehmeyer, *Liederkomponist*, 7 ff. and passim. For Reger's letter to publishers Breitkopf and Härtel, on January 11, 1899, see Reger, *Meister*, 61.

13. Of primary importance is his missionary work for Wolf; see Reger's article, "Nachlass," 2 ff. Reger edited Wolf's "Christnacht" and the *Italienische Serenade* for publication. However, Walker indicates in "Italian Serenade" (161–174) that Reger made only minor emendations in *Italienische Serenade*. Fritz Stein, *Thematisches Verzeichnis der im Druck erschienen Werke von Max Reger* (Leipzig, 1953), 523, cites the compositions by Wolf that Reger edited.

14. Louis, *Gegenwart*, 222.

15. Niemann, *Gegenwart*, 147 ff. Mahler complained repeatedly to Strauss about his neglect as composer. See Mahler, Strauss, *Briefwechsel*, 16, 18, 43, 53, and 75. However, Muck, *Berliner*, vol. 1, reprints programs from several concerts in Berlin that featured Mahler's works, which indicates that his music was performed there more frequently before 1915 than one might assume.

16. The periodical *Der Morgen* recognized Strauss as "Leader of the Moderns": See Strauss, *Recollections*, 12 ff.; Louis, *Gegenwart*, 98; Finck, *Strauss*, 286; Newman, *Strauss*, 96; Gysi, *Strauss*, 9; Steinitzer discusses his term *Sprechlied* in *Strauss*, 25.

17. "Many of Strauss's most ambitious songs are absolutely formless," Newman asserts, "with no more organization than a jellyfish" (*Strauss*, 93; see also *Studies*).

18. Trenner, *Dokumente*, 81, drew these comments from a newspaper interview of Strauss by Max Marschalk in the *Vossische Zeitung*, October 15, 1918. Strauss felt that although Beethoven, Brahms, and Meyerbeer had brilliant melodic ideas, they did not develop them sufficiently. Only Mozart did so to perfection, according to Strauss, who learned this rare skill from studying Schubert's dances, on the advice of Brahms (see *Dokumente*, 4 and 80). Strauss's comments to Stefan Zweig, made when the composer was about seventy years old, show that his early manner of developing melody had undergone no basic change (Zweig, *Gestern*, 336, or Trenner, *Dokumente*, 230).

19. See Wiora, *Lied*, Elaine Brody and Robert Fowkes, *The German Lied and Its Poetry* (New York, 1971), and Stein, *Lied*. So, too, did earlier authors: see Müller, *Geschichte*, and Pamer, "Lied," 939–955.

20. Schuh, *Strauss*, 471–472. Schuh's examples include the whole-tone passage in "Leises Lied," the quasi-polytonal close of "Für funfzehn Pfennige," and the bold harmonic innovations in "Notturno" that foreshadow *Salome*.

21. Wolf's statement is drawn from Heinrich Werner's unpublished diary, the entry for January 30, 1895. Frank Walker provided this information. Würz, *Reger, eine Sammlung*, 3:128: "Regers Lieder," quotes Reger's complaint. For Pfitzner's comment, see the introduction of the composer's privately printed *Meine Liedertexte*. I am grateful to Frau Professor Mali Pfitzner, widow of the composer, for a copy of this book.

22. Of course, Moerike's poems had been set before Wolf, by Schumann, for instance. "He may have been drawn to Moerike by Schumann's song settings" (Walker, *Wolf*, 112). Hans Joachim Erwe lists other composers who set Moerike before Wolf (*Musik nach Eduard Mörike*, 2 vols., Hamburg, 1987). But Wolf's remarkable settings of a large number of Moerike's poems qualify the composer as Moerike's prime missionary. Prawer (*Mörike*) recognizes (especially in the foreword, ii, and 36, 38, and 41) the debt of the literary world to Wolf: "The publications of [Wolf's *Moerike-Lieder*] represents a critical turning point in Moerike's afterlife. It was these songs, above all, that carried his name far beyond Germany's borders. They fundamentally altered the established concept of Moerike's personality and art."

23. The length of this list can be reckoned if I cite just those poets whose names begin with *H*—Otto Erich Hartleben, Karl Henkell, Hermann Hesse, Paul Heyse, Hugo von Hofmannsthal, Arno Holz, and Ricarda Huch.

24. Kahle, *Dichtung*, 338. Frisch, *Early Works*, 79 ff., discusses Dehmel, his influence on Schoenberg's early published lieder, and the notorious trial. See also *Richard Dehmel* (Leipzig, 1926), by the leading critic Julius Bab. Chapter 3 of Otto Eduard Lessing, *Masters of Modern German Literature* (1912, reprint, New York, 1967), provides interesting contemporary studies of the poet.

25. Schoenberg, *Letters*, 35. Armin Knab, Theodor Streicher, and Hermann Zilcher composed lengthy Dehmel cycles. Theodor Courvoisier, Paul Gräner, Joseph Haas, Humperdinck, Joseph Marx, Pfitzner, Reger, Schoeck, Sibelius, Richard Trunk, and Zemlinsky set Dehmel's protest poetry and verse for children. Otto Julius Bierbaum (1865–1910), another opponent of the straitlaced, especially in his *Irrgarten der Liebe*, also attracted many lied composers when his poetry first appeared: Ludwig Thuille, Gräner, J. Haas, Siegmund Hausegger, Humperdinck, Kienzl, Reger, Schillings, Strauss, and Trunk. Bierbaum, founder of the *Überbrettl*, the artistic cabaret entertainment of Berlin (1901)—see Bierbaum's *Eine emp-*

findsame Reise im Automobile von Berlin nach Sorrent (Berlin, 1903)—also wrote verse that Oscar Strauss, Viktor Hollaender, and Schoenberg set as *Überbrettl* songs.

26. Löns—unhappy in childhood, unlucky in early maturity, and killed in action in World War I—became a symbol of the Wandervogel movement, as I shall discuss in Chapter 2. Many collections of *Lönslieder* (for guitar) appeared during World War I. Löns's poetry was also set as concert lieder by Yrjö Kilpinen (78 songs!), Schoenberg (*Jeduch*, unfinished), and Felix von Woyrsch, among others.

27. Liliencron was a professional soldier who had been decorated for bravery. Though Wolf never set Liliencron's verse, d'Albert, Ansorge, Haas, Pfitzner, Reger, Schillings, Rudi Stephan, Strauss, and Zilcher did. Other composers attracted to Morgenstern include Reger, Kienzl, Kilpinen, Joseph Marx, Strauss, Trunk, and Weingartner.

28. Schoenberg's attention may have been drawn to George when he attended meetings of the Ansorge Society (discussed in Chapter 2), where George's poetry was well represented. Songs to Mombert's poems were composed by Ansorge, Berg, and J. Marx. Knab wrote complete cycles on Mombert and George.

29. Courvoisier (his complete Op. 18), Schoeck, Strauss, and Georg Vollerthun, among others, set Michelangelo's verse. Heyse's Italian and Spanish translations (with Emanuel Geibel) were set by such composers as Bausznern, Goehler, Haas, Arnold Mendelssohn, Pfitzner, Schreker, and especially J. Marx. Verse of other Latin authors in German translation set by lieder composers includes: Lope de Vega (by Felix Woyrsch, Op. 14), Dante (Schoeck), Petrarch (Schoenberg), and Giordano Bruno (Klose). Lieder on the works of Paul Verlaine were composed by Ansorge, J. Marx, Reger, Schoeck, and Trunk (the complete Op. 42, *Zwölf Lieder*). Schreker's *Zwei lyrische Gesänge* and Marx's "Jugend und Alter" are set to Walt Whitman's poetry.

30. Strauss, *Recollections*, 127 ff. Strauss and Thuille, *Freundschaft*, paints a clear picture of Strauss senior's discipline, e.g., his instruction (180) that Richard compose simpler modulations. The complete edition of Strauss's songs prints only twenty-two of Strauss's earliest songs (from his childhood and student days): *Richard Strauss Lieder: Gesamtausgabe*, ed. Franz Trenner, 4 vols. (London, 1964–65). Del Mar, *Strauss*, inventories forty-two songs (3:248–249) from these years, including lost and unfinished songs later discovered and published by Willi Schuh (1968). However, Petersen cites forty-five lied titles from Strauss's earliest years, including unpublished sketches (*"Ton und Wort,"* 186–188). Further, she believes (14, n. 15) that Strauss's first published cycle, Op. 10, was actually finished November 12, 1885, not 1882–83, and that this cycle originally included a ninth song, "Wer hats getan?" (Gilm), that was "forgotten until the 1970s" (99).

31. James Huneker, *Overtones: A Book of Temperaments* (New York, 1904), 22, cites Strauss's Ritter comment. On the early influence of Wagner, see Trenner, *Dokumente*, 19, and Strauss, *Recollections*, 127 ff. Op. 22, written before Op. 21, provides the possible stylistic link between the songs of Strauss's youth and his maturity. Robertson, *History*, 607, discusses verse of social protest.

32. Interesting early comments on Wagner's influence were made by Max Hehemann, *Max Reger* (Munich, 1917), 32 and 36; Rolle, "Liederkomponist," 150–155; and Guido Bagier, *Max Reger* (Stuttgart, 1923), 52. Hehemann considers the influence especially evident in Op. 48. See also Wehmeyer, *Liederkomponist*, passim.

33. Strauss, *Recollections*, 13–17 and passim.

34. Finck, *Strauss*, 283. Finck's comment was taken from a review he wrote in 1900.

Newman, *Strauss*, 96. The Strauss songs to which Newman was referring are "Himmelsboten" (Op. 32, no. 5); "Glückes genug" (Op. 37, no. 1); and "Die Ulme zu Hirsau" (Op. 43, no. 3).

35. Hugo Riemann, *Grosse Kompositionslehre* (Stuttgart, 1913), 3:236. Reger and Riemann had tangled earlier: see Riemann, "Degeneration," and Reger's reply, "Degeneration," 49–51.

36. Reger, *Briefe*, 94. See also Reger's treatise on modulation, *Modulationslehre*, and his two articles in response to criticism of it: "Ich bitte ums Wort!" and "Mehr Licht!"

37. "Lasst mich ruhen" (pub. 1860), which moves from E major to G sharp, is one of several similar examples by Liszt. After 1875, Liszt frequently treated tonality in his songs in this way. Carl Loewe did so earlier, in "Die Glocken zu Speier" (1837), Op. 67, no. 2, which proceeds from B-flat minor to F-sharp minor. Schubert also provides fascinating examples, and Richard Kramer has interesting things to say about them in *Distant Cycles: Schubert and the Conceiving of Song* (Chicago, 1994), passim. John Daverio's "The *Wechsel der Töne* in Brahms's *Schicksalslied*," *Journal of the American Musicological Society* 46 (1993): 84–113, provides engaging comments on the work's "progressive tonal scheme" (85).

38. Mozart, letter to his father, Vienna, September 26, 1781 (*Letters*), 2:769.

39. See Lawrence Kramer's similar analysis (126 ff.) of this song in his "Decadence and Desire: The *Wilhelm Meister* Songs of Wolf and Schubert," in *Music at the Turn of Century*, ed. Joseph Kerman (Berkeley, 1990). Deborah J. Stein, *Hugo Wolf's "Lieder" and Extensions of Tonality* (Ann Arbor, 1985), studies Wolf's harmonic and tonal complexity according to Heinrich Schenker theory. So, too, did Felix Salzer in discussing some Wolf lieder: see *Structural Hearing* (New York, 1962). Schoenberg drew attention to the tonal complexity in his own "Lockung" (Op. 6, no. 7): though in E-flat major, "no E♭ chord sounds as a pure tonic even once during the song's course" (Schoenberg, *Harmonielehre*, 430).

40. Frisch, *Early Works*, 211 ff., provides an engaging comparison of the styles of Schoenberg and Reger. Further, the early published lieder of Schoenberg and Alma Schindler (Mahler) show interesting similarities. Both composers, students of Zemlinsky, admired Brahms's piano parts, which they sought to surpass in weight and mass. Both showed Wolf's influence in their finely wrought declamation, harmonic language, and motivic structure. Interestingly enough, some of Schindler's early lieder are more individual than the three of Schoenberg mentioned. But in my review-article, "The *Lieder* of Alma Maria Schindler Mahler," *Music Review* 49 (1988): 190–204, I question the chronology of her published songs.

41. Schoenberg worked on three important compositions at the time of his break with tonality, the Second Quartet (May 9, 1897, to August 1908), the two songs of Op. 14 (1907–08), and *Hanging Gardens*. Of these, the quartet's fourth movement ("Entrückung": Transcendence)—composed in August 1908 on a text by George—and *Hanging Gardens* clearly mark Schoenberg's transition to atonality. The term *atonal* has, of course, gained wide currency despite Schoenberg's own dislike of it.

42. Schoenberg, *Letters*, 35. See Walter Frisch, "Schoenberg and the Poetry of Richard Dehmel," *Journal of the Arnold Schoenberg Institute* 9 (1986): 137–179.

43. Quoted in Reich, *Schoenberg*, 49.

44. "Am Strande" (1908?) and the *Hanging Gardens* (1908–09) were followed by only two more sets of songs, Op. 22 (1913–16), and, twenty years later, Op. 48 (1933). Op. 22 is for voice and orchestra.

45. Schoenberg, "My Evolution," 151.

46. Quoted in Walter Kolneder, *Anton Webern: An Introduction to His Works*, trans. Humphrey Searle (Berkeley, 1968), 33.

Chapter 2: Preservation of Tradition

1. Mayer argues in *Persistence,* 84, 95, and 97, that "the magnates of capital and the professions never coalesced sufficiently to contest seriously the social, cultural, and ideological pre-eminence of the old ruling class." Their "supreme ambition was not to besiege or overturn the seignorial establishment but to break into it." Sheehan, *Imperial Germany,* 62–92, also argues that the new industrial class "struggled for titles."

2. "The bourgeoisie was monarchist to the core and outdid itself in fawning loyalty to the Kaiser." This Marxist view, drawn from Gerhart Eisler, Albert Norden, and Albert Schreiner, *The Lesson of Germany* (New York, 1945), 58, is similar to James Billington's conclusion in *Fire in the Minds of Men* (New York, 1980) and to that of the popular historian Barbara Tuchman in *The Proud Tower* (New York, 1966). She states: "National tended to outweigh class traits among the German Socialists: they were more obedient than bold" (416). Billington asserts: "The German Social Democrats failed 1) to take—or even to share—power in imperial Germany and 2) to prevent—or even to resist energetically—German entrance into World War I" (370). See Tom Kemp, *Industrialization in Nineteenth-Century Central Europe,* 2d. ed. (London, 1985), 99 and 102.

3. Mayer, *Persistence,* 84; George Henschel, *Musings and Memories of a Musician* (Reprint, New York, 1979, from the 1919 edition), 340–341.

4. Austria's landed aristocracy of at least two dozen families "controlled over 250,000 acres apiece. . . . Nearly 60 per cent of the active labor force worked the land." The inner circle of the highest aristocracy remained "closed to new ideas and [new] blood right down to the fall of the Habsburgs," Mayer notes (*Persistence,* 27 and 109). Kemp records, in *Industrialization,* 79, that in Germany: "The lords were, on the whole, not great proprietors on the scale of those of the Habsburg Empire." Industrialization developed much later in Austria than in Germany. Advancement into the aristocracy through ennoblement was greatly restricted (see Sheehen, *Imperial Germany,* 25 and passim).

5. McGrath, *Dionysian Art,* 89 ff., particularly, also 5, 20, 59 ff., and passim. In *"Alte unnennbarer Tage!"* Eckstein includes an eye-witness account of the student life of Wolf, Mahler, Lipiner, and Viktor Adler. See also Castle, *Geschichte,* 1559 ff., a fine source on Mahler and other members of this student group. Walker, *Wolf,* 217–218, discusses pan-Germanic demonstrations in the Vienna Wagner Verein. On Viennese at the turn of the century, see also Schorske, *Vienna,* and Jarausch, *Students.*

6. See Schubert's friend and benefactor Leopold von Sonnleithner, in "Bemerkungen," 697, and Maurice J. E. Brown, *Schubert: A Critical Biography* (London, 1961), 108. More recent research indicates that "Diabelli . . . earned a small fortune from brisk sales of Schubert songs over the years." After 1821 Schubert "assumed a position at the summit of Viennese musical life. It was unthinkable that publishers would have rushed to engrave his works unless there was a constant and steady demand." (Otto Biba, "Schubert's Position in Viennese Musical Life," *Nineteenth-Century Music* 3:2 (1979), 110.

7. For a discussion of the lied in concert life before 1870, see my article "The Lied in 19th-Century Concert Life," *Journal of the American Musicological Society* 18 (1965): 207–218.

8. Helm, *Musikalische Welt,* 62.

9. Gutmann, *Erinnerungen,* 90.

10. Wolf, *Kritiken,* 360 (*Criticism,* 273).

11. Raucheisen, interview with the author.

12. Emilie Bittner, interview with the author.

13. Although the first public performance of *Pierrot Lunaire* occurred in Berlin in October 1912, its first private performance, Emilie Bittner assures me, occurred in the home of Alma Mahler. Bittner was present on that occasion.

14. Correspondence of Wilhelm von Wymetal to Conrad Ansorge (November 30, 1903). The letter was in the possession of Dorothea Ansorge-Lippisch. Lieder were probably performed at the Dehmel and George evenings, since Ansorge set texts by both poets. I am very grateful to Frau Ansorge-Lippisch for valuable information about Conrad Ansorge and his society.

15. Societies dedicated to the arts were abundant in fin de siècle. Literary Vereine contributed to concert life almost as significantly as musical groups by sponsoring works of unknown composers. Wolf's *Moerike-Lieder*, we recall, were first performed in the Vienna Wagner Verein. Societies were formed for Wolf, Mahler, Strauss, Pfitzner, Reger, Ansorge, Julius Weismann, Theodor Streicher, Richard Wetz, Martin Plüddemann, Joseph Haas, and Alban Berg. They remained in vogue until the Third Reich, when all societies were forced to disband.

16. Michael Raucheisen accompanied singers often in hotels like the Vier Jahreszeiten and the Bayerische Hof in Munich and the old Waldorf Hotel in New York. Frieda Hempel also performed at such events: see her *Gesang*, passim, and Linda L. Tyler, "'Commerce and Poetry Hand in Hand': Music in American Department Stores, 1880–1930," *Journal of the American Musicological Society* 45 (1992): 75–120. The Überbrettl of Berlin and the Elf Scharfrichter of Munich, though short-lived, were sensationally successful. Überbrettl songs, though light in character, were not light in quality, e.g., Schoenberg's cabaret songs. It was common at that time to refer to an "Aria and Lieder Concert," in that order. However, Rudolf Louis reported in 1909 that the orchestral lied had replaced the "concert aria which has completely died out" (*Gegenwart*, 245). See C. Schumann and Brahms, *Briefe*, 1:549.

17. Walker, *Wolf*, 272. The term *interval* (*Zwischenpausen*) refers to musical offerings at concerts other than those of the main soloists, the *Konzertgeber*. Raimund von Zur Mühlen (1854–1931) was among the first to give Liederabende devoted exclusively to songs. Ivor Newton devotes a chapter of his book *At the Piano: Ivor Newton, The World of an Accompanist* (London, 1966), to Zur Mühlen. Pianoforte lieder were common at symphony concerts of the Berlin Philharmonic Orchestra from its founding in 1882 to World War I. For instance, performances of orchestral songs—Schubert's "Erlkönig," in Berlioz's orchestration (given December 10, 1890)—increased considerably in frequency in Berlin after 1900. Richard Strauss conducted orchestral versions of his songs and those of Mahler on December 4, 1899, April 9, 1900, December 12, 1904, and October 13, 1915. See Muck, *Berliner*, 1:355, 405, and 458, and 3:3, 4, 79, 96, 153 and passim, for the years before 1900.

18. Helm, "Wiener Musikleben," 8:39 (1917).

19. Quoted in Gutmann, *Erinnerungen*, 103.

20. Ehlers, "Zur Konzertreform," 109.

21. See Paul Marsop, "Zur Bühnen und Konzertreform," *Die Musik* 18 (1906): 79–99, 215–230. Marsop discusses Batka's monograph, *Handbook for the Concert Manager*, on page 248 of *Die Musik* 19 (1906). See also pages 246–258 on the concert reform movement.

22. Marsop, "Der Musiksaal der Zukunft," 5:3–4n (1902). See Marsop's "Zur Reform des Concertwesen," 54, and Ehlers, "Konzertreform," 110, on banishing arias from song recitals.

23. Ehlers, "Die Verdunklung der Konzerträume," *Die Gesellschaft* 1 (1902), 308. Marsop added: "Indirect lighting," which was used "mainly in lecture rooms, art classes, and schools," is the best type of lighting for "theatres and concert halls. . . . Anyone seated in the gallery and thereby unfortunate enough to have had to stare into the bright lights of a chandelier for an entire evening certainly would recognize the benefits of indirect lighting" ("Bühnen und Konzertreform," 250). Lengthy articles, pro and con, appeared shortly after 1900 on the subject of dimming lights during recitals.

24. Marsop, "Vom Musiksaal," 170.

25. Ehlers, "Verdunklung," 316; Marsop, "Zur Bühnen," 256 and 316. Marsop discusses the Nuremberg concert in "Vom Musiksaal," 166–167.

26. Mauke, "Lebende Lied" n.p. Mauke and Weingartner continued their dispute in other issues of the newspaper, Mauke on August 23 and Weingartner on August 30. Weingartner rejected Mauke's appeal for special atmosphere, dress, and perfume in performing lieder. I wish to thank Carmen Weingartner, Weingartner's widow and herself a fine conductor, for bringing these articles to my attention.

27. Wagnerians experimented with ways to adopt the hidden orchestra of Bayreuth for concerts. They also urged that amphitheater structures be adapted for all future concert halls and opera houses, using Bayreuth as the model. The Prince Regent Theater in Munich is an example. Such halls, Wagnerians argued, were more democratic and acoustically superior to halls with tiers of boxes and loges. Wagnerians also sought to curtail applause, as it was at Bayreuth, where applause at the close of the first and third acts of *Parsifal* is proscribed.

28. Mahler and Strauss, *Briefwechsel*, 96–97.

29. Strauss's letter is published in translation in *Musical Quarterly* 36 (1950): 1–8, with an introduction by Alfred Mann ("The Artistic Testament of Richard Strauss"). Lang's editorial comment follows on page 8.

30. Niemann, *Gegenwart*, 48 ff., discusses the "Brahms school." I wish to thank Carl August Weismann, former violist of the Freiburg Opera and Symphony Orchestra, for allowing me to study "Fernrohr," the unpublished autobiography of his father, Julius Weismann. Material quoted above was drawn from pages 15 and 17. A friend of Brahms's, Heinrich von Herzogenberg (1843–1900) of the Hochschule für Musik (Berlin)—to whom Weismann refers—was one of Germany's foremost professors of composition. Pfitzner surveys his student days at the Frankfurt Conservatory with Knorr and James Kwast in *Reden, Schriften, Briefe*, ed. Walter Abendroth (Berlin-Frohnau, 1955), 185 and 187. Mali Pfitzner, the composer's widow, presented me with a copy of this book. The Peter Cahn quotation is from *Das Hoch'sche Konservatorium in Frankfurt am Main (1878–1978)* (Frankfurt am Main, 1979), 92, 191, passim. Conservative composers were appointed senior professors of composition in other schools, e.g., Gustav Jenner (1865–1920)—Brahms's only student—became director of music at the University of Marburg, and Felix Draeseke (1835–1913) was professor of composition in Dresden. These academics generally had little success as composers except Draeseke, who in his youth was a New German radical but in later life became a severe conservative. He attacked the moderns (Strauss) in an article called "Die Konfusion in der Musik" (1906). Changes in the curriculum came after World War I when, for instance, Bernhard Sekles (1872–1934) became professor of composition in the Frankfurt Conservatory and Schoenberg and Hindemith were made professors in conservatories in Berlin. On Thuille as professor of composition, see Andrew D. McCredie, "Ludwig Thuille als Kompositionslehrer und Theoretiker," in Edelman et al., *Thuille*, 43–48.

31. Pfitzner, *Reden*, 188.

32. Strauss suggested (1902) that this "momentary" overcharged writing should be overlooked because Schoenberg, "is *very* talented" (see Stuckenschmidt, *Schoenberg*, 63). Schoenberg had not yet embarked on his radical excursions. Strauss, familiar with Schoenberg's sextet (*Verklärte Nacht*, 1899), asked Schoenberg on July 19, 1902, for the score of his *Pelleas und Melisande*, which Schoenberg had not yet completed (it was finished February 28, 1903; see *Schoenberg*, 62). Stuckenschmidt cites Strauss's severe comment but adds that Strauss, as director of the Vienna Opera, was "in favor of [performing] works of Schoenberg and Ernst Krenek" (73). Mahler's comment is from A. Mahler, *Memories*, 112. Mahler is supposed to have declared himself "incapable of 'reading' the score [of Schoenberg's Second String Quartet (1908)]" (see Norman Lebrecht, *Mahler Remembered* [London, 1987], 255).

33. Schoenberg, *Harmonielehre*, 440.

34. The first letter is dated October 14, 1904. The second was written January 13, 1905 (see Reger, *Briefe*, 124, 134). The *Schlichte Weisen* and Reger's volkstümlich songs are discussed in Chapters 7 and 11.

35. Quoted in Bauer-Lechner, *Recollections*, 131. See also Graeme Alexander Downes, "Mahler and Progressive Tonality," Ph.D. diss., University of Otago.

36. Hofmannsthal to Strauss, October 18, 1908; Strauss to Hofmannsthal, August 16, 1916(?) (Strauss and Hofmannsthal, *Briefwechsel*, 50, 359).

37. Pfitzner examines the three methods of setting texts in *Impotenz*, 90 ff., and *Inspiration*, 67 ff. The first book received sharp critical rebuke from Alban Berg. For a recent reprint of *Inspiration*, see *Hans Pfitzner Schriften*. Pages 294 and 295 provide interesting comments by Pfitzner about the way he unites words and music in the lied.

38. Newman, *Strauss*, 94–95. Newman drew Strauss's remarks from Hausegger, *Gedanken*, 398–399, which reprints a questionnaire Hausegger sent to several composers, Strauss among them, inviting them to explain how they wrote lieder.

39. More-recent commentary on Schumann's influence on Mahler's "Des Antonius von Padua Fischpredigt" includes David Anniss Pickett, "Gustav Mahler as an Interpreter" (Ph.D. diss., University of Surrey, 1988), 1:99. Bauer-Lechner, *Recollections*, 169, cites Mahler's judgment of Schumann: "Nobody has mastered the perfected, self-contained form of the lied as he did." Del Mar, *Strauss*, 3:323. On the Schumann-Mahler link, see also Reinhard Kapp, "Schumann-Reminiszenzen bei Mahler," *Österreichische Musikzeitschrift* 37 (1982): 241–248.

40. Walker, *Wolf*, 60. The songs that Wolf probably had in mind were "An*," "Wanderlied," and "Morgentau." Youens entitles her first chapter, on Wolf's early songs, "Too Much like Schumann," (*Hugo Wolf*). On Wolf's early affinity for Schumann, see also Hans Eppstein, "Entwicklungszüge in Hugo Wolfs frühen Liedkompositionen," *Svensk tidskrift för musikforskning* 66 (1984): 49–50. The manuscript of "Was soll ich sagen" is located in the City Library, Vienna.

41. Bernhard Adamy prints Pfitzner's uncompleted biography in Pfitzner, *Sämtliche Schriften*, 134–161. Page 161 reproduces the manuscript of Pfitzner's sonnet to Schumann. *Hans Pfitzner Sechs Sonette* (six sonnets) were privately printed in 1949, on his eightieth birthday, the year of his death. I am grateful to the composer's widow for a copy of this publication. Pfitzner eagerly accompanied singers of Schumann's pianoforte songs. Further on Pfitzner's involvement with Schumann, see Abendroth, *Pfitzner*, 189, 237, 347, and 349. Williamson, "In the Footsteps of Schumann," *Music of Pfitzner*, 48–82, has much of consequence to say on the Pfitzner lied.

42. Pfitzner specialists contend that no composer captures the rustling and deep mystery of the German forest as do Schumann and Pfitzner (see Abendroth, *Pfitzner*, 355, and Hans Joachim Moser, "Hans Pfitzner als Liederkomponist," *Hellweg* 4 [1924]). Bert Vos and Preston

Barba, *German Lyrics and Ballads, from Klopstock to Modern Times* (New York, 1925), 386, provides the comment on Goethe.

43. See Wehmeyer, *Liederkomponist,* 184 and passim. Her discussion of the Stimmungslied (175 ff.) is of special interest. Several lesser masters of the late-romantic lied were also strongly influenced by Schumann. Hans Sittner, president of the Akademie für Musik und Darstellende Kunst in Vienna, an authority on Wilhelm Kienzl, drew special attention to Schumann's influence on Kienzl in a letter to me. The 1990 Koch International compact disk "Wilhelm Kienzl Lieder/Songs" (314020), performed by Steven Kimbrough (baritone) and Dalton Baldwin (piano), presents a fine selection of the composer's songs. In Chapter 11 I consider the influence of Schumann on structure in the fin-de-siècle lied.

Chapter 3: End of the Romantic Era

1. Abrams, *Mirror,* 21–22. My article "Romanticism Today," *Musical Quarterly* 76 (1992): 93–109, discusses the question of why romanticism remained for decades a field strewn with snares and pitfalls thwarting investigation.

2. Abrams, *Mirror,* 21.

3. Mozart, letter to his father, July 3, 1778 (*Letters,* 2:558).

4. Geoffrey Hartman, *Beyond Formalism* (New Haven, 1970), 301.

5. Sachs, *Rhythm,* 273. Sachs also illustrates how "emotional content" in C. P. E. Bach is closely allied to the expressiveness of the early Italian baroque (323). Abrams, *Mirror,* 22.

6. Paul Henry Lang considers "extreme subjectivism" a central factor of romanticism in *Music in Western Civilization* (New York, 1941), 737, as do most music historians.

7. Mahler, *Briefe,* 190, 207, 31–32, 36, 38, and 42.

8. A limited number of copies (120) of *Krämerspiegel* were printed in 1921 for private circulation. The English publishers Boosey and Hawkes finally published the songs in 1959, without translations of the poems, explaining "they are not translatable" and advising readers: "One should not attribute more importance to Alfred Kerr's verses than they deserve." The firm misled English readers further, stating that the poems were "all too spicy." Barbara A. Petersen, *"Die Händler und die Kunst:* Richard Strauss as Composers' Advocate," in *Richard Strauss: New Perspectives on the Composer and His Work,* ed. Bryan Gilliam (Durham, 1992), 115–132, explores Strauss's problems with publishers. Mahler also had negative experience with von Hase. His letter inquiring whether von Hase would publish his Seventh Symphony went unanswered (Reilly, *Mahler und Adler,* 51–52). Mahler quipped that von Hase was "probably planning to publish the complete works of Wallnöfer." An Adolf Wallnöfer (1854–1946), singer and composer, did exist.

9. Mathilde Schoenberg left Arnold early in the summer of 1908. He quoted the phrase "alles ist hin" (all is lost) from the folk song "Ach du lieber Augustin" in the trio of the second movement of his F-Sharp Minor Quartet (July 27, 1908). Newlin states that the quotation and its treatment was of "real emotional significance" (*Bruckner,* 235). Schoenberg dedicated the quartet to "My Wife." Mathilde returned to Arnold that summer. See Stuckenschmidt, *Schoenberg,* 94 ff., on the affair and 168–169 concerning Schoenberg's later feelings about it. Schoenberg, born September 13, 1874, was still thirty years of age when he composed "Alles," on September 9, 1905.

10. The literary theorist Robert M. Browne pursued this train of thought vigorously in correspondence with me.

11. Walker, *Wolf,* 363.

12. See Walker, *Wolf,* 221–222, 280, 305, and 313, for his uncompromising specifications to printers and performers of his music.

13. Johann Gottlieb Fichte, *Grundlage der gesamten Wissenschaftslehre* (Leipzig, 1794), 303. The English translation is from Walzel, *Romanticism,* 29.

14. Peckham, *Studies,* 217–218; Stephenson, *Romanticism,* 7. In the text above, I have replaced the given English translation of "avoiding reality" with "flight from the world of man," which is closer to Stephenson's "Verschlingung von Weltflucht," in *Romantik in der Tonkunst* (Cologne, 1961), 5. See Hans Tischler, "Classicism, Romanticism and Music," *Music Review* 14 (1953): 205–208. Gurlitt drew his concept of the alienated romantic from Stephenson's study: see Riemann, *Musik-Lexikon* (1967, ed. Gurlitt), 814 ff.

15. The poet Novalis (1772–1801) portrays his search for such fulfillment in his chief work, the unfinished *Heinrich von Ofterdingen* (1802). Heinrich's search for the magnificent flower he beheld in a dream forever impels him onward. The blue flower symbolizes the romanticist's goal. His plight is to seek happiness in a nebulous shadowland, a utopia of illusion, a state in which, as Novalis puts it, "reality becomes dreams and dreams become reality." For John Daverio, the contributions of Novalis's contemporary Friedrich Schlegel (1772–1829) embody the essence of romanticism in music, not only for his time but for the entire century: see Daverio's *Nineteenth-Century Music and the German Romantic Ideology* (New York, 1993).

16. Goethe to Eckermann, September 24, 1827. English translation from Babbitt, *Rousseau,* 309. On Wagner, see Leon Botstein, "Wagner and Our Century," in *Music at the Turn of Century,* ed. Joseph Kerman (Berkeley, 1990), 168.

17. Kuno Franke, *A History of German Literature* (New York, 1903), 504. Franke's contribution to German literary criticism is outstanding. Otto Eduard Lessing dedicated to him his *Masters in Modern German Literature* (1912, reprint, New York, 1967): "Dem Bahnbrecher deutscher Kultur in Amerika" (The pioneer of German culture in America).

18. Babbitt, *Rousseau,* 264 and 265. See Walzel, *Romanticism,* 232 and 236, for a discussion of the Jean Paul comment viz. romantic irony.

19. Stephenson, *Romanticism,* 12.

20. English translation by Alma Elise Luseky from Walzel, *Romanticism,* 130. Reprinted with permission from Putnam Publishing Company. The original German poem is untitled, see Tieck, *Frühe Erzählungen und Romane,* 833–835. Mitchell discusses how nature gives Mahler initial comfort but, in the end, "arouses his melancholy" (*Early Years,* 89).

21. See Niemann, *Brahms,* 352 and 434. Niemann's observation has the ring of authenticity. Nevertheless, there are few truly romantic Brahms works. Among his romantic lieder are "O wüsst ich doch den Weg zurück" (Groth), "Todessehnen" (Schenkendorff), "Der Tod, das ist die kühle Nacht" (Heine), "Immer leise wird mein Schlummer" (Lingg), and "Auf dem Kirchhof" (Liliencron). Brahms sought to soften the pessimism in several significant choral works, e.g., *Rhapsodie* (for alto and male chorus), *Schicksalslied,* and *Gesang der Parzen.* He refused to conclude *Schicksalslied,* which sets the Hölderlin poem, as the poet did: with the fall of man. After a long struggle, he concluded the work with the music of the opening section, which expresses the serenity of the gods. For Stephenson's comment, see *Romanticism,* 12.

22. Myers, *Civilization,* 361; Wolf, quoted in Walker, *Wolf,* 219.

23. Quoted in A. Mahler, *Memories,* 109. Alma Mahler shows how anti-Semitism was the source of Mahler's persistent feelings of social isolation. One example: after acquiring new friends in a summer resort, he found their homes "closed to him" in the fall in Vienna. At once he felt "rebuffed as a Jew and, avoiding new acquaintances for the future, fell back on his boyhood friends."

24. The German of these lines reads, "Ach nein, ich ließ mich nicht abweisen. Ich bin von Gott, und will wieder zu Gott!" See Ludwig Achim von Arnim and Clemens Brentano, *Des Knaben Wunderhorn* (Berlin, no date given), 1:454.

25. Hartman, *Formalism*, 303–304. Peckham, *Romanticism*, 56, discusses the concept of wanderers alienated from their society as the essence of romantic behavior. "If the crisis is severe, this . . . estrangement spreads through personal contact and through literature, the arts, philosophy, theology, and so on. . . . In time, a network of this kind of estranged individual establishes itself throughout a culture by means of various kinds of contact and communication, everything from personal conversation to performance of music."

26. Quoted in Bauer-Lechner, *Recollections*, 174. Mahler nearly succumbed to a dangerous hemorrhage on February 24, 1901. See my article "Mahler's Dirges for His Death: February 24, 1901," *Musical Quarterly* 64 (1978): 329–330, and Feder, "Mahler Dying," 125–148.

27. Pfitzner's "Abschied" is another. The prevailing mood of the text is of tranquility and awe for the Almighty, the creator of the woods and the evening's peace. The music, however, enshrouds the poem with deep nostalgia. Its strong atmosphere and prominent melody are immersed in sadness. They cover the poem like a mournful veil, blurring peaceful stillness and transforming forest tranquility into elegiac lamentation.

28. The eminent Pfitzner scholar Erwin Kroll generalizes that Pfitzner was most successful when he set poems of "dejection . . . of loneliness and of fear of abandonment" (*Pfitzner*, 89 and 128). Such themes dominate the subjects of Pfitzner's *Sechs Jugendlieder* but recur only occasionally in his mature works. Nevertheless, the critic Conrad Wandrey called Pfitzner "an undertaker of Romanticism." Pfitzner retorted furiously even against the label *romantic*, acknowledging the presence of a "weary-world renouncing theme" only in some works. He argued that in most he struck out in many other directions (Pfitzner, "Offener Brief," 729). Wandrey was referring to "Nachtwanderer," an early work (Op. 7, no. 2) in his statement that Pfitzner had "sympathy for death." In "Nachtwanderer," a horseman ends his ride through sinister darkness as a victim of the spirits of romanticism. The same harshness dominates "Herr Oluf" (Op. 12), which depicts another night ride that ends in death. Such harshness stamps even the seemingly playful fairy tale discussed above, "Hast du von den Fischerkindern."

29. Abrams, *Mirror*, 26 and 28–29. Modern criticism, according to Stanley Edgar Hyman (*The Armed Vision* [New York, 1952], 7, 14, 307, and passim) began in 1924 "with the publication of I. A. Richards's *Principles of Literary Criticism.*" Contrary views came after World War II, the most recent from the New Historicism, which challenges the concept of "sanitizing" a work while analyzing it. New Historicism aims to establish romanticism as a nineteenth-century phenomenon. Such scholarship runs counter to the long-established view of "romantic" music as denoting both a period and "a universal phenomenon of all times [and] zones . . . since classical antiquity" (Lang, *Western Civilization*, 738).

30. Wolf, *Briefe Grohe*, 45. The commission, issued by Max Burckhard, the director of the Vienna Burgtheater, was for incidental music for Ibsen's *The Feast at Solhaug* (see Walker, *Wolf*, 281).

31. The period that followed World War I, when musical styles were undergoing fundamental change, proved to be a time of crisis for many—Franz Mittler (1893–1970), for instance. Before the war, Mittler, at age sixteen, had composed lieder that were published by the best presses (Universal Edition, Associated Music Publishers). After the war, this gifted young—

but still unknown—composer, like many others, found himself in a netherland, confronting a new musical world that was rejecting his revered late-romantic style. On Mittler, see Diana Mittler-Battipaglia, *Franz Mittler* (New York, 1993).

32. For these labels see the following: "music in transition," Andrew J. Broekema, *The Music Listener* (Dubuque, ca. 1978); "in transition," Roland Nadeau and William Tesson, *Listen* (Boston, 1976; "transition from the romantic to the modern period," Richard Wink and Lois Williams, *Invitation to Listening* (Atlanta, 1976). Stanley Sadie interrupts the customary sequence of periods as baroque, classical, romantic, followed by a special term, "turn of the century," and finally twentieth century: see *S. Sadie's Music Guide* (Englewood Cliffs, N.J., 1986). For the Wagnerian designation of "the twilight of the gods," see Beekman Cannon, Alvin Johnson, and William Waite, *The Art of Music* (New York, 1960). "The Road to the Present" is Lang's title (*Western Civilization*). Homer Ulrich's comment is interesting, owing to diversity of terms noted: the fin de siècle "has not yet received a satisfactory all-embracing name" (*For Listening* [New York, 1970], 280). Thus Ulrich and Paul Pisk (*A History of Music and Musical Styles* [New York, 1963]) suggest "expanded resources" (550).

33. Weingartner, *Lebenserinnerungen*, 363–364, records Weingartner's first impressions of Wolf's *Moerike-Lieder*.

34. Louis, *Gegenwart*, 216–217. Batka is one of several early critics who challenged this narrow view of the Wolf lied. See "Zur Würdigung," 273 ff. The *post-Wagnerian* designation occurs in Martin Bernstein, *An Introduction to Music* (1937; Englewood Cliffs, N.J., 1972), Lang, *Western Civilization*, William Fleming and Abraham Veinus, *Understanding Music* (New York, 1958), Wink and Williams, *Invitation*, David Hughes, *A History of European Music* (New York, 1974), *The Schirmer History of Music* (New York, 1982), and, in 1995, La Grange, *Vienna*, 785: "The Wagnerian Hugo Wolf."

35. Hugo Riemann, "Die Romantik in der Instrumentalmusik," *Spemanns goldenes Buch der Musik* (Berlin, 1900), 197. Niemann, *Gegenwart*, 63 ff. Einstein, *Romantic*, 226 ff., 361, and passim. Dahlhaus "Romantik," 412. Castle discusses neoromanticism in the fin de siècle in poetry, architecture, sculpture, and painting in German-speaking Prague as an influence of Wagner and a reaction to naturalism (see *Geschichte*, 1344 ff.).

36. Joseph Machlis, *Introduction to Contemporary Music* (New York, 1961), 55; Lang, *Western Civilization*, 991. Specialists often disagree on which composers are postromantic, e.g., for Hughes (*European Music*, 44), both Brahms and Bruckner are postromantic, but not for Donald Jay Grout (*A History of Western Music* [New York, 1980–88]) and Leon Plantinga (*Romantic Music* [New York, 1984]). Two sources used by specialists, the *Music Index* and RILM, add further confusion. Each suggests a different term as ideal for musical styles of the fin de siècle. *The Music Index* (Ann Arbor, Mich.), as of 1979, uses *neoromantic* as its one and only designation. RILM (*Répertoire International de Littérature Musicale*), however, suggests *post-romantic*. RILM compiled (for the years 1971 to 1988) titles of books, articles, reviews, dissertations, etc., according to which term each used in its title. Here are their totals: post-Wagnerian (20 listings), neoromantic(ism) (19), postromantic(ism) (8,803), and late romantic(ism) (111). If, however, we examine the enormous total for postromantic, we find the result grossly inflated: it includes studies of Schubert and Schumann and explorations that authors specifically designated as *late romantic*. Publications that used no terms in their titles were also included in the *postromantic* total: problems, indeed, for RILM compilation procedure. I thank Daniel Rubey, chief librarian of the Lehman College library, for his search of RILM's compilation of abstracts with references to *postromantic*.

37. Carl Dahlhaus strenuously objects to a broad application of the term *late romantic*. "It is absurd to yoke Strauss, Mahler, and the young Schoenberg, composers who represent modernism in the minds of their turn-of-the-century contemporaries, with the self-proclaimed antimodernist Pfitzner, calling them all 'late romantic'" (*Nineteenth-Century Music*, trans. J. Bradford Robinson [Berkeley, 1989], 334). But every period, and even every political organization, has its conservatives and progressives. In part III of this book I explore the late-romantic elements of thought that these four composers share in common.

38. See chap. 1, n. 3, above.

39. Jerome J. McGann, *The Romantic Ideology* (Chicago, 1983), 3, 13–14.

Chapter 4: Declamation

1. Quoted in Newman, *Wagner*, 4:453–454. Wagner often wrote about the enunciation problem: see, for example, his *Bericht*, 11 and passim. My article "Theatrical Declamation and German Vocal Music of the Late Romantic Period," *Seminar* (1978): 169–186, gives all quotations and terminology in the original German.

2. Winter, *Singschule*, is among early attempts to found German schools of singing, but these all retained important aspects of Italian pedagogy.

3. Schmitt, *Aussprache*.

4. Schmitt, *Gesangschule*, 43.

5. Plüddemann, *Übungen*, 71 ff. "Das Wandern ist des Müllers Lust" is the first line of Schubert's song "Das Wandern," from *Die schöne Müllerin*.

6. Newman, *Wagner*, 3:311. Newman comments further: "But after *Flying Dutchman* will come *Tannhäuser, Lohengrin* and—*Tristan!* At the thought of this last [Wagner's] heart almost fails him. Since the necessary human instruments for his greater works do not exist, he says, he will have to create them. . . . The king [Ludwig II] fully agreed with him that a School must be founded" to train "a new kind of opera singer and actor," (318). On the collaboration, see Hey, *Vortragsmeister*, 62 and 222.

7. See Jung, "Gesangsaussprache," 45–47; Plüddemann, "Verrottung," 21–29—a heated appeal for correct German free from dialect—and, most important, Oberländer, *Übungen*, "Exercises to Master Dialect-Free Speech," which was first published in Berlin, ca. 1882, and underwent its tenth edition in Munich, 1917, in which twenty thousand copies were printed. I thank Frau Bender, wife of the outstanding bass Paul Bender (1875–1947, debut 1900), for his copy of this book, which is well marked from use. On Siebs's commission, see his *Bühnenaussprache*, particularly page 7, on the aim to help actors "free themselves from dialects and provincialisms."

8. Wolf, *Kritiken*, 117 (*Criticism*, 92); Strauss, from the foreword to his opera *Intermezzo*.

9. See Wilhelm Altmann, "Kritik," *Die Musik* 1 (1901), 346, for the first review and Hans Bossardt, "Kritik," *Die Musik* 1 (1901), 343, for the second; Plüddemann, *Übungen*, 26.

10. *The New Grove* and *The New Harvard Dictionary of Music* are among several reference books in which *Sprechstimme* and *Sprechgesang* are incorrectly identified as synonyms; see the Glossary, below.

11. Schumann, "Wüllner," 19; Lehmann, *Sing*, 239. A common modern misconception is that singers are forced to employ Sprechgesang in order to sing Wagnerian roles correctly. The great Wagnerian baritone Friedrich Schorr offered his experience to prove this opinion false. "There does not appear to me to be any fundamental difference between the melodic style of

Wagner and Verdi. I build my phrases in Wagner exactly the same way I do in Verdi. Wagner is not responsible for the false 'Sprechgesang' . . . heard in recent times." See Herbert Biehle, *Die Stimmkunst* (Leipzig, 1931), 2:177.

12. On late-romantic recitation, see the Glossary and von Possart's *Kunst* and, to some extent, his *Erstrebtes und Erlebtes* (Berlin, 1916).

13. The Destinn review is from the *Neue musikalische Presse* (Leipzig), 1903, 97, and the censure of Wagner singers (of ca. 1900) is from Georg Münzer, "Humperdinck," 61.

14. See, for instance, Ernst Wolf's "Gesang mit Text," entry no. 435 in *Spemanns Goldenes Buch der Musik* (Berlin, 1904).

15. Gura, *Erinnerungen*, 118 ff.

16. Hunnius, *Kunst*, 78, provides the Stockhausen quotation. See "Kritik," *Die Musik* 1 (1901), 342, for Erich Urban's review of von Dulong's concert. Paul Marsop suggested the screen: see "Zur Bühnen und Konzertreform," *Die Musik*, 255 ff.

17. Weingartner, "Nochmals das 'lebende Lied.'"

18. Plüddemann, "Loewe," 330. The recording by von Possart is *Concert Record* (Grammophone GC-2-41078).

19. The singer Gerhard Hüsch provided me with much valuable information on lied performance during the fin de siècle.

20. The story comes from Hans Halm, a former director of the Music Division of the Bavarian State Library. No innovation was involved in Wüllner's recitation of this Shakespearean excerpt. Hermann Linde recited the same scene at a concert on November 13, 1880, which included music of Mozart and Chopin (see the program files of the *Archiv der Gesellschaft der Musikfreunde*, Vienna).

21. Hanslick, *Concertsaal*, 214, and Plüddemann, *Balladen*, vols. 2 (foreword) and 3.

22. Gerhardt recorded the Wolf song twice, in 1907 and 1938. The first recording, released in 1908 (HMV 2-43183 [3765]), illustrates the excesses of youth she mentioned but certainly not the second of 1939 (HMV GR 21). Incidentally, Wolf had himself already musically pictured *Fäden* with a descending portamento. Gerhardt was referring in "der Schleier fällt" to the final song of Schumann's *Frauenliebe und Leben*, Op. 42. "Ludwig Wüllner," *Der Kunstwart* 26 (1913), 19.

23. *Clipping Files*, "Wüllner," Lincoln Center Music Research Division. The review in question, written by Philip Hale, is simply entitled "Music." It was stamped December 9, 1908, by a library clerk.

24. Plüddemann, *Balladen*, vols. 1 (concluding remarks), 2–3. In the wake of late-romantic naturalism, Schubert's "Erlkönig" was recorded (ca. 1930) in a manner the manufacturing company, French Columbia (LFX 336 LX361, LO219), called a "dramatized version." Each character in the ballad was performed by a separate singer: Georges Thill, Claude Pascal, and Henri-Bertrand Etcheverry. Schubert himself once joined in a similar performance of his "Erlkönig." But Albert Stadtler notes that the occasion was considered a joke and not (as it had been in the recording) as a serious attempt toward achieving naturalism: "An odd effect was made, as I still well remember, by the attempt (only among ourselves, of course) to sing *Erlkönig* as a trio. Schubert sang the father, Vogl the *Erlkönig*, Josefine the child and I played" (Deutsch, *Memoirs*, 153).

25. Quoted in Deutsch, *Memoirs*, 116 and 337.

26. E. F. Taubert, "Kritik," *Die Musik* 10 (1904): 294–295.

27. See Hans Emge, "Liebe zum bel canto" (manuscript). Emge, a prominent voice teacher, active professionally from around 1920 to around 1960, numbered Gerhard Hüsch among his students.

28. E. F. Taubert, *Berliner Post* (n.d.): see Franz Ludwig, *Ludwig Wüllner* (Leipzig, 1913), 158–159. For further on Wüllner, see "Memoriam," *Kaleidoscoop* (Rotterdam), 1954, pp. 19–34, and Herbert Biehle, "Köpfe im Profil: Ludwig Wüllner," *Die Musik* 19 (1927): 337–40.

29. Louis, *Gegenwart*, 307–308, and Smolian, "Schwinden," 59 and 115 ff. Curiously enough, Louis observed, most great singers of lieder came from countries other than Germany, especially from Holland (*Gegenwart*, 310–311).

30. Louis, *Gegenwart*, 309–310.

31. J. A. Fuller-Maitland, *Brahms* (London, 1911), 179.

32. From Schoenberg's preface to *Pierrot Lunaire*.

33. John S. White, *The Salome Motive* (New York, 1947), 13. See also my early article on the subject, "The Influence of Theatrical Declamation upon Composers of the Late Romantic Lied," *Acta Musicologica* 34 (1962): 18–28.

34. Northcote, *Duparc*, 57–58; Friedrich Klose, *Meine Lehrjahre bei Bruckner* (Regensburg, 1927), 316.

35. For example, Strauss wrote, "My vocal style has the pace of a stage play": see his *Recollections*, 156.

36. Excerpt from Bahr's *Gesammelte Aufsätze über Hugo Wolf*, quoted in *Hugo Wolf*, trans. Ernest Newman (London, 1907), 25.

37. Frank Walker, indefatigable biographer of Wolf, arranged interviews for me with Wolf's friends and members of his family. The comments above were made by Wolf's niece Cornelia Strasser.

38. Plüddemann, *Balladen*, vols. 1 (concluding remarks), 2–3; Strauss, *Betrachtungen*, 181. For Wolf's letter to Emil Kauffmann, June 5, 1890, see *Briefe Kauffmann*, 13, translation from Walker, *Wolf*, 429.

39. From the foreword to Strauss's opera *Intermezzo*, 1.

40. Many specialists offered me valuable information on recitation in Germany and Austria during the fin de siècle. I should like, in particular, to thank the actor Ernst Grill, pupil and associate of Ernst von Possart; Ludwig Voss, grandson of von Possart; Hans Halm, former chief of the Music Division of the Bavarian State Library; and Artur Kutscher, formerly of the Department of German Literature: Division of Theatrical Studies, of the University of Munich. I am also grateful to the Theater Museum (Clara Ziegler Stiftung, Munich) for making its fine private record library available to me. Volbach, *Sprache* is a practical study of Late Romantic recitation. Lehmann, *Sing*, 230.

41. Josef Kainz, "Prometheus," Black G & T 41224 (1902). Alexander Moissi, "Prometheus," HMV DB519 (1912). Though Kainz's disc dates from 1902, his performance illustrates the type of recitation Wolf heard in Vienna in 1889, the year he set "Prometheus." On Kainz, see Bang, *Kainz*. On Moissi, see Böhm, *Moissi*. The English translation of "Prometheus" used in the following discussion is by Philip Lieson Miller, in *Ring of Words*, 34. Reprinted with permission of Philip Lieson Miller.

42. Decsey, *Wolf*, 2:138.

43. The graphs in the examples above diagram Kainz's and Moissi's speech inflections as they appeared on the screen of an oscilloscope. I am grateful to Paul Balkin, formerly of the Department of Physics at Hunter College, for operating this instrument and helping me to take readings from it.

44. Decsey *(Wolf,* 2:146 ff.) and Bieri *(Wolf,* 106) are among Wolf specialists who criticized "Der Gärtner" for poor declamation.

45. While a critic on the *Salonblatt* (see Wolf, *Musical Criticism,* e.g., 268, 274, and passim), Mahler also criticized Reichmann severely: he asserted that Reichmann "frequently sang out of tune" (La Grange, *Mahler,* 1:478). Lafite, however, thought Reichmann sang Schubert's "Erlkönig" with dramatic intensity (*Schubertlied,* 93–94).

46. Wolf, *Briefe Köchert,* 61.

47. Plüddemann, *Balladen,* foreword, vol. 4; Mahler, quoted in Decsey, "Stunden," 40:143–144.

48. Lorraine Gorrell discusses free rhythm in Wolf and Debussy, *The Nineteenth-Century German Lied* (Oregon, 1993), 285 ff. Klose's manuscripts, his wife notes in correspondence with me, are on file in the University Library in Basel.

49. Translation by Ernest Newman, *The Hugo Wolf Society* (London, ?1931), 4:16.

50. Decsey, "Stunden," 40:143–144. Yet Mahler made several affirmative comments on the importance of declamation in the lied. For instance: "The ideal lied begins with the words. The music almost takes care of itself, if the performer enunciates thoughtfully and declaims with sharp accentuation." He added: "If a singer does not sing *Mutter* but stretches the first syllable to *Mu-ter* [*sic*], the entire effect is immediately destroyed" (quoted in Bauer-Lechner, *Erinnerungen* [Killian], 167).

Chapter 5: Naturalistic Description and the Reaction It Provoked

1. Wolf to Oskar Grohe, August 11, 1890, *Briefe Grohe,* 34; Decsey, *Wolf* 3:46, for the "Gesang Weylas" comment.

2. The song's early publication by B. Firnberg of Frankfurt am Main included the performance direction translated in the text in part: "Bis zu der Stelle ⊕ muss die rechte Hand viel leiser als die linke gespielt werden, es soll dadurch die Vorstellung erweckt werden, das Musik aus dem Hause durch das geschlossene Fenster von der Strasse aus vernommen wird." This instruction is absent from the modern critical edition prepared by Hans Rectanus. Dynamic indications for the passage, however, are the same in both editions. Consequently, the pianist using the critical edition is instructed—without the reason being given—to play the music for the right hand pianissimo and that of the left hand mezzo-forte with "viel pedal" (generous use of the pedal).

3. Einstein, introduction to Georg Benda's *Ariadne auf Naxos* (Leipzig, 1920), vi; Einstein, *Romantic,* 8; On Strauss, see W. P. James, "Music Pure and Applied," *Music and Letters* 2 (1921): 373–385; Helm, "Wiener Musikleben," 7:445–446 (1916), cites the enthusiasm of audiences for vivid stage effects. Helm provides another surprising example: "In order to render vividly the magic-fire music [in *Die Walküre*] they conceived the idea of filling pails . . . with inflammable liquid and lighting them. The flames leaped towards the ceiling" (6:433). On descriptiveness in music, viz., naturalism, see my article "The Impact of Naturalism on Music and the Other Arts during the Romantic Era," *Journal of Aesthetics and Art Criticism* 30 (1972): 537–543.

4. Wolf to Grohe, February 22, 1896, *Briefe Grohe,* 219.

5. Quoted in Gutmann, *Erinnerungen,* 72.

6. Reger instruction in the score; Wolf, quoted in Walker, *Wolf,* 209. The song is "An eine Aeolsharfe," from the *Moerike-Lieder.*

7. Franz Strauss and his wife, Alice, son and daughter-in-law of the composer, permitted me to examine Strauss's notebooks.

8. Wolf, *Briefe Mayreder,* 26–28. Charles Rosen mentions the interesting curiosity of "horn calls" where "there are no horns" mentioned in the poetry. He observes: "In Romantic music these horn calls come from landscape; they appear in Schubert and Beethoven with a novel aura of the sublime and the melancholy derived from the new ambitions of landscape painters and poets. In the extraordinary triumph of landscape, we can see both painter and poet using elements of Nature—foliage, rocks, mountains, and above all the unifying power of light—the way a musician uses harmonies and motifs" (*The Romantic Generation* [Cambridge, 1995], 116, 117, 135).

9. All three quotes in Dahlhaus, *Absolute Music,* 28–29 and 31.

10. Niemann, *Wagner,* 162 ff.

11. Schellenberg's remarks in this chapter are drawn from two of his articles: "Konrad Ansorge," *Der Türmer* 32 (1929), 70, and "Über musikalisches Illustrieren," *Nord und Süd* 20 (1915), 490.

12. Goethe's comments were drawn from the poet's letter to Adalbert Schöpke. Schellenberg quotes Goethe's remarks in "Über musikalisches," 490.

13. Schopenhauer, *Wille und Vorstellung,* 3:310.

14. Riemann's comment was drawn from the English translation of his dictionary [J. S. Shedlock, London, 1908]. See also the entry on musical aesthetics. The *New Harvard* finds the "dichotomy between absolute and program music" carried on for more than a century to be "essentially misleading, for it obscures the complex intertwining of extramusical associations and 'purely' musical substance that can be found even in pieces that bear no verbal clues whatever" ("Absolute Music").

15. Pfitzner, *Gesammelte Schriften,* 3:93. Stephani, *Tonarten* and "Der Stimmungscharakter der Tonarten," *Die Musik* 15 (1905): 20–24. For Helmholz see his *Die Lehre von Tonempfindungen* (Braunschweig, 1863), esp. 502 ff. See also Richard Hennig, *Die Charakteristik der Tonarten* (Berlin, ?1897), and Hennig, "Gibt es eine 'Charakteristik der Tonarten?'" *Bayreuther Blätter* 40 (1917): 92–121; Mendelssohn, "Allerlei," 217–218. Riemann discusses the topic during his analysis of some of Bach's fugues, *Katechismus der Fugen-Komposition* (Leipzig, 1906), 1:156 ff.: see, in particular, his "Lehre von Tonvorstellungen," 1–26. Steblin, *Key Characteristics* is a recent analysis. Charles A. Culver, *Musical Acoustics* (New York, 1956), 140.

16. Prochazka, *Franz,* 49; Stephani, *Tonarten,* 81; Berlioz, *Grand traité d'instrumentation et d'orchestration modernes* (Paris, ?1844), 33; on D'Indy and Franck, see Cooper, *French Music,* 113.

17. Wolf, *Kritiken,* 213 (*Criticism,* 164). Wolf often veiled tonality through augmented chords to evoke feelings of discomfort and disorientation as in "Zur Warnung," "Abschied," "Bei einer Trauung," and "Das verlassese Mägdlein."

Chapter 6: The Height of Naturalism in Music

1. Wolfram Humperdinck, son of the composer, provided me with unpublished letters and documents written about *Königskinder* by the composer. The quotation is from a letter the composer wrote to an archivist, a Dr. Distl, November 2, 1898. See W. Humperdinck's biography of his father: *Humperdinck,* 238–39, which reproduces part of the letter in question.

2. Istel's "Rousseau" is one of few monographs on early melodrama that mentions the genre's second flowering. See also my article "The Joining of Words and Music in Late Romantic Melodrama," *Musical Quarterly* 42 (1976): 571–590. Rousseau's earliest melodrama, *Pygmalion* (1770), was followed by those of Georg Benda (1722–95) and preceded by *Sigismund* (?1761) by Johann Ernst Eberlin (1702–62). A large number of melodramas were written and performed in the nineteenth century. Beethoven, Mendelssohn, Joseph von Lindpaintner (1791–1856), Liszt, Theodor Gerlach (1861–1940), and Pfitzner contributed significant examples. In Liszt's time the genre became fashionable in drawing rooms. Melodrama, however, appeared to be in decline when Humperdinck "revived" it. At that time, conservative Wagnerites denounced melodrama, citing comments of Wagner, who disliked it.

3. Humperdinck's statement is drawn from his diary (1897) and Cosima Wagner's is from Nodnagel, "Melodram," 155.

4. From Humperdinck's letters, the first to Arthur Seidl (August 4, 1895) and the second to Arthur Smolian (August 5, 1895).

5. See Goethe's "Über *Proserpina*," *Sämtliche Werke* (Stuttgart, 1893), 14:255; see also Georg Benda's *Ariadne auf Naxos* (Leipzig, 1920), prepared by Alfred Einstein, page viii, in which the same warning is issued—a point that is particularly noteworthy; for, as Einstein observes, Benda's melodramas had extraordinary influence: on Mozart, Beethoven (in *Fidelio*), the Schubert lied, the ballads of Zumsteeg, and even on the oratorios of Haydn.

6. Humperdinck's comment on "relative pitch" is from the composer's unpublished memorabilia. His remark on musically trained actors is from one of his diaries. His original plan, to set *Königskinder* as an opera, was frustrated (1895) by its author, Elsa Bernstein-Porges (pseud. Ernst Rosmer), who permitted her text to serve as a melodrama but not as an opera libretto. She withdrew her objection, however, in 1907, enabling Humperdinck to revise the melodrama as an opera.

7. Leopold Hirschberg, "Loewes Op. 9," *Allgemeine Musik-Zeitung* (?December 8, 1916).

8. Strauss, *Eltern*, 204, 211, 221, 250, 252, 258, and 276. See also Tschirch, "Strauss," 658.

9. See Del Mar, *Strauss*, 2:357. Jerome McGann's reference to the "double awareness: of the actual differentials—political, economic, ideological—which separate the Romantic period from our own," is quoted above in Chapter 3.

10. Max Steinitzer's excellent monograph on the subject, *Melodram*, enumerates (60 ff.) the extensive literature on fin-de-siècle melodrama.

11. Steinitzer, *Melodram*, mentions Burmeister's humorous "Der Kuckuck," with music after Chopin's *Mazurka*, Op. 30, no. 2, among other similar examples (32). See page 40 on *gesprochene Lieder*.

12. Richard, *Schillings*, 23, is the perceptive critic; Wilhelm Altmann, "Kritik," *Die Musik* 11 (1904): 75–76, provides the *Hexenlied* comment. Mahler was among the *Hexenlied*'s many admirers. Incidentally, Schillings was regarded early in the twentieth century as one of the most important composers in Germany. His opera *Mona Lisa* (1915) had more than two thousand performances. However, after World War I, his thoroughly late-romantic style was eclipsed by the new avant garde: Schoenberg, Hindemith, Schreker. Schillings's interest in composition declined radically during his eclipse.

13. The recording is on both Deutsche Grammophon 35000-2 and Polydor 67047-9. The Theater-Museum (Munich) provided an opportunity for me to study these recordings. Two earlier melodramas of Schillings's, *Kassandra* and *Das Eleusische Fest* (Op. 9, nos. 1 and 2)— both of 1900 and both on texts by Schiller—are available on a 1994 compact disk, recited by

Martin Neubauer and orchestrated and conducted by Konrad Bach and the Thüringian Symphony Orchestra (Marco Polo 8.223660).

14. The unrevised text had been set as a melodrama by Emil Kaiser.

15. An article in *Neue musikalische Presse,* January 1903, 136, compares Wüllner's and von Possart's styles; Tschirch, "Reisen," 658; Kienzl, *Deklamation,* 154; the English judgment is Rockstro, "Melodrama," 3:107. I wish to thank Helene Kienzl, the composer's widow, for materials pertaining to Wilhelm Kienzl.

16. Donal Henahan, "Claire Bloom in a Twist on Homer," *New York Times,* November 7, 1990, C:14. Claire Bloom performed with Brian Zeger, pianist, at the 92nd Street Y, New York, on November 5, 1990, and in Purchase, New York, at the State University College on November 8, 1990. The ever-helpful Burnett Cross alerted me to the Purchase performance. *Enoch Arden* was recorded by Claude Rains and pianist Glenn Gould in 1962 (Columbia MS 6341 and CBS MP 39754). Three more recent recordings were made of this work: Gert Westphal, reciter, and John Buttrick, pianist, 1984 (in German, with Adolf Strodtmann's translation, Jecklin Disco, JD 592-2); Lucy Rowan, reciter, and Stephen Hough, pianist 1987 (in English, Musical Heritage Society, 921077), and Erik Rhodes, reciter, and Gordon Manley, pianist, 1990 (in English, New Records, 501).

17. Zilcher, "Selbstbiographie" (unpublished, 1942), 17. In his youth Zilcher accompanied such outstanding artists as Raimund von Zur Mühlen and Caruso on their American tours. I thank the conductor Heinz Reinhart Zilcher, son of the composer, for much useful information about his father.

18. Letter to von Possart, July 12, 1903. Schillings's correspondence has been deposited in the music division of the Bavarian State Library (Munich). The letters had been in the possession of Ludwig Voss, grandson of von Possart, who made them available for me.

19. Letter to von Possart, September 1, 1907. Schillings's comment on the Goethe text is from a letter to von Possart, December 6, 1910.

20. Strauss to Hofmannsthal, July 10, 1917 (*Strauss Hofmannsthal Briefwechsel,* 372). But Strauss later had a partial change of heart: "I am now, more than before, in favor of purely spoken dialogue: partly without music altogether, partly melodramatic, partly only with short musical phrases. . . . Spoken dialogue has . . . the advantage of greater intelligibility and quicker completion" (October 23, 1923; 502). On Strauss's winning of von Possart to his side, see Strauss, *Eltern,* 204.

21. Louis, *Gegenwart,* 227, where, in a footnote, *Königskinder, Enoch Arden, Hexenlied,* and the great reciter von Possart are mentioned as examples.

22. Humperdinck, *Humperdinck,* 237–238. On Schoenberg's opportunities to hear *Königskinder,* see Heuberger, "Königskinder," 235–243, and Stephan, "Geschichte des Melodrams," 186. Other composers experimented with various kinds of "Sprechstimmen" and with systems of notating them, e.g., John B. McEwen (1868–1948), *Poems for Inflected Speech, with Musical Accompaniment,* and Michael Fabianovitch Gnessin (1883–1957), "Musical Reading," *Grove* (5th ed.) 4:482, and 8:26, the article on *Sprechgesang.* These titles and descriptions serve as English terminology for Sprechstimme, not Sprechgesang.

Chapter 7: Pan-German Nationalism

1. Tom Kemp, *Industrialization in Nineteenth-Century Central Europe,* 2nd ed. (London, 1985), 99. Pascal's informative *Naturalism* provides a long list of "forgotten" authors (some slightly better known than others), e.g., Felix Dahn, Karl May, Arno Holz, and, of course, the outstanding Gerhart Hauptmann (93 ff.).

2. Stern, *Cultural*, xxvi. Stern's *Gold*, 181 ff., speaks of the "speculative fever [that] gripped Germans of all classes" before 1870.

3. According to Kemp, Germany's rapid industrialization wrought enormous social and economic upheavals: "Industrialization was destroying something precious in the old Germany" (*Industrialization*, 105 and passim). Stern identifies the conservative revolution as "a European phenomenon," in *Cultural* (xxiii); however, he concludes that "only in Germany had it become a decisive intellectual and political force." John Weiss is another historian who speaks of the period from 1870 to 1933 as a conservative revolution: see *Conservatism in Europe 1770–1945: Traditionalism, Reaction, and Counter-Revolution* (New York, 1977), 84–89.

4. Even "men of independent and humane minds" Georg Brandes, Maximilian Harden, and Christian Morgenstern and the liberal *Freie Bühne* and *Der Kunstwart* were favorably disposed to Langbehn (Pascal, *Naturalism*, 40).

5. Father Friedrich Jahn, *Deutsches Volksthum* (Lübeck, 1810), introduced *Volkstum* as a German equivalent of "nationality": see either *Trübners Deutsches Wörterbuch* or Jacob and Wilhelm Grimm, *Deutsches Wörterbuch*. *Deutschthum* implies intrinsic German character. Herder coined the terms *volkstümlich* and *Volkstümlichkeit* to indicate folkish popularity. After Herder, *Volkstümlichkeit* evidently came to mean the commonality of the people, their inherent characteristics. Paul de Lagarde, outspoken nationalist and exponent of the radical right, dreamt that the rebirth of Deutschthum would cure Germany's woes. Capitalism divided the nation into conflicting classes. Liberal parliamentarians added the clash of opposing parties, which further weakened the nation's will to power. Deutschthum would heal the nation's greed, materialism, and isolate its enemy, the Jews, who were seen as gnawing at the nation's core.

6. *Völkisch* is now a term used in English by specialists in several disciplines for the nationalist ideology under discussion: see, e.g., McGrath, *Dionysian*, Stern, *Cultural*, Kemp, *Industrialization*. On *Heimatkunst*, see Pascal, *Naturalism*, 40.

7. On Treitschke, see Andreas Dorpalen, *Heinrich von Treitschke* (New Haven, 1957), 180. George E. Berkley, *Vienna and Its Jews* (Cambridge, Mass., 1988), 73 ff. The sketch appears on the second page of a series of unnumbered pages that begin after page 126. Robert S. Wistrich, *The Jews of Vienna in the Age of Franz Joseph* (Oxford, 1989), 215 ff., examines "aggressively racist" action of university students. "Racial hygiene" is Pascal's term (*Naturalism*, 214).

8. Hoeckner's *Jugendbewegung*, 5, is still the best source for the German youth movement, the musical aspect in particular. Hoeckner, however, does not discuss the antiliberal, antidemocratic aspect of the youth movement. A more recent study is Stachura's *Youth Movement*.

9. Quoted in Hoeckner, *Jugendbewegung*, 44. Hoeckner drew this comment from "Wandervogel und Volkslied," *Wandervogel*, 4 (1910), 81 ff. For the last two quotations, see 187 and 213.

10. Hoeckner, *Jugendbewegung*, see 44 and 26, respectively, for Breuer's comments.

11. *Volksliederbuch für Männerchor*, ed. Rochus Freiherr von Liliencron, 2 vols. (Leipzig, 1906), introduction. See n. 43, below, for some of the composers involved.

12. Moser, *Lied*, 264, prints the original German verse.

13. Both passages are from the short foreword written by the editors, Joseph Joachim, Carl Krebs, and Humperdinck of *Im Volkslied: Moderne Preislieder*, vol. 1 (Berlin, 1903), the collection published by *Die Woche*. See also "Im Volkston," *Die Woche* 15 (1903), 643.

14. Heinrich Neumann, "Im Volkston," *Die Woche* 17 (1903), 731–732.

15. The name Austro-Hungarian Empire is used here to distinguish that multiethnic state from Austria, the German-speaking area. Historians from 1920 to our generation agree that chauvinistic nationalism arose in Austria and Germany in the 1870s and replaced the liberal nationalism of earlier decades; see, for instance, Carleton Hays, *Essays in Nationalism* (New York, 1926), George Mosse, *The Crises of German Ideology* (New York, 1964), and Geoff Eley, *Reshaping of the German Right* (New Haven, 1980).

16. Wistrich, *Age of Franz Joseph*, 211. On Judaeophobia in Germany, see Jehuda Reinharz, *Fatherland or Promised Land: The Dilemma of the German Jew, 1893–1914* (Ann Arbor, 1975). Schönerer was anti-Hapsburg, anti-Catholic, and anti-Austrian. He was attracted by Teutonic paganism, even trying to resurrect old Germanic names for the months of the year (see Andrew G. Whiteside, *Georg Ritter von Schönerer and Austrian Pan-Germanism* [Berkeley, 1975]).

17. Berkley, *Vienna*, 63. Stern, *Gold*, 498–499. Gerson Bleichröder, Bismarck's banker, amassed a wealth equaled only by Alfred Krupp's. He rose to "eminence" as late as the 1850s and 1860s, the decade Stern calls the "halcyon days."

18. Nationalists identified "Americanization," the mixing of ethnic groups, as the ultimate sin. Wistrich, *Joseph*, 226 ff., discusses restriction of Jewish immigration. The United Christian manifesto of 1889 and other programs were fashioned to exclude Jews from the professions and the civil service. Immigration into Vienna of Jews from Russia, the country noteworthy for most oppressive restrictions, rose rapidly. Vienna's Jewish population grew from "6,000 in 1860 to 147,000 in 1900, or nearly nine percent of the city's total population" (Berkley, *Vienna*, 35). In Austria and Germany many felt that "the pariahs [the Jews] had become the true power" (Stern, *Gold*, 495).

19. Batka, "Melodrama," 226. Actually, Humperdinck used only two folk tunes, modified to his taste, besides quoting a fragment from two others in his fairy-tale opera. See Humperdinck, *Humperdinck*, 224–225.

20. On Wolf, see Walker, *Wolf*, 217; see Pascal, *Naturalism*, 41, on Bartels.

21. Walker, *Wolf*, 55n. and 53 ff. Goldschmidt's secular oratorio, *Die sieben Todsünden*, was successfully performed in Berlin, Vienna, and Hanover and published in 1880. Goldschmidt had engaged Wolf, then in financial need (1877), to correct the score for its performance in Vienna. On Wolf and Goldschmidt and other interesting Wolfian subjects, see Margarete Saary's *Persönlichkeit und Musikdramatische Kreativität Hugo Wolfs* (Tutzing, 1984).

22. Peter Pulzer, *The Rise of Political Anti-Semitism in Germany and Austria* (Cambridge, 1988), 47, gives 1867 as the time of the first anti-Semitic reaction. Stern observes that "the very term *anti-Semitism* was first invented in Germany in the 1870s" (*Gold*, 495). Wistrich, *Age of Franz Joseph*, 209 ff., gives similar dates. On Lueger and anti-Semitic ideology in musical Vienna, see La Grange, *Vienna*, 135 ff., a careful revision of his earlier study (*Mahler* 1:497 ff.). La Grange's discussion of the subject in each book is entitled "New Anti-Semitic Campaign— Second Philharmonic season." On Lueger, see also Bauer-Lechner, *Mahler*, 111; Stuckenschmidt, *Schoenberg*, 144; and Schorske, *Fin-de-siècle*. Schorske also discusses Schönerer.

23. Quoted in La Grange, *Vienna*, 118 ff. The article in question, entitled "The Jewish Regime at the Vienna Opera" and signed E. Th., appeared in the *Deutsche Zeitung*, November 6, 1898, two days before the actual concert on November 8, which was Mahler's first appearance as conductor of the Philharmonic. For more on Mahler and anti-Semitism, see these two articles in *Nineteenth-Century Music* 18 (1995): Karen Painter, "The Sensuality of Timbre: Responses to Mahler and Modernity at the *Fin de siècle*," 236–256, and K. M. Knittel, "'Ein

hypermoderner Dirigent': Mahler and Anti-Semitism in *Fin-de-siècle* Vienna," 257–276. Meyer, *Münchner Philharmoniker*, 170 ff., presents additional examples of such criticisms of Mahler by the press in Munich, 1910.

24. Quoted in La Grange, *Mahler*, 1:555, and *Vienna*, 222. Helm later reviewed Mahler's performance of Bruckner favorably.

25. Louis, *Gegenwart*, 182; quoted in La Grange, *Mahler*, 1:549.

26. Lueger, quoted in Berkley, *Vienna*, 104, 106, and passim; Schnitzler, quoted in Pascal, *Naturalism*, 74.

27. The *Schlichte Weisen* by Alexander Ritter, Strauss's mentor, was the forerunner by many years of the others mentioned. Ritter and Strauss drew texts for their *Schlichte Weisen* from poetry of the nationalist Felix Dahn. Reger also turned to Dahn for his *Schlichte Weisen*, but only once: "Du meines Herzens Krönelein" (Op. 76, no. 1). *Drei schlichte Weisen* (Op. 18) of Max von Schillings are not lieder as Moser implies (*Lied*, 188) but pieces for violin.

28. Georg Goehler, "Gustav Mahlers Lieder," *Kunstwart und Kulturwart* 24 (1910), 146. Ida Dehmel, widow of the poet, observed that "from earliest childhood, [Mahler's] relationship to the [*Wunderhorn*] had been particularly close" (see A. Mahler, *Memories*, 93). Humperdinck, d'Albert, Thuille, Schoenberg, Strauss, Graener, Knab, Kienzl, Haas, Joseph Weismann, Courvoisier, and Zilcher are among others who "suddenly" discovered this collection of folk poetry. Curiously enough, the first three men selected *Wunderhorn* verse for their songs for the *Woche* competition in 1903.

29. Quoted in A. Mahler, *Memories*, 79–80. The year this conversation took place is uncertain. Alma Mahler entered the event in her diary under winter 1905. But the meeting between the composers (Schoenberg, Zemlinsky, and Klaus Pringsheim were also present) occurred during a summer's night when Mahler was at Maiernigg. Streicher began to set *Wunderhorn* texts long before this occasion, the composer's daughter assured me—while he was still in his teens. I am grateful to Margarete Streicher and the singer Gerda Ratz Streicher, descendants of the composer, for information about Streicher. For more on Streicher see Richard Bruce Wursten, "The Life and Music of Theodor Streicher: Hugo Wolf Redivivus?" (Ph.D. diss., University of Wisconsin, 1980).

30. Pamer, "Lieder," 17, 111, comments on "Tamboursg'sell" and "Zu Strassburg." His study addresses other songs, e.g., "Le Deserteur" (see example 37 in the text above), in vol. 16 (1929), 122, of the same periodical. La Grange quotes these examples of Pamer, along with other folksongs that he says "bear a certain likeness to Mahler's" melodies (*Vienna*, 738; see also 750 and 752).

31. See Klusen, "Gustav Mahler und das Volkslied seiner Heimat," *Journal of the International Folk Music Council* 15 (1963), 31. The music in example 35b is quoted from František Bartoš, *Národní písně moravské* (Prague, 1901), 23, no. 25b. Bartoš's example 46 (on page 39 of the same collection) has a similar melodic curve. The "township of Iglau, . . . situated at the Western edge of Moravia," Ernst Krenek informs us, during Mahler's childhood was "largely inhabited by Germans [as] a 'linguistic island'" (see his "Gustav Mahler," in Bruno Walter, *Gustav Mahler*, trans. James Galston [New York, 1941], 158).

32. Quoted in Bauer-Lechner, *Erinnerungen*, 11. On the influence of Czech (Bohemian) folk music on Mahler, see Vladimir Karbusicky, *Gustav Mahler und seine Umwelt* (Darmstadt, 1978), 52, 54, and passim, and Constantin Floros, "Gustav Mahler und die 'böhmische Musik,'" *Musica* 45 (1991): 160–168. Susan Filler inventories in her important contribution *Gustav and Alma Mahler: A Guide to Research* (New York, 1989) discussions of the role of folk music in

Mahler's melodic style: see 219 ff. My article "The Trend towards the Folklike, Nationalism, and Their Expression by Mahler and His Contemporaries in the Lied," *Chord and Discord* 11 (1963): 40–56, is an early study of the subject.

33. See "Verlorne Müh'!" "Wer hat dies Liedlein erdacht?" "Des Antonius von Padua Fischpredigt," "Rheinlegendchen," and "Lob des hohen Verstandes."

34. "The texts of the *Gesellen* [Wayfarer] songs are my own," Mahler wrote in a letter to the critic Max Marschalk (Mahler, *Briefe,* 186). Variants of the first stanza appear in other Volkslieder: in "Horch was kommt von drausen rein?" published by Hans Breuer in his *Zupfgeigenhansl* and in "Ich bleibe mit meinen Schmerz allein." The text surfaces in widely distributed folk-song collections, from the Rhenish Palatinate to the mountains of Saxony. Even Mahler's title, *Lieder eines fahrenden Gesellen,* was not original. Rudolf Baumbach used it for the collection of folklike verse he wrote in 1878. Four of these poems were set to music by Arthur Foote: *Vier Gesänge aus Lieder eines fahrenden Gesellen von Rudolf Baumbach,* Op. 39. The Wanderlied was a favorite subject of composers long before Mahler's *Wayfarer* songs, as Luise Eitel Peake tells us in "Kreutzer's *Wanderlieder:* The Other *Winterreise,*" *Musical Quarterly* 65 (1979): 83–102.

35. La Grange notes, *Vienna,* 228, that the *Deutsches Volksblatt* "questioned" Mahler's "declamatory style" and that Helm writing in the *Deutsche Zeitung* found "errors in diction." These were more likely errors in *declamation* than in diction.

36. Wehmeyer (*Liederkomponist,* 102–108, 154–163, 167–172 and passim) is most informative on Reger's retreat from Wolf's influence. About half of the songs in the first four volumes of the *Schlichte Weisen* are devoid of literary devices. They occur infrequently in the other songs. None appears in volumes 5 and 6 of the *Kinderlieder.* The songs from his middle years (Opp. 31–75) are rich in literary devices, but these devices appear in only half of his earlier songs. Reger's observation was drawn from Hermann Unger, *Max Reger* (Bielefeld, 1924), 37, an important source for later Reger specialists.

37. Reger decided to orchestrate "Mariä Wiegenlied" because it is sung so often at concerts: see his letter to Bote and Bock, his publisher (Reger, *Briefe,* 302). Arrangements of *Schlichte Weisen* songs by Reger and various editors are listed in Fritz Stein, *Thematisches Verzeichnis der in Druck ershienenen Werke von Max Reger* (Leipzig, 1953).

38. *Oberbayerische Tanzlieder* (Op. 77), *Altbayerische Humoresken* (Op. 64), *Bayerische Ländler* (Op. 36), and specifically "Boarisch" of Op. 104; see Roth, *Schmid,* 44, 50, and passim.

39. On Courvoisier and the Volkslied, consult Kroyer, *Courvoisier,* 33, 47, and passim, and the composer's foreword for Schumann's *Frauenliebe und Leben,* published in Munich (1921) by Drei Maskenverlag. The *Sieben alte deutsche Gedichte,* Op. 23 (1909–10) is one of the first cycles in which Courvoisier put his theories into practice. Others include giant collections: Op. 27, *Geistliche Lieder* (1917–19), five volumes (fifty-two songs); Op. 28, *Kleine Lieder zu Kinderreimen* (1916–1919), four volumes (fifty-two songs); Op. 29, *Lieder auf alte deutsche Gedichte* (1912–25), two volumes (thirty-four songs).

40. La Grange (*Vienna,* 242, 228–230) outlines critical opinion during the fin de siècle of Mahler's folkish lieder. Hanslick quote is on page 229. The public reacted more sympathetically. Berliners "encored *Rheinlegendchen*" (242) and Viennese were enthusiastic over "Hans und Grethe," "Erinnerung," and "Scheiden und Meiden" (231). Strauss's letter to Mahler, too, was positive: "Your songs . . . gave me and the audience much pleasure; but the establishment critics did not find them serious enough. Anything that does not contain a certain dose of boredom 'lacks style' at a concert" (Gustav Mahler and Richard Strauss, *Gustav Mahler*

Richard Strauss Correspondence, ed. Herta Blaukopf and trans. Edmund Jephcott [Chicago, 1984], 47).

41. The first was Mahler's angry retort to a technical analysis of "Der Schildwache Nachtlied" (see Decsey, "Stunden" 144–145). Bauer-Lechner, *Recollections,* 33–34, provides the "Rheinlegendchen" comment.

42. Reger, *Briefe,* 287: Reger's letter of September 9, 1914. His twelve *Geistliche Lieder* (Op. 137) are all choralelike; they are the strictest and most consistently four-part polyphonic writing of any of Reger's songs. Bach evidently was Reger's model. The melody assigned to the voice is doubled in the upper line of the four-part instrumental accompaniment.

43. The Kaiserliederbuch, as the collection was referred to colloquially, was entitled *Volksliederbuch für Männerchor* (2 vols. [Leipzig, ?1906]) and "published at the instigation of the German kaiser, Wilhelm II." Forty composers, including Bruch, Humperdinck, Strauss, and Thuille, were motivated in their work by love of folk song and patriotism, the editor Rochus Freiherr von Liliencron announced in the introduction: 610 lieder were selected from well over 8,000 suggested. Included are four examples by Wagner: "The Pilgrim's Chorus" (*Tannhäuser*), no. 3a; "The Battle Hymn" (*Rienzi*), no. 263a; "The Helmsman's Song" and "The Song of the Sailor," nos. 304a and 304b (both from *Der fliegende Holländer*); as well as these nineteenth-century lieder, e.g., "Der Lindenbaum" (Schubert), no. 218; "Die Lotosblume" (Schumann), no. 443; and "In stiller Nacht" (Brahms), no. 53. The foreword to the special edition of *Im Volkston,* vol. 2, by Carl Krebs for *Die Woche,* gives the results of the contest. The prize songs are published in the special edition.

44. Richard Strauss, "Ein vergeblicher Versuch volkstümlich zu schreiben," *Das deutsche Volkslied* 7 (1905), 43. Strauss's arrangements for male chorus in the *Volksliederbuch* are "Geistlicher Maien" (no. 88), "Misslungene Liebesjagd" (no. 287), "Tummler" (no. 324), and "Kuckuck" (no. 577).

45. Bach, *Ballad,* 22–23, and *Grove* (1890), which defines *Kunstlied,* in contrast with *Volslied,* as "more regular and finished compositions which are written with conscious art by men who have made music their study." The fifth edition of *Grove* (1954) does not make this naive distinction: "Even a song by a great master, if it happens to be simple enough, may come to be called a *Volkslied."*

46. From Humperdinck's diary for June 1900. According to Otto Neitzel, Humperdinck regarded Volkslieder as building blocks ("Humperdinck," 71). And so did many other late romantics. Ida Dehmel remarked that Mahler, like herself, considered folk poems, "not complete in themselves, but blocks of marble which anyone might make his own." She notes that Mahler had "appropriated some few bits from the *Wunderhorn"* (see A. Mahler, *Memories,* 93).

47. Mahler made another change of title before deciding on "Rheinlegendchen," from "Tanzreime" to "Tanzlegendchen" (Bauer-Lechner, *Erinnerungen,* 12). The manuscript is in the Pierpont Morgan Library, Lehman Deposit. The tempo of the typical waltz at about 1880 would have been too fast for "Hans und Grethe." The qualifying adjective *gemächlich* guides the performer to the tempo of the Ländler. The indication "Gemächlich" in "Rheinlegendchen" produces a similar effect.

48. Ludwig Erk (1807–83), *Deutscher Liederhort* (1856), rev. 1893–94, 3 vols., by Franz Magnus Böhme (1827–98), is a distinguished collection of Volkslieder. Erk censured the work of Zuccalmaglio, *Volkslieder.* (Andreas Kretzschmer [1775–1839] had begun the collection, which was completed after his death by Zuccalmaglio.) According to Wiora (*Zuccalmaglio,* 11),

Zuccalmaglio did not compose any of the tunes, as Erk had charged. All are genuine, but "tinted" by their editor in "romantic color." Brahms's tart reply is from a letter to Philipp Spitta (April 3, 1894) that Wiora quotes on pages 19–20. Wiora's discussion of "Weder Glück noch Stern" (44) resolves questions raised by scholars in connection with Mahler's setting of that text.

49. Lang, *Knab,* 58n36. A questionnaire entitled "Crises of the Volkslied" was sent to sixty-six experts in music: "Zur Krisis des deutschen Volksliedes, 66 Antworten zur Umfrage der 'Zeitschrift für Musik,'" *Zeitschrift für Musik* 3C (1930), 366.

50. Knab, "Meine Lieder," 42.

51. Like Wolf, Knab published collections of lieder devoted to a single poet. But Knab shaped his collections slowly, adding new songs for decades. He finally completed eight *Georgelieder* (1904–21), eight *Dehmel* songs (1905–25), and twelve *Mombertlieder* (1905–23). These volumes of concert lieder thus mix earlier and later styles. Aside from concert lieder Knab wrote many collections of folkish songs. Kinderlieder are important among them. Knab arranged well over two hundred folk songs; see Lang, *Knab,* 63. I am grateful to P. Ivonne Knab for information on the composer that she provided in correspondence.

52. Armin Knab, "Vom einfachen," 125. Knab objected also to the excessive subjectivity of Romantic poets, their "cult of personality," the "Ich" (I) poets, who wrote of themselves; see Lang, *Knab,* 47 ff. For further comments on this subject by Knab, see "Denken und Tun," 62–64, and an interview with his wife, "Gespräch mit Yvonne Knab," *Armin Knab,* ed. Franz Krautwurst et al. (Tutzing, 1991), 59 ff.

53. See Hoeckner, *Jugendbewegung,* 99 ff. The *Zupfgeigenhansl* (1909) was the father of all of these popular collections. See above, Chap. 1, n. 26, for more on Löns.

Chapter 8: The Ballad and the Kinderlied

1. Quoted and translated by Walker (*Wolf,* 266); original German is from Wolf, *Brief Köchert,* 8. Wolf set "Dem Vaterland" first as a lied (May 12, 1890) and shortly thereafter (June 4) as a choral piece. Dissatisfied, he revised his choral setting in 1894 and again in 1897–98.

2. Bilke, "Plüddemann," 89, and Schemann, *Plüddemann,* 47, respectively, are sources of the first and second comments. Plüddemann's introduction to *Balladen und Gesänge,* 2:ii, comments on Paul Bulss (1842–1902), who sang this ballad for the kaiser. Plüddemann dedicated several of his ballads to this esteemed singer.

3. The eight ballad types are: 1) traditional narrative songs that have been handed down orally; 2) medieval French verse set to music, known as *ballades;* 3) the art ballad found in the literature of the late eighteenth, the nineteenth, and the early twentieth centuries; 4) the art ballad in music for solo voice and piano (and/or orchestra)—the topic of the present chapter; 5) the choral ballad (Schumann, Brahms, and Wolf); 6) instrumental compositions for piano (Chopin and Brahms), for other solo instruments (Dvořák and Vieuxtemps), and for orchestra; 7) sentimental drawing-room songs of the late nineteenth and early twentieth centuries; and 8) twentieth-century popular (commercial) music. Further, specialists in literature distinguish the ballad from the romance. The romance is more subjective and lyrical, less dramatic, than the ballad. Narration, less important in romance than in ballads, serves in romance mainly to give greater scope to the lyrical elements. Courtly love and knightly deeds are the favorite

subjects of romance. On the ballad in German literature, see Walter Hinck, *Die deutsche Ballade von Bürger bis Brecht* (Göttingen, 1968).

4. Plüddemann, "Loewe," 320 ff. Plüddemann's introductions (*Vorwort*) and concluding remarks (*Nachwort*) to his published ballads are most informative.

5. See Bach, *Ballad;* Spitta, "Ballade," 405–461; König, "Ballade," 3–47. The fine article "Ballade," in *Musik in Geschichte und Gegenwart* by Otto Heinrich Mies, draws much information from the ground-breaking study by Spitta just cited. See also my "The Ballad as Conceived by Germanic Composers of the Late Romantic Period," *Studies in Romanticism* 12 (1973): 499–515, which concentrates on Plüddemann's ballads.

6. Spitta, "Ballade," 427–428, and passim; Dannreuther, *Romantic,* 286.

7. Wolf, *Kritiken,* 362.

8. Plüddemann, *Balladen,* concluding remarks, 1:viii (1892) and (in the same volume) concluding remarks to the third edition (1889), ii–iii, respectively.

9. König, "Ballade," 20; Bach, *Ballad,* 41; and Plüddemann, *Balladen,* 1:ii.

10. Plüddemann, *Balladen,* 1:viii.

11. Plüddemann, *Balladen,* 1:iv.

12. Plüddemann, "Josef Reiter," *Neue Musikalische Rundschau* 1 (1896), 78.

13. "Der Raubschütz" is incomplete (Vienna City Library, MH 6679/C). Only the title page survives of three Eichendorff songs that were to form a group. The final two are ballads, "Das zerbrochene Ringlein" and "Der traurige Jäger." There are other title pages and sketches of ballads extant in Vienna City Library deposits, e.g., MH 6733/C, marked "Konvolut von Skizzen" (1878), a large collection of sketches with many separate title pages and many pieces of just a few bars in length. Other title pages and sketches of ballads, e.g., three on Friedrich Hebbel (1813–63) texts (MH 6681/C), are also in the Vienna City Library deposit. Early unpublished ballads of Wolf, printed posthumously, have been reprinted in the complete edition of his compositions (see vol. 7:1–2); 7:3 prints Wolf's early setting (1875) of Goethe's ballad "Der Fischer."

14. Schur, *Wolf,* 35, and Walker, *Wolf,* 104, respectively, are sources for the two quotations. Heinrich Werner, *Hugo Wolf in Maierling* (Leipzig, 1913), 17, recounts Wolf's admiration of "Archibald Douglas."

15. Bauer-Lechner, *Erinnerungen,* 119 (*Recollections,* 130).

16. Fuller Maitland, *Masters,* 276–281. Batka, *Plüddemann,* 26–27, compares Sommer to Wolf: "I have not read anywhere . . . that people have had enough of Hans Sommer or Hugo Wolf because both are far behind Franz Schubert in naive freshness." Valentin's *Sommer* is a more recent monograph. Sommer's Op. 8 and Op. 11 (both of 1885) contain his most significant ballads.

17. Morold, "Reiter," 21. Twenty-one ballads of this self-taught musician were published between 1893 and 1900 by Th. Rättig of Vienna and Leipzig. Reiter's ballads were sung repeatedly after their introduction to the public by Ernst Appel. Plüddemann's scathing review of Reiter's ballads is cited above in note 12. Reiter, an avid collector and arranger of Volkslieder, published several anthologies.

18. Moser, *Lied,* 223. Mattiesen entered music unconventionally, from philosophy. He composed many more lieder than ballads and therefore was annoyed by the statement, widely circulated and repeated even in the article on the ballad in *Die Musik in Geschichte und Gegenwart* (*MGG*), that he "is almost exclusively a ballad composer" (1133).

19. Louis, *Gegenwart,* 237; Plüddemann, "Loewe," 329. Plüddemann thought that the lied and opera, in contrast to the ballad, lent themselves perfectly to contemporary subjects.

20. Plüddemann had a substantial number of advocates. Wilhelm Schmid of Nuremberg published forty-eight of his *Balladen und Gesänge* in eight volumes. Schemann's *Plüddemann* presents a good bibliography, of which Bilke's and Batka's works are the most noteworthy (see notes 2 and 16, above). See also Schemann, "Ballade," 34–41. Suppan discusses Plüddemann's efforts to found a ballad school in Graz, "Plüddemann," 2–3. This article also contains a useful bibliography. Schemann, *Plüddemann,* 110–113 and passim, discusses concerts of his works. Helm, "Wiener Musikleben," 249, comments on Plüddemann's concert of March 4 and on the Wolf performance that followed. Helm also mentions Josef Reiter here (and passim) as another ballad composer seeking to be known as Loewe's follower.

21. See "Preisausschreiben," *Die Woche,* 8 (1906), 629, the issue for April 14. Prizes were announced December 22, 1906. The volume of prize ballads is entitled *Preisgekrönte Balladen komponiert für die Woche* (Berlin, 1908). The contest's results are given on page 111.

22. Kienzl, *Lebenswanderung,* 155. Kienzl performed his Op. 73 on such occasions.

23. See Franz Magnus Böhme, *Deutsches Kinderlied und Kinderspiel* (Quedlinburg, 1897). Friedrich Zimmer (1855–1919) worked on several collections of folk and especially folklike Kinderlieder, one of these—*Volkstümliche Spiellieder und Liederspiele für Schule und Kinderstube* (Quedlinburg, 1879)—in "close association . . . with Ludwig Erk" (32). Wilhelm Stölten discusses these collections and lists them in *Friedrich Zimmer, ein deutscher Volkserzieher* (Berlin-Zehlendorff, 1933), 268–269.

24. For valuable studies by Humperdinck's contemporaries on his lieder see, Besch, *Humperdinck;* Batka, "Humperdinck," 3–20; Bekker, "Humperdinck"; Münzer, "Humperdinck," 59–72; and Neitzel, "Humperdinck," 62–84.

25. Quoted in Walker, *Wolf,* 226 and 287–288.

26. Humperdinck, *Humperdinck,* 193, 275. Wolfram Humperdinck gives this information (193 ff.) about the the two earlier versions of *Hänsel und Gretel.* The composer called the first version "Ein Kinderstuben-Weihfestspiel von Adelheid Wette—'Hänsel und Gretel' in Musik gesetzt von Onkel." The four songs were "Tanzduett," "Echolied," "Schlummerlied," and "Kikerki-Lied." Wolfram Humperdinck doubts the often-stated theory (e.g., in Walker, *Wolf,* 288, and Hans Joachim Moser, *Geschichte der deutschen Musik* 3 [1928], 386) that Hugo Wolf suggested the idea to Humperdinck to develop *Hänsel und Gretel* into an opera (*Humperdinck,* 201n).

27. Wolfram Humperdinck's discussion of his father's songs in *Humperdinck* is based on Thamm, *Humperdinck.* The total number of songs by Humperdinck is about seventy; see Wilhelm Pfannkuch, "Engelbert Humperdinck," *MGG,* 6:946 ff., which lists lied manuscripts not cited by Thamm. See also R. J. Pascall's similar inventory of lieder, "Engelbert Humperdinck," in *The New Grove.*

28. "S'Sträussle" (1889), "Jäger und Senn'rin" (1895), and "Oi' Schwalb' macht koi'n Sommer" (1901) are examples.

29. Dorothy Gordon printed a selection of thirteen of Blech's Kinderlieder for American audiences: see *Inky Jimmy and Soppy Sally* (New York, 1942). Universal Edition published Blech's Kinderlieder in six volumes: Opp. 21, 22, 24, 25 (each containing eight songs) 27, and 28 (each with nine). A festive publication for Blech's sixtieth birthday, Jacob, *Leo Blech,* discusses the lied and includes a work list. See also Rychnovsky's three studies, each entitled "Leo Blech."

30. See Kroyer, *Courvoisier,* 49–50.

31. Braunfels's *Verkündigung* (Annunciation) was performed on March 4, 1992, by the Cologne Symphony Orchestra and Chorus, Dennis Russell Davies, conductor, and recorded for EMI (CDS5 55104-2). I am grateful to Michael and Wolfgang Braunfels, sons of the composer, for information about their father. A large number of Braunfels's lieder remained unpublished and (as of 1957) are still in his home in Überlingen, on Lake Constance. Braunfels's work includes: Op. 1 (written before 1905), published Ries and Erler; Op. 2, *Lieder im Volkston* (before 1905, manuscript); Op. 4, *Sechs Lieder Gesänge* (completed 1905), Ries and Erler; Op. 7, *Fragmente eines Federspiels* (1910–11), Ries and Erler; Op. 13, *Nachklänge Beethovenscher Musik* (1909), Ries and Erler; Op. 19, *Drei chinesische Gesänge* (1914), published Tischer and Jagenberg; Op. 26, *Auf ein Soldatengrab* (1915), published Universal Edition; Op. 27, *Zwei Gesänge von Hölderlin* (1916–18), Universal Edition; Op. 29, *Drei Gesänge von Goethe* (?manuscript); Op. 53, *Die Gottminnende Seele* (1935–36), published Dr. Gerig, Cologne; Op. 58, *Romantische Gesänge* (1918–42), Dr. Gerig; Op. 59, *Der Tod der Kleopatra* (manuscript); Op. 62, *Von der Liebe süss und bitterer Frucht* (1945), Dr. Gerig; and *Trauer-Tanz und Werbelieder,* Op. 65 (manuscript, incomplete, 1947). The major part of Braunfels's lieder, especially those composed after the *Fragmente,* are orchestral songs.

32. Oppenheim, *Zilcher,* 70 ff., discusses these songs.

33. On Schmid's Kinderlieder, see, Roth, *Schmid,* 37 ff.

34. The best study of Haas is by Laux, *Haas.* Publications of the Haas Gesellschaft (founded in 1949) provide additional important information on the composer. On Haas's Kinderlieder, see Mies, "Haas."

35. Haas, "Kinderlied," 174–177.

36. Other Kinderlieder by Haas, some in the idiom of Gebrauchsmusik, include: *Sechs dreistimmige Kanons über Sprüchlein* (1913), no opus number; *Sechs Lieder für dreistimmigen Kinder- oder Frauen-chor, a cappella* (Op. 44, 1916); *Sechs Krippenlieder für eine Singstimme oder Kinderchor mit Klavier* (Op. 49, 1919); *Zehn Marienlieder für ein- bis zweistimmigen Frauen- oder Kinderchor mit Begleitung der Orgel oder Harmonium* (Op. 57, 1922); and *Schelmenlieder für eine Singstimme oder Kinderchor und Klavier* (Op. 71, 1929). Haas wrote other kinds of communal music besides Kinderlieder: the curious *Lieder der Sehnsucht* (Op. 77, 1929), for instance, which is Gregorian chant, provided a linear-modal piano accompaniment to aid amateurs in singing chant.

37. *Trali Trala* (Op. 47, 1918) represents a small step back with its descriptive touches and occasional tricky piano parts. Although probably written for performance by adults, its humor has great appeal for children. Further, "Der Mutter vorzusingen" (no. 4) and "Wiegenlied" (no. 12) are among Haas's finest lieder; see Laux, *Haas,* 88.

Chapter 9: The Twilight of Late Romanticism

1. From Wolf's unpublished diary, entry of December 27. Frank Walker, who owned a copy of the diary, provided me with this entry.

2. Mackintosh, *Symbolism,* 3.

3. Peter Russell corrects several authors, the present one included, on the number of poems in Rückert's *Kindertotenlieder.* His count of 425 is based on the first complete edition of 1872, edited by the poet's son, Heinrich Rückert, and printed by Sauerländer (Frankfurt am Main). See Russell, *Light,* chap. 3, esp. pp. 35–37 of this interesting and informative study.

Conrad Beyer, however, the earliest prominent Rückert scholar, indicates—in *Nachgelassene Gedichte Friedrich Rückerts* (Vienna, 1877), 342—that the total number of *Kindertotenlieder* poems Rückert composed is 428. He adds, contrary to the contentions of Russell and La Grange (*Vienna,* 825n1), that a "few *Kindertotenlieder* were published during the poet's life." Beyer's statements are probably correct because Heinrich Rückert, the poet's son, and a Professor Spiegel, another authority, advised Beyer on the publication of his book.

4. Mahler reshaped this motive as the principal idea of the Adagietto of his Fifth Symphony, as well as of the song, "Ich bin der Welt abhanden gekommen." Incidentally, eyes and blindness had similar significance for Maurice Maeterlinck in his symbolist play *Pelléas et Mélisande.* The blind man, wise Arkel (wise because he is only partially blind), and the lovers' meeting place, "Blindman's Well," all suggest "the blindness of humanity in the face of blinding fate" (Joseph Kerman, *Opera as Drama* [New York, 1956], 186).

5. Floros, *Mahler,* 321: "The Glockenspiel [in Mahler] fulfills a symbolic function as a rule . . . when called upon to play long held single tones."

6. Edward Reilly, correspondence with the author. The sketch of "Nun will die Sonn'" is in the Gesellschaft der Musikfreunde (Vienna). See Mitchell, *Mahler: Songs and Symphonies,* 3:133–138, for a detailed discussion of the sketch. Russell's observation is pertinent: "In very few poems in all of the *Kindertotenlieder* is the affirmation of 'eternal light' as explicit as it is [in "Nun will die Sonne"]; and at no other point is the juxtaposition of personal loss and universal salvation so sharply . . . stated as in the final couplet of this poem." See *Light,* 45, 51, and 57.

7. Mahler had replaced the final word *Haus* (house) with *Schoss* (womb or lap) in the manuscript copy of "In diesem Wetter," giving an entirely different conclusion for Rückert's poem. The implications of this change are discussed in detail in my article "Mahler's Dirges for His Death: February 24, 1901," *Musical Quarterly* 64 (1978): 329–353.

8. Mitchell discusses his concept of the organizing frame in *Songs and Symphonies,* passim, particularly 142n49.

9. Mitchell, *Songs and Symphonies,* 349, 397, and 350. The author's explanation of how Mahler expresses the symbolism occurs on 395, 396, and 414. Hermann Danuser identifies the motive and chord in question as this work's *Grundgestalt* and *Grundakkord* (fundamental figure and chord); see *Lied,* 31. On the other hand, Zoltan Roman (and Helmut Storjohann) believe that Mahler's treatment of this motive anticipates "one of the organizing principles of the dodecaphonic system of composition"; see Roman, "Aesthetic Symbiosis and Structural Metaphor in Mahler's *Das Lied von der Erde,*" *Festschrift für Kurt Blaukopf* (Vienna, 1975), 116.

10. See A. Mahler, *Memories,* 206, for "the only true reality." Mahler asserted that the part of nature we see "is only its surface . . . its most superficial part. . . . People [overlook] Nature's secrets, its divine countenance, which we can only surmise" (Bauer-Lechner, *Erinnerungen,* 140). Mahler's comment, "My need to express myself," is drawn from Mahler, *Briefe,* 187 (*Selected Letters,* 179). Mahler's comment on the manuscript's title page reads: "Dies habe ich unter hinterweltlichen (metaphysichen) Schmerzen zur Welt gebracht." The manuscript in question is now in Lehman Deposits of the Pierpont Morgan Library. The conductor George Alexander Albrecht considers the mystical in his book on Mahler symphonies; see "Was uns mit mystischer Gewalt hinanzieht," in *Die Symphonien von Gustav Mahler* (Hameln, 1992).

11. Mahler ceased writing programs for his symphonies after his Fourth Symphony, mainly because, as he noted, "programs . . . are always misinterpreted" (La Grange, *Vienna,* 522). Interestingly enough, his earlier programs, like those of his contemporaries, are replete with detailed imagery. However, revision of these programs (and programs for later sympho-

nies) tends gradually to grow less descriptive of the external world and more detailed about life's hidden core. Two examples of the change: the 1893 version of the First Symphony's "scandalous Huntsman's Funeral"—"Forest animals accompany the hunter's coffin. . . . Hares . . . Bohemian musicians, singing cats, toads, crows . . . stags, deer, foxes and other four-legged and feathered animals," which in the 1900 revision becomes, "A funeral procession passes by: all the misery and sorrow of the world strikes our hero with biting irony" (quotations from La Grange, *Mahler*, 1:748 and 749); and the "shocking" scherzo of the Second Symphony. The 1896 version is described as "a dance viewed as if from a distance, through a window, without hearing the music. . . . Partners seem absurd . . . crazy . . . as if deformed by a concave mirror." The 1901 revision carries the program, "The spirit of unbelief and negation . . . takes possession . . . turmoil of appearances . . . despairs of himself and of God . . . disgust of existence" (see Bauer-Lechner, *Erinnerungen*, 23, for the 1896 version, and A. Mahler, *Memories*, 213, for the 1901 version). See also Stephen Hefling's provocative comparison of program music by Mahler and Strauss, "Miners Digging from Opposite Sides: Mahler, Strauss, and the Problem of Program Music," *Richard Strauss: New Perspectives on the Composer and His Work*, ed. Bryan Gilliam (Durham, 1992), 41–52.

12. Bauer-Lechner, *Erinnerungen*, 11 (*Recollections*, 32 ff.).

13. Newlin, *Bruckner*, 199–200.

14. Chiari, *Symbolisme*, 54. According to Valéry, Mallarmé was jealous of the "magic spell of Beethoven or Wagner. . . . He tried desperately to find a means of regaining for [poetry] the important and marvelous qualities which all-too-powerful Music was stealing from it" (Rollo Myers, *Modern*, 66). Valéry's discussion is from *Pièces sur l'art* (Paris, 1934). For Mallarmé's comment, see Guy Michaud, *Mallarmé*, trans. Marie Collins and Bertha Humez (New York, 1965), 113.

15. For Mahler's first remark, see Bauer-Lechner, *Recollections*, 32; for his second observation, see Bauer-Lechner, *Erinnerungen*, 44; Mahler's Third Symphony comment occurs in Mahler, *Briefe*, 163.

16. Hertz, *Tuning*, xii–xiii. Mitchell, *Songs and Symphonies*, 372, 397, and passim; Danuser, *Lied*, 36. For the Bethge translation, I have adapted Deryck Cooke's translation of the Mahler song (immediately following): see Mitchell, *Songs and Symphonies*, 337. Translation used by permission of Faber and Faber.

17. Lilian R. Furst, "German Romanticism and French Symbolism," in *Counterparts: The Dynamics of Franco-German Literary Relationships, 1770–1895* (Detroit, 1977). Rückert's use for evocative purposes of unusual syntax, diction, and orthography in *Kindertotenlieder* was recognized in 1877 but was seen as idiosyncratic: e.g., the archaic "von *wannen* alle Strahlen"; the evocative "verb*lenden* Geschicke"; the suggestive "Ihr spühtet" (referring to "eyes" [*Augen*]); and in its context, *Zelt* (literally, "tent") as opposed to *Welt* (world); see Conrad Beyer, *Nachgelassene Gedichte Friedrich Rückerts* (Vienna, 1877), 345–346. Moerike, Stein concluded, "anticipates [symbolist] technique to an amazing extent"; see his "Mörike," 22–38; Walter Höllerer, "Eduard Mörike," *Zwischen Klassic und Moderne* (Stuttgart, 1958), 321–356, and his bibliographical references for further studies of symbolist affinities in Moerike. Leon Plantinga, *Romantic Music* (New York, 1984), 456, also recognized that the "ambiguities of literal meaning [in Moerike] anticipate the manner of the symbolists Baudelaire, Verlaine, and Mallarmé." E. L. Stahl discusses "The Genesis of Symbolist Theories in Germany" in *Modern Language Review* 41 (1946): 306–317. Chiari, *Symbolisme*, 60, and Bertocci, *Symbolism*, 67,

discuss earlier examples, e.g., Jouffroy's conception of poetry in *Cours d'esthetique* (1827), as a sequence of symbols that reflect the invisible.

18. Swedenborg's *Hieroglyphica* (English: *A Hieroglyphic Key* [London, 1784]) formulates the author's doctrine of correspondences, which, he indicated, had been well known in the ancient world but was forgotten by the time of the Greeks.

19. Schopenhauer, *Welt als Wille,* 217. I wish to thank William Pohle of the Philosophy Department of Lehman College for invaluable suggestions on these pages. Thomas Carlyle, incidentally, was among a host of literary interpreters of the concept of the artist as privileged: "In a work of art . . . wilt thou discern Eternity looking through Time; the Godlike renders visible." See his *Sartor Resartus* (Oxford, 1913), 160.

20. Quoted in Chiari, *Symbolisme,* 133–134.

21. Quoted in A. Mahler, *Erinnerungen,* 288. La Grange revives (in *Vienna,* 826) the question of why Mahler set Rückert's poetry, which "many commentators have criticized . . . on literary grounds." In seeking to justify Mahler's choice, La Grange skirts one of Mahler's main objectives as a lieder composer. The mature Mahler never sought masterpieces of poetry from Goethe, Eichendorff, and Moerike, as did Wolf and others. He selected Bethge, translator of poems in *Das Lied von der Erde,* who certainly was no better a poet than Rückert. And Mahler considered the *Des Knaben Wunderhorn* poems to be "not complete in themselves, but blocks of marble which anyone might make his own" (see chap. 7, n. 46). Further, Mahler had no special interest in the subject of children's death as such, otherwise he might, perhaps, as La Grange mentions, have selected better literary examples from Eichendorff's *Auf meines Kindes Tod.* As a lied composer, Mahler's search was always for poetry with special inner meaning, verse that he might alter and, through his music, infuse with deeper meaning. His discovery of Rückert was momentous for Mahler. Rückert, an orientalist, was fascinated by the Eastern philosophy that had attracted Fechner, who had opened a new world for Mahler: the world of symbolism. Mahler's interest in Rückert's *Kindertotenlieder* was centered on the mystical aspect of life's renewal after death. La Grange notes inaccurately that I, too, criticized Rückert's poetry in the *Kindertotenlieder* in my article "Mahler's Dirges for His Death" as a "sentimental" treatment of the subject. My comment was just the opposite: the poetry Mahler selected for the third and fourth songs, in contrast to the poetry in the other three songs, with its depths of symbolism, "tends to be maudlin." La Grange also misquotes my praise for Rückert, which was not for his "spellings"—a German poet obviously knows how to spell German—but for his "unusual syntax, diction, and *orthography.*"

22. Hoffmann added: "The perfume of dark red carnations has a singular magic over me," E. T. A. Hoffmann, "Höchst zerstreute Gedanken," *Kreisleriana* (Leipzig, ?), 1:393–394. "Involuntarily I fall into a dreamy state, and I hear them, as if coming from afar, the ebb and flowing deep tones of the basset horn." Samuel Cramer, poet-hero of Baudelaire's *La Fanfarlo* (1847), kept Swedenborg's books on his night table. Baudelaire considered "correspondences" part of mystical reality, i.e., the visible world conceived as a reflection of the inner invisible world.

23. Quoted in Myers, *Modern,* 67.

24. Music stimulated the experiments of the French symbolists. Rimbaud created a musical "vowel-sonnet" and René Ghil a "verbal instrumentation"—expressed in his *Traité du Verbe* (1886)—in which each consonant and vowel possessed musical value. The radical alteration of French poetry, free verse was the idea principally of Gustave Kahn (1856–1936) and Jules Laforgue (1860–87), though others, e.g., Jean Moréas, also claimed its invention. Laforgue was, in this connection, deeply influenced by Walt Whitman's *Leaves of Grass*, which he translated into French. Block's *Mallarmé*, 60–61, provides a good bibliography and helpful references on symbolism, Wagner, and music. Contributors to the *Revue Wagnérienne* include Mallarmé, Vincent d'Indy, René Ghil, Joris-Karl Huysmans, Gabriel Fauré, Camille Saint-Saens, Liszt, Catulle Mendés, and Florent Schmitt. Hertz's *Tuning* is a fine study of the subject.

25. Sams, *Wolf*, 159; Walker, *Wolf*, 253. Wolf also suggests terra firma and the sense of rising to higher levels with mediant modulations in other songs ("Morgenstimmung" [Reinick], "Auf einer Wanderung" and "Jägerlied," both poems by Moerike), although not necessarily with symbolist implications in text and music.

26. Stein draws attention to the way Moerike isolates *Ängste* and *quäle* in "Mörike," 33–34, where he strongly affirms Moerike's symbolist affinities.

27. Wolf often reduces music to stark essence in those of his *Spanish* (Sacred) *Songs* that concern contrition, e.g., "Mühvoll komm' ich beladen," "one of [Wolf's] most penetrating of psychological studies," according to Ernest Newman (*Wolf*, 213).

28. See the penetrating study by Adams, *Holzweg*, particularly 8, 7, 10, 15. On George and music, see Osthoff's article in the supplementary volume of *MGG*, 442–447, and particularly his book, *Stefan George*. Osthoff discusses the influence of Mallarmé, i.e., French symbolism, on George in chapter 9 and passim. See also Brinkmann, "Schönberg," chap. 11, n. 27, and Hertz, *Tuning*, 135 ff. Guy Michaud discusses Mallarmé's Tuesday-evening gatherings, which were attended by George, Oscar Wilde, Arthur Symons, and Debussy; see his *Mallarmé*, trans. Marie Collins and Bertha Humez (New York, 1965), 121 ff.

29. Schorske, *Fin de siècle*, 349; MacDonald, *Schoenberg*, 175; Lawrence Kramer, *Music and Poetry: The Nineteenth Century and After* (Berkeley, 1984), 161; Hertz, *Tuning*, 153. Hertz draws interesting symbolist parallels among George, Verlaine, and Mallarmé.

30. Translation amended and drawn from Schoenberg, "The Relationship," 142–144.

31. Wellesz, *Schönberg*, 120; Schoenberg, "Relationship to Text," 141 and 145; Ulrich K. Goldsmith, "The Renunciation of Woman in Stefan George's *Das Jahr der Seele*," *Studies in Comparison*, ed. Hazel E. Barnes, William M. Calder III, and Hugo Schmidt (New York, 1989), 113.

32. The second song suggests G major to Anton Webern, B major to Hertz (*Tuning*, 142), and "the related tonalities of G and D" to Kramer (*Music and Poetry*, 163 ff.). In the third song, Webern discerns tonal feeling but no specific key. Kramer hears "an oscillating bass that seems to swing . . . from D to G to C and return through G to D" minor, which soon "disintegrates." He declares that "tonal motives in *Das Buch* tend to focus on the related tonalities of G and D, a disposition introduced into the cycle by the second and third songs." Lessem, *Schoenberg*, 44, hears C minor/E flat in the opening bars. Webern's comments about tonality are drawn from MacDonald, *Schoenberg*, 175–176.

33. Schoenberg speaks of achieving an artistic fusion "on a higher plane" at the close of "Das Verhältnis zum Text," *Der Blaue Reiter* (Munich, 1912), 27–33. See Reich, *Schönberg*, 56–57, for the comment "art is the cry of distress." Bailey, *Programmatic*, 79 ff., discusses the Schoenberg symphony "inspired" by Mahler and the "Jacobleiter." Stuckenschmidt, *Schoenberg*, 233 and 234, examines the "obsession" of Berg, Webern, and Schoenberg for Strindberg. Schoenberg composed Op. 22 between 1913 and 1916.

34. See, for instance, Walker, *Wolf*, 193, and Del Mar, *Strauss*, 313.

35. Hans Joachim Moser esteemed Ansorge one of Germany's first impressionists and

"Meine weissen Ara" a fine example of impressionism (*Lied,* 187). Karl Laux concluded more recently in his article on Ansorge: "Ansorge . . . was strongly stimulated by impressionism, which he disseminated in Germany above all in his songs" (*MGG,* 1:510). The composer expressed his resentment over the impressionist label in a letter to Ernst Ludwig Schellenberg, author of articles on Ansorge. Obituaries on Ansorge as an "impressionist composer," were written by Walter Dahms (*Magdeburgische Zeitung,* February 15, 1930) and Kurt Schubert (*Tonkünstler Zeitung,* March 5, 1930). I am again grateful to Dorothea Ansorge-Lippisch, the composer's late daughter, for this information.

36. See Palmer, *Impressionism,* 19, for Debussy's "more convincing realism." In France, the term *impressionist* was applied to Debussy as early as 1887, pejoratively at first. By 1905 the label had changed in France from a scornful to a respected designation; see Jarocinski, *Debussy,* 11. Jarocinski believes that the German art historians Richard Hamann and Werner Weisbach were the first non-Frenchmen to speak of musical impressionism, but the two provided examples from Wagner, Liszt, and Bruckner (17). Debussy's music was "very little known in Germany" before World War I, Jarocinski argues (18). He credits German musicologists for firmly establishing the concept of musical impressionism internationally. Schoenberg (see *Harmonielehre,* 438, 443, and 450) and other central European specialists knew Debussy's music before the war: Niemann, *Gegenwart,* devotes an entire section of his book (229 ff.) to Debussy, the Monet of musical impressionism, "its leader and master" (232). Ronald L. Byrnside's careful study "Musical Impressionism: The Early History of the Term" (*Musical Quarterly* 66 [1980]: 522–537), warns of the "looseness with which [the term *musical impressionism*] was often applied to Debussy's music" (536).

37. Schoenberg, *Harmonielehre,* 450; Joseph Marx, "Lied und Landschaft," *Betrachtungen,* 10 ff. On the Marx lied, see Robert Schollum, *Das Österreichische Lied des 20. Jahrhunderts* (Tutzing, 1977). This engaging study also considers several lesser-known early twentieth-century lied composers (Wilhelm Kienzl, Julius Bittner, and Alexander Zemlinsky), as well as Mahler, Schoenberg, Berg, and Webern.

38. The dates of musical impressionism are given by Hans Albrecht in his article on impressionism in *MGG* and are generally accepted. Although impressionists continued to paint in their inimitable style after 1886, their last official exhibition as a group occurred in that year. Younger followers—Seurat, Van Gogh, Gauguin, Lautrec—revolted against the realism of impressionism. Many of them worked in their studios, exploring different aspects of inner reality, instead of out-of-doors as had the impressionists. Palmer interprets the late appearance of musical impressionism as the "inevitable, ubiquitous time-lag" of music; see his *Impressionism,* 18.

39. Vallas, *Debussy,* 8–10.

40. Schoenberg, *Harmonielehre,* 450. Jarocinski vigorously rejected the impressionist label. His important monograph was published first in Polish (*Debussy, a Impresionizm i synmbolizm,* 1966), then translated into several languages, e.g., French (1970), English (1976), and Italian (1980). Numerous scholarly studies of impressionism vs. symbolism followed, international in scope.

41. Schoenberg, *Harmonielehre,* 450; Moser, *Lied,* 189, called Ritter "the father of German impressionism."

42. Zilcher's imaginative pedal effects are already apparent in his Op. 10 and are discussed by Oppenheim in *Zilcher,* 65 ff. Visual and aural colors were blended by Schreker and, of

course, Scriabin. After 1920 a multitude of such musical procedures fell under the umbrella of musical impressionism.

43. Denis Stevens, *A History of Song* (New York, 1961), 261, dispenses typical non-Germanic opinion of Reger; Reger, *Briefe*, 127.

44. Schoenberg, *Harmonielehre*, 450. Alfred Machner, "Rudi Stephans Werk, Eine Beschreibung als Studie zur Stilwende in der Musik um 1910," Ph.D. diss., Breslau, 1943, has long been the most complete discussion of the composer. I wish to thank Frau M. H. Stephan for making this dissertation available to me. Early Stephan publications include: Hugo Kauder, "Rudi Stephans Lieder," *Musikblätter des Anbruchs*, 3 (1921): 196–198; Karl Holl, *Rudi Stephan* (Mainz, 1922); and eighteen mature songs of the composer, ed. Holl (Mainz, 1921). Five of these songs, orchestrated by Stephan, are also published by Schott. There is a recording of *Liebeszauber* with the Berlin Radio Symphony, conducted by Hans Zender; Dietrich Fischer-Dieskau soloist (Koch Schwann). Hans Schneider's commendable series of short studies, *Komponisten in Bayern* (Composers in Bavaria), includes Brand, *Stephan*, the best source available on Stephan.

45. See Schoeck's letter (June 13, 1907) in Vogel, *Schoeck*, 54. See Puccini, *Turandot*, act 1, piano vocal score (G. Ricordi), 58. The tune, "Moon-Lee Wah," in thoroughly Western harmonization, is quoted in August Wilhelm Ambros, *Geschichte der Musik*, vol. 1 (Leipzig, 1862), in the chapter on Eastern music. The conductor Ludwig Rottenberg (1864–1930) and Ernst Toch (Op. 29) also set Bethge's Chinese lyrics.

46. The Weismann Archive (Duisburg, Germany: W. Falke, former curator) was a good source of information on Weismann. See Theodor Haas, "Bittners chinesische Lieder," *Musikblätter des Anbruch* 4 (1922), 156, and Haas's "Die Lieder Julius Bittners," *Neue Musik-Zeitung* 45 (1924), 18. Bittner was the subject of numerous articles, reviews, and two books: Specht, *Bittner*, and Ullrich, *Bittner*. His Singspiel *Das Höllisch Gold* was well received. Bittner wrote his own libretti and the texts of five of the six Chinese songs discussed. The first poem, by Pang Tschi Yü herself, was translated by Klabund (pseudonym). Many of Bittner's lieder were composed for his wife, a fine contralto. Bittner specialized in two unrelated professions: law and music. He served as judge until 1920 and worked on questions involving copyright from 1920 to 1922. He was also admired in Vienna as the composer of several successful operas.

47. Hans Bethge, *Die chinesische Flöte, Geleitwort* (Stuttgart, 1955), afterword, 74.

48. I should like to thank Carmen Weingartner-Studer, author, orchestral conductor, and widow of Felix Weingartner, for copies of Weingartner's *Japanische Lieder*. Other songs on Japanese verse include: Kienzl, "Frühlingsahnung" (Op. 87); Braunfels, *Von der Liebe süss und bittre Frucht, Vier Gesänge nach dem Japanischen* (Op. 62; Bethge), and Wetz, "Nun wird es Herbst," Op. 27, no. 4.

49. Madsen, *Art Nouveau*, 29.

50. The eroticism of art nouveau was immediately apparent in the revival exhibition in New York (1960), as is evident in Hilton Kramer's review: "The Erotic Style: Reflections on the exhibition of 'Art Nouveau,'" *Arts* 34 (1960). Its "peculiar eroticism . . . seems to color everything." But the eroticism was often veiled: "The idealism of Art Nouveau is—though often but not always, euphemistic and oblique—an erotic idealism . . . afraid of a robust sexuality . . . not the thing in itself, but its appearance and atmosphere were wanted" (23, 26). Madsen explores the style's inner meaning, its procreative symbolism in *Art Nouveau*, 30 ff. and passim.

51. Art nouveau was variously expressed in different countries. In Germany, the stress was

on the floral. Jugendstil became a luxuriant architectural style, whose floral decoration resembles that of the baroque and rococo. The English artist Aubrey Beardsley and, occasionally, the Austrian Gustav Klimt entwined their art-nouveau works with decadent motifs, giving their women a sinister mien. I shall refer to the style as *Jugendstil* throughout this book. The relatively few comments on musical Jugendstil early in our century include Hanslick, *Zeit*, 77; Gysi, *Strauss*, 19; and Moser, *Lied*, 191.

52. Berg's remark is drawn from Stuckenschmidt, *Schoenberg*, 133. See Erich Urban, *Die Musik* 1 (1901), 342, on Magda and Franz Henri von Dulong.

53. Bethge's "Am Ufer" departs radically from Li-Tai-Po's original, in which almost no Jugendstil symbols appear. Bethge's "translation" is a twenty-two line poem. The original Chinese poem comprises only nine lines. Reference to the young men is brief: "Who are these wandering young men / Gathering by the willow trees? / Their horses disappear into the flowers." Bethge's model was probably the translation by Hans Heilmann, who inserted Jugendstil symbols into the text. Bethge augmented these symbols: the alliterative series of flower words is one example. Interestingly enough, Heilmann, Bethge, and Mahler shared a contemporary view of their subject, absent in Li-Tai-Po's original. Li-Tai-Po's thought is centered on "the legendary beauty of Xishi, who once collected lotus flowers" on the river bank pictured in the text. Mitchell prints and discusses the translations just mentioned in *Songs and Symphonies*, 267 ff. See also Hermann Danuser's fine article, "Mahlers Lied 'Von der Jugend'— ein musikalisches Bild," in the Stenzl, *Art Nouveau*, 151–169.

54. La Grange prints the entire poem of 1884 in *Mahler*, 1:831–832, no. 7. Its two relevant lines are: "Und müde Menschen schliessen ihre Lider, / Im Schlaf auf's Neu, vergess'nes Glück zu lernen!" (And weary men close their heavy lids / to learn lost happiness anew in sleep!). Bethge's closing lines read: "Die Erde ist die gleich überall, / Und ewig, ewig sind die weisen Wolken." Those of Mahler: "Die liebe Erde allüberall / Blüht auf im Lenz und grünt aufs neu! / Allüberall und ewig blauen licht die Fernen, / Ewig . . . ewig!"

55. A. Mahler, *Memories*, 160. Klimt portrayed Beethoven as a knight in armor, "whose features recall Mahler": Blaukopf, *Mahler*, ex. 213; ex. 231 illustrates Mahler's use of Secessionist typeface for his Rückert lieder. Mahler's plan to conduct Beethoven's Ninth Symphony at the Secession's opening ceremony, April 15, 1902, never took place: see La Grange, *Vienna*, 512 ff.

56. The exhibit in the Museum of Modern Art in New York City in 1960 sparked this revival in the United States. See *Art Nouveau*, ed. Peter Selz and Mildred Constantine (New York, 1959). Carl Dahlhaus observes that the revival occurred concurrently with the new interest in Mahler's music. He sees no stylistic connection between the two, however ("Rätselhafte Popularität," *Mahler*, 10). The revival stimulated studies of musical Jugendstil, e.g., Johannes Schwermer, "Jugendstil-Musik in der ästhetischen Enklave," *Neue Zeitschrift für Musik* 136 (1965): 2–5; Theodor Adorno, *Gustav Mahler* (Tübingen, 1966), 216; Udo Dammert, "Der Jugendstil in der Musik," *Musica* 20 (1966): 53–58; Hans Hollander, "Musik und Jugendstil," *Neue Zeitschrift für Musik* 132 (1971): 411–413; Neuwirth, *"Parsifal,"* 175–198; Weber, "Jugendstil," 171–174.

57. Dahlhaus, "Jugendstil," cited in Stenzl, *Art Nouveau*, 81 ff.

58. Frisch, "Jugendstil," 143, 144, and 145. *Synaesthesia* is defined in *Webster's Unabridged Dictionary* (1928) as "the concomitant experiences of different types of sensations, as when sounds are apprehended as having characteristics of colors. . . . Other [senses] have been added[:] . . . temperature *sense*, sexual *sense*, . . . sense of the heart . . . and any special faculty of sensation." Synaesthesia thus involves the psychological blending of all the senses. For fin-de-siècle musicians, a whole realm of feeling resides within intersensorial synaesthesia.

59. Frisch, "Jugendstil," 148 and 150–151.

60. Baudelaire, *Painter,* 116. Baudelaire took synaesthesia beyond the intersensorial in his famous sonnet "Correspondences," in which, as noted above, he declares that all elements of outer reality (phenomena) and inner reality (ideas) are interrelated. Here, perfumes have the "sweet" "sound" of oboes, the "color" of green meadows, and the "freshness of children's skin."

61. J. K. Huysmans, *Against the Grain* (A rebours) (New York, 1931), 132–133; Kandinsky, *Spiritual,* 59. Scriabin envisaged (1915) but never realized a work he called "Mysterium," in which light, color, scents, and physical contact were to intermingle. Enid Starkie, *Baudelaire* (Norfolk, 1958), 235, inquires into perfume concerts, Baudelaire, and synaesthesia in general. The Law of Seriality formulated by Paul Kammerer (1880–1926)—and once supported by Albert Einstein, Wolfgang Pauli, and C. G. Jung—is also related to synaesthesia. It holds that in addition to "the causality of classical physics, there exists a second basic principle in the universe which tends towards unity, a force of attraction comparable to universal gravity. But while gravity acts on all mass without discrimination, this other universal force acts selectively to bring like and like together both in space and time." See Arthur Koestler, *The Case of the Midwife Toad* (New York, 1973), 140.

62. Mackintosh, *Symbolism,* 14; Dahlhaus, "Jugendstil," 87 and passim; Frisch, "Jugendstil," 146. Kandinsky, Frisch notes, was deeply involved in the Jugendstil milieu in his formative years in Munich. But Peg Weiss, whom Frisch cites as evidence, speaks of Kandinsky's stay in Munich as being a time of more than one influence—"naturalistic impressionism and lyric symbolism (Jugendstil)"—and adds: "The lyric symbolism or Jugendstil works outnumbered the others" (*Kandinsky,* 42). Evidently a lyric symbolism and Jugendstil—not Jugendstil alone as Frisch implies (144 ff.)—were influences on Kandinsky then. Further, Kandinsky expressed symbolist views throughout *Spiritual:* e.g., he speaks of "spiritual inner life" (40), theosophy, and Mme Blavatsky (32–33) and refers, in typical symbolist language, to Maeterlinck (33 and 75), who "takes us into a world"—that inner world referred to throughout this chapter—where "souls . . . [are] eternally menaced by some invisible and somber force" in works such as "Les Sept Princesses" and "Les Aveugles."

63. Dahlhaus, *Nineteenth,* 332. Reinhold Brinkmann is another adversary of musical Jugendstil in "On the Problems of Establishing Jugendstil as a Category in the History of Music with a Negative Plea," *Miscellanea Musicologica, Adelaide Studies in Musicology* 13 (1984): 19–48. Lectures, symposia, articles, and books on art nouveau continue to proliferate, e.g., the Symposium of the International Musicological Society at the University of Adelaide, Australia, September 23–30, 1979, where advocates by far outnumber adversaries.

64. Hertz, *Tuning,* xii.

65. The quotation of decadents "playing with fire" is from Jackson, *Nineties.* Originally published around 1913, this book is still one of the best discussions of decadence in English literature. Dawson's text is from his poem "Non sum qualis eram bonae sub regno Cynarae." The motto of Des Esseintes (in Huysmans, *A rebours*) is a line from Flaubert, spoken by the Chimera in Flaubert's *Tentation de Saint-Antoine:* "I look for new scents, larger flowers, untried pleasures!"

66. Strindberg wrote in his diary in 1897: "What is woman? The enemy of friendship . . . the necessary evil, the natural temptation . . . a never ending source of tears. . . . Just as she was created from a crooked rib, so is her entire nature crooked and warped and inclined to evil" (quoted in J. P. Hodin, *Edvard Munch* [New York, 1974], 81). See also Kokoschka's play *Mörder, Hoffnung der Frauen* and Félicien Rops's painting *Vengeance d'une Femme*.

67. Quoted in Jessie M. Tatlock, *Greek and Roman Mythology* (New York, 1917), 113–115.

68. The quotation by Benn is drawn from a lecture Donald Mitchell gave for the British Broadcasting Corporation (?1971) on "What is Expressionism?" I am grateful to Mitchell for a typescript and a tape of his informative lecture. Bahr, *Expressionismus*, 123.

69. Though the designation *expressionism* occurred as early as 1850, it gained prominence from 1901 to 1908, after the obscure artist Julien-Auguste Hervé entitled his exhibit in Paris *Expressionismes*. Willet suggests (*Expressionism*, 25) that Kandinsky, who exhibited in Paris with Gabriele Münter, might have brought the term to Germany when he returned there in 1907. Peter Selz, however, disagrees: "The original derivation of the term *Expressionism* is still not known." It did not take root from the Hervé exhibit. "Theodor Däubler recalled," Selz notes, ". . . that the word *expressionisme* was first used by Matisse": see Selz, *Expressionist*, 256. After the term gained currency in Germany (1910), it was applied to all the arts.

70. A study of early performances of *Pierrot Lunaire*, undertaken by W. Heinitz at the phonetic laboratory of the University of Hamburg, throws considerable light on Schoenberg's intention in composing the work. Heinitz examined the recitation of two Sprechstimme artists trained by Schoenberg. He discovered that the two differed from each other to an extraordinary degree with respect to rendition of pitch. Heinitz concluded that Schoenberg's notation could not be realized accurately. See Heinitz, "Sprechtonbewegungen," 1–3. In actual fact, the creation of a weird atmosphere was the composer's primary consideration. Precise rendition of pitch and rhythm was of secondary importance. Performers today, however, are more careful to follow Schoenberg's indications for pitch and rhythm than to create the expressionist atmosphere intended.

71. The term *abstract expressionism* was in use as early as 1919 in an article by Oswald Herzog, "Der abstrakte Expressionismus." Paul F. Schmidt applied the term to Kandinsky in 1920 and so, too, did Alfred H. Barr (1929) in a lecture and in the catalogue of the Museum of Modern Art (New York City): see Selz's *Expressionist*, 126, 184, and 342n49. The term is useful, for it distinguishes the free and partly representational style of early expressionists from the later development of expressionism in Germany. *Abstract expressionism* has been in popular use in New York since World War II to describe a group of artists active there immediately after the war.

72. Quoted in Samuel, *Expressionism*, 103–104. Engelke's comments were drawn from a letter he wrote while serving in France as a soldier. The date of the letter and of the poet's death are incorrectly given in this book. The letter in question was written near Cambrai on October 7, 1918. Engelke, born October 21, 1890, died of wounds October 13, 1918, in a British field hospital. See Gerrit Engelke, *Das Gesamtwerk* (Munich, 1960), 498, which reprints the poet's *Rhythmus des neuen Europa* (1921) and unpublished poetry and correspondence.

73. Kasimir Edschmid, *Über den Expressionismus in der Literatur und die neue Dichtung* (Berlin, 1919), 57. Spurning romantic individualism, Terfloth argues persuasively on the importance of the universal in German expressionist theater ("Universal," 128–134). Jacob Wassermann (1873–1934) referred to "the collective emotion" as "entselbstete Leidenschaft."

Chapter 10: Expressive Aesthetics in Performance

1. Quoted in Hunnius, *Kunst,* 62.

2. Riesenfeld, "Wüllner," 364; Feodor Chaliapin, clipping files, Music Research Division of the Library and Museum of the Performing Arts at Lincoln Center, New York City.

3. Bauer-Lechner, *Erinnerungen,* 22. On Lekeu and French music, see Cooper, *French Music,* 55 ff.

4. Walker, *Wolf,* 212; Mahler to Adler, in Pamer, "Mahler," 127. Mahler's *Kindertotenlieder* comment, letter to Arthur Seidl, February 17, 1897, Mahler, *Briefe,* 229.

5. Otto Neitzel on Wüllner, *Kölnische Zeitung,* March 1896, see Ludwig, *Wüllner,* 174.

6. *Richmond News Leader,* December 4, 1907, in Bispham, clipping files, Lincoln Center.

7. *Appleton Post* (Wisconsin), November 3, 1909, and A. F. on "Bispham on Wüllner," *Musical America* 9 (1909), 20, in Bispham, clipping files, Lincoln Center.

8. Ernst Wolf, "Gesanglehre—Das Portament," *Spemanns goldenes Buch der Musik* (Berlin, 1900), entry 437. The following recordings present instructive illustrations of the portamento and the mannered style in question: Ernestine Schumann-Heink (1861–1939, debut 1878), Schumann, "Mondnacht," Victrola 88197 (ca. 1908); Emma Eames (1865–1952, debut 1889), Schubert, "Who Is Sylvia?" Victrola 88013 (1905); and Katharina Senger-Bettaque (1862–?, debut before 1879), Wolf, "Gesang Weylas," Barbara Migurski and Richard Warren, Jr., *Treasures from the Yale Collection of Historical Sound Recordings,* P1993, CD 1. Portamentos were also generously applied in instrumental music, as a recording of Strauss's *Ein Heldenleben,* with the New York Philharmonic, conducted by Willem Mengelberg, RCA Victor M44 (1928), illustrates. A parting of the ways evidently took place in the New York Philharmonic when Arturo Toscanini followed Mengelberg as chief conductor. The timpanist Saul Goodman indicates in an interview—"Saul Goodman talks to Burnett Cross on Tape," June 1990 (unpublished)—that Mengelberg's portamentos infuriated Toscanini when he attended a rehearsal. He left, refusing to appear as guest conductor. When Toscanini returned four weeks later he insisted that the strings eliminate portamentos entirely. Emma Eames later in life apparently also had misgivings about the portamento; see *Memories.* Two of many contemporary expressions of distaste for generously applied portamentos: Alan Blyth censured two portamentos, "ugly, both," in Lilli Lehmann's recording of Schubert's "Erlkönig" 800 04; RLS 766 (1906), *Song on Record,* vol. 1: *Lieder,* ed. Alan Blyth (Cambridge, 1986), 76–77. Strauss, notes Del Mar (*Strauss,* 3:275), perhaps "allowed his enthusiasm to get the upper hand at the expense of taste in his over-use of the vocal portamento" in "Wie sollten wir geheim sie halten" (Op. 19, no. 4). See also Bos, *Accompanist,* 99 ff.

9. "The words marked with > are to be emphasized forcefully."

10. Weingartner, *Conducting,* 28. On changing attitudes toward tempo in nineteenth-century music, see my article "Tempo as an Expressive Element in the Late Romantic Lied," *Musical Quarterly* 59 (1973): 497–518.

11. Retards and holds were freely made in the following recordings. Schubert, "Who Is Sylvia?": Emma Eames, Victrola 88013 (1905) and David Bispham (debut 1890), Columbia 30020 (1906–07); Schubert, "Wohin?": Marcella Sembrich (1858–1935, debut 1877), HMV AGSB 88 (1906); Schubert, "Ständchen": Julia Culp (debut 1903), Victor 6066 (1915); Johanna Gadski (debut 1889), Victor 88112 (1908); Paul Reimers (1878–1942, debut 1902), Victor 55045 (1914). Minne Nast's rendition (G & T 43193X) of Schubert's "Heidenröslein" (1902), with its sudden retards and excessively long holds, reduces fin-de-siècle performance to caricature. The degree to which the late-romantic style is mannered is especially evident when singers ren-

dered arias of Handel, as reviews indicated they did, with continual changes of tempo, dynamics, and timbre.

12. See Weingartner, *Conducting*, 28, on the Luftpause. Frederick Niecks, "Tempo Rubato from the Aesthetic Point of View," *Monthly Musical Record* 43 (1913), 117.

13. Quoted in Liess, *Marx*, 153.

14. Quoted in Bauer-Lechner, *Recollections*, 46, trans. altered; Steinitzer, *Strauss*, 52.

15. Quoted in Bauer-Lechner, *Recollections*, 46.

16. Kullak, *Vortrag*, 118; Niecks, "Chopin," 145; August Schmid-Lindner, pianist and associate of Reger; *Musical Courier*, March 6, 1912, reviews Henschel's performance. For an example of Mahler's performance, see Mahler's Welte-Mignon Piano Rolls (*Mahler Plays Mahler*, Pickwick, CD GLRS 101).

17. A note in Marx's "Nocturne" on page 1 alerts the performer: "In this piece the metric double rhythm [i.e., the multiple time signatures in the voice part] is to be regarded (with all rubato freedom of delivery) as to have the second half of the bar correspond in length of time to the first 3 eighths (or 4 eighths) of the bar. [The $\frac{2}{2}$ should not be converted into a kind of $\frac{7}{8}$.] This [instruction] does not affect the delivery of rubatos and ritardandos." Mitchell, *Songs and Symphonies*, 342, 410, and 495n148.

18. Carl Philip Emanuel Bach, *Essay on the True Art of Playing Keyboard Instruments* (New York, 1949), 149, trans. and ed. William J. Mitchell; *Mozart Briefe und Aufzeichnung: Gesamtausgabe*, ed. Wilhelm A. Bauer and Otto Erich Deutsch (Kassel, 1962), 2:83; Leopold Mozart, *A Treatise on the Fundamental Principles of Violin Playing* (London, 1959), 224, trans. and ed. Editha Knocker; Johann Nepomuk Hummel, *Ausführliche theoretisch-practische Anweising zum Pianofortespiel* (Vienna, 1928), 418 and 427; Carl Guhr, *Über Paganinis Kunst die Violine zu Spielen* (Mainz, ?1830), 66–67.

19. Wagner, *Conducting*, 36 and 35; Kullak, *Vortrag*, from the foreword; see also Seidl, *Dirigenten*, 24, and Spitteler, *Essays*, 63. Weingartner, *Conducting*, 28. "The Wagnerian tradition of Bayreuth—especially under the baton of Felix Mottl (1856–1911)—has, indeed, overdone the slower tempos to such an extent that German musicians' slang coined the verb *vermottln* for the exaggeration of *adagio* and *lento*"; (Sachs, *Rhythm*, 324).

20. Leo Fall and Siegfried Fall were both "solo repetiteurs" for Brahms, they are discussed in Hans Emge, "Liebe zum bel canto" (unpublished manuscript). Emge was the outstanding voice teacher of Gerhard Hüsch and others. Elena Gerhardt's slow tempi are evident in these recordings: Schubert, "An die Musik," HMV 043202, and Schubert, "Du bist die Ruh'," City Road (London), both recorded in 1911 with Nikisch. Gerhardt's two recordings of Wolf's "Und willst du deinen Liebsten sterben sehen" impressively illustrate her earlier preference for slower tempi; see Chap. 4, n. 22 above.

21. The development of the modern piano from the Viennese instrument (the ideal of Mozart and Hummel) occurred largely in the first half of the nineteenth century: heavier action, thicker strings and thicker soundboard, cast-iron frame, and double escapement. Cross stringing, which gave the modern piano its powerful timbre, was not generally introduced until about 1855 (Sachs, *Instruments*, 396–397).

22. Strauss, *Richard Strauss Lieder, Gesamtausgabe*, ed. Franz Trenner, 4 vols. (London, 1964–65), vol. 1: *Revisionsbericht*, 345, quotes both of Strauss's remarks. Walker, *Wolf*, 428.

23. Paul Bekker, "Zur Charakteristik der Stimmen," *Die Musik* 4 (1905), 174.

24. Hey, *Vortragsmeister*, 68.

25. Hey discusses the Tiefgriff der Stimme in *Gesang-Unterricht*, vol. 3, passim, and *Der* *kleine Hey* (Mainz, 1912), vol. 4, passim. Carl Adelmann, "Julius Hey, *Deutscher Gesangunterricht,*" *Bayreuther Blätter* 1 (1888): 317–328, offers an informative contemporary criticism of Hey's vocal method. A recording by Anton Sistermanns (1865–1926), bass-baritone, provides an illustration of "low larynx" sound as taught by his teacher Stockhausen; see Migurski and Warren, *Treasures from the Yale Collection,* CD 1, ex. 19. Monika Hunnius, another student of Stockhausen's, notes (*Kunst,* 91) that Stockhausen taught the dangerous method noted. A Dr. Goliner, a physician, held that the Tiefgriff der Stimme, as taught before 1900, is "deleterious to the larynx"; see his "Das Stimmorgan und seine Pflege, eine ärztliche aufklärung für alle Sänger," *Neue Musik-Zeitung* 8 (1887): 181–182. Lehmann, *Sing,* 248.

26. Other examples of Wagner's preference for dark timbre: his introduction of the covered orchestra pit (at Bayreuth, which shaded orchestral timbre, but see note 55, below) and of deep brass instruments (bass trumpet, Wagner tubas, bass and contra-bass trombone, and contra-bass tuba). String instruments, too, were affected; larger violas (eighteen-inch instruments) replaced the smaller ones then and now in practice.

27. Walker, *Wolf,* 205.

28. See Tchaikovsky's Sixth Symphony (1893), Allegro vivo, bars 160–161, and Mahler's Seventh Symphony (1904–05), the Scherzo (after cue 161).

29. Mitchell indicates, in *Lieder eines fahrenden Gesellen* (London, 1977), introduction, that this edition alone "represents the composer's final intentions." Reilly, "A Catalogue of the Musical Manuscripts of Gustav Mahler" (manuscript in preparation), discusses differences among manuscripts of the same work by Mahler. Winternitz examines Mahler's revision of "Der Schildwache Nachtlied" (*Autographs,* 1:130–131).

30. The seven Schoenberg songs are: "Abschied" (Op. 1, no. 2), "Die Aufgeregten" (Op. 3, no. 2), "Warnung" (Op. 3, no. 3), "Freihold" (Op. 3, no. 6), "Verlassen" (Op. 6, no. 4), "Am Wegrand" (Op. 6, no. 6), and "Lockung" (Op. 6, no. 7). Lang, *Knab,* 43 and 83.

31. See Lafite, *Sänger,* 78 ff., on fin de siècle performances of Schubert lieder.

32. Moore, *Unashamed,* 19–20.

33. Percentages were derived from study only of Wolf's mature lieder: the *Moerike, Eichendorff, Goethe, Michelangelo,* and *Spanish* and *Italian Songbooks,* and *Lieder nach verschiedenen Dichtern.* Percentages on Strauss, Reger, and Pfitzner lieder were drawn from complete editions of their songs.

34. The songs are "Der Arbeitsmann" (Op. 39, no. 3) and "Lied an meinen Sohn" (Op. 39, no. 5). Strauss composed almost all his dramatic songs in the decades around 1900: both these two and "Die Ulme zu Hirsau" (Op. 43, no. 3) of 1899, "Von den sieben Zechbrüdern" (Op. 47, no. 5) of 1900, "Lied des Steinklopfer" (Op. 49, no. 4) of 1901, and "Frühlingsfeier" (Op. 56, no. 5) of 1906. Notable exceptions: "Drei Masken" (no. 4, *Krämerspiegel,* Op. 66, 1918) and "Lied der Frauen" (Op. 68, no. 6). These lieder all climax in double not triple forte.

35. Among them are "Sie haben heut' abend Gesellschaft" (Op. 4, no. 2, 1888–89), "Zorn" (Op. 15, no. 2, 1904), "Gegenliebe" (Op. 22, no. 4, 1907), and "Der Weckruf" (Op. 40, no. 6, 1931).

36. Recordings include Lehmann, Schubert, "Du bist die Ruh,'" Berlin Odeon 50432 (July 2, 1907; mm. 22–23 and 46 contain subtle diminuendos. Striking diminuendos occur on *erhellt,* mm. 59–60, and its repetition, mm. 73–74). Also Schubert, "Ständchen," Gadski, Victor 88112; Reimers, Victor 5504; and Culp, Victor 6066. And Friedrich Brodensen, Schubert, "Sei mir gegrüsst," Parlophone 2-5631, P1290-II, recorded with Felix Günther, piano. Examples of dynamic shadings introduced into Schubert's "Erlkönig": transcriptions for piano

solo by Liszt (185?), Victor Felix (ca. 1870), and especially Liszt's and Reger's orchestrations of the song. More recently see Kalmus Song Series: *Franz Schubert Songs*, vol. 1. On "Erlkönig," see also n. 60, below.

37. Walker, *Wolf*, 305. Walker discusses (280) the extreme care Wolf exercised when proofreading his songs for publication.

38. Gerhardt, Raucheisen, Culp, and Huesch indicated that less adept singers often fooled audiences in this manner. Recorded examples of hushed conclusions include: Schumann-Heink, Schumann, "Mondnacht," Victrola 88197 (ca. 1908–09); Brodensen (see above, n. 36); Gerhardt, Schubert, "Suleikas Zweiter Gesang," Berlin, HMV DB-1544 (1929).

39. Hunnius, *Kunst*, 175; Weingartner, "lebende Lied"; Hanslick, *Concertsaal*, 214. Leopold Schmid is another critic who considers both Mühlen and Wüllner the most modern and distinguished of concert singers: "Tonkünstler der Gegenwart," *Spemanns*, entry 1302 (photograph of Wüllner, entries 1155–1157).

40. Sonnleithner, "Bemerkungen," 697–701. By "prevailing taste" (see Deutsch, *Memoirs*, 116–117), Sonnleithner was referring to the impassioned lied performance of the 1860s. Was that style known before 1830? Members of Schubert's circle—Franz von Hartmann, Josef von Spaun, and Sonnleithner—provide answers in their discussion of the performance style of Michael Vogl (1768–1840), a principal singer of Schubert's songs. They agree that Vogl was cultivating a "new" style of interpretation. Hartmann: Vogl was "the first to introduce . . . the declamatory . . . [and] make us intellectually and emotionally aware of it." Von Spaun: "Some people have criticized Vogl for . . . his somewhat theatrical manner of performance" but this "heightened the effect in a great many songs." Sonnleithner: He "overstepped the permissible limits more and more as he lost his voice" and "merely helped himself out as well as he could, in the manner of the experienced opera singer, where his voice and strength did not suffice" (Deutsch, *Memoirs*, 116–117, 273, 365).

41. Hummel, *Ausführliche*, 423; Deutsch, *Memoirs*, 337.

42. "Arbitrary slackening or accelerating of the pace is now [1846] being applied often to a caricature," Czerny complained in *Die Kunst des Vortrags der ältern und neuen Clavier-compositionen—Die Fortschritte bis zur neuesten Zeit*, Supplement or Part 4 (Vienna, ca. 1846), 31 para. 72, to his three-volume *Piano Forte School*. Wagner, *Conducting*, 43. On (2), Wagner remarked: "It is obviously the delicate duty of the executants" to link "with an appropriate modification of tempo" an Allegro to an Adagio "so unobtrusively . . . that a change in the movement is hardly perceptible" (48). On (3), Wagner wrote: *"Our conductors so frequently fail to find the correct tempo because they are ignorant of singing"* (19). This third principle was most important for late romantics. It explains by implication why instrumental lyricism came in the nineteenth century to be called "free declamation" by Liszt and others, as well as why the term *declamatory style*, certainly in use before Liszt, found its way into the Rieman-Einstein lexicon (under *rubato*) as a chief characteristic of tempo in the second half of the nineteenth century and why late romantics, e.g., Mahler, in their penchant for intense expression, wanted even the timpani to sing.

43. See the commentary in a footnote on page 404 of Liszt, "Dirigiren." On Fritz Steinbach, see Blume, *Brahms*, passim. Kullak, *Vortrag*, 115.

44. Arthur Laser, *Der moderne Dirigent* (Leipzig, 1904), 7. Hans Emge discusses Wüllner and Zur Mühlen in his "Liebe zum bel canto" manuscript, 4.

45. Orel, "Strauss," 12–13, and Strauss, *Betrachtungen*, 161. On Pfitzner's accompaniment of Schumann's *Liederkranz*, see Abendroth, *Pfitzner*, 384. The older Strauss did not play with the freedom that Orel indicated when, in 1943, he accompanied singers on *Richard Strauss begleitet Hilde Konetzni, Anton Dermota, Alfred Poell,* Preiser, CD Mono 93261.

46. Pfohl, *Nikisch,* 70.

47. Bos, *Accompanist,* 44.

48. Frederick Dorian, *The History of Music in Performance* (New York, 1942), 283; Bos, *Accompanist,* 45, on Brahms's approval of the license; Henschel, *Recollections,* 17. I am indebted to Elena Gerhardt, Michael Raucheisen, and August Schmid-Lindner for this information.

49. Helm, "Wiener Musikleben," 8:274 (1917).

50. Weingartner, *Conducting,* 31. On unconventional time signatures: in 1888 Wolf exclaimed, "I wrote ['Jägerlied'] in $\frac{5}{4}$ time, and perhaps I may say that seldom has $\frac{5}{4}$ time been so fittingly employed as in this composition" (Walker, *Wolf,* 202). Further, Pfitzner was fond of the expansive $\frac{3}{2}$ and $\frac{2}{2}$, and did not shy away from $\frac{5}{8}$ and $\frac{5}{2}$. More unusual signatures enriched the lied in the first two decades of the twentieth century, figures with the "denominator" of 16 — $\frac{12}{16}$ and $\frac{9}{16}$, as often found in Reger, and $\frac{18}{8}$ in Klose's *Bruno Lieder* (see ex. 20).

51. Information gathered from interviews with these musicians.

52. Weingartner, *Conducting,* 22; Pfitzner, "Werk und Wiedergabe," 74.

53. Bos, *Accompanist,* 86 and 24, respectively.

54. Wilhelm Altmann, "Kritik," *Die Musik* 1 (1901), 447. Review by Evaire C. Witker, clipping files, Lincoln Center. Philip Miller indicates that it was unusual for accompanists' names to appear on early recordings of lieder.

55. Adherents of Wagner criticized the composer's covered orchestra pit at Bayreuth because it "shaded" orchestral brilliance (Marsop, "Unsichtbares," 331–338). Weingartner offered suggestions to correct the "defect"; see "Vorschlag," 173–177. *Der Merker* sent a questionnaire (1915) to leading conductors of opera inviting comments on Wagner's covered orchestra. Nearly all conductors preferred the natural brilliance of the orchestra to the timbre of the covered orchestra. Their replies appear at the conclusion of Weingartner's article (177–187). Strauss, incidentally, had a solution similar to Weingartner's in 1895.

56. Strauss probably made this statement in 1933. Strauss, *Recollections,* 45. Toscanini disliked the "languors" of German conductors like Felix Mottl and Karl Muck. He tended to select faster tempi the older he grew. This point is important in view of Toscanini's influence on conductors in the twentieth country. Wagner, *Conducting,* 35. A review of Sergiu Celibidache conducting the Munich Philharmonic in Carnegie Hall in *New York Magazine* (May 8, 1989, 86–87) presents an illuminating example of a modern American critic's attitude toward late-romantic languors. The critic, appalled by the conductor's "elongated tempi," describes his interpretation of Bruckner's Fourth Symphony: it was "played like an LP record slowed to half-speed. . . . If Celibidache's musical message is always this repulsively self-indulgent and egocentric, he can keep it to himself." Another example, but a contrary one: Gilbert Kaplan discloses that the famous Adagietto from Mahler's Fifth Symphony is taken much slower today than it was by Mahler and his associates. "A timing of seven and a half minutes" is given for the Adagietto in Mahler's first performance of the symphony (1904), "seven minutes" for the movement in his reading of the symphony in Saint Petersburg (1907), and "just over seven minutes" in Mengelberg's recording (1926). Kaplan clocked the Adagietto in recent recordings: Leonard Bernstein, "some 11 minutes"; Bernard Haitink, "about 14 minutes"; and "more than a quarter of an hour" in concert performances of the symphony under Bernstein and Hermann Scherchen (Kaplan, "A Dirge? No. It's a Love Song," *New York Times,* July 19, 1992, sec. 2, 19 and 22).

57. Bauer-Lechner, *Recollections,* 46.

58. A Schubertiade was in progress in 1992 at the 92nd Street Y, in New York City. Hermann Prey founded the first Schubertiade in Vienna (1983) to perform all of Schubert's music. He worked with Omus Hirshbein of the 92nd Street Y on the similar venture in New York, scheduled from 1988 to 1997. Edward Rothstein, *New York Times,* January 31, 1992, C-13, reviewed Prey's master class of January 29. Flagstad with Edwin McArthur, London FFrr X5262 ARL 3256 (1956); Fischer-Dieskau with Gerald Moore, Electrola (Odeon) E90 921 WALP 535 (?1952–54) and Deutsche Grammophon 2561 020 (1969–72), vol 2. Further, Fischer-Dieskau makes a slightly early entry in the earlier recording in measure 97 but not in the later one. See two Prey recordings, one with Karl Engel: Schubert, Phillips Lied Edition, 6599 383 (?1973–74), and one with orchestra, conducted by Gary Bertini, RCA ARLI-3002 (1977). I wish to thank Don MacCormack and David Thomas of the Rogers and Hammerstein Archive of Recorded Sound of the New York Public Library of the Performing Arts for dates and record numbers of the recordings mentioned.

59. Lilli Lehmann, Berlin, Odeon 80004 (1906); David Bispham, Columbia 30019 (?1906–08); Johanna Gadski with Frank LaForge, piano, Victor 88040 (1906); Sophie Braslau, Columbia, set 89, 67431-D 98498, (?1928). Lehmann's tempo is elastic throughout. She sings the music of the "Erlkönig" in hastened tempo and with further accelerandos. Her tempo for the child is slower, a steady but frightened heartbeat; she paces the father's music still slower, but reassuringly calm. Gadski, in contrast, generally maintains an even pulse, though she sings "Willst feiner Knab" a shade faster than the father's previous comment. The opening bars in Gadski's recording are abridged, perhaps to fit her performance onto the disc. (Fin-de-siècle singers, of course, always had to consider timing of performances in preparing phonograph records.) Bispham slackens and accelerates tempo freely, but he often returns to an established basic pulse. Braslau's conception is especially free: she depicts the Erlkönig (mm. 57–72) appreciably faster than the music for the child (mm. 72–79). Further, these artists all introduced holds and retards to stress key words, e.g., "*Leid's* getan" (m. 130) or "*ächzende* Kind" (mm. 139–40). And they decreased tempo at significant cadences, but again with great individuality. Most noteworthy: they occasionally altered the notation. Gadski, for instance, changed "seh' es genau," measure 108, from the written (♩ ♩ ♪) to (♩ ♫). Finally, the recording with orchestra of "Erlkönig" by Ernestine Schumann-Heink, Nimbus CD 7811 (from Victor C11339-1, 1911): though her pace is stricter than Gadski's, she does modify tempo (e.g., "reicht den Hof"), change some time values, and introduce portamentos and striking changes of vocal timbre.

60. Johannes Messchaert, *Eine Gesangstunde, Allgemeine Ratschläge nebst gesangstech-nischen Analysen von einigen Schubert-Liedern,* Edition Schott, No. 119, ed. by Franziska Martienssen, published with the piano-vocal scores (Mainz and Leipzig, 1927). The publication includes lessons on three Schubert songs: "Meeresstille," "Erlkönig," and "An die Leyer." I thank Frau Paul Bender for a copy of the publication. Liszt's piano-solo transcription of "Erlkönig," is an example that shows the tradition in its initial stages. He marked the passage that reads "Willst feiner Knabe" *un peu plus animé* and the "ich liebe dich" *molto appassionato ritèn* and introduced other tempo modifications later in his orchestral version of this song. Liszt's solo piano transcription was published (185?) in Vienna by Diabelli, no. 6534. Alan Walker notes that "as soon as [Liszt] entered Vienna . . . Schubert song transcriptions started [1838] to pour from his pen." "Erlkönig" is one of his first; see "Liszt and the Schubert Song Transcriptions," *Musical Quarterly* 75 (1991), 249.

Chapter 11: Structural Principles and the Common Aesthetic

1. The special kinds of unity and integration Beethoven introduced among the separate movements of works such as his Fifth and Ninth Symphonies inspired many later composers: numerous "cyclical" symphonies, symphonic poems, and motivically integrated operas followed. One perhaps can understand why—in the spirit of fin-de-siècle partiality for such unity and integration—Max von Schillings composed recitatives for Mozart's *Die Entführung aus dem Serail* to replace the spoken text and why Wolf criticized Handel's *Saul:* "Much of this work appears antiquated and pale, especially the [alternation] of arias and recitatives" (Wolf, *Kritiken,* 157 [*Criticism,* 121]).

2. Laux, *Haas,* 87, discusses cyclic unity in Haas. Richard Kramer suggests the existence of other cyclical conceptions among Schubert's lieder (*Distant Cycles,* passim). In one example, stimulated by the research of another scholar, Kramer charges that the sequence of Heine songs in Schubert's *Schwanengesang,* published months after the composer's death, "is the wrong one. . . . When the [six Heine] songs are withdrawn from *Schwanengesang* and their sequence revised, an integral cycle is reinstated so elegant in concept as to force us to a revision of the idea of cycle itself." (125). A song cycle may be defined, as it is by Rufus Hallmark, as "a group of songs for voice and piano constituting a literary and musical unit" (*The New Harvard Dictionary of Music*). Hallmark, ed., *Nineteenth-Century German Lieder* (forthcoming), will include an essay on song cycle.

3. Winternitz, *Autographs,* vol. 2, pl. 162.

4. "Zur Ruh, zur Ruh!" (Justinus Kerner) is an early example (1883). Walker commented, in a letter to me, on the subtlety and complexity of the Wagner influence on Wolf: "One would have to write a book" on this subject. Yet Walker found few mature lieder that show Wagner's unmistakable influence. (Incidentally, Wolf used opus numbers for his lieder until 1876.)

5. Pfitzner, *Hans Pfitzner Sämtliche Schriften* 4:443. Patrick McCreless's study of the role played by *Stimmung* (mood) in creating unity in Schumann's *Liederkreis* is well worth consultation; see "Song Order in the Song Cycle: Schumann's *Liederkreis,* Op. 39," *Music Analysis* 5 (1986): 5–28.

6. Some studies, like the influential early work by Paul Mies, *Stilmomente und Ausdrucksstilformen in Brahms'schen Lied* (Leipzig, 1923), 8 ff. and 15 ff., divide strophic songs into two categories, those with a single melody and those with more than one melody, a twofold division that is more involved than necessary for the present discussion.

7. Sachs discusses symmetry and seriation with much insight in *Commonwealth,* 206–207.

8. Weber and Schubert applied strophic form repeatedly. Schubert wrote the greatest number early in his life. Over 70 percent of his songs from 1815 are simple strophics. The number decreases continually so that only 17 of 115 songs (15 percent) from between 1824 and 1828 are in this form. Schumann wrote fewer strophic songs. Brahms, despite his avowed classicism, turned to strophic form mainly in his folkish lieder. Mahler is quoted in Bauer-Lechner, *Erinnerungen,* 119.

9. "Um Mitternacht" approximates strict strophic form more closely than any other *Moerike* song. Wolf strove for a different shade of meaning, however, by accenting the third line of the second stanza differently from the corresponding line in the first stanza. Hans Eppstein's "Zum Schaffensprozess bei Hugo Wolf" (*Die Musikforschung* 37 [1984]: 4–20) is a brief but rewarding discussion of Wolf's structure and creative process.

10. Walker, *Wolf,* 205.

11. His keys of D major and F-sharp minor are tertial relations common in nineteenth-century sonata form, e.g., the main subjects of the first movement of Brahms's Second Symphony.

12. Mitchell, *Songs and Symphonies*, 106 and 190. Mitchell outlines "Das Trinklied"'s third strophe on page 177.

13. Newlin, "Bruckner, Mahler, Schoenberg" (Ph.D. diss., Columbia University, 1945), was among the first to argue that it is a symphony. Stephen E. Hefling argues similarly in "*Das Lied von der Erde:* Mahler's Symphony for Voice and Orchestra—or Piano," *Journal of Musicology* 10 (1992), 303 ff. Mitchell, *Songs and Symphonies*, 468n76; by Danuser, see *Das Lied*, e.g., 39, 42, or 44 and "Gustav Mahlers Symphonie 'Das Lied von der Erde' als Problem der Gattungsgeschichte," *Archiv für Musikwissenschaft* 40 (1983): 276–286.

14. Bauer-Lechner, *Recollections*, 147.

15. "Zugvogel" is a fine expression of romantic pessimism, to which Pfitzner was strongly inclined (see Chap. 3, above).

16. Sachs, *Commonwealth*, 297.

17. In late Victorian and Wilhelmian interior design, the right or left window drape might be broader and more elaborate than its companion; see Frances Lichten, *Decorative Art of Victoria's Era* (New York, 1950), 133.

18. Mahler treated "Wo die schönen Trompeten blasen" similarly. The text in the second of its two D-major sections (mm. 130–162) is one line shorter than the corresponding first D-major section (mm. 40–72). Mahler assigned the "missing" parallel phrase (mm. 142–145) to the piano part to create the structural orderliness associated with folkish songs.

19. Gerd Sievers, *Die Grundlagen Hugo Riemanns bei Max Reger,* (Ph.D. diss., Hamburg, 1949), 213 and 222. Wehmeyer, *Liederkomponist,* 251 ff.

20. Westrup and Harrison censured *through-composed* as the "literal American translation of G. *Durchkomponiert.* It is not English"; see *New College Encyclopedia of Music* (New York, 1960), 657. *The New Grove* (1980) indexes *through-composed* without criticism. In the past century, some English critics have regarded *folk song* as awkward English for *Volkslied*, also to no avail.

21. Authorities have defined *through-composed* in a variety of ways. Maurice J. E. Brown, the Schubert authority, distinguishes in Schubert "between *durchkomponiert* song and episodic song. I take *durchkomponiert* to mean the type of on-running song in which different melodies and musical moods are bound together by a basically unchanging type of accompaniment, e.g., 'Gretchen am Spinnrade,' 'Der Zwerg,' 'Die junge Nonne.' The episodic structure consists of independent episodes, which may recur, in which unity is obtained (if at all) by stylistic integrity, e.g., 'Prometheus,' 'Der Neugierige,' and 'Kriegers Ahnung'" (letter to the author). Mies recognizes in Brahms (*Stilmomente u. Ausdrucksstilformen im Brahmsschen Lied* [Leipzig, 1923]) two kinds of through-composed song, those with one melody and those with more than one. Wehmeyer, in analysis of the Regerlied (*Liederkomponist,* 238 ff.), identifies five kinds: *Kontrastformen, Steigerungsformen* (see below), *Inhaltliche Bogenformen* (songs unified by a dynamic curve), *Ausdruckskonstanteformen,* and *Episodisch wechselnde Formen* (see below).

22. Hans-Herwig Geyer, *Hugo Wolfs Mörike-Vertonungen* (Kassel, 1991), 179–211, undertakes a long and detailed analysis of "An die Geliebte."

23. Wehmeyer, *Liederkomponist,* 242 ff., provides examples of different kinds of Steigerungsformen.

24. Songs with prominent stock accompaniment figures include: Wolf's "Auch kleine

Dinge" and "Bedeckt mich mit Blumen," Strauss's "Traum durch die Dämmerung" and "Wiegenlied," and Reger's "Der Himmel hat eine Träne geweint" and "Ruhe" (Op. 62, no. 3). See Wehmeyer, *Liederkomponist,* 247–249, for a fine discussion of Ausdruckskonstante forms.

25. Wehmeyer calls digressive rambling forms *Episodisch wechselnde Formen* (*Liederkomponist,* 249–250).

26. Pamer, "Lieder," 16, 135. La Grange, *Mahler* 1:790, provides a similar analysis.

27. They measure, for instance, the "exposition" of the first movement differently. For Danuser, "Herr dieses Hauses!" (bar 112) marks the beginning of the exposition's repetition (*Das Lied,* 38 and 42 ff.). Mitchell, however, identifies that passage as "a continuous development," not the exposition's restatement (*Songs and Symphonies,* 186). With respect to the final movement, *Abschied,* we receive different analyses not only from Danuser and Mitchell, but also from Robert Bailey, whose discussion Mitchell quotes on page 384. For Mitchell's comment on fluidity in Mahler's forms, see p. 446, n. 8.

28. Traces of strophic form are apparent in Songs 9, 10, and 12. In addition, these elements of musical form, prefigured in the late-romantic lied, are also evident in *Hanging Gardens:* structural frames (Songs 3, 6, 10, and 14), period structure (Song 10), traditional thematic development (Songs 2 and 15), imitation (Songs 3 and 8), and asymmetric melodic structure. Wellesz, *Schoenberg,* 118. Stroh, "Schoenberg," 36 and passim. Lessem, *Schoenberg,* 42. Further analyses of this cycle can be found in Brinkmann, "Schönberg," Ehrenforth, *Ausdruck,* and Anthony Payne, *Schoenberg* (New York, 1969), 28–30.

29. Stroh, "Schoenberg," 35 and 41 ff.

30. Pamer, *Mahler Lieder,* 16, 135 ff., for instance. Transitional structures, that come between strophic and through-composed categories, are numerous, especially in Reger. Wehmeyer provides a subtle example: though Reger's "Wiegenlied" (Op. 43, no. 5) is strophic "hardly a passage in the different strophes is the same." Its strophic contour is evident because each is separated by a pause from its neighbor; further, each is derived from the stanzaic framework of the poetry (*Liederkomponist,* 236).

31. Hermann Unger, "Reger Aussprüche," *Max Reger, eine Sammlung von Studien aus dem Kreise seiner persönlichen Schüler,* ed. Richard Würz, vol. 2: *Regers Persönlichkeit* (Munich, 1921), 79–80, 127–128. "Waldeinsamkeit" (no. 3), "Beim Schneewetter" (no. 6), and "Zum Schlafen" (no. 59) are almost as strict as "Daz iuwer min engel walte!" Wehmeyer, *Liederkomponist,* 225, cites examples (e.g., "Beim Schneewetter," no. 6) of poems Reger altered for purely musical reasons.

32. Like Mahler, Reger created asymmetrical designs by inserting instrumental interludes only in some, rather than in all strophes of a song: "Schmeichelkätzchen," "Mein Schätzelein," and "Es blüht ein Blümlein." Also like Mahler, Reger altered the sequence of phrases within a strophe as a means of varying it ("Herzenstausch," no. 5). And he often presented the initial phrase of a second strophe a tone higher (or lower) than the corresponding phrase of the first strophe, after which he might modulate still further and conclude the song in a distant key or suddenly return to the original key. "Es blüt ein Blümlein" (no. 20) and "Des Kindes Gebet" (no. 22) are examples.

33. See Volker Freund, *Hans Pfitzners Eichendorff-Lieder* (Hamburg, 1986), which reconsiders the old theory that Pfitzner's lieder, owing to their careful structural design, are in essence absolute music. Freund, however, concludes, after some interesting anaylsis, that the theory is absurd (215).

Chapter 12: Late-Romantic Expansiveness

1. Mahler's *Symphony of a Thousand* (his Eighth Symphony) and Schoenberg's even more expansive *Gurrelieder* are examples of the era's most imposing ensembles. Riemann's "Degeneration," *Deutscher Musikerkalender* (1908), appeared in 1907. Reger's reply (*Neue Musikzeitung* 29 [1907]: 49–51) has the same title. Newman, *Strauss*, 96.

2. Quoted in Lies, *Marx*, 155.

3. Wolf, *Briefe Mayreder*, 44; Strauss, from the foreword of his opera *Intermezzo*.

4. Ernst Krause, *Richard Strauss* (Leipzig, 1955), 158; Bauer-Lechner, *Erinnerungen*, 147.

5. Hermann Grabner, *Regers Harmonik,* 2nd ed. (Wiesbaden, 1961), 1: a noteworthy monograph originally published in 1921.

6. Annegert Fauser, in *Der Orchestergesang in Frankreich zwischen 1870 und 1920* (Regensburg, 1994), 6 ff., suggests three periods for the development of the orchestral song in France: the first, beginning in 1834–35; the second, after 1870, with songs by Franck, Duparc, and Saint-Saens; and the third, with an outburst of activity, during the fin de siècle. Max Kalbeck, *Johannes Brahms*, vol. 1b: 1856–1862 (Berlin, 1912), 474. The five are "Memnon," "Gruppe aus dem Tartarus," "Greisengesang," "An Schwager Kronos," and "Geheimes." The second and fourth are the songs that were withdrawn. According to Kalbeck, *Brahms*, 474, the two were performed by the Viennese Academic Choral Society and by the Viennese Choral Society for Men. They were finally published by Oxford University Press. Liszt, *Briefe*, 56. My article "The Orchestral Lied: An Inquiry into Its Style and Unexpected Flowering around 1900," *Music Review* 37 (1976): 209–226, is restricted to a study of representative examples of the genre. This chapter explores the genre in terms of late-romantic aesthetics. Two further studies on the orchestral lied should be noted: Hermann Danuser, "Der Orchestergesang des Fin de Siècle," *Die Musikforschung* 4 (1977): 425–452, and, specifically on Mahler, Elisabeth Schmierer, *Die Orchesterlieder Gustav Mahler* (Kassel, 1991).

7. Only "Träume" was scored by Wagner. Reger mentions spas and watering places: "Max Reger über seine Bearbeitung Brahms'scher Werke," ed. Erich H. Müller, *Simrock Jahrbuch* 1 (1928), 70. See Louis, *Gegenwart*, 237, on the decline of the concert aria.

8. Haas, interview with the author; Bleyle, correspondence with the author.

9. Bauer-Lechner, *Recollections*, 130.

10. La Grange, *Mahler*, 1:764.

11. A. Mahler, *Memories*, xxii–xxiii. The final piano-vocal version of "Des Antonius Fischpredigt" is July 8, 1893. (The date of its conception is uncertain.) The song was expanded into the Scherzo of the Second Symphony (July 16, 1893), then orchestrated as a song (August 1, 1893). See Bauer-Lechner, *Erinnerungen*, 7 and 10. I quote from the typescript of Hefling's article, which he kindly forwarded to me (1987). This article, "The Composition of 'Ich bin der Welt abhanden gekommen,'" which includes a careful study of Mahler's sketches for his lieder, is published in Hermann Danuser, ed., *Gustav Mahler: Wege der Forschung* (Darmstadt, 1992).

12. Trenner, in the complete edition of Strauss's songs, vol. 4; see also the indexes by Asow and Trenner of Strauss's works. Strauss may have orchestrated more pianoforte songs than indicated in these sources. He arranged "Der Arbeitsmann" (Op. 39, no. 3) especially for Hans Hotter, as he noted in a letter to the singer (see Strauss, *Welt*, 408). Hotter, however, informed me that he did not recall ever having received the letter. Nor is the manuscript mentioned in the complete edition. The National Library (Vienna) possesses a manuscript (a full orchestral score) of this song, but not in Strauss's hand. However, Trenner's *Richard Strauss, Verzeichnis*

(Vienna, 1985), 67, indexes an orchestrated version of "Arbeitsmann," completed December 12, 1918.

13. Strauss, *Eltern*, 188. Steinitzer, *Strauss* (1920), 131, notes Strauss's rise as conductor. Strauss's opinion of Pauline as interpreter of his songs was always high; see, for instance, Trenner, *Dokumente*, 78 ff., and an interesting letter by poet Karl Henckell to the composer (Strauss, *Welt*, 152).

14. Strauss, *Eltern*, 208, and Strauss, *Welt*, 152, record Strauss's comment to his parents; for those of the press, see, for instance, "The Strauss Festival," *Musical Courier* 48:10 (1904), p. 26. Strauss also orchestrated for Pauline's concerts Schubert's "Ganymed" (January 7, 1897) and Beethoven's "Wonne der Wehmut" (January 14, 1898).

15. Edwin Evans, "The Recent Richard Strauss Festival in London," *Musical World* 3 (1903), 130.

16. The tribute was for Ursuleac's performance in the revival (June 19, 1940) of *Die Ägyptische Helena*. Strauss orchestrated "Zueignung" on that day, as well as three other songs for her (September 3, 5, 10, 1933): "Frühlingsfeier" (Op. 56, no. 5), "Mein Auge" (Op. 37, no. 4), and "Befreit" (Op. 39, no. 4), which she performed in Berlin, October 1933. Strauss added a fourth song, "Lied der Frauen" (Op. 68, no. 6), September 22, 1933; see Strauss and Krauss, *Briefwechsel*, 27 ff.

17. Strauss and Krauss, *Briefwechsel*, 148. Trenner observes in notes for the complete edition of Strauss lieder, vol. 4, that Strauss arranged his pianoforte songs "when times were politically disturbed," in 1918, 1933, and 1940. But in 1940, as we have seen, Strauss played through his Brentano songs "quite by accident," and only then decided to orchestrate them. Moreover, the group of four from 1933 were orchestrated as a special tribute to Ursuleac. Further, Willi Schuh (Strauss, *Eltern*, 236) and concert programs indicate that Strauss probably orchestrated "Wiegenlied" in 1900, not around 1916, as given by Trenner. Moreover, "Cäcilie" should have been included as a fourth song among the "three" that Trenner notes that "Strauss orchestrated in 1897."

18. Orel, "Strauss," 12–13.

19. Strauss and Krauss, *Briefwechsel*, 27.

20. Decsey, *Wolf*, 2:42. "Seufzer," composed April 12, 1888, was scored May 28, 1889. On the other hand, "Wer sein holdes Lieb verloren," composed October 7, 1889, was not orchestrated until December 1–4, 1897. Wolf orchestrated most of his pianoforte songs about two years after he composed them. Walker, *Wolf*, 221.

21. In a letter to Oskar Grohe, April, 16, 1890, in Wolf, *Briefe Grohe*, 13 ff.; see also 40, 41, 91, and 123.

22. Wolf, *Briefe Kauffmann*, 41. Kauffmann became Wolf's close friend and ardent adherent. Zumpe, *Erinnerungen*, 55.

23. Wolf, *Briefe Grohe*, provides the "Prometheus" comment (170) and the one on "Er ist's" (14). Günter Raphael of Breitkopf and Härtel reduced Wolf's four horns to two, besides eliminating *many* doubled and added wind parts. Wolf's original score was published by Peters. Weingartner, *Lebenserinnerungen*, 1:364.

24. Lieder calling for large orchestra include "Prometheus," "Wo find' ich Trost," and "Mignon" ("Kennst du das Land").

25. Twenty-three of these songs are now extant. Five were lost in a streetcar in 1893 (Wolf, *Grohe*, 123): "Ganymed," "Geh', Geliebter," "Er ist's," "Anakreons Grab," and "Mignon." Wolf reorchestrated the last two immediately. Though "Er ist's" and the first version of "Mignon" reappeared later, scores for "Ganymed" and "Geh', Geliebter" have never been recovered. Fragmentary sketches survive for "Geh', Geliebter" and "Epiphanias," along with an incomplete "Christblume I" (see Walker, *Wolf,* 498).

26. The six additional songs are "In der Frühe," "Karwoche," "Gebet," "An den Schlaf," "Neue Liebe," and "Wo find ich Trost?" And, as mentioned in Chapter 11, Wolf carefully grouped together songs with similar subjects and arranged "Gesang Weylas," "Denk' es o Seele," and "Er ist's," bringing the total to twelve arrangements.

27. A complete index of Pfitzner's work that would be of the scope of those for Wolf, Mahler, Strauss, and Reger is a primary need and most evident in the area of orchestral song. *MGG* reproduces (10:1174) an orchestration (in manuscript) of the pianoforte song "Trauerstille" (Op. 26, no. 4), not mentioned in the indexes of Helmut Grohe and John Williamson. Nor is there mention made of six songs by Schumann that Pfitzner orchestrated: "Belsatzar" (Op. 57), "Der arme Peter" (Op. 53, no. 3), "Verratene Lieb" (Op. 40, no. 5), "Dichters Genesung" (Op. 36, no. 5), "Der Soldat" (Op. 40, no. 3), and the "Provenzialisches Lied" (Op. 139, no. 4). Abendroth (*Pfitzner,* 189 and 446n147) suggests that these Schumann songs, which have "all disappeared," may have been in the archive in the Strasbourg Conservatory. Two ballads by Loewe ("Erlkönig" and "Odins Meeresritt") that were orchestrated by Pfitzner and published by Brockhaus are widely indexed.

28. Abendroth, *Pfitzner,* 208. Pfitzner conducted and accompanied at innumerable Liederabende during these years (209).

29. This orchestra, one of Europe's finest, was conducted by Hans von Bühlow (1880–85), Richard Strauss (1885–86), Fritz Steinbach (1886–1903), Wilhelm Berger (1903–11), and Reger (1911–14).

30. The first quotation appears in Stein, *Reger,* 64, the second in Rudolf Louis, *Münchener Neuerste Nachtrichten,* January 9, 1914 (reprinted in Reger, *Briefwechsel mit Herzog,* 547).

31. Reger's letters to the editor of Simrock, *Simrock Jahrbuch,* vol. 1 (Berlin, 1928), ed. Erich H. Müller, December 19, 1913 (65), and letters for July 26, 1914 and November 22, 1914 (67 and 69). Reger, *Briefe,* 302 and 127, respectively, mention the "Mariä Wiegenlied" and "Aeolsharfe" comments. For the "Mein Traum" remark, see Reger, *Briefe zwischen der Arbeit,* 39.

32. Reger, *Simrock,* provides the composer's three remarks, in this order: April 17, 1914, April 4, 1914, and November 6, 1915 (66–70).

33. Louis, *Gegenwart,* 237. Schmierer, *Orchesterlieder,* 11 ff., presents a good summary of conservative censure of the orchestral lied.

34. "The quotation by Schoenberg on his *Kammersymphonie,* Op. 9," writes R. Wayne Shoaf, archivist of the Arnold Schoenberg Institute, "was first published on a record jacket for Dial 2 [a record company] in 1950. The text itself was written in 1949."

35. David P. Schroeder, "Alban Berg and Peter Altenberg: Intimate Art and the Aesthetic of Life," *Journal of the American Musicological Society* 46 (1993): 261–294, is an engaging study of the work.

36. Mayer, *Persistence,* 3–4.

37. Timothy L. Jackson's observations are interesting, e.g., he studies motivic interconnection between the older lied and "Im Abendroth," one of the four last songs, see "*Ruhe, meine Seele!* and the *Letzte Orchesterlieder,*" in *Richard Strauss and His World,* ed. Bryan Gilliam (Princeton, 1992), 90–137. "Malven," composed for Maria Jeritza (November 23, 1948), is the last song Strauss wrote.

Glossary

Declamation. 1) The art of reciting or speaking before an audience with studied rhetorical expression, intonation, and gesture. Two types of recitation were in vogue in fin-de-siècle Germany: the older, grandiloquent theatrical style of such actors as Josef Kainz and Ernst von Possart and a later, more natural style, similar to that of daily speech. 2) In music, the art of reflecting *prosody or suggesting speech. Fin-de-siècle singers considered declamatory techniques to be of great importance. Outstanding performers applied techniques ranging from great subtlety to overpowering emotional intensity but not to the exclusion of lyrical singing. Dramatic, epic, and prose texts of emotional content lend themselves best to declamatory treatment, especially when they are set within a singer's speaking range. In actual practice, singers apply declamatory techniques more in dramatic opera and ballads than in the lied. See also *Deklamationslied*.
Discussion: Chapter 4.

Deklamationslied (declamatory song). The composer's reflection in the lied of *prosody or recitation of poetry. During the fin de siècle, this genre represented the ideal fusion of poetry and music in lied. Important as a concept, the term *declamatory song* has inherent problems. First, it embraces a variety of styles in a broad continuum that extends from lyrical song, in which the composer seeks only to reflect prosody, to many kinds of speechlike compositions. Second, it can be applied to a mixture of genres: passages of declamatory writing appear in every kind of lieder, including *volkstümlich song. Third, the term discloses little about the piano part—whether it serves to support the declamation through such musical means as harmonic shading or whether it illustrates descriptive imagery in the text. More precise terms were introduced during the fin de siècle: *gesteigerte Sprache* (elevated speech), *lyrische Rezitativ* (lyrical recitative), *Parlando ballad style, Prose lyrique, and *Sprechlied. But these concern the voice part only. The term *naturalistic lied* refers to both voice and piano parts.
Discussion: Chapters 1 and 4.

Gedichte für Singstimme und Klavier (poetry for voice and piano). A title for sets of lieder or, occasionally, for separate songs. Schumann reintroduced the term, after sporadic applications by earlier composers, to indicate a "new" concept of lied composition in which the music reflects subtleties of the poetry. After around 1850, *Gedichte* came to signify not only this new concept of lied but also an alternative term for the widely current *Lieder and *Gesänge. Conservatives preferred *Lieder* and *Gesänge*: Robert Franz, who disapproved of the literary implications of *Gedichte*, argued that it brought "declamation too much into the foreground." Although Brahms called his Op. 19 *Fünf Gedichte* (1858–59), the title was later changed to *Lieder und Gesänge* (1870). Wagner, always the radical, designated his songs on texts by Mathilde Wesendonck *Fünf Gedichte* (1857–58). Surprisingly enough, late romantics seldom used the term, despite their approval of its implications. They preferred specific references to the poetry on which the songs were set in their titles, like *Des Knaben Wunderhorn* (Mahler and Streicher), rather than the indiscriminate *Gedichte*. Strauss and Mahler, among others, did, however, entitle early lieder Gedichte. The point escaped general notice because their original title was later changed to Lieder, the term that was gaining widespread currency early in the twentieth century for every kind of German song. Wolf resisted, however, preferring to call the published version of all of his mature song collections Gedichte.

Note: On Brahms, see Margit L. McCorkle, *Johannes Brahms, Thematisch-bibliographisches Werkverzeichnis*, ed. Donald M. McCorkle (Munich, 1984), 66–68. *Acht Gedichte* was Strauss's original title for Op. 10 (Aibl. 1887, 1888, 1897, 1898). The publisher, Universal Edition, changed the title to *Lieder* in 1907. I thank Barbara Petersen for this information. Mahler's published *Lieder und Gesänge* and *Lieder eines fahrenden Gesellen* bore the titles *5 Gedichte componiert von Gustav Mahler* and *Gedichte von einem fahrenden Gesellen*, respectively, in manuscript. Also see Wiora, *Das deutsche Lied*, 74 ff., on *Gesänge* and *Gedichte*.

Lieder und Gesänge. Collective term after around 1850 for various kinds of German art song. *Lieder* and *Gesänge* underwent fundamental changes of meaning from the late eighteenth and early nineteenth centuries to the twentieth century.

Lied, Lieder (German lyric poem or German lyric song). During the late eighteenth and early nineteenth centuries, *lied* designated a vocal medium in miniature, one of several *species, uncomplicated, tuneful (*liedhaft*), often in strophic form, intended for performance in the home. This concept of lied persisted throughout much of the nineteenth century. Even after around 1850 sophisticated musicians—Clara Schumann, Brahms—regarded the lied condescendingly as a "ditty" (*Liedchen*). Recall Clara Schumann's complaint (1866) that Stockhausen charged one-and-a-half talers and sang only "little lieder"; Brahms depreciated his *Vier Ernste Gesänge* (1896) humorously as "kleine Liederchen"; and Wolf was stung by the thirst of performers and public alike for his "Liederchen." Lieder were not given serious consideration for public performance until the late decades of the nineteenth century. *Lied* is now the standard modern term for a German song. In recent English dictionaries of music (*New Grove, New Harvard*), *Lied* is defined as a song in the German vernacular. The *New Harvard* makes this distinction: in German, a Lied is "any song (folk, work, children's, political)"; in English, it is an "art song."

Gesang, Gesänge (German song or German poem). In the late eighteenth and early nineteenth centuries, Gesänge by composers J. F. Reichardt, J. A. P. Schulz, and E. Kunzen were songs with simple melody and uncomplicated form. *Gesang* also designates songs about states of feeling, *Gesänge der Wehmut* (Zumsteeg), *Heitere Gesänge* (Loewe), and throughout the century, it referred to songs of different ethnic peoples, *Hebräische Gesänge* (Loewe), *Gesänge des Orients* (Strauss).

In poetry, *Gesang* signified simple, hymnlike verse for such poets as Friedrich Klopstock, Goethe, and Moerike, which composers set in a variety of ways, though not necessarily as hymnlike songs. *Gesang* also served for ethnic poetry in German translation: *Gesänge der Serben* (Siegfried Kaller); Brahms set several poems from this collection.

In the mid-nineteenth century, *Gesänge* became a general title for collections of songs in a variety of styles. Robert Franz's *Gesänge* consist of several kinds of poetry, as does Brahms's Op. 43, *Vier Gesänge*. Adolf Jensen's Gesänge often are settings of a single poet or are drawn from one literary source. *Gesänge* was also used to distinguish the expansive songs, especially of the fin de siècle, from "simple" lieder: see Brahms's complex, philosophical *Vier ernste Gesänge*, Op. 121 (1896), Reger's Opp. 62, 68, 70, and 75 (which are also known as *symphonic lieder*), Strauss's songs for large orchestra (Opp. 33, 44, 51) and Schreker's *Zwei lyrische Gesänge*, expansive lyrical songs.

In the twentieth century, *Gesang* is less frequently applied; often it is replaced by *Lied.*

Melodielied (lyrical song). A genre of the lied in which a prominent melody is usually assigned to the voice part while the piano part functions as accompaniment, providing harmonic support. Form in Melodielieder, especially in early nineteenth-century songs, is generally simple and clear-cut. Schubert's Melodielieder became classic models, owing to their melodic appeal and the imaginative treatment of piano parts, which can be simple accompaniment ("Gute Nacht"), involve descriptive imagery ("Wohin"), contain constructive motives ("Gefror'ne Tränen"), or share the melody with the voice part ("Mut"). Late-romantic examples, though more complex harmonically and freer in form, are noteworthy also for attractive melody and for piano parts that serve as accompaniment: "Verborgenheit" (Wolf), "Ging heut' Morgen übers Feld" (Mahler), "Zueignung" (Strauss), "Der Gärtner" (Pfitzner), and "Mariä Wiegenlied" (Reger). German lied specialists apply *Melodielied* to any genre of song—folk song, *volkstümlich song, *Stimmungslied—with a prominent melody.
Discussion: Chapter 7.

Parlando ballad style. Martin Plüddemann's name for the declamatory vocal composition that is most appropriate for epic narration, a distinctive element of the traditional ballad. Composers, Plüddemann argues, should distinguish this element of the ballad as sharply in music as poets did in literature. Loewe's contribution, his ability to narrate musically through the parlando ballad style, heightens interest in narrations and thus captures the essence of the ballad in music. Parlando ballad style—in comparison with opera, especially Wagnerian music drama—is less dramatic and more objective, cooler and less emotional and in comparison to the lied, less warmly lyrical. Impassioned passages are more suggested musically than realized. Before Loewe, musical interest slackened during narrations as composers chiefly relied on dull secco recitatives. As applied by Loewe and Plüddemann, the parlando ballad style confirms the ballad as a genre distinct from the lied.
Discussion: Chapter 8.

Prosody. Tone or accent of a syllable in verse, involving meter, variation of meter, and other tools: rhyme, alliteration, caesuras, and even punctuation, which serve to center attention on key words. Composers sought musical analogues for these tools. In example 81, we see Wolf's musical rendering of the alliteration of *wurzel* and *wachsen*.

Meter. When a reader grasps a pattern of accents in verse, the expectation is that the pattern will continue. But verbal sense even within the same poetic meter dictates that each word should receive an individual degree of emphasis. Pulse in music, on the other hand, may be shaped in two different ways: into unvaried metronomic patterns of accents or, like meter in poetry, into subtly shaded patterns. The two are evident in the different ways Jan Václav Tomášek (1774–1850) and Wolf set the same line of poetry (ex. 82). Tomášek applied its basic trochaic meter mechanically, hardly differentiating words according to their meaning. Wolf, however, stressed each word according to its relative importance in the context (compare

auf dei - nem Grab   zu wur - zeln   und zu   wachsen.

(Upon your grave to root and to grow; trans. Philip Lieson Miller, *The Ring of Words*)
Example 81.   Wolf: "Denk'es o Seele" (Moerike), mm. 23–26.

Thyr- sis bot   ihr für   ein Mäul- chen zwei,   drei Schäf - chen gleich   am   Ort

Thyr- sis bot ihr   für ein Mäul - chen zwei,   drei   Schäfchen gleich am Ort,——

(Thyrsis bid her for a kiss / Two, three lambs on the spot)
Example 82.   (a) Tomášek, "Die Spröde" (Goethe), Op. 54, no. 20, mm. 23–27; (b) Wolf:
"Die Spröde," mm. 22–25.

Thyrsis and *für*) by providing different time values in each measure and by interrupting the
trochaic meter (m. 3) to focus attention, as did Goethe, upon *drei*.

Variation of meter. This technique draws attention to the words on which poets center
meaning. Moerike, for instance, in "An eine Aeolsharfe," quoted below, varies meter unexpectedly, by thrusting together two accented syllables, *wand* and *die-* (ll. 1 and 2), then two
unaccented: *-se* and *Ge-* (ll. 3 and 4). The reader is thus inclined to pause between each metric
variation, giving the key word, *Geheimnisvolles* (mysterious), special attention.

Ángelehnt an die Éfeuwand	Supported by the ivy-covered wall
diéser álten Terrásse	of this old terrace,
Dú, einer luftgebornen Múse,	o mysterious harp
Geheímnisvólles Saítenspiél.	of an aerial muse

(translated by Philip Miller, *The Ring of Words*)

Although Wolf inserted rests (see asterisks in ex. 83b) for the metric variations in question,
Brahms was unwilling to interrupt the flow of his melody to support the poet's irregular meter
(ex. 83a).

Early and late romantic composers differ markedly with respect to treatment of prosody.
Late romantics characteristically stressed accented syllables in a variety of ways: by setting
them to dissonances, by syncopation, by sudden changes of dynamics, and by including
unaccented notes and normally accented notes. Significantly enough, Wolf allowed the
stressed syllable to fall on the main beat of the bar—on *Kind* (child)—only once, in "Mignon"
(ex. 84). Beethoven and Schubert, in early nineteenth-century fashion, set nearly every stressed
syllable in "Mignon" on an accented beat, thus placing Goethe's text more within the bonds of
conventional musical accentuation than Wolf's (ex. 85).
    Discussion: Chapters 1, 2, 4.

Species of German song. During the late eighteenth and early nineteenth centuries
German songs were identified by diverse names, rather than the all-inclusive *Lieder*. The long
list includes: *Arien, Arietten, Balladen, *Gesänge, Kantaten, Romanzen, Oden, *Gedichte,* and
Volkslieder. Several of these types or classes of song—ballads, romances, odes—were so called
by virtue of their poetry. Arien, Arietten, and Kantaten, derived from Italian opera or cantata,
are songs with lyric-dramatic scenes; see Schubert's *Die Allmacht*, an aria-lied hybrid. Beethoven entitled *Adelaide* a cantata. These various song species were gradually replaced during
the mid-nineteenth century by *Lieder* and/or *Gesänge* and in our century by the all-inclusive
lied. Although modern authors (Kinsky and Halm, *Beethoven* [cited below] and McCorkle,

Example 83.   (a) Brahms: "An eine Aeolsharfe" (Moerike), Op. 19, no. 5, mm. 1–13; (b) Wolf: "An eine Aeolsharfe," mm. 1–9.

Brahms [cited above]) call species of early German art songs *Arietten, Kantaten,* and the like, according to how they are designated by their composers, these critics generally refer to the songs in their commentaries simply as *lieder.*

Discussion: Chapters 7 and 8.

Note: Beethoven's inscription for *Adelaide* (Op. 46) reads, "Eine Kantate für eine Singstimme mit Begleitung des Clavier" (A cantata for voice with piano accompaniment). His Op. 75, *Sechs Gesänge,* was originally called *6 deutsche Arietten* (6 German arias). Op. 128, *Der*

(What have they done to you, poor child? trans. Philip Lieson Miller, *The Ring of Words*)
Example 84.   Wolf: "Mignon" (Goethe), mm. 53–56.

Example 85.   (a) Beethoven: "Mignon" Op. 75, no. 1, mm. 42–45; (b) Schubert: "Mignon," mm. 11–14.

Glossary

Kuss (The kiss) is an "Ariette mit Klavierbegleitung"; see Georg Kinsky and Hans Halm, *Das Werk Beethovens: Thematisch-bibliographes Verzeichnis seiner sämtlichen vollendeten Kompositionen* (Munich, 1955), 109, 200, 387. Breitkopf and Härtel published these songs, as well as the aria "In questa tomba obscura" in *Sämmtliche Lieder*. The publisher Simrock also changed titles of Brahms to *Lieder und Gesänge:* op. 70 (*Vier Gesänge*), op. 84 (*Fünf Romanzen und Lieder*); see McCorkle, *Brahms*, 11, 22, 301, and 350. On lied hybrids, see Wiora, *Das deutsche Lied*, 72 ff., and Moser, *Deutsche Lied*, 287.

Sprechgesang (speechlike singing). Crisp and chiseled enunciation is the most striking feature of Sprechgesang. Such consonants as *k, t, d,* and *g* are enunciated explosively, and elision of words is avoided. Elevated speech is another feature of the style. Vocalists would hover between singing and speaking dramatic passages, especially those that lay within their speaking range. Sprechgesang, in short, induces its practitioners to place the vocal art at the service of distinct enunciation. The style was prominent in Germany and Austria during the fin de siècle, in Wagnerian dramas at Bayreuth, in the ballad, and even in the lied. Its use declined after World War I.
Discussion: Chapter 4.

Sprechlied (speech-song). A special kind of lied in which the voice part is contoured after the inflections of speech. The term was applied early in the twentieth century in either a panegyric or pejorative sense.
Discussion: Chapter 1.

Sprechstimme (speaking voice). A style of recitation developed by Schoenberg, often confused with *Sprechgesang. The original concept and the notational system involved derive from Humperdinck's *Die Königskinder* (1897), the melodrama version, which contains the composer's request for "reciters" with musical ability. Schoenberg's Sprechstimme became an important part of expressionism and is evident in works like *Pierrot Lunaire* (1912), in which the composer gives instruction on its rendition. The artist is to execute the rhythm precisely, leaving each given note immediately, with either a falling or rising inflection, as in speech, but in so doing, the artist must never create the effect of "songlike speech melody," "realistic-natural speech," or "song." Schoenberg's instruction is vague on aesthetic objectives, however. Further, he permitted reciters under his guidance to deviate to an extraordinary degree in rendering pitch, provided they contributed fully to his implied aesthetic intent: the creation of a hallucinatory atmosphere. The consequence is that Sprechstimme artists today tend primarily to follow Schoenberg's instruction regarding pitch and rhythm rather than the underlying objective: achieving the atmosphere he intended.
Discussion: Chapter 6.

Stimmungslied. A genre of the lied in which evocation of mood is the composer's chief purpose: a mood that, in master lieder, is gentle, intimate, and shaded with nuances of the finest kinds. The voice and piano parts serve equally toward this end, the first with delicate, all-pervading lyricism and the second with characteristic configurations sustained throughout the lied—undulating eighths or sixteenths, ostinato-like patterns—that serve to create and sustain the mood. Favored subjects include love, idealized nature—sunny meadows, moonlit nights—and poetry of languorous melancholy. Pictorialism, though it may occur, is of secondary importance to evocation of atmosphere. Schumann was the first to compose a large number of Stimmungslieder. Such songs as his "Im wunderschönen Monat Mai," from the *Dichterliebe,* served as models for the late-romantic composers. Their mastery of the genre and debt to Schumann are evident in such lieder as "Nachtzauber" (Wolf), "Ich atmet' einen linden Duft" (Mahler), "Freundliche Vision" (Strauss), and "Abschied" (Pfitzner). Discussion: Chapter 2.

Symphonic lied (style). A term in vogue during the fin de siècle for lieder of great density and expansiveness. The piano parts are virtuosic, involve prominent solos, and often suggest the multicolored fin-de-siècle orchestra. Great demands are made also upon the singer, whose vocal line interprets the poem often in declamatory or free rhapsodic style within a flood of instrumental sound. Nearly all late romantics contributed symphonic lieder, including Wolf ("Prometheus"), Strauss ("Der Arbeitsmann"), Reger ("Reinheit"), and Schoenberg ("Dank"). Symphonic lieder have been censured by some critics as songs for "piano with vocal accompaniment," celebrated by others as the most modern of concert lieder. Discussion: Chapter 12.

Volkstümliches Lied (folklike song). The adjective *volkstümlich*, said to have been coined by Johann Gottfried von Herder for folkish expressions, came into general use after 1850 for products inspired by genuine folk art. The musical roots of this interest are traceable to late eighteenth century, when composers, delighting in ideals of simplicity, favored *Singspiel* above Italian *opera seria* and the unpretentious lied over the sophisticated aria. Some volkstümlich songs (Schubert's "Heidenrösslein" and "Das Wandern," for instance) attained such popularity that they were commonly believed to be folk songs. Later songs, particularly from the fin de siècle, underwent fundamental changes. Volkstümlich songs became complex, emotive, and highly personal orchestral songs, conceived for professional singers. An aesthetic incongruity had evolved: rural, folkish texts were given sophisticated urban settings. Discussion: Chapter 8. *Note:* See *Trübners Deutsches Wörterbuch* (Berlin, 1956), vii, under the entry for *Volkstum*. See also Christian Gottfried Krause's *Abhandlung von der musikalischen Poesie* (Berlin, 1747 and 1752), where the term *volkstümliches Lied* was used in the sense discussed above.

Wort-Ton Problem (word-tone conflict). This describes the debate over how much attention the composer should pay to subtleties of poetry when setting a poem to music. Two theoretical extremes emerge. In one, which we may call the literary-lied style, scrupulous attention is given to the materials of poetry: subject, tone and attitude, imagery, and *prosody. Fine points of *declamation, however, became a central concern for New German theorists. Wolf's art, his innovative declamatory principles, served as model. Through syncopation, for instance, Wolf effectively emphasized consecutive accented syllables by placing the first syllable in each group on an accented beat and the second on a syncopated note, producing two degrees of stress (ex. 86, mm. 3 and 5).

Early nineteenth-century composers like Schubert and Schumann rarely used syncopation for purposes of declamation. But early twentieth-century composers, following Wolf, often

Example 86. Wolf: "Lied vom Winde" (Moerike), mm. 15–20.

(That is really bad weather / rain and storm, and snow!)
Example 87.   Strauss: "Schlechtes Wetter" (Heine), Op. 69, no. 5, mm. 3–9.

did, sometimes applying chains of syncopation for the purpose. Wolf's innovative principles of declamation accordingly came to be regarded by contemporaries as the essence of the literary-lied style.

In the second extreme, criticized particularly by New German theorists, composers tend to favor the materials of music over those of poetry, with these consequences: They are loathe to interrupt melody with rests to replicate pauses the poet created through metric variation (compare exx. 82a and 82b). Attractive melodies are repeated with new words, often with little or no melodic change to reflect the different text. If the melody is too short (or too long) for the text, the text is altered to coordinate the two. Although rhythmic motives may be derived from the text, they are shaped independently of the meter of the text. In example 87 we see how Strauss features an iambic rhythm (see the asterisks) in the piano and voice parts with much charm but in so doing divides *schlechtes* into two parts and gives *regnet* considerably longer duration than poetic meter suggests.

In actual practice, the two theoretical extremes are not mutually exclusive categories but opposite ends of a continuum, with the mass of nineteenth-century lieder distributed at various points between. Even master composers like Wolf who favored one concept of composition were occasionally influenced by the other, sometimes even in a single song, a fact that New German theorists tend to overlook.

Discussion: Chapters 1, 2, 4.

Note: Cleanth Brooks and Robert Penn Warren, *Understanding Poetry* (New York, 1938), is still one of the best discussions of the materials of poetry.

Select Bibliography

Abendroth, Walter. *Hans Pfitzner* (Munich, 1935).

Abrams, M. H. *The Mirror and the Lamp: Romantic Theory and the Critical Tradition* (New York, 1953).

Adams, Jeffrey. "*Holzweg und Kohlengarten*: The Failed Projects of Naturalist Poetry and George's Myth of Symbolism." In Gregorio C. Martin, ed., *Selected Proceedings of the Pennsylvania Foreign Language Conference,* Duquesne University, Department of Modern Languages, 1988.

Babbitt, Irving. *Rousseau and Romanticism* (New York, 1932).

Bach, Albert. *The Art Ballad* (Edinburgh, 1890).

Bahr, Hermann. *Expressionismus* (Munich, 1916).

Bailey, Walter B. *Programmatic Elements in the Works of Schoenberg* (Ann Arbor, 1984).

———. "Prophetic Aspects of Musical Style in Early Unpublished Songs of Arnold Schoenberg." *Musical Quarterly* 74 (1990).

Bang, Hermann. *Josef Kainz* (Berlin, 1910).

Batka, Richard. "Engelbert Humperdinck," *Die Musik* 8 (1908–09).

———. "Der Kampf ums Melodrama." *Neue Musikalische Rundschau* 1 (1897).

———. *Martin Plüddemann und seine Balladen* (Prague, 1896).

———. "Zur Würdigung Hugo Wolfs." *Kranz: Gesammelte Blätter über Musik* (Leipzig, 1903).

Baudelaire, Charles. *The Painter of Modern Life and Other Essays.* Trans. Jonathan Mayne (London, 1964).

Bauer-Lechner, Natalie. *Erinnerungen an Gustav Mahler* (Leipzig, 1923). (*Gustav Mahler in den Erinnerungen von Natalie Bauer-Lechner.* Ed. Herbert Killian, with notes by Knud Martner [Hamburg, 1984].) (*Recollections of Gustav Mahler.* Trans. Dika Newlin. Ed. Peter Franklin [Cambridge, 1980].)

Bekker, Paul. "Engelbert, Humperdinck." *Westermann Monatshefte* (January 1908).

Bertocci, Angelo Philip. *From Symbolism to Baudelaire* (Carbondale, Ill., 1964).

Besch, Otto. *Engelbert Humperdinck* (Leipzig, 1914).

Bieri, Georg. *Die Lieder von Hugo Wolf* (Bern, 1935).

Bilke, Rudolf. "Martin Plüddemann." *Die Musik* 7 (1907–08).

Blaukopf, Herta, and Kurt Blaukopf. *Gustav Mahler: Leben und Werke in Zeugnissen der Zeit* (Stuttgart, 1994).

Blaukopf, Kurt, and Soltan Roman. *Mahler, a Documentary Study* (New York, 1976).

Block, Haskell. *Mallarmé and the Symbolist Drama* (Detroit, 1963).

Blume, Walter. *Brahms in der Meiniger Tradition* (Stuttgart, 1933).

Böhm, Hans. *Moissi der Mensch und Künstler* (Berlin, 1927).

Born, Karl Erich. "Structural Changes in German Social and Economic Development at the End of the Nineteenth Century." *Imperial Germany.* Ed. James J. Sheehan (New York, 1976).

Bos, Coenraad V. *The Well-Tempered Accompanist, As Told by Ashley Pettis* (Bryn Mawr, Pa., 1949).

Brand, Juliane. *Rudi Stephan* (Tutzing, Germany, 1993).

Breuer, Hans. *Der Zupfgeigenhansl.* 156th ed. (Leipzig, 1930).

Brinkmann, Reinhold. "Schönberg und George." *Archiv für Musikwissenschaft* 26 (1969).

Castle, Eduard. *Geschichte der deutschen Literatur in Österreich-Ungarn im Zeitalter Franz Josephs,* vol. 2: 1890–1918 (Vienna, n.d.).

Chiari, Joseph. *Symbolisme from Poe to Mallarmé* (New York, 1956).

Cooper, Martin. *French Music: From the Death of Berlioz to the Death of Fauré* (London, 1951).

Courvoisier, Walter. "Introduction" to Robert Schumann, *Frauenliebe und Leben* (Munich, 1921).

Dahlhaus, Carl. *The Idea of Absolute Music.* Trans. Roger Lustig (Chicago, 1989).

———. "Rätselhafte Popularität." *Mahler: Eine Herausforderung.* Ed. Peter Ruzika (Wiesbaden, Germany, 1977).

———. *Realism in Nineteenth-Century Music.* Trans. Mary Whittal (Cambridge, 1985).

Dahlhaus, Carl, and Hans Heinrich Eggebrecht. "Romantik." *Brockhaus Riemann Musiklexikon* (Mainz, Germany, 1979).

Dannreuther, Edward. *The Romantic Period* (Oxford, 1905).

Danuser, Hermann. *Das Lied von der Erde* (Munich, 1986).

Decsey, Ernst. *Hugo Wolf.* 4 vols. (Leipzig, 1903).

———. "Stunden mit Mahler." *Die Musik* 39, 40 (1911).

Del Mar, Norman. *Richard Strauss,* 3 vols. (London and Philadelphia, 1962–73).

Deutsch, Otto Erich. *Schubert: Memoirs by His Friends.* Trans. Rosamond Ley and John Nowell (New York, 1958).

Diez, Werner. *Hans Pfitzners Lieder* (Regensburg, Germany, 1968).

Eames, Emma. *Some Memories and Reflections* (New York, 1927).

Eckstein, Friedrich. *"Alte unnennbarer Tage!"* (Vienna, 1936).

Edelmann, B., et al. *Ludwig Thuille* (Tutzing, Germany, 1993).

Ehlers, Paul. "Die Verdunklung der Konzerträume." *Die Gesellschaft* 1 (1902).

———. "Zur Konzertreform." *Die Musik* 9 (1903).

Ehrenforth, Karl H. *Ausdruck und Form. Arnold Schönbergs Durchbruch zur Atonalität in den George-Liedern Op. 15* (Bonn, 1963).

Einstein, Alfred. *Music in the Romantic Era* (New York, 1947).

Evans, Edwin. "The Recent Richard Strauss Festival in London." *Musical World* 3 (1903).

Fauser, Annegret. *Der Orchestergesang in Frankreich zwischen 1870 und 1920* (Regensburg, 1994).

Feder, Stuart. "Gustav Mahler Dying." *International Review of Psychoanalysis* 5 (1978).

Finck, Henry T. *Richard Strauss* (Boston, 1917).

Floros, Constantin. *Gustav Mahler.* Vol 2: *Mahler und die Symphonik des 19. Jahrhunderts in neuer Deutung* (Wiesbaden, Germany, 1977).

Frisch, Walter. *The Early Works of Arnold Schoenberg, 1893–1908* (Berkeley, 1993).

———. "Music and Jugendstil." *Critical Inquiry* 17 (1990).

Fryhold, Edmund von. "Die Technik der musikalischen Deklamation." *Die Musik* 4 (1905).

Fuller Maitland, J. A. *Masters of German Music* (London, 1894).

Gura, Eugen. *Erinnerungen aus meinem Leben* (Leipzig, 1905).

Gutmann, Albert. *Aus dem Wiener Musikleben: Künstler-Erinnerungen 1873–1908* (Vienna, 1914).

Gysi, Fritz. *Richard Strauss* (Potsdam, Germany, 1934).

Haas, Joseph. "Das alte und das neue Kinderlied." *Joseph Haas, Reden und Aufsätze* (Mainz, 1964).

Haas, Theodor. "Bittners chinesische Lieder." *Musikblätter des Anbruch* 4 (1922).

———. "Die Lieder Julius Bittners." *Neue Musik-Zeitung* 45 (1924).

Hallmark, Rufus, ed. *Nineteenth-Century German Lieder* (New York, forthcoming).

Hanslick, Eduard. *Aus dem Concertsaal: Kritiken und Schilderung aus den letzten 20 Jahren des Wiener Musikleben* (Vienna, 1870).

———. *Aus neuer und neuester Zeit* (Berlin, 1900).

Hausegger, Friedrich von. "Zum Jenseits des Künstlers." *Gedanken eines Schauenden* (Munich, 1903).

Hausegger, Siegmund von. *Alexander Ritter* (Berlin, 1907).

Heinitz, W. "Die Sprechtonbewegungen in Arnold Schoenbergs 'Pierrot Lunaire.'" *Vox* 1 (1925).

Helm, Theodor, *Frommes Musikalische Welt, Notiz-Kalender für 1879* (Vienna, 1879).

———. "Fünfzig Jahre Wiener Musikleben (1866–1916)." *Der Merker* (1915–20).

Hempel, Frieda. *Mein Leben dem Gesang* (Berlin, 1955).

Henschel, George. *Personal Recollections of Johannes Brahms* (New York, 1907).

Hertz, David Michael. *The Tuning of the Word: The Musico-Literary Poetics of the Symbolist Movement* (Carbondale, Ill., 1987).

Heuberger, Richard. "Königskinder." *Im Foyer* (Leipzig, 1901).

Hey, Julius. *Deutscher Gesangs-Unterricht.* 3 vols. (Mainz, 1884–86).

———. *Richard Wagner als Vortragsmeister "1864–1876"* (Leipzig, 1911).

Hoeckner, Hilmar. *Die Musik in der deutschen Jugendbewegung* (Wolfenbüttel, Germany, 1927)

Holl, Karl. *Rudi Stephan* (Mainz, 1922).

Hollander, Hans. *Musik und Jugendstil* (Zurich, 1975).

Humperdinck, Wolfram. *Engelbert Humperdinck* (Frankfurt, 1965).

Huneker, James. *Overtones: A Book of Temperaments* (New York, 1904).

Hunnius, Monika. *Mein Weg zur Kunst* (Heilbronn, Germany, 1927).

Istel, Edgar. "Jean-Jacques Rousseau als Komponist seiner lyrischen Scene Pygmalion." *Publikationen der Internationalen Musikgesellschaft* 1 (1901).

———. "Ludwig Thuille." *Musical Quarterly* 18 (1932).

Jackson, Holbrook. *The Eighteen Nineties* (reprint, New York, 1966).

Jacob, Walter. *Leo Blech* (Hamburg, 1931).

Jarausch, Konrad H. *Students, Society and Politics in Imperial Germany: The Rise of Academic Illiberalism* (Princeton, N.J., 1982).

Jarocinski, Stefan. *Debussy, Impressionism and Symbolism.* Trans. Rollo Myers (London, 1976).

Jung, Erdmann. "Beitrag zur Gesangsaussprache." *Musikalische Wochenblatt* 9 (1878).

Kahle, Wilhelm. *Geschichte der deutschen Dichtung* (Münster, Germany, 1954).

Kandinsky, Wassily. *Concerning the Spiritual in Art.* Trans. Michael Sadler (reprint, New York, 1966).

Kienzl, Wilhelm. *Meine Lebenswanderung* (Stuttgart, 1926).

———. *Die musikalische Deklamation* (Leipzig, 1885).

Knab, Armin. "Meine Lieder." *Westermanns Monatshefte* 114 (1913).

———. "Vom einfachen Liedsatz." *Völkische Musikerziehung* 2 (1936).

König, Adolf. "Die Ballade in der Musik." *Musikalisches Magazin* 9 (Langensalza, Germany, 1904).

Kramer, Lawrence. "Decadence and Desire: The *Wilhelm Meister* Songs of Wolf and Schubert." *Music at the Turn of Century.* Ed. Joseph Kerman (Berkeley, 1990).

Kramer, Richard. *Distant Cycles: Schubert and the Conceiving of Song* (Chicago, 1994).

Kroll, Erwin. *Hans Pfitzner* (Munich, 1924).

Kroyer, Theodor. *Walter Courvoisier* (Zurich, 1928).

Kullak, Franz. *Der Vortrag in der Musik am Ende des 19. Jahrhunderts* (Leipzig, 1898).

Lafite, Carl. *Schubertlied und seine Sänger* (Vienna, 1928).

La Grange, Henry de. *Gustav Mahler,* vol. 1 (New York: 1973).

———. *Gustav Mahler,* vol. 2: *Vienna: The Years of Challenge (1897–1904)* (New York, 1995).

Lang, Oskar. *Armin Knab.* 2nd ed. Ed. Paula Yvonne Knab (Würzburg, Germany, 1981).

Laux, Karl. *Joseph Haas* (Düsseldorf, ?1954).

Lehmann, Lilli. *How to Sing.* 3rd ed. Trans. Richard Aldrich (New York, 1949). (*Meine Gesangkunst* [Berlin, 1902].)

Lessem, Alan Philip. *Music and Text in the Works of Arnold Schoenberg* (Ann Arbor, 1979).

Liess, Andreas. *Joseph Marx* (Graz, Austria, 1943).

Liszt, Franz. "Ein Brief über das Dirigiren." *Allgemeine deutsche Musik-Zeitung* 10 (1883).

———. *Franz Liszts Briefe,* vol 2, ed. La Mara (Leipzig, 1893).

Louis, Rudolf. *Die deutsche Musik der Gegenwart.* 2nd ed. (Munich, 1909).

Ludwig, Franz. *Ludwig Wüllner* (Leipzig, 1913).

McCredie, Andrew, ed. "Art Nouveau and Jugendstil and the Music of the Early Twentieth Century." *Miscellanea Musicologica* 13 (Adelaide, Australia, 1984).

MacDonald, Malcolm. *Schoenberg* (London, 1976).

McGrath, William J. *Dionysian Art and Populist Politics in Austria* (New Haven, 1974).

Machner, Alfred. "Rudi Stephans Werk, Eine Beschreibung als Studie zur Stilwende in der Musik um 1910" (Ph.D. diss. University of Breslau, 1943).

Mackintosh, Alastair. *Symbolism and Art Nouveau* (Woodbury, N.Y., 1978).

Madsen, Tschudi Stephan. *Art Nouveau.* Trans. R. I. Christopherson (New York, 1967).

Mahler, Alma. *Gustav Mahler: Memories and Letters.* 4th ed. Trans. Basil Creighton. Ed. Donald Mitchell and Knud Martner (London, 1990).

Mahler, Gustav. *Gustav Mahler Briefe 1879–1911.* Ed. Alma Maria Mahler (Berlin, 1924).

———. *Selected Letters of Gustav Mahler.* Trans. Eithne Wilkins, Ernst Kaiser, and Bill Hopkins. Ed. Knud Martner (New York, 1979).

———. *Unbekannte Briefe.* Ed. Herta Blaukopf (Vienna, 1983).

Mahler, Gustav, and Richard Strauss. *Gustav Mahler, Richard Strauss Briefwechsel von 1888–1911.* Ed. Herta Blaukopf (Munich, 1980). (*Gustav Mahler–Richard Strauss Correspondence, 1888–1911.* Trans. Edmund Jephcott [Chicago, 1984].)

Marsop, Paul. "Der Musiksaal der Zukunft." *Die Musik* 5 (1902), 9 (1903), 12 (1904).

———. "Unsichtbares Orchester und deutsches Bühnenhaus." *Der Merker* 6 (1915).

———. "Vom Musiksaal der Zukunft." *Die Musik* 12 (1904).

———. "Zur Bühnen und Konzertreform," *Die Musik* 18 (1906); 19 (1906).

———. "Zur Reform des Concertwesen." *Die Gegenwart* 35 (1889).

Marx, Josef. *Betrachtungen eines romantischen Realisten* (Vienna, 1947).

Mauke, Wilhelm. "Das lebende Lied—Ein Kapital Zukunftsmusik." *Frankfurter Zeitung* (August 10, 1899).

Mayer, Arno J. *The Persistence of the Old Regime* (New York, 1980).

Mendelssohn, Arnold. "Allerlei." *Die Musik* 28 (1908).

Meyer, Gabriele. *100 Jahre Münchner Philharmoniker* (Munich, 1994).

Mies, Paul. "Joseph Haas, ein moderner Meister des Kinderliedes." *Halbmonatsschrift für Schulmusikpflege* 18 (1924).

Miller, Philip. *The Ring of Words* (New York, 1963).

Mitchell, Donald. *Gustav Mahler: Songs and Symphonies of Life and Death* (London, 1985).

———. *Gustav Mahler: The Early Years* (London, 1980).

Moore, Gerald. *The Unashamed Accompanist* (New York, 1956).

Morold, Max. "Hans Pfitzner als Liederkomponist." *Hellweg* 4 (1924).

———. *Josef Reiter* (Vienna, 1904).

———. "Josef Reiter." *Neue Zeitschrift für Musik* 106 (1937).

Moser, Hans Joachim. *Das deutsche Lied seit Mozart*. 2nd ed. (Tutzing, Germany, 1968).

Mozart, Wolfgang A., *The Letters of Mozart and His Family*. 2nd ed. 3 vols. Trans. Emily Anderson (New York, 1966).

Muck, Peter. *Einhundert Jahre Berliner Philharmonisches Orchester*. 3 vols. (Tutzing, Germany, 1982).

Müller, Günther. *Geschichte des deutschen Liedes von Zeitalter des Barock bis zur Gegenwart* (Munich, 1925).

Münzer, Georg. "Engelbert Humperdinck." *Monographien moderner Musiker*, vol. 1 (Leipzig, 1906).

Myers, Bernard, S. *Art and Civilization*. 2nd ed. (New York, 1967).

Myers, Rollo. *Modern French Music* (New York, 1971).

Neitzel, Otto. "Engelbert Humperdinck." *Nord und Süd* 97 (1898).

Neuwirth, Gösta. "*Parsifal* und der musikalische Jugendstil." *Richard Wagner: Werk und Wirkung*. Ed. Carl Dahlhaus (Regensburg, 1971).

Newlin, Dika. *Bruckner, Mahler, Schoenberg*. 2nd ed. (New York, 1978).

Newman, Ernest. *Hugo Wolf* (reprint, New York, 1966).

———. *The Life of Richard Wagner*, vol. 3: 1859–1866; vol. 4: 1866–1883 (New York, 1941, 1946).

———. *Musical Studies* (reprint, New York, 1969).

———. "Notes for *The Hugo Wolf Society*" (London, 1931).

———. *Richard Strauss* (reprint, New York, 1969).

Niecks, Frederick. "Misconceptions Concerning Chopin." *Monthly Musical Record* 43 (1913).

———. "Tempo Rubato from the Aesthetic Point of View." *Monthly Musical Record* 43 (1913).

Niemann, Walter. *Johannes Brahms*. Trans. Catherine Alison Phillips (reprint, New York, 1969).

———. *Die Musik der Gegenwart*. 5th–8th ed. (Berlin, 1913).

———. *Die Musik seit Richard Wagner* (Berlin, 1913).

Nodnagel, Ernst Otto. "Das naturalistische Melodrama." *Jenseits von Wagner und Liszt* (Konigsberg, Germany, 1902).

Northcote, Sydney. *The Songs of Henri Duparc* (London, 1949).

Oberländer, Heinrich. *Übungen zum Erlernen einer dialektfreien Ausprache*. 10th ed. (Munich, 1917).

Oppenheim, Hans. *Hermann Zilcher* (Munich, 1921).

Orel, Alfred. "Richard Strauss als Begleiter seiner Lieder." *Schweizerische Musikzeitung* 1 (1952).

Osthoff, Wolfgang. *Stefan George und 'Les deus musiques': Tönende und vertonte Dichtung im Enklang und Wiederstreit* (Stuttgart, 1989).

Palmer, Christopher. *Impressionism in Music* (New York, 1973).

Pamer, Fritz Egon. "Das deutsche Lied im neunzehnten Jahrhundert." *Handbuch der Musikgeschichte,* vol. 2. 2nd ed. Ed. Guido Adler (Berlin, 1930).

——. "Gustav Mahlers Lieder." *Studien zur Musikwissenschaft* 16 (1929); 17 (1930).

Pascal, Roy. *From Naturalism to Expressionism* (New York, 1973).

Peake, Luise Eitel. "Kreutzer's *Wanderlieder:* The Other *Winterreise.*" *Musical Quarterly* 65 (1979).

——. *The Song Cycle: A Preliminary Inquiry into the Beginnings of the Romantic Song Cycle and the Nature of an Art Form* (Ph.D. diss. Columbia University, 1968).

Peckham, Morse. "On Romanticism: Introduction." *Studies in Romanticism* 9 (1970).

——. *Romanticism and Behavior* (Columbia, S.C., 1976).

Petersen, Barbara. *"Ton und Wort": The Lieder of Richard Strauss* (Ann Arbor, 1980).

Pfitzner, Hans. *Hans Pfitzner: Gesammelte Schriften,* vol. 3 (Augsburg, Germany, 1926–29).

——. *Hans Pfitzner: Sämtliche Schriften,* vol. 4. Ed. Bernhard Adamy (Tutzing, Germany, 1987).

——. *Meine Liedertexte* (Munich, 1941).

——. *Die neue Aesthetic der musikalischen Impotenz* (Munich, 1920).

——. "Offener Brief von Hans Pfitzner an den Herausgeber der 'völkischen Kultur' Dr. Wolfgang Nufer." *Die Musik* 26 (1934).

——. *Reden, Schriften, Briefe.* Ed. Walter Abendroth (Berlin-Frohnau, 1955).

——. *Über Musikalische Inspiration* (Berlin, 1943).

——. "Werk und Wiedergabe." In *Gesammelte Schriften.*

Pfohl, Ferdinand. *Arthur Nikisch* (Hamburg, 1925).

Plüddemann, Martin. *Die ersten Übungen für die menschliche Singstimme* (Munich, 1885).

——. Introduction and concluding remarks to *Balladen und Gesänge.* 8 vols. (Nuremberg, 1891–99).

——. "Josef Reiter." *Neue Musikalische Rundschau* 1 (1896).

——. "Karl Loewe." *Bayreuther Blätter* 15 (1892).

——. "Noch ein Wort zur Verrottung und Errettung der deutschen Sprache." *Bayreuther Blätter* 4 (1881).

Possart, Ernst von. *Die Kunst des Sprechens* (Berlin, 1909).

Prawer, S. S. *Mörike und seine Leser: Versuch einer Wirkungsgeschichte* (Stuttgart, 1960).

Prochazka, Rudolf. *Robert Franz* (Leipzig, 1894).

Reger, Max. *Beiträge zur Modulationslehre* (Leipzig, 1903).

——. "Degeneration und Regeneration in der Musik." *Neue Musikzeitung* 29 (1908).

——. *Grosse Kompositionslehre* (Stuttgart, 1913).

——. "Hugo Wolfs künstlerischer Nachlass." *Süddeutsche Monatshefte* (February 1904). Reprinted in the *Mitteilungen des Max Reger Instituts, Bonn* (May 1966).

——. "Ich bitte ums Wort!" *Neue Zeitschrift für Musik* 71, no. 4 (1904).

——. *Max Reger: Briefe eines deutschen Meister* (Leipzig, 1928).

——. *Max Reger Briefe zwischen der Arbeit.* Ed. Ottmar Schreibe (Bonn, 1956).

——. *Max Reger Briefwechsel mit Herzog Georg II. von Sachsen-Meiningen.* Ed. Hedwig Müller von Asow and E. H. Müller von Asow (Weimar, 1949).

——. "Max Reger über seine Bearbeitung Brahms'scher Werke." Ed. Erich H. Müller. *Simrock Jahrbuch* 1 (1928).

——. "Mehr Licht!" *Neue Zeitschrift für Musik* 61:11 (1904).

Reich, Willi. *Schoenberg: A Critical Biography.* Trans. Leo Black (New York, 1971).

Reilly, Edward. *Gustav Mahler und Guido Adler zur Geschichte einer Freundschaft* (Vienna, 1978).

Richard, August. *Max Schillings* (Munich, 1922).

Riemann, Hugo. "Degeneration und Regeneration in der Musik." *Deutscher Musikerkalender* (Max Hesse, 1908).

———. "Ideen zu einer 'Lehre von Tonvorstellungen.'" *Jahrbuch der Musikbibliothek Peters* 21, 22 (1914–16).

———. "Die Romantik in der Instrumentalmusik." *Spemanns goldenes Buch der Musik* (Berlin, 1900).

Riesenfeld, Paul. "Ludwig Wüllner." *Nord und Süd* 105 (1903).

Robertson, John George. *A History of German Literature* (Edinburgh, 1953).

Rockstro, William Smyth. "Melodrama." *Grove's Dictionary of Music and Musicians.* 2nd ed. (1904–10).

Rolle, Hugo. "Max Reger als Liederkomponist." *Neue Musik-Zeitung* (1928).

Roth, Hermann. *Heinrich Kaspar Schmid* (Munich, 1921).

Rückert, Friedrich. *Kindertotenlieder* (Frankfurt a.M., 1872).

Russell, Peter. *Light in Battle with Darkness: Mahler's* Kindertotenlieder (Bern, 1991).

Rychnovsky, Ernst. "Leo Blech." *Monographien moderner Musiker,* vol. 2 (Leipzig, 1907).

———. "Leo Blech." *Die Musik* 7 (1907–08).

———. *Leo Blech* (Prague, 1905).

Sachs, Curt. *The Commonwealth of Art* (New York, 1946).

———. *The History of Musical Instruments* (New York, 1940).

———. *Rhythm and Tempo* (New York, 1953).

Sams, Eric. *The Songs of Hugo Wolf* (New York, 1962).

Samuel, Richard H., and R. Hinton Thomas. *Expressionism in German Life: Literature and the Theatre 1910–1924* (Cambridge, 1939).

Schellenberg, Ernst Ludwig. "Konrad Ansorge." *Der Türmer* 32 (1929).

———. "Über musikalisches Illustrieren." *Nord und Süd* ?20 (1915).

Schemann, Ludwig. *Martin Plüddemann und die deutsche Ballade* (Regensburg, 1930).

———. "Über die Bedeutung der Ballade für unsere Zeit und unsere Zukunft." *Bayreuther Blätter* 20 (1897).

Schillings, Max von. "Königskinder." *Neue musikalische Rundschau* 1 (1897).

Schmitt, Friedrich. *Friedrich Schmitts System zur Erlernung der deutschen Aussprache* (Munich, 1874).

———. *Grosse Gesangschule für Deutschland* (Munich, 1954).

Schoenberg, Arnold. *Arnold Schoenberg Letters.* Trans. Eithne Wilkens and Ernst Kaiser. Selected and ed. Erwin Stein (New York, 1965).

———. *Harmonielehre* (Leipzig, 1911).

———. "My Evolution" (1952). *Musical Quarterly* 75 (1991).

———. "The Relationship to the Text." *Style and Idea.* Trans. Leo Black. Ed. Leonard Stein (New York, 1975).

———. *Style and Idea.* Trans. Dika Newlin (New York, 1950).

Schopenhauer, Arthur. *Die Welt als Wille und Vorstellung,* vol. 3 (Wiesbaden, Germany, 1949).

Schorske, Carl E. *Fin-de-Siècle Vienna* (New York, 1980).

Schroeder, David P. "Alban Berg and Peter Altenberg: Intimate Art and the Aesthetic of Life." *Journal of the American Musicological Society* 46 (1993).

Schuh, Willi. *Richard Strauss, Jugend und frühe Meisterjahre, Lebenschronik 1864–1898* (Zurich, 1976).

Schumann, Clara, and Johannes Brahms. *Clara Schumann, Johannes Brahms: Briefe aus den Jahren 1853–1896.* Ed. Berthold Litzmann (Leipzig, 1927).

Schumann, Wolfgang. "Ludwig Wüllner." *Der Kunstwart* 26 (1913).

Schur, Gustav. *Erinnerungen an Hugo Wolf.* Ed. Heinrich Werner (Regensburg, 1922).

Seidl, Arthur. *Moderne Dirigenten* (Berlin, 1902).

Selz, Peter. *German Expressionist Painting* (Berkeley, 1957).

Selz, Peter, and Mildred Constantine. *Art Nouveau* (New York, 1969).

Sheehan, James. *Imperial Germany* (New York, 1976).

Siebs, Theodor. *Deutsche Bühnenaussprache* (?Berlin, 1898).

Smolian, Arthur. "Vom Schwinden der Gesangkunst." *Neue musikalische Presse* (Leipzig, 1903).

Sonnleithner, Leopold von. "Bemerkungen zur Gesangkunst IV." *Recensionen und Mitteilungen über Theater und Musik* 45 (1860).

Specht, Richard. *Julius Bittner* (Vienna, 1921).

Spitta, Philipp. "Ballade." *Musikgeschichtliche Aufsätze* (Berlin, 1894).

Spitteler, Carl. *Musikalische Essays* (Basel, Switzerland, 1947).

Stachura, Peter D. *The German Youth Movement, 1900–1945* (New York, 1981).

Stahl, E. L. "The Genesis of Symbolist Theories in Germany." *Modern Language Review* 41 (1946).

Steblin, Rita K. *A History of Key Characteristics in the Eighteenth and Early Nineteenth Centuries* (Ann Arbor, 1983).

Stein, Fritz. *Max Reger* (Potsdam, 1939).

Stein, Jack. "Poem and Music in Hugo Wolf's Moerike Songs." *Musical Quarterly* 53 (1967).

———. *Poem and Music in the German Lied from Gluck to Hugo Wolf* (Cambridge, Mass., 1971).

Steinitzer, Max. *Richard Strauss* (Berlin, 1911, 1920, 1921).

———. *Zur Entwicklungsgeschichte des Melodrams und Mimodrams* (Leipzig, 1919).

Stenzl, Jürg, ed. *Art Nouveau, Jugendstil und Musik,* Festschrift for Willi Schuh (Zurich, ?1980).

Stephan, Rudolf. "Zur jüngsten Geschichte des Melodrams." *Archiv für Musikwissenschaft* 17 (1960).

Stephani, Hermann. *Der Charakter der Tonarten* (Regensburg, 1923).

Stephenson, Kurt. *Romanticism in Music* (Cologne, Germany, 1961).

Stern, Fritz. *Gold and Iron* (New York, 1977).

———. *The Politics of Cultural Despair* (Berkeley, 1961).

Stockhausen, Julius. *Der Sänger des deutschen Liedes* (Frankfurt, 1927).

Strauss, Richard. *Betrachtungen und Erinnerungen* (Zurich, 1949). (*Recollections and Reflections.* Trans. L. J. Lawrence. Ed. Willi Schuh [London, 1953].)

———. *Briefe an die Eltern, 1882–1906,* ed. by Willi Schuh (Zurich, 1954).

———. *Richard Strauss und Ludwig Thuille: Briefe der Freundschaft 1877–1907.* Ed. Alfons Ott (Munich, 1969).

———. *Die Welt um Richard Strauss in Briefen.* Ed. Franz Grasberger (Tutzing, Germany, 1967).

Strauss, Richard, and Clemens Krauss. *Briefwechsel zwischen Richard Strauss und Clemens Krauss* (Munich, 1964).

Strauss, Richard, and Hugo von Hofmannsthal. *Richard Strauss Hugo von Hofmannsthal Briefwechsel.* 5th ed. Ed. Willi Schuh (Zurich, 1978).

Stroh, Wolfgang Martin, "Schoenberg's Use of Text: The Text as a Musical Control in the 14th *Georgelied,* Op. 15." Trans. Barbara Westergaard. *Perspectives of New Music* 6 (1968).

Stuckenschmidt, H. H. *Schoenberg: His Life, World, and Work.* Trans. Humphrey Searle (New York, 1978).

Suppan, Wolfgang. "Martin Plüddemann und seine Grazer Balladenschule." *Neue Chronik zur Geschichte und Volkskunde der innerösterreichischen Alpenländer Südost-Tagespost,* suppl. 59 (1960).

Terfloth, John H. "The Universal Element in German Expressionist Drama." *Educational Theatre Journal* 14 (1962).

Thamm, Eberhard. "Der Bestand der lyrischen Werke Engelbert Humperdinck" (Ph.D. diss., University of Mainz, 1951).

Tieck, Ludwig. *Frühe Erzählungen und Romane,* vol. 3 (Munich, 1963).

Trenner, Franz, ed. *Richard Strauss: Dokumente seines Leben und Schaffens* (Munich, 1954).

Tschirch, Emil. "Mit Strauss auf der Reisen." *Die Musik* 16 (1924).

Ullrich, Hermann. *Julius Bittner* (Vienna, 1968).

Valentin, Erich. *Hans Sommer* (Braunschweig, Germany, 1939).

Vallas, Léon. *The Theories of Claude Debussy.* Trans. Maire O'Brien (New York, 1967).

Vogel, Werner. *Othmar Schoeck* (Zurich, 1976).

Volbach, Fritz. *Die Kunst der Sprache* (Mainz, 1912).

Wagner, Richard. *Bericht an Seine Majestät den König Ludwig II von Bayern über eine in München zu errichtende deutsche Musikschule* (Munich, 1865).

———. *On Conducting.* Trans. and ed. Edward Dannreuther (London, 1897).

Walker, Frank. "The History of Wolf's Italian Serenade." *Music Review* 8 (1947).

———. *Hugo Wolf.* 2nd ed. (New York, 1968).

Walzel, Oskar. *German Romanticism.* Trans. Alma Elise Luseky (New York, 1932).

Wandrey, Conrad. "Hans Pfitzner." *Völkische Kultur* 26 (1934).

Weber, Horst. "Jugendstil und Musik in der Oper der Jahrhundertwende." *Die Musikforschung* 27 (1974).

Wehmeyer, Grete. *Max Reger als Liederkomponist* (Regensburg, 1955).

———. "Max Reger Auseinandersetzung mit dem Lied." *Max Reger: Festschrift aus Anlass des 80. Geburtstages des Meisters am 19. März 1953* (Leipzig, 1953).

Weingartner, Felix. *Lebenserinnerungen,* vol. 1 (Zurich, 1928).

———. "Nochmals das 'lebende Lied.'" *Frankfurter Zeitung* (August 30, 1899).

———. *Über das Dirigiren* (Berlin, 1896). (*On Conducting,* trans. and ed. Ernest Newman [Leipzig, 1925].)

———. "Ein Vorschlag für das Verdeckte Orchester." *Der Merker* 6 (1915).

Weiss, Peg. "Kandinsky in Munich: Encounters and Transformations." *Kandinsky in Munich: 1896–1914* (New York, 1982).

Wellesz, Egon. *Arnold Schönberg* (New York, 1969).

Werner, Heinrich. *Hugo Wolf in Maierling* (Leipzig, 1913).

Willet, John. *Expressionism* (New York, 1970).

Williamson, John. *The Music of Hans Pfitzner* (Oxford, 1992).

Winter, Peter. *Vollständige Singschule* (Mainz, 1824).

Winternitz, Emanuel. *Musical Autographs from Monteverdi to Hindemith* (Princeton, N.J., 1955).

Wiora, Walter. *Das deutsche Lied* (Wolfenbüttel, Germany, 1971).

————. *Die rheinisch-bergischen Melodien bei Zuccalmaglio und Brahms* (Bad Godesberg, Germany, 1953).

Wolf, Hugo. *Hugo Wolf: Briefe an Melanie Köchert.* Ed. Franz Grasberger (Tutzing, Germany, 1964). (*Hugo Wolf: Letters to Melanie Köchert.* Trans. Louise McClellan Urban [New York, 1991].)

————. *Hugo Wolf: Briefe an Rosa Mayreder.* Ed. Heinrich Werner (Vienna, 1921).

————. *Hugo Wolfs Briefe an Emil Kauffmann.* Ed. Edmund Hellmer (Leipzig, 1903, 1911).

————. *Hugo Wolfs Briefe an Oskar Grohe.* Ed. Heinrich Werner (Leipzig, 1905).

————. *Hugo Wolfs musikalische Kritiken.* Ed. Richard Batka and Heinrich Werner (Leipzig, 1911). (*The Musical Criticism of Hugo Wolf.* Trans. Henry Pleasants [New York, 1978].)

Würz, Richard, ed. *Max Reger, eine Sammlung von Studien aus dem Kreise seiner persönlichen Schüler* (Munich, 1921).

Youens, Susan. *Hugo Wolf: The Vocal Music* (Princeton, N.J. 1992).

Zuccalmaglio, Wilhelm von, and Andreas Kretzschmer. *Deutsche Volkslieder mit ihren Originalweisen* (Berlin, 1840).

Zumpe, Herman. *Persönliche Erinnerungen* (Munich, 1905).

Zweig, Stephan. *Die Welt von Gestern* (Berlin, 1955).

Index

Abrams, M. H., 35, 36, 38, 45, chap. 10
 passim, 245
Ansorge, Conrad, 10, 113, 159, 196, 244,
 250n28, 253nn14,15, 280n35
——*Amaranths Waldeslieder,* 201
——*Fünf Gesänge* (Op. 14), 159, 196
——"Meine weissen Ara," 159
——*Vigilien,* 201
——*Waller im Schnee,* 10, 201

Bach, Albert, 120, 126
Bahr, Hermann, 62, 72, 171
Bailey, Robert, 225, 293n27
Balzac, Honoré de, 152, 158
Barbi, Alice, 22, 194, 248n10
Bartók, Béla, 121, 195, 197
Batka, Richard, 22, 259n34
Baudelaire, Charles, 148, 152, 159, 169,
 283n60
Beethoven, Ludwig van, 21, 26, 89, 191n1,
 249n18; ex. 85
Benda, Georg, 89, 265n2
Berg, Alban, viii, 6, 158, 167, 244, 253n15,
 255n37
Berkley, George, 107, 110–111
Berlioz, Hector, 11, 75, 81, 85, 232, 241n3,
 253n17
Bethge, Hans, 150, 164, 165, 167
Bispham, David, 56, 95, 96, 178, 197,
 290n59; fig. 5
Bittner, Emilie, 20, 253n13
Bittner, Julius, 20, 164–165, 281n46
Blech, Leo, 135, 138
Bleichröder, Gerson von, 111, 268n17
Bleyle, Karl, 20, 21, 233
Bloom, Claire, 95
Blyth, Alan, 285n8
Böhme, Franz Magnus. *See* Erk, Ludwig,
 and Franz Magnus Böhme
Bos, Coenraad V., 194, 196
Brahms, Johannes, 6, 14, 21, 26, 27, 28, 31,
 40, 42, 59, 96, 113, 120, 121, 161
——"An eine Aeolsharfe," ex. 83
——"Der Tod, das ist die kühle
 Nacht," 40, 257n21
——"Nachtigall," 188
——*Schicksalslied,* 251n37, 257n21
——"Unbewegt laue Luft," 184
——*Vier ernste Gesänge,* 194, 298
Brandt, Marianne, 6, 248n9
Braslau, Sophie, 197, 290n59
Braunfels, Walter, 137, 138, 164, 275n31
Breuer, Hans, 108, 270n34

Bruckner, Anton, 18, 112, 244, 259n36
Byron, George Gordon, Lord, 39, 152

Chaliapin, Feodor, 177, 196
Chopin, Frédéric, 21, 91, 115
Conrad, Michael Georg, 72, 107
Courvoisier, Walter, 80–81, 135, 269n28;
 ex. 38
——"Das grosse Loch," 136–137; fig. 8
——*Geistliche Lieder,* 118, 199, 270n39
Cross, Burnett, 266n16, 285n8
Culp, Julia, 20, 60, 177, 178, 190, 192,
 288n38

Dahlhaus, Carl, 46, 82, 168, 169, 260n37,
 282n56
Dahn, Felix, 129, 266–67n1, 269n27
Dannreuther, Edward, 125
Danuser, Hermann, 150, 208, 225, 293n27,
 294n6
Debussy, Claude, 71, 168, 280n36
Decsey, Ernst, 4, 65, 74, 239
Dehmel, Richard, 9–10, 11, 15, 21, 137, 140,
 158, 253n14, 269n28, 271n46
Del Mar, Norman, viii, 32, 90, 250n30,
 285n8
Destinn, Emmy, 55
Dulong, Magda von, 59, 167
Duparc, Henri, 62, 294n6

Ehlers, Paul, 24, 25, 253n23
Eichendorff, Josef von, 18, 79, 127, 158,
 200, 228; ex. 51c
Einstein, Alfred, 46
Erk, Ludwig, and Franz Magnus Böhme,
 121; exs. 34b, 37b

Fechner, Gustav Theodor, 152
Fichte, Johann Gottlieb, 38, 151
Finck, Henry, 7, 12
Fischer-Dieskau, Dietrich, 197
Flagstad, Kirsten, 197
Floros, Constantin, 145
Franck, César, 85, 294n6
Franz, Robert, 203, 297
Friedrich, Caspar David, 39, 186
Frisch, Walter, 168–169, 170, 251n40
Fuller Maitland, John Alexander, 61,
 129

Gadski, Johanna, 191, 197, 290n59
George, Stefan, 9, 10, 16, 21, 142, 151, 155,
 156–158, 159, 250n28, 251n41, 253n14

Gerhardt, Elena, 58, 60, 178, 184, 190, 192, 194, 261n22, 286n20, 288n30
Goehler, Georg, 113, 166
Goethe, J. W. von, 5, 9, 21, 33, 39, 57, 64–69, 83, 84, 85, 104, 153, 159, 165, 200, 244
Gould, Glenn, 95
Graener, Paul, 10, 63, 76, 227, 244, 269n28
Grainger, Percy, 27, 122
Gura, Eugen, 20, 70, 188, 248n10
Gutheil-Schoder, Marie, 132
Gutmann, Albert, 20, 22

Haas, Joseph, viii, 113, 140, 162, 185, 199, 233, 244, 253n15, 275n36, 275n37
————*Flaischlenlieder*, 163
————"Graue Tage," 164; ex. 49c
————*Rum bidi bum!* 139
Hafiz, 10, 165–166
Hanslick, Eduard, 6, 18, 22, 81–82, 119, 192, 249n17
Hase, Oskar, 37, 109n8
Hauptmann, Gerhart, 107, 267n1
Hefling, Stephen, 208
Hegel, G. W. F., 182
Heger, Robert, 182
Heilmann, Hans, 164
Heine, Heinrich, 40, 171, 200, 207, 304
Helm, Theodor, 6, 18, 22, 76, 112, 117, 194, 248n9, 263n3, 274n20
Henahan, Donal, 247n5, 266n16
Henckell, Karl, 11, 249n23
Henschel, George, 17, 182, 183, 194
Hensel, Walter, 121
Hertz, David Michael, 149, 157, 170, 279nn29,32
Herzogenberg, Heinrich von, 27, 250n30
Hey, Julius, 52, 53, 186
Hindemith, Paul, 44, 113, 245, 254n30
Hitler, Adolf, 18
Hoffmann, E. T. A., 152, 186
Hoffmann von Fallersleben, 139, 200
Hofmannsthal, Hugo, 29, 103, 151, 249n23
Holland, Bernard, 247n5
Holz, Arno, 155, 249n23, 267
Hummel, Johann Nepomuk, 184, 192, 193
Humperdinck, Engelbert, 89, 90; melodrama, chap. 6 passim; mentioned, 6, 87, 104, 105, 110, 120, 133–135, 162, 267nn11,28, 274n27; ex. 27b
————"Am Rhein," 134
————"Die Lerche," 134
————*Hänsel und Gretel*, 111, 133, 134, 142
————*Junge Lieder*, 133–134; ex. 41
————*Königskinder*, 88, 89–90, 104, 133, 265n6, 302; ex. 27a
Hunnius, Monike, 191, 287n25
Hüsch, Gerhard, 196, 197
Huysmans, Joris Karl, 169, 171

Jackson, Timothy, 245
Jäger, Ferdinand, 70, 188
Jarocinski, Stefan, 170
Jean Paul, 40, 152
Joachim, Amalie, 20, 90
Jöde, Fritz, 108, 109, 121, 122
Jung, Carl Gustav, 153, 283n61

Kainz, Josef, 64, 65–69, 94, 262nn41,43, 297
Kandinsky, Vasily, 168, 169, 172
Kant, Immanuel, 148, 151
Kaplan, Gilbert, 289n56
Keats, John, 39
Kemp, Tom, 17
Kerr, Alfred, 37, 256n8
Kienzl, Wilhelm, 20, 94–95, 109, 133, 162
Klimt, Gustav, 168, 171, 285n55
Klose, Friedrich, 62, 72, 166, 289n50; ex. 20
Klusen, Ernst, 114, 115
Knab, Armin, 121–122, 187, 223, 269n28, 272n50; ex. 51c
————*Alte Kinderreime*, 140; ex. 42
————*Mombert-Lieder*, 188–189
Knorr, Iwan, 27, 254n30
Kramer, Lawrence, 157, 279n32
Krauss, Clemens, 238
Kullak, Franz, 182, 184, 193

Lagarde, Paul de, 107, 113, 122
La Grange, Henry-Louis de, 270n40, 276nn3,11, 278n21
Lang, Paul Henry, 26, 46, 256n6, 259n32
Langbehn, Julius, 107, 122
Laser, Arthur, 193
Lehmann, Lilli, 20, 54, 59, 64, 70, 191, 290n59
Lenau, Nikolaus, 39
Lessem, Alan Philip, 226, 279n32
Liliencron, Detlev von, 10, 21, 249n27
Liszt, Franz, 3, 27, 120, 129, 184, 192, 193, 226, 229, 232, 265n2
Li-Tai-Po, 164, 282n53
Loewe, Carl, 32, 125, 128, 129, 133, 200, 202, 241, 299
————"Archibald Douglas," 127
————"Erlkönig," 57
————"Heinrich der Vogler," 126
Löns, Hermann, 10, 123, 250n26
Louis, Rudolf, 3, 4, 45, 60, 104, 112, 130, 243, 249n17, 253n16, 262n29
Lueger, Karl, 112, 113

McCreless, Patrick, 291n5
Mackintosh, Alastair, 142, 169
Maeterlinck, Maurice, 160, 276n64

Mahler, Alma, 20, 168, 253n13, 257n23, 269n29
Mahler, Gustav: on anti-Semitism, 7, 18, 42, 43, chap. 7 passim; and Schumann, 32, 255n39; symbolism, 37, chap. 9 passim; declamation, 71, 74, 263n50; performance, 127, 128, 180–182, 190, 195; structure, chap. 9 passim, exx. 64, 68, 70; volkstümlich song, 114–17, 119, 123, 269n31; mentioned, 18, 28, 38, 46, 74, 83, 129, 142, 164, 168, 172, 178, 186, 188, 191, 202, 209, 212, 237, 240, 241, 243, 253nn15,17, 256n3, 263n45, 297
———Das klagende Lied, 116, 127
———Das Lied von der Erde (The Song of the Earth), 43, 147, 150, 164, 167, 168, 183, 207–208, 209, 231, 293n27; ex. 46
———Des Knaben Wunderhorn, 29, 42, 114, 115, 203, ex. 34
"Das irdische Leben," 128, 149, 172, 210; ex. 68
"Der Schildwache Nachtlied," 86, 119, 181, 235, 271n41
"Des Antonius von Padua Fischpredigt," 32, 27, 115, 204, 237, 269n33
"Es sungen drei Engel," 234; ex. 52a
"Lied des Verfolgten im Turm," 79, 148, 212; ex. 70
"Lob des hohen Verstandes," 204, 270n33; exx. 23d, 25b
"Rheinlegendchen," 119, 127, 235, 270n39, 271n47; ex. 78
"Scheiden und Meiden," 114; ex.52c
"Trost im Unglück," ex. 34a
"Um schlimme Kinder," 114, 203–204
"Urlicht," 42, 86, 180, 213, 219–225, 235; ex. 74
"Verlor'ne Müh'," 204, 270n39
"Wer hat dies Liedlein erdacht," 32, 270n33
"Wo die schönen Trumpeten blassen," 180, 214, 292n18
"Zu Strassburg auf der Schanz," 114, 115, 127, 234, 269n30
———Kindertotenlieder, 29, 114, 143–147, 149, 158, 170, 201, 207–208, 231, 276n6; exx. 43, 44
———Lieder eines fahrenden Gesellen (Songs of a Wayfarer), 37, 41, 44, 116, 212, 233, 235, 270n34, 298, 299; ex. 79
———Lieder und Gesänge, 29, 114, 115, 121, 204, 212, 234, 270n34, 271n47, 298, exx. 25a, 36
———Sieben letzter Lieder
"Der Tamboursg'sell," 114, 115, 116, 128, 187, 269n30
"Ich atmet' einen Lindenduft," 32, 303

"Revelge," 114, 115, 127, 183, 235
"Um Mitternacht," 183, 234
———Symphony No. 2, 178, 201
———Symphony No. 3, 149, 234
Mallarmé, Stéphane, 142, 148, 149, 153, 156, 158, 159, 171, 279n28
Mann, Heinrich, 111
Mann, Thomas, 39, 111
Marsop, Paul, 25
Marx, Joseph, 6, 63, 160, 164, 165, 179, 180, 185
———"Im Maien," 187, 229; ex. 59
———"Nocturne," 183; ex. 55
———"Tuch der Tränen," ex. 51b
Mattiesen, Emil, 129, 130, 273n18
Mauke, Wilhelm, 26, 82
Mayer, Arno, vii, 245, 248n1
Mayer, Friederike, 70
Mendelssohn, Felix, 89, 111, 113, 162
Messchaert, Johannes, 20, 197, 248n10, 290n60
Meyer, Conrad Ferdinand, 33
Meyerbeer, Giacomo, 112, 249n18
Michelangelo, 10, 250n29
Miller, Philip Lieson, 64–69 passim, 289n54, 300, 301
Mitchell, Donald, 147, 150, 183, 208, 225, 234, 284n68, 287n29, 293n27
Mittler, Franz, 258n31
Moerike, Eduard, 9, 154–155, 200, 203, 209, 213, 215–216, 240, 249n22, 298
Moissi, Alexander, 64–69, 94, 262n43
Mombert, Alfred, 10, 250n28
Monet, Claude, 159, 160
Moore, Gerald, 188, 196, 197
Morgenstern, Christian, 10, 267n4
Moser, Hans Joachim, 33, 130, 162, 269n27, 279n35
Mottl, Felix, 232, 286n19
Mozart, W. A., 14, 35, 89, 91, 134, 184, 249n18
Müller von Königswinter, Wolfgang, 43

Newlin, Dika, 149, 292n13
Newman, Ernest, 7, 8, 9, 12, 30, 205, 217, 229, 249n17, 251n34, 260n6
Niecks, Frederick, 180, 182
Niemann, Walter, 4, 7, 42, 46, 82
Nietzsche, Friedrich, 10, 21, 82, 113, 151
Nikisch, Arthur, 184, 194, 286n20
Novalis, 42, 152, 186, 257n15

Orel, Alfred, 193, 237

Pamer, Fritz Egon, 114, 224
Pataky, Hubert, 164
Peckham, Morse, 35, 38, 258n25

Performance: vocal pedagogy, Italian and German, 51–53; enunciation, 53–54, 70–71, 126; Sprechgesang, 5, 54–55, 87, 302; theatrical techniques, 55–58, 71, 178; naturalism's influence on, chap. 4 passim; parlando style, 71, 128, 299; expressive aesthetics, 177, 179–180, 191–193, 196; tempo, 181–184, 192–193, 194–195, 285n8, 288n42; timbre and dynamics, 184–191, 235–236, 237; low larynx, 186, 196–197; creative interpretation, 194
Petersen, Barbara, 250n30
Pfitzner, Hans: and New German aesthetics, 9, 30, 31; lied composition, 9, 30, 31, 42, 71, 230; stylistic development, 27, 29–30, 254n30; mentioned, viii, 21, 45, 72, 83, 109, 186, 188, 195, 196, 209, 226, 253n15, 254n30
——"Abschied," 258n27, 303
——*Alte Weisen*, 201, 228
——"An den Mond," 8, 159
——"Das Alter," 227
——"Der Trompeter," 242
——"Die Heinzelmännchen," 242
——"Du milchjunger Knabe," 227
——"Hast du von den Fischerkindern," 43–44, 258n28; ex. 4
——"Herr Oluf," 63, 78, 258n28
——"Hussens Kerker," 79–80
——"Ich fürcht' nit Gespenster," 227
——"In Danzig," 9, 191
——"Klage," 242
——"Lethe," 241
——"Mir glänzen die Augen," 227
——"Nachtwanderer," 258n28
——"Schön Suschen," 180
——"Sie haben heut' Abend Gesellschaft," 75, 207, 287n35; ex. 67
——"Singt mein Schatz," 79
——"Sonett Nr. 92" 230; ex. 76
——"Sonst," 78, 241
——"Stimme der Sehnsucht," 79
——"Trauerstille," 296n27
——"Unter der Linden," 210
——*Von deutscher Seele*, 200, 227
——"Wanderers Nachtlied," 227
——"Wandl' ich in dem Morgentau," 75
——"Wenn sich liebes," 227
——"Zorn," 287n35
——"Zugvogel," 210
Plüddemann, Martin, 51, 54, 58, 59, 62, 64, 113, 124, 125, 126, 130, 230, 253n15, 274nn19,20, 299; ex. 23a
——"Der Kaiser und der Abt," 57, 71
——"Der Taucher," 77, 127
——"Der wilde Jäger," 77, 127
Poe, Edgar Allan, 98, 149

Poisl, Josephine, 216
Possart, Ernst von. *See* Von Possart, Ernst
Prey, Hermann, 197
Prokofiev, Sergei, 113

Rains, Claude, 95
Raucheisen, Michael, 18, 196, 199, 253n16, 288n38
Rauchenberger, Johanna von, 97
Reger, Max: influences on, 6, 11; development, 6, 11, 12–13, 28; and Schumann, 33, 20; on dynamics, 187, 188, 190; mentioned, 7, 27, 28, 45, 71, 113, 135, 179, 182, 191, 194, 195, 225, 253n15, 296n29
——*Achtzehn Gesänge*, 28
——"Aeolsharfe," 162, 243; ex. 49a
——"All' mein Gedanken," 184; ex. 56
——"An die Hoffnung," 185, 242
——"Aus den Himmelsaugen," 33
——"Der Alte," 80, 81
——"Der Himmel hat eine Träne geweint," 33
——"Der König bei der Krönung," 216
——"Der Schmerz ist der Schmied," 78
——"Ein Drängen," 13, 14, 28
——"Flieder," 226
——"Friedhofsgang," 180
——*Fünf neuen Kinderlieder*, 120, 229
"Wiegenlied," ex. 75
——"Gute Nacht," 78
——"Hymnus des Hasses," 12
——"Leichtsinniger Rat," 219
——"Mein Herz," 226
——"Mein Traum," 118, 243
——"Notturno," 34
——"Pflügerin Sorge," 78
——"Reinheit," 303
——"Ritter rät den Knappen dies," 187
——"Ruhe," 292; ex. 57a
——*Schlichte Weisen*, 28, 117–118, 120, 121, 139, 199, 214, 227, 231, 269n27, 270n36
"Am Brünnele," 118
"Beim Schneewetter," 293n31
"Daz iuwer min engel walte," 227
"Der verliebte Jäger," 77
"Des Kindes Gebet," 293n32
"Du meines Herzens Krönlein," 118, 120
"Es blüht ein Blümlein," 293n32
"Gottes Segen," 120
"In einem Rosengärtelein," 118, 120
"Mariä Wiegenlied," 118, 243, 270n37
"Mein Schätzelein," 293n32
"Mit Rosen bestreut," 118
"Schlecht' Wetter," 227
"Schmeichelkätzchen," 293n32

"Vorbeimarsch," 118
"Waldeinsamkeit," 117, 118, 293n31
"Wenn die Linde blüht," 118
"Zum Schlafen," 118, 293n31
"Zwei Mäuschen," ex. 23b
———"Sehnsucht," 172
———"Spatz und Spätzin," 219
———"Traum durch die Dämmerung,"
219
———"Trost," 219
———"Verklärung," 190; ex. 62
———"Wehe," 78, 187
———"Wenn in bangen trüben
Stunden," 231; ex. 77
———"Wir Zwei," 219
———Zwölf geistliche Lieder, 120, 227,
231, 271n42
Reichmann, Theodor, 70, 126, 188, 263n45
Reilly, Edward, 145–146, 276n6, 287n29
Reinick, Robert, 124, 200
Reiter, Josef, 122, 129, 130, 273n17
Rheinberger, Joseph, 27, 133
Riemann, Hugo, 12, 46, 84, 214, 229,
251n35, 264n15
Rimbaud, Arthur, 148
Ritter, Alexander, 113, 269n27
———"Noch eine Nachtigall?" fig. 9
Roman, Zoltan, 276n9
Rosmer, Ernst (pseudonym), 134, 265n6
Rousseau, Jean-Jacques, 88, 89, 264n2
Rückert, Friedrich, 41, chap. 9 passim
Rückert, Heinrich, 275n3
Russell, Peter, 276nn3,6

Sachs, Curt, 36, 256n5, 286n19
Saint-Saëns, Camille, 231, 296n7
Salzer, Felix, 251n39
Sams, Eric, 153
Satie, Erik, 86
Schacko, Hedwig, 105
Schalk, Joseph, 111
Schellenberg, Ernst Ludwig, 83
Schelling, Friedrich von, 151
Schillings, Max von, 27, 89, 93, 96, 97, 98,
109, 113, 179, 269n27, 291n11
———Das Hexenlied, chap. 6 passim;
exx. 28, 29, 30, 31
———Glockenlieder, 162, 209, 243
Schlaf, Johannes, 107
Schlegel, Friedrich, 257n15
Schmid, Heinrich Kaspar, 118, 120, 122
———"Aus Feld und Wiese," 138
———"Des Apfelbaumes Frühlings-
traum," ex. 51a
———"Nüsse knacken," 138
———Ringelreihen, 138
———Türkisches Liederbuch, 120, 166
Schmid-Lindner, August, 178, 182, 194

Schmitt, Friedrich, 51–52, 59, 61, 186
Schnitzler, Arthur, 113
Schoeck, Othmar, 6, 165, 185
———"In der Herberge," 164
Schoenberg, Arnold: break with tradition,
vii, 16, 27, 34, 61, 168, 169, 170, 172, 173,
199, 225, 228; influences on, 6, 10, 14;
development, 14–16, 225–226; symbol-
ism, 168, 169, 170; mentioned, viii, 7, 12,
47, 112, 142, 152, 153, 160, 188, 214
———"Abschied," 225–226
———"Alles," 15, 37, 225
———"Am Strande," 251n44
———"Am Wegrund," 37
———Chamber Symphony, No. 1, 244
———"Dank," 14, 303
———Das Buch der hängenden Gärten
(Hanging Gardens), 15, 16, 37, 86, 156–
157, 225, 226, 293n28
———"Der verlorene Haufen," 132
———"Der Wanderer," 15
———"Die Aufgeregten," 15, 225
———Die glückliche Hand, 104, 158
———Die Jacobsleiter, 158
———"Erhebung," 225
———"Erwartung," 14, 169, 225
———"Freihold," 15, 37, 225
———"Ghasel," 15, 225
———Gurrelieder, 104, 294
———"Hochzeitslied," 15
———"Ich darf nicht dankend," 15, 225
———"Jane Grey," 15, 132, 225
———"Jesus Bettelt" ("Schenk mir
deinen goldenen Kamm"), 14
———"Litanie" (String Quartet No. 2),
37
———"Lockung," 15, 225, 251n39
———Pelleas und Melisande, 162
———Pierrot Lunaire, 20, 61, 63, 104,
172, 253n13, 284n70, 302
———Seraphita, 158
———"Traumleben," 15, 225
———"Verlassen," 15, 225
———"Waldsonne," 14, 225
———"Wie Georg von Frundsberg," 37,
225
Scholz, Bernhard, 26, 27
Schönerer, Georg von, 18, 110, 113, 268n16
Schopenhauer, Arthur, 82–83, 150, 151, 152
Schorr, Friedrich, 260n11
Schorske, Carl, 157
Schreker, Franz, 162, 195
———Vom ewigen Leben, 195
———Zwei lyrische Gesänge, 201, 298
Schubert, Franz, 9, 12, 18, 21, 32, 44, 75,
129, 153, 157, 192, 199, 232, 242, 243
———"Das Wandern," 52, 303
———"Der Doppelgänger," 57

Schubert, Franz (*continued*)
———*Die schöne Müllerin,* 90, 196
———"Erlkönig," 125, 180, 197, 253n17, 261n24, 263n45
———"Gute Nacht," 299
———"Heidenröslein," 303
———"Mignon," 300; ex. 85
———"Prometheus," 64–69, 292n21; exx. 6, 9, 11
———"Wohin?" 180, 299
Schuh, Willi, 8, 100, 249n20, 250n30
Schumann, Clara, 18, 21, 298
Schumann, Robert: his influence, 31–34, 200, 229; mentioned, 113, 201, 241, 303, 249n22
———*Dichterliebe,* 18, 32, 303
———"Die Loewenbraut," 22
———*Frauenliebe und Leben,* 18, 201; fig. 1
———"Im wunderschönen Monat Mai," 32, 302
———*Liederkreis,* 200
———*Manfred,* 42
———"Mondnacht," 60
Scriabin, Alexander, 169, 283n61
Sekles, Bernhard, 27
Sergel, Albert, 134, 137
Shakespeare, William, 57, 60
Shostakovich, Dmitri, 113
Sieb, Theodor, 52
Sistermans, Anton, 188
Smolian, Arthur, 60
Sommer, Hans, 88, 130, 201
———*Der Waldschratt,* 88
———"Die Räuberbrüder," 129
———"Sir Aethelbert," 129; ex. 39
———"Wüstenklänge," 129
Sonnleithner, Leopold von, 59, 192
Specht, Richard, 70
Spies, Hermine, 20
Spitta, Johann Philipp, 125
Stein, Jack, 151
Steinitzer, Max, 4, 7, 70, 91
Stephan, Rudi, 162, 163
———*Liebeszauber,* 162
———"Papel im Strahl," ex. 49b
Stephani, Hermann, 84, 85
Stephenson, Kurt, 39, 40, 42
Stern, Fritz, 106, 111, 267n3, 268nn17,22
Stockhausen, Julius, 18, 22, 52, 56, 177, 186, 191, 192, 232, 287n25
Stoeker, Adolf, 113
Strauss, Franz, 84, 237
Strauss, Paulina, 62, 236
Strauss, Richard: criticism of, 7, 9, 12, 30–31, 172, 217, 229; declamation, 7–8, 70, 72, 80, 85, 210; development, 11, 158–159, 162, 199, 228; naturalism, 54, 62, 63, 76, 77–78, 81; performance, 191, 197, 288n45, 289n55; structure, 205–207, 225, 226, 231, 241, 244; mentioned, 26, 27, 28, 45, 46, 82, 83, 113, 168, 190, 201, 209, 226, 227, 241, 244, 245, 253nn15,17, 254n32, 259n37, 267n11, 269nn27,28, 270n40
———*Acht Gedichte* (Op. 10), 185
———"Allersellen," 207
———"Amor," 81, 238
———*Ariadne auf Naxos,* 29
———"Befreit," 10, 295n16
———"Blindenklage," 85
———"Breit über mein Haupt," 85
———"Cäcilie," 236, 237, 295n17
———"Das Lied des Steinklopfers," 78
———"Das Rosenband," 236, 238
———*Das Schloss am Meere,* 90, 103
———"Das Tal," 243
———"Der Arbeitsmann," 10, 85, 287n34, 303
———"Der Einsame," 243
———"Die Georgine," 11
———"Die heiligen drei Könige," 78, 79
———"Die Nacht," 33
———"Die Zeitlose," 11
———"Du meines Herzens Krönelein," 193
———*Ein Heldenleben,* 103
———*Enoch Arden,* 90, 91, 95, 97, 98, 100–103; exx. 32, 33
———"Freundliche Vision," 33, 196, 303
———"Frühlingsfeier," 171, 237, 238, 287n34
———"Für funfzehn Pfennige," 7, 63, 210
———"Gefunden," ex. 26
———"Hab' ich euch denn je geraten," 79
———"Hat gesagt—bleibt's nicht dabei," 79
———"Herr Lenz," 180
———"Himmelsboten," 217
———"Hochzeitlich Lied," 78
———"Hymnus," 78
———"Ich liebe Dich," ex. 80a
———"Ich trage meine Minne," 206–207
———"Im Abendroth," 296n37
———"Im Spätboot," 33
———*Krämerspiegel,* 29, 31, 33, 37, 287n34
———"Leises Lied," 158, 190
———"Liebeshymnus," 236, 238
———"Lied an meinen Sohn," 10, 172, 188; ex. 1a
———"Lied der Frauen," 190, 238
———"Malven," 296n37
———"Mein Auge," 295n16

————"Meinem Kinde," 237, 238
————"Morgen," 236
————"Muttertändelei," 32, 237, 238
————"Nachtgang," 33
————"Nächtlicher Gang," 41
————"Nur Mut," 205; ex. 65
————"O wärst du mein," ex. 19
————"Pilgers Morgenlied," 7
————"Rückleben," 80
————"Ruhe, meine Seele," 7, 238, 245, 296n37
————*Salome,* 62
————"Schlechtes Wetter," 29; ex. 87
————"Ständchen," 4, 190
————"Traum durch die Dämmerung," 33, 194, 293n24
————"Und dann nicht mehr," 210
————*Vier letzte Lieder (Four Last Songs),* viii, 47, 297n37
————"Von den sieben Zechbrüdern," 128, 287n34; ex. 24
————"Von dunklem Schleier umsponnen," 85
————"Waldseligkeit," 33, 190, 237
————"Wenn," 14
————"Wer hat's getan?" 250n30
————"Wiegenlied" (Op. 41 no. 1), 190, 237, 295n17
————"Winterliebe," 79
————"Wozu noch Mädchen," 211
————"Xenion," 244
————"Zueignung," 205, 237, 295n16, 299; ex. 8oc
Stravinsky, Igor, viii, 86, 245
Streicher, Theodor, 21, 62, 114, 253n15, 269n28
————*Dehmel Sprüche,* 244
————*Hafis Lieder,* 165
————"Leitspruch," 244
————"Was du forderst," 71
Strindberg, August, 15, 142, 152, 171, 283n66
Strodtmann, Adolf, 100
Stroh, Wolfgang Martin, 226
Swedenborg, Emanuel, 151, 152, 158

Tagore, Rabindranath, 166
Tchaikovsky, Pyotr Ilyich, 21, 186
Tennyson, Alfred, Lord, 95, 100, 129
Thuille, Ludwig, 27, 109, 162, 231, 267n11
Tieck, Ludwig, 41, 152
Tischler, Hans, 39
Tomáček, Jan Václav, 299; ex. 82a
Toscanini, Arturo, 285n8, 289n56
Treitschke, Heinrich von, 107
Trenner, Franz, 250n30, 295n17
Trunk, Richard, 185, 196

————"Die Gänse," 138
————"Nachtigallen," 75
————*Zehn Kinderlieder,* 138
Tschirch, Emil, 94

Uhland, Ludwig, 103, 128
Ursuleac, Viorica, 237

Valéry, Paul, 152, 277n14
Verlaine, Paul, 148, 156, 159, 171
Von Possart, Ernst, 54, 55, 57, 64, chap. 6 passim, 297

Wagner, Cosima, 88
Wagner, Richard: and New German aesthetics, 3, 11; Wagner societies, 5, 12, 18, 45, 111, 252n5, 253n15; Wagnerian, 12, 127, 153, 186, 188, 201, 299, 302; Bayreuth, 26, 55, 96, 178, 184, 188, 254n27, 289n55, 302; post-Wagnerian, 35, 45–46; tempo, 184, 192, 193, 197, mentioned, 27, 29, 39, 44, 45, 52, 54, 55, 59, 70, 81–82, 120, 121, 122, 126, 127, 129, 133, 148, 153, 160, 169, 186, 197, 229, 242, 250n31, 250n32, 259nn35,36, 261n11, 265n2
————*Der fliegende Holländer,* 42, 186, 260n6
————*Die Meistersinger,* 88, 112
————*Lohengrin,* 42, 260n6
————*Opera and Drama,* 81, 84
————*Parsifal,* 172, 254n27
————*Ring des Nibelungen,* 52, 54, 76, 233
————*Siegfried Idyll,* 234
————*Tannhäuser,* 260n6, 271n43
————*Tristan und Isolde,* 11, 40, 42, 53, 83, 168, 178, 181, 182, 186, 260n6
————*Wesendonk Lieder,* 232, 297
"Träume," 294n7
Walker, Frank, 38, 239, 288n37, 291n4
Walter, Bruno, 183
Walter, Gustav, 18, 20, 22
Weber, Carl Maria von, 62, 134
Webern, Anton, 16, 158, 167
Weingartner, Felix, 25, 45, 57, 59, 60, 82, 96, 165, 180, 184, 192, 195, 196, 239, 289n55
————*Japanische Lieder,* 165; ex. 50
————"Liebesfeier," 165
————*Musik zu Goethes Faust,* 88
Weismann, Julius, 27, 164, 166, 253n15, 269n28
Weiss, John, 248, 267n3
Wellesz, Egon, 226
Wette, Adelheid, 134
Whitman, Walt, 195, 250n29
Wildenbruch, Ernst von, 93
Wilhelm II, 106, 109, 110, 115, 123, 124

Williamson, John, 242
Winternitz-Dorda, Martha, 133
Wolf, Hugo: and New German aesthetics, 3–4; modern lied, 3, 53, 63; *Salonblatt*, 6, 20, 42, 126; influence, 6, 70, 71; Moerike, 9, 153, 249n22; early songs, 32, 127, 155, 200, 273n13, exx. 57, 60, 61; naturalism, 62, 63, 69, 76, 77, 80, 81; declamation, chap. 6 passim, 179; performance, 70, 185, 186, 191; *volkstümlich*, 70, 185, 186, 191, 196, 209; ballad, 126, 127, 129, 130; symbolism, 153–155; tempo and dynamics, 181, 188, 189; structure, chaps. 9 and 11 passim; mentioned, viii, 3, 9, 18, 21, 22, 32, 38, 44, 45, 46, 62, 71, 78, 82–86, 111, 113, 124, 127, 133, 142, 162, 165, 191, 227, 229, 230, 245, 291
———"Abschied," 200, 218, 264n17; ex. 73
———"An den Schlaf," 181; ex. 53a
———"An die Geliebte," 215–216, 292n22
———"An eine Aeolsharfe," 77; ex. 83b
———"Auch kleine Dinge," 292n24
———"Auf ein altes Bild," 240, 241
———"Bedeckt mich mit Blumen," 292n24
———"Bei einer Trauung," 264n17
———"Bitt' ihn, o Mutter," 180
———"Coptisches Lied II," 184
———"Das verlassene Mägdlein," 77
———"Dem Vaterland," 124
———"Denk' es, o Seele!" 240; ex. 81
———*Der Corregidor*, 80, 241
———"Der Feuerreiter," 6, 63
———"Der Gärtner," 70, 77
———"Der Genesene an die Hoffnung," 200
———"Der Jäger," 128
———"Der Knabe und das Immlein," 76
———"Der Rattenfänger," 127
———"Der Sänger," 127
———"Die Geister am Mummelsee," 127, 128, 185; ex. 58
———"Die Spröde," 299–300; ex. 82
———*Drei Gedichte von Michelangelo*, 185
———"Ein Stündlein wohl vor Tag," 201, 203
———"Elfenlied," ex. 72
———"Epiphanias," 76, 82, 86
———"Er ist's," 240, 295n25, 296n26
———"Erstes Liebeslied eines Mädchens," 186
———"Fussreise," 70; ex. 71
———"Ganymed," 153
———"Gesang Weylas," 71, 75
———*Goethe-Lieder*, 5, 69, 241
———"Grenzen der Menschheit," 31, 85

———"Gutmann und Gutweib," 86
———"Harfenspieler II and III," 240, 241
———"Heimweh," 18, 76
———"Im Frühling," 210
———"In der Frühe," vii, 70, 153, 154–155; ex. 48
———*Italienisches Liederbuch (Italian Songbook)*, 5, 14, 30, 69, 72–73, 200, 240, 241
———"Jägerlied," 279n25, 289n50
———"Karwoche," 76
———"Lied vom Winde," 77; ex. 86
———"Man sagt mir," 72–74; ex. 22
———"Mausfallensprüchlein," 118
———"Mein liebster ist so klein," 218
———"Mignon" ("Kennst du das Land?"), 240 241, 295nn24,25; ex. 84
———*Moerike-Lieder*, 5, 46, 127, 200, 253n15, 292n22; exx. 25c, 53a, 58, 71, 72, 73, 81, 83, 86
———"Morgenstimmung," 279n25
———"Mühvoll komm' ich und beladen," 279n27
———"Nachtzauber," 32, 158
———"Nimmersatte Liebe," 211; ex. 69
———"Nixe Binsefuss," 128
———"Nur wer die Sehnsucht kennt," 14, 15
———*Penthesilea*, 239, 240
———"Peregrina I and II," 201
———"Prometheus," vii, 5, 11, 64–69, 189
———"Ritter Kurts Brautfahrt," 111
———"Schlafendes Jesuskind," 241
———"Schmerzliche Wonnen," 181; ex. 53b
———"Seufzer," 155, 180
———"Sie blassen zum Abmarch," 184
———*Spanisches Liederbuch (Spanish Songbook)*, 5, 14, 133, 155, 200, 241, 279n27
———"Storchenbotschaft," 128
———"Um Mitternacht," 291n9
———"Und steht Ihr früh am Morgen auf," 163; ex. 47
———"Und willst du," vii, 58
———"Verborgenheit," 299
———"Verschling der Abgrund," 76
———"Was soll der Zorn," 30–31; ex. 3
———"Wo find' ich Trost?" 155
———"Zur Ruh, zur Ruh," 291n4
———"Zur Warnung," 63; ex. 25c
Woyrsch, Felix, 166, 250n26
Wüllner, Ludwig, 20, 54, 56, 57–58, 59, 60, 61, 64, chap. 6 passim, 177, 192

Yeats, William Butler, 43
Youens, Susan, 255n40

Zelter, Carl Friedrich, 21
Zemlinsky, Alexander, 14, 21, 28, 158, 166, 251n40
Zerner, Ruth, 248n1
Zilcher, Hermann, 83, 85, 96, 162, 185, 266n17, 269n28
——"Abend," 138
——"Aus dem hohenlied Salomonis," 201
——*Dehmel-Zyklus*, 201, 229
——*Eichendorff* cycle, 202
——*Fünfzehn kleine Lieder*, 201
——"Wo sind alle die Blumen hin?" 138
Zuccalmaglio, A. W. F. von, 121, 271n48
Zumpe, Herman, 110, 240
Zumsteeg, Johann Rudolf, 126, 129, 298
Zur Mühlen, Raimund von, 177, 191, 192, 194, 196, 253n17, 266n17, 288n39